Maine Mapmaker's Kitchen

Creative, healthy recipes for home, camp, and afloat

Maine Mapmaker's Kitchen

Creative, healthy recipes for home, camp, and afloat

by Jane Crosen with Richard Washburn

with illustrations by the author

Waterbird Press
Penobscot, Maine

Waterbird Press

110 McCaslin Road
Penobscot, Maine 04476
www.mainemapmaker.com
207–326–4850

First edition, 2009

Text design and illustrations by Jane Crosen, with production assistance from Ann Ahearn.
Cover design and color page layouts by Ann Ahearn with Jane Crosen; map, illustration, and
fabric appliqué by Jane Crosen; cover photography by Ann Ahearn and Richard Washburn.

Typeset in Goudy and Perpetua
Printed on 60-lb Cougar Natural 10% recycled text with soy inks
Printed by Penmor Lithographers, Lewiston, Maine, U.S.A.

Library of Congress Cataloging-in-Publication Data is available on file.

ISBN 978-0-9796403-2-2 2795

10 9 8 7 6 5 4 3 2 1

Photo Credits

Pages 2, 43, 221, 260, Richard Washburn; page 230, Robert Crosen; page 282, Jane Crosen. Page 168, at home in Penobscot: Test kitchen, Stephen Fay; onion pulling, Nancy Crosen; salsa making, Jane Crosen; all others, Richard Washburn. Overleaf, Washburns gathering: Top left, Richard Washburn; all others, Betsy Butterworth. Page 280, Crosen camp: Top right, Glenn Crosen; middle left, Robert Crosen, Sr.; middle right and bottom left, Robert Crosen; bottom right, Nancy Crosen. Overleaf, rustic camp kitchens: Top left, middle and lower right, Richard Washburn; all others, Jane Crosen.

Contents

Dedications & Appreciations

To my Grammie, Hilda Hancock, who cooked with a little of this and that herself, and didn't mind a moppet making "little messes" in her kitchen.

To my Mom, Joyce Crosen, for her Downeast home-cooking know-how and taste for adventure in travel and eating; and my Dad, Robert Crosen, for carrying on the comfort food tradition, offering good leads on recipes, and turning up several gems from the family camp photo archives.

To my Grandma, Gwendolyn Crosen, a creative cook who sparked an early interest in baking and ethnic cooking, especially Persian and Middle Eastern.

To my Aunt Sally (Crosen) Bonello, who gave me two blank journals that begged to be filled up with kitchen and camp adventures.

To the Washburns, all enthusiastic and capable cooks—Dolly, Betsy and Herb, Jon and Vonuo, Art and Dot, Jesse and Didi, Sarah and Beau, Tanya and Terrence—for so many warm and wonderful family meals, where the conversation naturally centers around food and cooking. A special thank-you to Betsy, whose gift subscription to *Cooking Light* guided many experiments in lightening up; Vonuo, for her intuitive, healthy way with Asian cooking; Paul Caldwell, Dot's dad, for turning us all on to *The Inquisitive Cook*; Tanya, for sharing some nice books on international cooking and food history; and Art and Dot, for several fun cuisine-themed gift baskets that got us cooking in new directions.

And to my larger family—beginning with the Findhorn Community in Scotland, which handed me an apron and sign-up rota, and gave me the first of many opportunities to "co-create" in the community kitchens during my time there in the mid-1970s.

To my friend Linda Best, for her generous heart, her gifts of cooking, healing, and nurturing, and her gentle nudges that I get this cookbook written—and make it both personal and practical.

To my walk-and-talk buddy Jan Carpenter, for her suggestions on making the cookbook more user-friendly for vegetarians, and on taking a wider view with essays connecting food, people, places.

To Carol and Ken Hyams, for their adventurous spirit in round-the-world cooking and for sharing inspiring cookbooks from their collection.

To the cookbook authors and editors at The Lyons Press/Globe Pequot I've worked with as copyeditor, for showing me the way. Also the Blue Hill Public Library, for its congenial ambience and fine collection of cookbooks (many of them cited in "Sources & Recommended Reading").

To the boatbuilding, publishing, and conservation communities of the Blue Hill area, comprising a lot of great cooks—especially WoodenBoat Publications in Brooklin, Brooklin Boat Yard, and the Great Pond Mountain Conservation Trust in Orland—for so many good times and fabulous potlucks. And WERU community radio, our cornucopia of alternative news, local voices, and music to cook by.

To the Blue Hill Food Co-op, Tradewinds, and John Edwards Market in Ellsworth, for carrying a healthy array of whole foods and natural ingredients from various sources, including our local organic farmers, and providing the perfect setting for serendipitous encounters with friends and neighbors.

Thanks to the Camp Muse, which encouraged much of the writing, editing, illustrating, and camp-kitchen pondering. And to Allene White for her sage advice: Test every recipe at least twice! (Not easy for a little-of-this-and-that experimenter, but it has made me a more precise, intentional cook. Most recipes have been tested and tweaked a number of times; there may still be a few variations from the "School of Intuitive Cooking" that could use another test, though.)

To all my sounding boards and previewers, everyone who offered feedback and cheered me on—not just Washburns (especially Betsy, Herb, and Vonuo) and Crosens (Dad, Glenn and Nancy, Aunt Sally and her friends Marion and Liz), but Alina and Robert Blakesley, Anne Martina, Linda Best, Kristen LaRiviere, Susan White, Lisa Black, Carol Hyams, Jan Carpenter and Bob Salesi, Heather Spangler, Denise and Lois Lock, Lucy Webb Hardy, Kathy Turok, Betsy Bott, Ronaele Marie, Sarah Herndon, Peter Stremlau, and many other friends, colleagues, and map buyers who have become friends. Special thanks to Joyce Kleffner and Richard Washburn for steering me straight on preserving and cooking techniques, and to Dean Lunt, Kate Gooding, and Stuart Shotwell for their publishing wisdom. Thanks also to Olga Lange, Richard Merrill, and to my friends at Downeast Graphics & Printing who've printed all my maps—especially designer Ann Ahearn, Charlie Ferden, and David Fickett—for their advice and expertise with design and prepress (Ann, you are a star!). And thanks to the folks at Penmor Lithographers for their fine job producing this book.

But most of all, to my husband and kitchen mate Richard Washburn, my partner and colleague in so many great meals and projects, for his constant love and support, culinary expertise and good sense, and help in shaping the book, inventing and testing recipes, and rounding up photos. He found his way into my heart (and kitchen) by fulfilling promises of roast chickens and other domestic delights. In 1988, the year of our wedding, we collaborated on our first collection of recipes, *We'd Like to Invite You All to Dinner! So we've cooked up this cookbook* . . . . This one picks up where our earlier book left off, and repeats a few favorites.

✹

Sources & Recommended Reading

In learning more about the cuisines of other regions and cultures, Richard and I have been inspired by the following cookbooks, using their recipes and techniques as a springboard to simple, healthy adaptations: *Tapas: The Little Dishes of Spain*, by Penelope Casas; *Greek Vegetarian Cooking*, by Jack Santa Maria; *Greek Meze Cooking*, by Sarah Maxwell; *The Classic Mediterranean Cookbook*, by Sarah Woodward; *The New Romagnolis' Table*, by Margaret and Franco Romagnoli; *From an Italian Garden*, by Judith Barrett; *Middle Eastern Cooking*, by Harry Nickles; *The Legendary Cuisine of Persia*, by Margaret Shaida; *An Invitation to Indian Cooking*, by Madhur Jaffray; *Regional Cooking of China*, by Margaret Gin and Alfred Castle; and a delightful, mostly vegetarian trip around the world, *Sundays at Moosewood Restaurant*, by The Moosewood Collective. (And these are just the cookbooks that have found their way to our shelves; there are others to get to know, like *Rustico* by Micol Negrin, *Classic Lebanese Cuisine* by Kamal Al-Faqih, *The Slow-Food Mediterranean Kitchen* by Paula Wolfert . . . .)

We've enjoyed many of the country-cooking, ethnic, and regional favorites in *Harrowsmith* magazine's third collection of family-heirloom recipes from readers across America and Canada. Another friendly melting pot is *The Best of New Mexico Kitchens*, with "house specials" from Southwestern homes and local restaurants. And *Cooking Light* magazine is always full of delicious ideas, a world bazaar of classic and innovative recipes on the theme of healthy proportions.

Among the cookbooks I've had the pleasure of copyediting are *Supermarket Confidential*, *Soup for Every Body*, and *Seduced by Bacon* by Joanna Pruess, each full of creative, mouthwatering recipes and practical comments. Drawing on her years spent living and cooking in France, Joanna has a gift for combining fresh ingredients in simple, authentic, appetizing ways. Several other cookbooks with a similar emphasis are nice to know: *French Farmhouse Cooking*, by Susan Herrmann Loomis; *Cooking Provence,* by Antoine Bouterin; and closer to home in rural Vermont, Ruth Cousineau's *Country Suppers* and Ellen Ecker Ogden's *From the Cook's Garden*.

Even closer to home, it's always fun sampling the eclectic recipes, food history, and commentary of our local columnists, Allene White, Sandy Oliver, and Harry Kaiserian (in the *Ellsworth American, The Working Waterfront, Maine Boats, Homes & Harbors,* and *The Weekly Packet*). Also the fresh, down-to-earth writing of our local cook's gardener, Barbara Damrosch, who, with her husband Eliot Coleman at Four Seasons Farm in Brooksville, keeps Hancock County cooks supplied with organic vegetables year-round—and informed about good varieties to grow in their own kitchen gardens.

Barbara Kingsolver takes home-grown and local to a grand level in *Animal, Vegetable, Miracle*, her landmark book about the year she and her family spent eating foods grown as close to home as possible. The book is packed with information on the ecology and politics of our food supply, tips on preserving harvests, animal husbandry, and simple rustic recipes centered on fresh foods in season.

For anything you need to know on preserving and storing food, we've supplemented our well-thumbed bibles, 1980s editions of Rodale's *Stocking Up* and Ball's *Blue Book,* with two newer sources, Janet Greene's *Putting Food By* and Janet Chadwick's *The Busy Person's Guide to Preserving Food.* Another trusted reference on ingredients, preparation, and equivalents is the 1964 edition of *The Joy of Cooking,* by the "Rombauer ladies," Irma and Miriam Rombauer.

An informative trip back in time is *The Art of Cookery*, by Hannah Glasse, a facsimile reprint of "America's most popular cookbook in 1776." Art history meets food history in *The Art of Food*, by

Claire Clifton, a guide to the past millennium of gathering, growing, and preparing food in the Old and New Worlds, as interpreted in historic paintings, with period recipes. The pioneering *Edible Wild Plants*, by Oliver Medsger, is a fascinating historical field guide to the indigenous food plants of North America and their preparation by native peoples and settlers.

A.D. Livingston's *Skillet Cooking for Home and Camp* and *The Freshwater Fish Cookbook* share cooking techniques and recipes from all over the place (even Maine), "unprissified" yet elegant in a rough-and-ready sort of way. Another adventurous cook is Betty Fusell, "the great experimenter," whose *Crazy for Corn* and *Home Bistro* offer innovative yet surprisingly simple combinations and techniques. At the other end of the adventure spectrum is *Cook's Illustrated*, a magazine in pursuit of "the best" recipes for classic dishes, whatever it takes—always interesting reading, though the ingredients and effort are often a bit rich for my taste.

From baking to bookmaking, I've been encouraged and inspired by Betsy Bott's *Made from Scratch*, "the feel-good, taste-good story" of her Vermont bakery-café, featuring vegetarian whole foods and whole-grain baking, with the back-story of the café and its grass-roots community woven among the recipes. *Simply Scones*, by Leslie Weiner and Barbara Albright, is less about whole ingredients, but full of elegant flavor combinations. *Baking with Julia*, by Dorie Greenspan, is a book of knowledge on the craft of fine baking; the chapters on rustic breads are especially enlightening. And for all of us born to bake and experiment, Richard and I highly recommend a friendly little kitchen science book called *The Inquisitive Cook: How a Pinch of Curiosity Can Improve Your Cooking*, by Anne Gardiner and Sue Wilson, which demystifies the hows and whys of food chemistry (and alchemy).

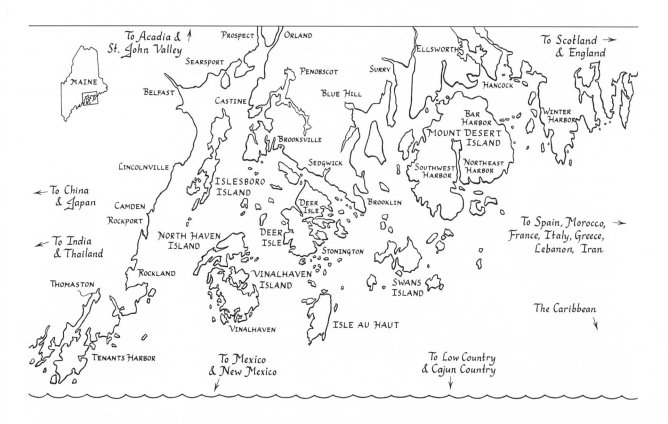

Introduction

While this collection of recipes featuring home-grown, home-made foods is firmly rooted in Maine, it grew out of a longtime taste for exploring. Some of you may already know me through my series of hand-drawn maps of Maine regions, made in much the same spirit as adventurous cooks explore different cultures and cuisines through recipes. Just as reading or making a map is a way to understand and appreciate a landscape, following and adapting recipes is a way to experience other countries and their regional and ethnic food traditions. A trip around the world, without having to cross the Portsmouth–Kittery bridge!

There's nowhere I'd rather be than home in Downeast Maine, which has many wonderful food traditions of its own. And yet my food cravings often reach out to other, older food traditions, usually from somewhere sunny and warm—Spain, Morocco, southern France, Italy, Greece; the Middle East, Far East; Mexico, the Caribbean; Carolina Low Country, Cajun country. What is it, the long, cold Maine winters and low-angle sun, a lack of vitamin D? Judging by the popularity of warm-climate cuisines, all of us New Englanders crave regular doses of vicarious travel to places with exotic cultures and long, leisurely growing seasons. In our cooking, my husband Richard and I hop regularly back and forth from Downeast Maine to the Mediterranean, India and Thailand, the Southwest, and home again.

Yet, despite the amazingly diverse offerings of today's global supermarkets, we'd really rather satisfy those cultural-cuisine cravings by relying on local foods, in season, wherever we can. Not only are they fresher and healthier, but usually "greener" in terms of farming practices, transportation, packaging, and storage—a better economy all around. Best of all are foods grown by a nearby farmer or in our own veggie garden. Here in Hancock County, where we live on the Blue Hill Peninsula, we're blessed to have some pockets of good farmland, kept productive by a circle of hard-working farmers, a thriving market-garden network, and a community that supports it, with a number of local producers offering artisan breads; free-range eggs, poultry, and lamb; organic and non-BGH dairy products; fresh local shellfish; native and organic fruits and vegetables. Many other parts of Maine enjoy a similar wealth of farmer's markets and local growers and bakers.

And so we mine cookbooks for good combinations based on various ethnic and regional cooking traditions, and see what we can make from what we have here and now, starting with our own garden. Granted, we buy imported cheeses, spices, wines, condiments, nuts, and numerous other things "from away" that make ethnic and regional dishes authentic . . . but we also take advantage of local foods, everything from fresh Maine shrimp and crabmeat, to native corn and beans, to foraged and pick-your-own berries, to wild crops like venison, mussels, and fiddleheads.

Trying to rely more on locally produced food means putting food by, and so you'll notice a theme of self-reliance running through this book, with recipe notes and practical advice on how to store and use garden and local harvests by freezing, drying, and canning.

Another facet of eating fresh local foods involves keeping a mental inventory of what's available right in your own refrigerator, and creatively recycling leftovers, either by "pot luck" (making good use of what's on hand) or by planning meals that will generate the makings of another, different meal—an old New England tradition. You'll find a number of recipes here made for making glorious reappearances—also versatile recipes that can be varied to suit your ingredients.

This kind of practicality also comes into play cooking in a camp kitchen (or canoe-camping, or camp-cruising in a kayak or small boat), where Richard and I have done most of our adventuring, relatively close to home in the wilds of Maine. You'll find camp cooking another strong theme, with some favorite camp recipes and notes on cooking in rustic conditions.

Many ethnic food traditions are based on vegetables and pulses, using only a small amount of animal protein, if any (something not always available or affordable). This way of eating is still very healthful and economical, so our repertoire includes a number of recipes that are either vegetarian or could easily be made so by leaving out the optional meat or fish.

But mostly this book is about combining healthy ingredients in authentic, creative, and delicious ways, with a minimum of fuss and preparation time. Where shortcuts are possible, they are taken. Fats, sugars, eggs, and rich dairy products are used with a lighter hand. Meats often appear in smaller amounts, combined with vegetables and pulses. Whole grains, flours, and pastas are favored, along with natural sweeteners and healthy oils. Most dishes and component recipes are made from scratch, even many of the condiments (marinades, sauces and dressings, pestos, salsas and chutneys).

If your kitchen and food preferences are anything like ours, you'll enjoy sampling from this collection of our household favorites. Maybe we can help widen your repertoire as exploring different cuisines has widened ours.

Some of the recipes are purely original. Some are adaptations of traditional recipes, synthesized from various cookbooks, which we've made so many times that our own signature touches have evolved (easier, healthier, different accent on flavoring). Some were inspired by dishes cooked by friends and family members. Some attempt to re-create memorable foods sampled at office and group potlucks, or at local bakeries and restaurants. Some are slightly updated Downeast comfort foods and family heirlooms. Most are good enough to make more than once, maybe a slightly different way depending on what you're in the mood for.

Because serendipity goes with the creative territory—I think most of us are hard-wired to deviate and innovate, follow recipes in a way that suits our taste or ingredients, make them our own. Like all cookbooks, this one is a collection of ideas, suggestions of good combinations, basic recipes for success with some variations to try. All in the spirit of culinary adventure!

Jane Crosen, Mapmaker
Penobscot, Maine 2008

Welcome

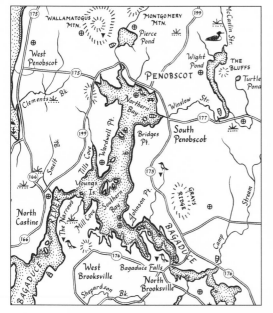

to Our Kitchen

A Well-Stocked Larder

Having plenty of staples on hand means different things to different people. For us, it means having enough key ingredients to be able to cook a variety of interesting dishes, whatever the season, without running to the store. Here's what we think of as a well-stocked larder. If this book speaks to you, and you live in Maine or rural New England year-round, your kitchen is probably a lot like ours.

FREEZER

To anyone living in a rural location, putting food by for winter seems just right. With winter's storms, iffy traveling, and unexpected power outages, it's reassuring to have a larder stocked with enough food to tide you over for a few days. With the ever-rising prices of gas and food, and a 12- to 25-mile drive to the nearest well-stocked grocery store, a "wintertime larder" frame of mind, for many of us practical Mainers, tends to prevail year-round.

Anyone with a substantial home garden soon invests in a chest freezer to preserve their harvest. Keeping the freezer full (to conserve electricity) becomes a way of life, and what better way to take advantage of good deals on meat, or fresh native crops like pick-your-own strawberries (page 230) and corn (page 182), while guaranteeing a supply of fresh local food at its best. Besides several kinds of green beans from the garden, we'll blanch and freeze a stash of home-grown shell beans (page 146), along with a selection of homemade sauces and salsas, including Genovese Pesto (page 21), frozen in small plastic containers. Green peppers, halved, seeded, and blanched, can be bagged and frozen, and used in cooking. In the wild food department, there are pint containers full of raspberries and blueberries (page 220), foraged from thickets near home and camp—a favorite summer ritual.

Then there's Maine shrimp, frozen at the height of shrimp season (page 70). Local sea scallops and mussels (page 66) also freeze well. Often we'll order a lamb from our neighboring organic farm, King Hill Farm (page 117), cut to our specs and packaged for the freezer. If Richard (or a friend) has gotten a deer, we'll have "free-range" venison cached away—and bacon and sausage, divided into meal-sized portions. The freezer is also a place to stash nuts, butter, and flours, to preserve freshness.

PANTRY & ROOT CELLAR

Our pantry, tucked under the stairs just a step away from the kitchen, is lined with shelves on either side filled with jars of home-grown herbs, gathered and dried (page 30): basil, marjoram, Greek oregano, thyme, winter and summer savory, sage, and lovage. Some years we may grow enough dill, cilantro, or epazote (page 158) to dry. Tarragon is tough, here in Maine, to keep going as a perennial, but some years we'll get a few extra sprigs to dry or use in herbal vinegars. There's a jar of dried calendula petals, which we use as "poor man's saffron" (page 185). And a jar of dried mint leaves, a wild variety that I love to gather late in the summer from a local stream. From these we top up our collection of smaller bottles, kept handy in an herb drawer beside the stove. The pantry shelves also usually hold a few bottles of herbal vinegar (page 49), another way to preserve garden herbs.

In a bountiful year, we'll put up (canned or frozen, depending on the chemistry of the sauce, see page 8) homemade tomato sauce and soup base, curried simmer sauce, red and green salsas, various fruit sauces, maybe some pickles, peperoncini or dilly beans, green tomato chutney or mincemeat, jams, jellies, and conserves. We've also started drying our own plum tomatoes (page 146).

Who could survive a day without onions or garlic—so the pantry always holds a big bag of onions and a basket of garlic, usually from our garden. Winter squashes, if we've grown enough to keep, do best in a dry airy room, so we keep them (along with the rest of the onion crop) in a storeroom upstairs. A good crop of potatoes goes into the root cellar, rinsed and well dried, then stored in 5-gallon plastic buckets with lids ajar and weighted with rocks (to discourage mice while allowing moisture to escape). Small sweet carrots, trimmed and rinsed, go in the refrigerator, while storage carrots go in the root cellar in buckets covered with sphagnum moss.

Fridge & Cupboard

One small shelf in the fridge is devoted to cheeses we like to use in cooking (page 135). Most of these are harder, aged cheeses with enough salt to keep fairly well, although they can become too hard to grate. (If this happens, refrigerate the cheese wrapped in a damp paper towel until it softens enough to grate.) All cheeses have a certain shelf life, so it's a good economy to keep an eye on them and use them up before mold settles in. (If spots of mold begin to appear, pare them off, rinse the cheese and pat dry, then rewrap in clean plastic or waxed paper.) If your household doesn't consume a lot of cheese, it's best to not get carried away with variety and stock just a few cheeses at a time.

It's nice to vary the menu with unaged cheeses, so we occasionally indulge in fresh mozzarella or locally made chevre—both too perishable and too delicious to hang around long. Also perishable are cultured cream cheese and sour cream, good to keep on hand as the base for a frosting, dip or spread, or to use in baking. A regular staple is part-skim ricotta, a high-calcium, low-fat fresh cheese with many uses. With little salt or enzymes acting as preservatives, ricotta, once opened, has a short shelf life, so any that we can't use within a week or so we'll freeze in smaller containers. When it comes time to make a ricotta dish, we let the frozen ricotta thaw gradually in the refrigerator. The consistency is not quite as creamy as fresh, but fine for cooking.

Also in the fridge are jars of Homemade Yogurt (page 211), along with numerous bags of nuts, seeds, and wheat germ, bought in bulk from the coop or natural food store. A selection of dried fruits keeps them company, on hand for cookies, quick breads, and granola. And of course butter, eggs, milk, and all the other usual staples. Oh, and the condiments—if your refrigerator is anything like ours, its doors are lined with all manner of jars—preserves, salsas, mustards, curry pastes, ginger (page 67). . . Plus oranges and lemons, and marinated green/ripe olives for cooking, salads, and snacking.

Handy to the stove is the wine cupboard, with cooking wine, vermouth, sherry, and marsala, which we use in sauces, marinades, and for deglazing pans (pages 125, 126). Other cupboard staples include an array of grains, pastas, lentils and dry beans (page 156), olive oil (light for sautéeing, extra-virgin for dressings and drizzling), and bottled condiments (tamari, chipotle and other pepper sauces, Worcestershire, toasted sesame oil). The baking area is lined with a battery of airtight jars holding whole-grain flours (page 207) and cupboards full of various sugars, sweet spices, home-brewed vanilla (page 263), orange oil, candied ginger, chocolate, and other things to inspire a baker's fancy.

Baking

Baking is fun—every cookie, muffin, scone, or loaf of bread a chemistry experiment. Combine flours with sugars, oils, leavening agents, salt, flavorings, and liquid, mix with love and heat, and poof! A delectable dessert or bread. Of course it's all the variables that make it exciting—not just which flours and fruits, nuts, and flavorings you choose to combine, but things like humidity, the size of your egg(s), and your precision in measuring.

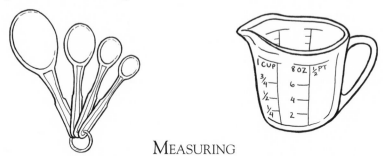

MEASURING

A lot depends on your measuring cups and how you fill and level them. To economize on steps and dishes, I take the shortcut of using my veteran Pyrex cup to measure all ingredients, liquid or dry, gauging the amount by eye. Many bakers, though, swear by using dry cups, which can be leveled off with a knife, giving a more accurate measure than leveling by eye. (As you'll see, I also use the measuring cup as a mixing bowl in muffin and quick bread recipes. Although mixing the liquid ingredients right in the cup isn't conventional, it gives you a truer total liquid measure, while greatly minimizing cleanup.) And the measuring spoons: full, or brim-full? I aim for brim-full with oils and other liquids, and level-off powders, spices, and other dry ingredients with a knife. If your measuring equipment or style is a little different, you may want to adjust the amounts slightly up or down. "Scant" calls for a measure slightly under the mark, "full" on the generous side.

And then the flours and grains: Not all whole-wheat pastry flours are created equal—some are more coarsely ground (stone-ground), others milled fine. The same with cornmeal, where you have a choice between corn flour (a finely milled cornmeal), regular coarse cornmeal, blue corn, white corn, and more. Not to mention oat flour and bran, wheat germ and bran, buckwheat flour, rice and semolina flours, and all the other possibilities a baker has to work with (page 207). It's these different textures, which take up moisture differently, along with the moisture content (depending on ambient humidity) and oil content (depending on how much of the germ is included) of the flours, that make it such a challenge to pin down the exact amount of liquid needed for a batter or dough that's just the right consistency. (And that's without getting into the different bread flours, both unbleached and whole-wheat, which are milled from harder wheat that has more protein and gluten, and handle differently when worked than the softer pastry flours.) Honey, too, when substituted for sugar, will alter the amount of liquid needed (usually less). This is why often a range like "1 to 2 tablespoons" is listed as a liquid additive. When in doubt, trust your instincts.

LIQUIDS

One thing idiosyncratic to my baking is the frequent use of milk "soured" with a little plain yogurt. This is a natural by-product of regularly making my own yogurt (page 211). It seems a waste to rinse out what yogurt is left clinging to the sides of the empty quart jar, so I swish the jar with a little milk (1/3 to 1/2 cup), to use in baking quick breads. You could simply substitute buttermilk, milk that's gone slightly sour, milk mixed with a little plain yogurt, or just regular milk—although the touch of acidity reacting with the alkaline component in the baking powder or soda helps to loft the flours. Another little habit of mine, with a similar effect, is using fresh-squeezed orange juice (or lemon juice, or cider) as part of the liquid in baking cookies and quick breads, not just as a flavoring but to compensate for a somewhat lighter measure of butter or oil.

BUTTER

Which brings us to that lovely stuff, butter. I adore butter in sparing amounts, but cringe at recipes (especially in older cookbooks) calling for butter in increments of a stick, cup, or pound. In most cookies, quick breads, and pastries, I find 2 to 4 tablespoons of butter is all it takes—combined with canola oil or light olive oil, two heart-healthy oils—to bring satisfying flavor and richness in proportion to the usual amount of flours. (The texture may be less delicate with less butter, but nuts, oats, wheat germ, and other wholesome ingredients bring flavor and a nice texture of their own.)

Dessert and bread recipes typically call for unsalted butter, for more precise control over the amount of salt, which plays a more important role than you'd think, lending structure to the flours in bread, and slowing the rate at which yeast ferments and breaks down gluten. But I prefer using salted butter (Kate's, homemade in Maine) for the simple practical reason that the two of us (one watching cholesterol) don't use that much butter, and it's easier to just work with one kind, salted, for both spreading and cooking, and dial back on the salt called for in a recipe. It takes 1/8 to 1/4 teaspoon of salt to bring 3 tablespoons unsalted butter (the usual amount in the cookie, scone, and cake recipes here) up to the salinity of salted butter—so that gives you a basic rule of thumb if using unsalted.

OVEN

Last but not least among variables is the oven. Gas or electric, low rack or high, how often you open the door to peek or rotate the pan(s), the calibration of your thermostat, all will affect your baking temperature and time. Also your baking pans: Pyrex, ceramic, and stoneware dishes bake more evenly than metal pans and hold heat longer, almost like using a baker's stone; hence you can go with a slightly lower temperature and longer baking time. Metal pans bake differently depending on thickness and whether the surface is dull or shiny. For example, cakes baked in venerable metal baking pans inherited from my Grandma, darkened over the decades with built-up oils, bake and brown up more quickly than in newer pans, because the dark surface absorbs more heat; pans with shiny surfaces, on the other hand, reflect heat so baked goods brown more lightly. Whatever the surface color, when using thin metal pans I give them a precautionary dusting of semolina or rice flour or coarse cornmeal to prevent scorched bottoms—especially with pizza, freeform yeast breads, and sugar-rolled cookies. Heavier stainless-steel pans take a bit longer but bake more evenly.

Unless noted otherwise in a recipe, rack position is generally the top third of the oven, especially for small items or thin layers of food or breads; thicker, denser items like round rustic breads, bundt cakes, roasts, whole fish, and casseroles bake more evenly in the center of the oven. If you notice, after following several of the recipes, that things take longer or shorter to bake than called for, it may be that your oven runs slightly hotter or cooler, so adjust heat and time to suit your own situation.

One last, energy-conservation note: Following convention and to give a common benchmark for baking times, the recipe directions call for a preheated oven. This is important for baking cookies, pastries, and breads. However, with casseroles, grains and potatoes, and most braised and roasted meat dishes, you can save energy by placing food in a cold rather than fully preheated oven. At the other end of the cycle, with most baking you can turn the oven off 5 minutes before the expected finish time, as it should hold the set temperature for about that long while the food finishes cooking.

You may notice the absence of a microwave—that's because we don't have one, being content with a gas stove and toaster oven. Microwave ovens are certainly handy for reheating quick meals at work and for people on the go. If you have one, by all means use any microwave shortcuts you're accustomed to.

Recipe Highlights

As noted earlier in the Introduction, four practical themes emerged from the growing collection of recipes. Thinking like a mapmaker, I came up with the idea of using symbols or icons to highlight recipes—mainly appetizers, soups, salads, and entrées—that lend themselves to certain parameters. Here is a "legend" of sorts:

 CAMP-FRIENDLY—Dishes with relatively few ingredients that are simple to prepare in rustic conditions such as you'd find car-camping, canoe-camping, camp-cruising, in a camp kitchen or in the galley of a small boat (or at home if the power goes out!). These dishes can be prepared using only a cooktop or camp stove and grill; parts of the meal can be premade or kitted up. See the Camp Kitchen section (page 281) for ideas on food planning and storage.

 POT LUCK—Dishes that make inspired use of the remains of another dish, creatively recycling leftovers into a uniquely delicious meal. The leftovers may be as simple as mashed potatoes, squash, vegetables, cooked meat, or one of the cross-referenced featured recipes in the book.

 RECYCLABLE—Dishes whose leftovers can be the makings of a whole 'nother meal. This is similar to "pot luck," but different in that "pot luck" makes serendipitous use of available leftovers, whereas here a dish is made with the intention of reusing leftovers in another meal.

 VEGETARIAN—Dishes that are vegetarian, or could be easily made so by leaving out a small amount of meat or fish (see "Vegetarian, Mostly," page 128).

YIELD VS. SERVINGS

The amounts for how much or how many servings a recipe yields vary somewhat by category.

WITH CONDIMENTS AND SAUCES, approximate yield is listed as liquid volume.

WITH BAKED GOODS, DESSERTS, AND SOME APPETIZERS, where there are variables in size, a range is given for how many cookies, muffins, turnovers, crostini, etc. the recipe should yield.

WITH SOUPS, SALADS, AND MOST ENTRÉES AND APPETIZERS, yields focus more on the number of people served rather than servings, considering that some may go for larger portions or seconds—and that when feeding a group, it's better to have plenty. Not to mention all the things you can do with leftovers!

A FEW USEFUL EQUIVALENTS

1/2 cup whipping cream	=	1 to 1 1/4 cups whipped
1/2 cup unpacked brown sugar	=	1/3 cup honey less 1 tablespoon liquid
1/2 lemon	=	1 1/2 tablespoons juice + 1 teaspoon zest
1/2 orange	=	3 to 4 tablespoons juice + 1 tablespoon zest
1 large egg	=	3 tablespoons liquid
1 1/2 teaspoons baking powder	=	1/2 teaspoon soda + 1 teaspoon cream of tartar
4 tablespoons salted butter	=	4 tablespoons unsalted butter + 1/4 teaspoon salt
1/8 teaspoon garlic powder	=	1 small to medium clove garlic
3 to 4 ounces cheese	=	1 cup grated/shredded
1 medium onion or apple	=	1 cup chopped
2 medium carrots	=	1 cup grated/shredded
2 cups diced potato or squash	=	1 cup cooked and mashed
1 cup dried lentils, beans, or rice	=	2 2/3 to 3 cups cooked
2 teaspoons fresh herbs	=	1 teaspoon dried

A NOTE ON PRESERVING

You'll find a number of recipes here for sauces, salsas, and other condiments, with notes on preserving. Mostly based on recipes and methods in '80s editions of the Ball *Blue Book* and Rodale's *Stocking Up*, they're household favorites that we've been putting up for years, following the earlier recommendations for water-bath processing. Although we have never had any food safety concerns in our home canning, the current wisdom, based on advances in food science, is that freezing is the safest method for preserving sauces that contain low-acid foods and oils which can harbor *Clostridium botulinum* bacteria. For the latest information on preserving, plus a selection of tested recipes, visit the National Center for Home Food Preservation website, www.uga.edu/nchfp.

Appetizers & Sandwiches

Fresh Salmon Pâté   10

Chicken Liver Pâté   11

Stuffed Mussels   12

Stuffed Mushroom Caps   13

Scampi Phyllo Tarts   13

Spanakópitas   14

Hummus   15

Lemon-Cream Cheese Spread   16

Italian Goat Cheese Spread   16

Crudités & Dips ~ *Tahini-Yogurt Dip,*
   Lemon-Sour Cream Dip, Guacamole   17

Cheese Nachos ~ *Garden Salsa*   18

Crostini with Fresh Mozzarella ~ *Genovese Pesto,*
   Tomato-Eggplant Tapenade   20

Chicken-Pesto Crostini or Sandwiches   23

Focaccia Grilled-Cheese Sandwiches   23

Salmon (or Steak) Sandwiches
   ~ *Dill-Horseradish Sauce*   24

Toasted Vegetable-Cheese Pockets   25

Ploughman's Lunch ~ *Green Tomato Chutney,*
   Cranberry Chutney   26

Mushroom-Cheese Baguette   27

Savory Potato Pasties   28

"Don't mind if I do . . ." Oh, it's all too easy to fill up on tempting hors d'oeuvres at a party or restaurant, then find yourself too full to do justice to the main course, much less dessert (sigh). Sometimes the best appetizers are the simplest ones—those that let you keep your appetite.

Eating out is an occasion, a chance to sample something different. At home or camp, though, with dinner on the way, all you need is a little something to take the edge off. We're generally content with just a few simple nibbles—a handful of almonds or pistachios, a sampling of marinated olives or cheese, crackers or sesame breadsticks ("Care for a cigar?").

For a dinner party, we'll dress this up a bit: grapes and special cheeses, colored peppers dipped in seasoned sour cream, crackers or bread with goat cheese or boursin, maybe some smoked scallops or mussels, all still so simple they hardly need recipes.

Then again, sometimes a special treat is called for, a hot or hearty hors d'oeuvre involving a little more preparation, an edible conversation piece. This chapter includes party offerings along with savory sandwiches that can double as a lunch or light meal.

Fresh Salmon Pâté

Smoked salmon pâtés I can take or leave, but a fresh salmon pâté sampled at Pilgrim's Inn in Deer Isle inspired me to re-create something similar at home. For many years since, this delicately flavored pâté has been on request for family holiday get-togethers.

The pâté at Pilgrim's Inn (circa 1984) was a feast for the eyes, the soft pink salmon sprinkled with crunchy spring green pistachios. More often I coat the pâté with parsley and almonds, which are a little less rich, and equally good.

SERVES 8 TO 10 AS APPETIZER

About 2/3 pound fresh salmon (preferably fillet)	Dash of salt
2 tablespoons water, white wine, or vermouth	A few grates white pepper
4 ounces cream cheese	1/3 to 1/2 cup whole raw almonds (or
2 tablespoons cream (or half-and-half)	lightly roasted pistachios, preferably
Juice of 1/3 lime (2 teaspoons)	unsalted), chopped
1/2 teaspoon dill weed	2/3 cup fresh parsley, chopped

Place salmon fillet skin-side down in non-stick pan with poaching liquid (water, wine, or vermouth). Cover and poach gently until just done (pink all the way through). Cool slightly, then discard skin, pick meat from bones, and crumble salmon between your fingers into a bowl until shredded, removing any fine bones.

Add cream cheese (the still-warm salmon will help soften it) and combine thoroughly, using fork or fingers. Add cream (or half-and-half), lime juice, dill, and salt and pepper to taste, remembering that the flavors will intensify. Chill for a couple of hours or until ready to serve.

When it's party time, form a bed of chopped nuts and parsley in shallow bowl or plate, and spoon pâté into the center. Pat into a flat, round cake, turning over and over until parsley and nuts are well pressed into the surface.

Serve with a bland, light cracker such as Bremner wafers or Breton crackers.

Chicken Liver Pâté

With a little thinking ahead, homemade chicken pâté makes a special appetizer offering (for carnivores, that is). Any light, crisp wheat cracker would make a good foil for this savory, relatively lean pâté.

SERVES 10 TO 12 AS APPETIZER

3/4 pound raw chicken livers and hearts

2 to 3 gizzards

1/3 cup dry sherry plus enough marsala to
    bring liquid measure to 1/2 cup

3/4 pound ground turkey

1 teaspoon dried sage

1 teaspoon dried chervil

1 teaspoon dried lovage

1/2 teaspoon dried thyme

1/4 teaspoon dried tarragon

1 clove garlic, minced

1/2 medium onion, minced

1 1/2 teaspoons salt

1 1/2 teaspoons ground white pepper

6 to 8 slices bacon

1/3 cup pistachios, lightly roasted and salted

Place chicken livers, hearts, and gizzards in bowl. Pour sherry and marsala over meat, cover bowl, and marinate for 6 hours in refrigerator.

Using your hands, thoroughly mix turkey with herbs, garlic, onion, salt, and pepper. Refrigerate for 3 to 4 hours to allow flavors to permeate the meat.

Line a 4 1/2 x 8 1/2-inch loaf pan with bacon strips, laying bacon across the width of the pan. Cut up the marinated chicken livers and add to turkey mixture; reserve marinade. Spoon half of mixture in bottom of loaf pan and press a couple tablespoons of the pistachios into the top. Distribute hearts and trimmed gizzards evenly over and sprinkle with a few more nuts. Preheat oven to 325°F.

Stir marinade into remaining turkey mixture and spoon half over contents of loaf pan. Add rest of pistachios and top off with the last of the turkey mixture. Fold ends of bacon strips over the top.

Cover loaf with foil and put in roasting pan filled about halfway with hot water. Bake on rack in middle of oven for 1 1/2 to 2 hours.

Let pâté cool 1 hour, then chill in refrigerator. Serve with wheat crackers or baguette rounds.

Stuffed Mussels

This simple but festive appetizer is a nice way to showcase fresh Maine blue mussels, whether locally farmed or wild ones you picked yourself (page 66). The robust flavor of the mussels stands up to the savory ingredients in the filling, which can be made ahead and refrigerated.

This recipe makes about 20 stuffed mussels, served on the "half-shell"—natural ramekins from large blue mussels picked at very low tide. If only smaller mussels are available, the filling can be served in large mussel shells saved from a previous meal, or perhaps gathered from the beach.

 SERVES 6 TO 8 AS APPETIZER

1 cup steamed mussel meats, chopped	1 medium to large egg
1 to 2 cloves garlic, minced	3/4 cup whole-wheat breadcrumbs
1 small onion, minced	1/2 cup beer
1 tablespoon mixed Italian herbs (basil, oregano, marjoram, savory, rosemary)	1/2 cup mussel broth
	2/3 cup shredded Gruyère cheese

This is a good way to use up leftover steamed mussels and broth (page 66). Otherwise, scrub about 2 dozen large mussels, steam, and remove meats, reserving 20 large shells plus 1 cup meats and 1/2 cup or more cooking broth. (Or, use enough smaller mussels to yield 1 cup meats, and bake filling in larger shells, saved or gathered.) Chop mussel meats, removing any pearls.

Combine first 5 ingredients (mussels through egg) in bowl. Add breadcrumbs alternately with broth and beer until a spoonable consistency.

Preheat oven to 375°F. Spoon filling into mussel shells and place on baking sheet. Sprinkle with Gruyère, and bake at for 10 to 15 minutes. Serve hot, eaten out of the shell or with a small fork.

SMOKED SEAFOOD

For a special treat, smoked shellfish, salmon, and trout are the simplest of appetizers, produced by a handful of Maine smokehouses including Ducktrap, Stonington Sea Products, Sullivan Harbor Farm, and Grindstone Neck of Maine. Most of them have some locally farmed or wild-caught seafood among their offerings, such as cherry- or hickory-smoked rope-cultured mussels, Maine shrimp, and sea scallops, and hot- and cold-smoked Bay of Fundy salmon.

Smoked mussels and scallops are as delicious as bacon-wrapped, but without the fat, and full of omega-3s. These flavorful nuggets are as irresistible as salted nuts, so spread the wealth by serving them surrounded by crudités like peppers, radishes, celery, and carrots with a dip (pages 18, 64)—or throw them into a pasta toss (page 76). Serve smoked salmon or trout on baguette rounds or crackers.

Stuffed Mushroom Caps

This very simple savory can be served as an appetizer, or as a garnish alongside grilled steak (or other entrée). The seasonings depend on what you have available for crumbs: If using grated dry wheat bread or plain crushed breadsticks (page 137), you'll want to season the crumbs with herbs, garlic, salt, and pepper. If using crushed sesame, garlic, sourdough, or other seasoned breadsticks or crackers, add the onions and herbs but hold back a bit on salt (if the crackers are salty) and other seasonings.

 SERVES 2 AS APPETIZER OR GARNISH

10 to 12 baby portabella mushrooms

1 tablespoon fresh onion, minced

1 tablespoon olive oil

2 tablespoons vermouth (or white wine with a little dry sherry)

1/8 teaspoon garlic powder

1 cup freshly grated breadcrumbs (or crushed breadsticks or crackers)

1/4 teaspoon dried marjoram or chervil

Salt and white pepper to taste

2 tablespoons grated Gruyère, Parmesan, or other flavorful aged cheese (optional)

Clean mushrooms and remove stems. Chop stems, and sauté along with minced onion in about half of the olive oil. Deglaze with vermouth (or wine/sherry), then add crumbs and seasonings.

Fill caps, and place in small oiled baking pan. Sprinkle with cheese if desired. Bake at 375°F for 10 to 15 minutes, or until mushrooms are steaming and tender and topping is nicely browned.

Variation

CRAB-STUFFED MUSHROOM CAPS: Use 1/2 cup bread or cracker crumbs in the filling, and add 1/2 cup fresh crabmeat. Top with 1/4 cup crumbs rubbed with a little olive oil and 1 tablespoon grated cheese.

Scampi Phyllo Tarts

Scampi in phyllo, what's not to like? Vonuo Washburn came up with the idea for these delicious bites.

 SERVES 8 TO 12 AS APPETIZER

Shrimp Scampi (page 73), without gremolata

24 mini phyllo tart shells (or make your own)

Make 1 recipe Shrimp Scampi, without the garnish; remove from heat after adding lemon juice. If using frozen phyllo shells, set in non-stick mini-muffin pan. (Otherwise, form tart shells using 8 sheets of 9 x 14-inch phyllo dough: melt 1 tablespoon butter with 2 1/2 tablespoons olive oil, and lay up a stack of 5 sheets, brushing between layers as on page 14. With a sharp knife, cut pastry into 15 3-inch squares; press into mini-muffin cups. Repeat, making 9 shells from 3 sheets of phyllo.)

Preheat oven to 350°F. Divide scampi among tart shells, filling each with a tablespoon of shrimp and a slight drizzle of sauce. Bake 6 to 8 minutes, or until tart pastry is nicely golden. Serve hot.

Spanakópitas

Anything made with phyllo (or fillo) takes a little more effort, but guarantees a delicious crispy treat, either as an appetizer or the focus of a light supper. As the Greek name suggests, Spanakópitas (properly spanakópitakia, "little spinach pies") are pastries wrapped around a spinach filling. We lighten the pastry by cutting the butter with olive oil, and season the traditional spinach-and-feta filling with a touch of nutmeg and savory herbs. As suggested by Richard's brother Art Washburn, fresh mushrooms are a nice addition, chopped fine and added raw to steam in the phyllo packets.

 SERVES 2 TO 4 AS MAIN DISH, 8 AS APPETIZER

1 tablespoon olive oil

4 to 5 scallions, chopped (*or* 1/2 large onion, or combination)

1/2 pound (5 to 6 cups) spinach, washed, stemmed, patted dry, and coarsely chopped

1/2 teaspoon dried cilantro

1/2 teaspoon dried basil

1/8 to 1/4 teaspoon nutmeg

Dash of salt (omit if using very salty feta)

2 tablespoons butter, melted

1/4 cup extra-virgin olive oil

1/2 cup (3 ounces) feta

2 to 4 baby portabella or field mushrooms, washed and finely chopped (1/2 to 2/3 cup)

16 sheets (about 5 ounces) 9 x 14-inch phyllo (fillo) dough, thawed and left wrapped

Sauté scallions and/or onions in oil until translucent. Add spinach, herbs, nutmeg, and salt. Cover sauté pan and cook just long enough to deflate spinach, then turn off heat.

Turn oven to 365°F and melt butter with oil in preheating oven in a small metal bowl. Meanwhile crumble or dice feta, chop mushrooms, and set aside.

Unfurl phyllo from its wrapper, and, taking sheets out gingerly one at a time, lay out the first "leaf" of dough on a clean countertop. Brush with melted butter-oil mixture, then cover with a second sheet of phyllo. Repeat 2 more times, for a total of 4 layers (do not brush top of fourth sheet). Cover remaining phyllo with plastic wrapper and damp dishtowel between batches to prevent dough from drying out; otherwise it will crack and be difficult to handle.

Cut assembled pastry into 2 strips 4 1/2 x 14 inches. Spoon 1/8 portion of filling in bottom left corner of strip of pastry; top filling with 1/8 portion of feta and mushrooms, and fold pastry up in a triangle, like a flag. Place on lightly oiled baking sheet. Repeat with 3 more batches of pastry, using up the rest of the filling.

Brush tops of Spanakópitas with butter/oil and bake at 365° for 15 to 18 minutes, or until pastry is nicely puffed and browned.

Serve piping hot as an appetizer, or as a main course along with brown rice and salad or stir-steamed summer squash (page 177).

NOTE: If using a 16-ounce box of frozen phyllo, packaged in 2 furls of dough each with 25 sheets of pastry, you'll use two-thirds of a roll in making a batch of Spanakópitas. To use up the remaining 8 or 9 sheets, layered and cut as described above, you might make a small batch of savory cheese pasties, another Greek appetizer, filled with a mixture of egg, ricotta, feta, lemon zest or nutmeg, and parsley, cilantro, or mint.

Hummus

This small recipe, scaled for eating up fresh or using leftover cooked chickpeas, can easily be doubled to serve a larger crowd for lunch or as a party appetizer. You can use canned chickpeas, but the soaked and cooked ones taste so much better. Traditionally hummus is made creamier using a larger proportion of tahini (sesame butter), which tends to be rich with an assertive sesame flavor; I like to underplay the tahini so the other flavors shine through.

Hummus is delicious as an appetizer, served on fresh bread or as a dip for vegetable crudités (see page 17), or as a lunch spread in pita pockets or on bread, along with a salad.

 MAKES 1 1/4 CUPS; SERVES 2 FOR LUNCH, 4 AS APPETIZER

1/2 cup dry chickpeas (1 1/4 cups cooked), cooked with small bay leaf (optional)	1/8 teaspoon ground cumin
	1/8 teaspoon ground coriander
1 small clove garlic, pressed and minced	Few grains cayenne pepper (optional)
2 tablespoons extra-virgin olive oil	Dash of salt (to taste)
1/2 to 1 tablespoon tahini sesame paste (or 1/2 teaspoon toasted sesame oil)	Fresh cilantro, chopped (or extra-virgin olive oil, paprika, and chopped parsley),
2 tablespoons fresh-squeezed lemon juice	as garnish

Soak chickpeas for several hours or overnight. Pour off soaking liquid, cover with water in small saucepan, bring to a boil, and cook for about 1 hour or until very tender. Drain cooking liquid from chickpeas and mash with fork. Gradually "whisk" in other ingredients with fork, all except the garnish. Taste and adjust seasonings, keeping in mind that flavors will intensify slightly as they get to know each other. Store chilled in airtight container or bowl covered with wrap until ready to serve.

Garnish with fresh cilantro or the traditional swirl of olive oil sprinkled with paprika and parsley.

Variation

ORANGE-CORIANDER HUMMUS: Substitute fresh-squeezed orange juice for lemon juice; omit cumin and use 1/4 teaspoon ground coriander.

Lemon-Cream Cheese Spread

This handful of fresh flavors came together as a spread for a Greek eliopitta (Olive Bread, page 202), served as a meze (appetizer). It's nice with crackers or vegetable dippers as well (page 17).

If you are lucky enough to get your hands on a Meyer lemon (available between October and February; I've found them at our local co-op), this is a nice way to feature it. Meyer lemons—a cross between a lemon and mandarin orange—are lovely, fruity and sweet, not at all bitter, and the rind so tender that it is more easily minced than grated. Otherwise, use zest and juice from an organic lemon.

 MAKES ABOUT 3/4 CUP

6 ounces Neufchatel cheese (lightened cream cheese, with 1/3 less fat)

1/2 teaspoon honey

1/2 teaspoon dried marjoram

2 to 3 thin slices Meyer lemon, finely minced, pulp, rind, and all (or 1/2 teaspoon lemon zest + 2 teaspoons juice and 1/4 teaspoon honey)

Using a fork, blend honey, marjoram, and lemon evenly with cream cheese; if it seems a little stiff, add a few more drops lemon juice until you have a good spreading consistency.

Serve as a spread for bread or crackers, or as a dip for sliced apples or veggie crudités (page 17).

Italian Goat Cheese Spread

This treatment for chevre not only makes a simple, delicious appetizer, but is a way to preserve the freshness of this perishable, creamy, tangy cheese by coating the surface with olive oil. Thanks to Lane Fisher who came to our camp as a guest bearing gourmet treats, including a spread made by a cheesemaker in Appleton, Maine, that inspired this approximation. It's rich and satisfying, so don't overindulge!

SERVES 2 TO 3 AS APPETIZER

3 ounces plain chevre

1 to 2 tablespoons chopped fresh basil (about 5 rolled leaves, thinly sliced)

1 tablespoon extra-virgin olive oil

1 tablespoon raw or lightly toasted pine nuts (see page 21 or 144)

Light sprinkle of salt (optional)

Few grates multicolored pepper

Place chevre in small bowl or 8-ounce plastic container. Sprinkle with basil and pine nuts, and salt and pepper to taste. Drizzle with oil.

Serve on small wheat crackers, baguette rounds, or pieces of good multigrain bread. Or, put a dab of spread on cucumber slices, halved cherry tomatoes, or bell-pepper strips.

Crudités & Dips

A colorful platter of mixed raw vegetables is healthy, eye-pleasing, and shouldn't spoil anyone's appetite. Anything fresh and juicy is a good candidate, peeled only if the skin is blemished or tough. Garden-fresh peapods, kohlrabi, sweet "candy carrots," and crunchy sweet rutabaga and Jerusalem artichokes are seasonal or root-cellar treats; otherwise bell peppers, celery, broccoli, and cauliflower are good grocery-store stand-bys any time of year.

 SERVES 4 TO 6 AS APPETIZER

Peapods (snow peas or sugar snaps), whole
Red, yellow, orange, green bell peppers, strips
Small sweet carrots, halved, julienned, or curls
Celery stalks, spears
Cucumbers, slices or spears

Rutabaga, peeled, 1/8–1/4-inch slices
Kohlrabi, peeled, 1/8-inch slices
Broccoli, cauliflower, or broccoflower, florets
Jerusalem artichokes, 1/8–1/4-inch slices
Assorted dips and spreads (pages 15–18)

Tahini-Yogurt Dip (MAKES ABOUT 3/4 CUP)

1/3 cup creamy tahini (sesame butter)
3 tablespoons water
2 tablespoons fresh-squeezed lemon juice
(or orange juice)
1/4 cup plain yogurt

Drop of honey (if using lemon juice)
1/8 teaspoon cumin (coriander w/ orange juice)
Few grains cayenne pepper (optional)
Few drops tamari (optional)
1 tablespoon minced scallions (optional)

Spoon tahini into small bowl or pitcher. Add water gradually, whipping it into the tahini with a fork until about the consistency of buttercream frosting. Gradually stir in lemon or orange juice, then yogurt, then remaining ingredients as desired. Adjust as desired for a thicker or thinner consistency by adding a little more tahini or water. (For a tahini salad dressing, see page 46.)

Tahini Magic

I first encountered tahini, and its magical transformation when whipped with water and other liquids, at the Findhorn Community in Scotland, where I lived, worked, and cooked for three years during my twenties. Every day the community kitchen would lay out a bounteous vegetarian lunch buffet of soups and salads, breads and grains, spreads and dressings, including several tahini-based ones that were fun to make. Tahini whipped with water made a simple spread, drizzled with honey, or could become a creamy dressing or dip spiked with yogurt, lemon juice, and a little cumin; or one tangy with orange juice, coriander, perhaps a few drops tamari and a tiny pinch of cayenne—flavor combinations that speak to me still. We also made a fudgy, cooked miso-orange tahini spread.

These tahini-based dips and dressings go especially well with carrots, napa, Chinese cabbage, broccoli, rutabaga (swedes in Scotland), Jerusalem artichokes, and other sweet brassicas and root vegetables. Like all other sesame products, tahini, though oil-rich, is an excellent source of calcium.

LEMON-SOUR CREAM DIP (MAKES 1 1/3 CUPS)

1 cup sour cream
3 tablespoons plain yogurt
1 tablespoon olive oil
1 tablespoon fresh lemon juice

2 teaspoons honey
1/4 teaspoon ground cumin (*or* 1 teaspoon
    fresh tarragon, 1/2 teaspoon dried)
Small dash cayenne or multicolored pepper

Combine ingredients in small bowl. Serve with raw vegetable dippers.

GUACAMOLE (MAKES 2/3 CUP)

With guacamole, the simpler and fresher, the better—so only make as much as you can consume at one sitting. This makes enough for two to share as an appetizer or garnish with Cheese Nachos.

1 ripe avocado, diced
1 tablespoon olive oil
2 tablespoons lemon or lime juice
1/4 teapoon ground cumin

Tiny pinch cayenne pepper
Salt and multicolored pepper to taste
2 tablespoons fresh cilantro, chopped,
    as garnish (optional)

Spoon avocado into small bowl and mash with fork. Stir in oil, juice, and seasonings. Garnish with cilantro if desired. Serve immediately with tortilla chips or bell pepper strips. Best eaten fresh.

Cheese Nachos

What could be better on a chilly night than a plate full of sizzling nachos laced with home-made, home-grown salsa from your own garden? Offer them as a hot appetizer, or the centerpiece of a quick light supper along with a salad, guacamole, toasted pumpkin seeds, and other Southwestern nibbles.

 SERVES 2 FOR SUPPER, 4 AS APPETIZER

6 white corn tortillas, 6-inch, sliced in quarters
1 1/2 cups (1 1/2 half-pint jars) Garden Salsa
    (or your favorite store-bought salsa; Green
    Mountain Gringo is especially good)

1 1/2 to 1 3/4 cups shredded Manchego cheese
    (or combination provolone/Monterey Jack)
Guacamole (above) and/or sour cream
Lettuce (optional)

Preheat oven to 400°F. Arrange tortilla wedges on pizza pan or baking sheet. Spoon about 1 tablespoon salsa on each tortilla quarter. Sprinkle with cheese, and bake for about 10 minutes or until cheese is bubbling and beginning to brown.

Serve with guacamole and lettuce, or round out the meal with refried beans, rice, and a salad.

GARDEN SALSA

Richard, the salsa maker in our house, takes his cue from what's fresh in our late-summer garden, going with earthy chili flavors or lighter and fresher notes depending on the ingredients at hand. For example, shallots, if you have an abundance, could replace some of the onions in a lighter salsa brightened with lime and cilantro (see variation). Basil, cilantro, cumin, and balsamic vinegar are the accents in a more robust salsa (main recipe). Either way, served fresh or cooked and put by, salsas made from vine-ripened plum tomatoes and fresh-picked, flavorful peppers are muy especiale.

There's always an element of hot-pepper roulette in using home-grown peppers. Peppers picked from the same plant can range from mildly hot to tongue-tingling, lip-burning hot—especially the membranes and seeds. It's a good idea to wear nitrile or latex gloves when seeding and chopping peppers in any quantity. Chances are, though, that even if a nibble of fresh pepper seems blistering hot, cooking will damp the heat a bit. We like growing Hungarian Hot Wax, an early pepper that ripens from pale green to yellow-orange to scarlet, adding color as well as varying amounts of heat.

Serve homemade salsa on Cheese Nachos, on Enchiladas (page 159; spoon a salsa stripe down the row of enchiladas before sprinkling on the cheese), or with steak. I'm not crazy for catsup, but somehow a little salsa is just the right mellowing agent on a charcoal-grilled burger.

5 TO 6 HALF-PINTS

4 1/2 cups fresh tomatoes, seeded and chopped

1 1/2 cups red or yellow onion, chopped

1/2 to 2/3 cup mildly hot peppers (combination of Hungarian Hot Wax, Lipsticks, and/or ancho chile peppers), diced

2 teaspoons salt

3 to 4 tablespoons fresh basil, chopped (*or* 1 1/2 tablespoons dried)

1/3 cup fresh cilantro, chopped (*or* 2 to 3 tablespoons dried)

2 tablespoons olive oil

1/4 teaspoon ground black pepper

1/2 teaspoon ground cumin

1 tablespoon balsamic vinegar (*or* 3 tablespoons fresh lime juice)

1 1/2 to 2 tablespoons red-wine or cider vinegar

Combine vegetables in ceramic or glass covered bowl, stir in salt, and refrigerate overnight (8 to 10 hours). Drain off excess liquid. (NOTE: If using meaty plum tomatoes, you can skip this step and simply add 1/2 to 3/4 teaspoon salt.) Add herbs, spices, and vinegar and mix well.

The salsa may be served garden fresh; any left over will keep 1 to 2 days in the fridge. Or it can be simmered 15 to 20 minutes and eaten with tortilla chips or in Cheese Nachos as a cooked salsa (which keeps longer, a week or so refrigerated), or frozen or canned in half-pint containers. (While we have enjoyed many seasons' worth of our salsa canned using the water-bath method, boiling for 20 minutes, freezing is the safest preservation method for this recipe since it contains oil and modest acidity—although omitting the oil and boosting the acidity would make it safe for processing. To explore the wider world of salsas and safe preserving of low-acid foods, visit www.uga.edu/nchfp.)

Variation

CILANTRO-LIME SALSA: Omit basil and cumin, and use 1/2 cup fresh chopped cilantro, along with 1 to 2 teaspoons fresh mint (if desired). Replace some of the onions with shallots, if available. For acidity, omit balsamic vinegar and use 1/4 cup fresh lime juice plus 2 to 3 teaspoons red wine vinegar.

Crostini with Fresh Mozzarella

Crostini—toasted slabs or rounds of bread dressed with olive oil or any number of intensely flavored tomato, eggplant, or olive-based spreads—are a rustic Italian classic. A crowd-pleaser at summer soirées, this appetizer takes just minutes to make if you have the ingredients on hand.

Our version features molten fresh mozzarella on toasted focaccia as a bland backdrop for a colorful choice of homemade spreads, Genovese Pesto or Tomato-Eggplant Tapenade, letting diners anoint their crostini as they wish. (Or, the crostini can be prepared in reverse, layering the mozzarella on top of the spread.)

Lacking pesto or tapenade, you could simply brush the bread with extra-virgin olive oil, add mozzarella and a sprinkling of fresh basil, minced shallots, and a few cherry tomato slices, and toast the crostini until golden (see first variation). Or, serve crostini toasts with a topping of warm Slow-Roasted Tomato-Onion Confit or Caramelized Onion-Tomato Sauce (see second variation below). The Chicken-Pesto Crostini or Sandwiches (page 23) are another satisfying alternative.

Either way, they're irresistible—don't spoil your appetite for dinner!

 SERVES 6 AS APPETIZER

1 loaf focaccia, about 10- to 11-inch diameter (or rounds of white or multigrain baguette, or Italian bread)	8 ounces fresh mozzarella, sliced in 1/4-inch rounds or half-moons
Extra-virgin olive oil	1/3 to 1/2 cup Genovese Pesto (page 21)
	3/4 cup Tomato-Eggplant Tapenade (page 22)

Use bakery-made focaccia, or make your own (page 206). Cut focaccia loaf in half, then slice each half crosswise into about a dozen 3/4-inch or 7/8-inch slabs, about 24 slices. (Or slice an equivalent amount of baguette rounds or Italian bread, enough to allow about 4 crostini per person.)

Lightly brush each piece of bread with olive oil, then cover with a single layer of mozzarella slices, or rounds if you are using bite-sized mozzarella balls. (Or if you prefer, spread half of the bread slices with pesto and half with tapenade, then cover with mozzarella.)

Bake in toaster oven (or near top of oven preheated to 400°F) until crusts are lightly toasted and cheese is melted and beginning to bubble (not browned). Serve immediately.

Variations

SUMMER GARDEN CROSTINI: Instead of using pesto or tapenade, arrange mozzarella on focaccia and sprinkle with a fresh garnish of chopped basil (or a mixture of basil, marjoram, and oregano), sliced cherry tomatoes, and minced shallots. Toast as described above.

CROSTINI WITH CARAMELIZED ONIONS & TOMATOES: Make 1 recipe Slow-Roasted Tomato-Onion Confit (page 176) or Caramelized Onion-Tomato Sauce (page 99). Serve warm on crostini toasts (focaccia slices or baguette rounds brushed with extra-virgin olive oil and lightly toasted).

GENOVESE PESTO

Every summer we grow a lush patch of Genovese basil, one of the most fragrant varieties—more than enough to eat fresh, so there's plenty to put by dried (page 30) or frozen as pesto. In high summer, when the basil patch is at its peak, I'll often make and freeze a double or triple batch of pesto to see us through to next year. I try to harvest the patch just before it begins to bolt, snipping the tops while leaving enough "understory" to produce a second growth for drying.

Fresh basil quickly darkens once chopped and exposed to air, so unless you're making a freezer batch it is best to only make as much pesto as you can consume right away. Leftover pesto, topped with a sealer coat of olive oil, will keep refrigerated for a couple of days, but freezing is the best way to preserve its fresh green color and flavor. Simply spoon the pesto into small plastic containers to freeze in the shape of a hockey puck. Whenever you need a tablespoon or two in a recipe or to serve with pasta, knock the frozen pesto out of its container and shave off what you need with a sharp knife; the fat content in the oil, cheese, and nuts keeps the frozen block soft enough to slice, and the frozen shavings will quickly melt once added to warm food.

Some recipes recommend that the cheese or garlic be left out of pesto you plan to freeze, to be added to the thawed pesto right before serving; I haven't noticed enough difference in taste or texture to offset the convenience of having the cheese and garlic already incorporated in the pesto.

MAKES 1 1/4 CUPS

2 3/4 to 3 cups fresh Genovese basil leaves, packed (discard any discolored parts)	1/2 cup extra-virgin olive oil
2 to 3 cloves fresh garlic, pressed	1/4 to 1/3 cup pine nuts, lightly toasted
1/3 teaspoon salt (scant 1/2 teaspoon)	1/4 to 1/3 cup grated Romano or Parmigiano-Reggiano cheese (or add later)

Wash, spin, and coarsely chop basil leaves; put half in blender along with garlic and salt. Add half the olive oil and pulse repeatedly, stirring and pushing leaves down into blade area with a chopstick between sets of pulses, until basil is minced and begins to form a paste. Add remaining basil and gradually pour in the rest of the oil, alternately pulsing and stirring until basil is uniformly minced.

Toast pine nuts in 325°F oven, frequently shaking pan, for just a couple of minutes, until they just begin turning light gold; cool. Add pine nuts to blender jar and pulse briefly a few times, enough to chop nuts without forming a purée. Finally stir in the cheese, then scrape mixture into small freezer containers for storage. (For a double batch, 3 half-pint containers work well.) Or reserve some fresh pesto for immediate use; refrigerate it covered with a thin coat of olive oil.

Serve pesto as a sauce or dressing for pasta, as a spread for sandwiches or crostini, or to enrich the flavor of soups, stews, and sauces.

Variation

PARSLEY-WALNUT PESTO: Replace the basil with fresh parsley, and replace the pine nuts with 1/2 to 2/3 cup very lightly toasted walnuts (page 268). Use half the amounts of garlic and cheese, and add 1/2 to 1 teaspoon each freshly grated lemon zest and lemon juice. Serve fresh (2 to 3 tablespoons per serving) tossed with a salad of pasta, wild or brown rice, shell beans, or green beans, cooked till tender or al dente and drained, garnished with cherry tomatoes or bell peppers.

Tomato-Eggplant Tapenade

Having sampled several jarred sundried tomato-eggplant pestos and tapenades over the years, I wanted to try a homemade version combining what I remembered of them with ideas from several Italian recipes. Blending the intense ripe flavors of tomatoes and garlic with the light freshness of eggplant and herbs, the tapenade can be served as a crostini or sandwich spread, or used as a pesto to brighten up a quick lunch of leftover cooked pasta.

The tapenade is best made ahead to allow the flavors to meld. If you're not used to eating raw garlic, roasting it ahead of time (for 20 minutes in a 350°F oven, wrapped in foil) will mellow its bite.

The proportions here are all about the big taste of sundried tomatoes, but you could adjust them to bring the eggplant more to the fore (see variation). Using reconstituted dried tomatoes, bought in bulk from the natural foods store (or home-grown and dried, page 146), is most economical, but alternatively you could use sundried tomatoes packed in oil, omitting the water and olive oil.

MAKES ABOUT 1 1/2 CUPS

8 to 9 dried tomato halves	1 teaspoon dried oregano (2 teaspoons fresh)
1/4 cup water, for soaking	1 teaspoon dried basil (2 teaspoons fresh)
2/3 medium (1/2 large) eggplant, peeled and sliced in 1/2 inch rounds	3 to 3 1/2 tablespoons tomato paste
1/4 cup extra-virgin olive oil	1/2 teaspoon light brown sugar
1 small clove garlic, pressed (*or* 1 to 2 cloves roasted garlic)	1/4 teaspoon salt
	Few grates "party" (multicolored) pepper
	1/2 teaspoon lemon juice

Snip dried tomatoes with scissors into small bowl or cup, cover with water, and soak for several hours or until thoroughly softened. (NOTE: Commercially dried tomato halves can be pretty salty; if the soaking water tastes briny, replace half of it with fresh water.)

Peel eggplant, slice in 1/2-inch-thick rounds, and arrange on liberally oiled baking pan. Cover with foil and bake in 350°F oven for about 10 minutes, then turn and bake another 10 minutes, or until translucent and tender. Turn oven off and let eggplant continue to bake another 5 minutes. Let cool, then put in glass or ceramic bowl and mash with a fork until fairly smooth and creamy (about 2/3 cup mashed eggplant). Set aside.

Place softened tomatoes with their soaking liquid in blender. Add oil and pulse until tomatoes are finely chopped, scraping blender from time to time to redistribute tomatoes around blade. Add garlic, herbs, and remaining ingredients and process just long enough to form a paste. Scrape into bowl with eggplant and mix thoroughly.

Refrigerate in airtight container; tapenade will keep for up to a week. Bring to room temperature before serving.

Variation

EGGPLANT-TOMATO TAPENADE: Use a larger proportion of eggplant, and reduce the amount of tomato paste. Add 1 to 2 tablespoon minced marinated ripe or semi-ripe olives to the tapenade, if desired.

Chicken-Pesto Crostini or Sandwiches

Leftover grilled chicken (especially dark meat) and tomato/basil-based pestos are a match made in heaven. This is a delicious and practical camp or camp-cruising menu item, with ingredients that may appear as part of lunch, an appetizer, or dinner.

  SERVES 2 FOR LUNCH, 4 TO 6 AS APPETIZER

1 to 2 leftover grilled (or roasted) chicken thighs, sliced

4 to 6 tablespoons Tomato-Eggplant Tapenade (page 22) or Genovese Pesto (page 21)

2 to 4 slices Italian Seed Bread (page 204), Sesame Semolina Bread (page 205), or other rustic multigrain bread

1 tablespoon raw or toasted pine nuts (optional)

Slice enough bread for two open-faced sandwiches or 4 to 6 appetizers. For crostini, lightly toast bread dry or brushed with extra-virgin olive oil. For sandwiches, simply slice fresh bread.

Generously spread bread or crostini toasts with tapenade or pesto. Sprinkle with pine nuts (raw or lightly toasted, page 21 or 144) if desired. Top with sliced chicken, and serve immediately, plain or accompanied by arugula or other fresh greens.

Focaccia Grilled-Cheese Sandwiches

This is one of our camp favorites, especially in the off-season, grilled on an old metal pie plate to round out a lunch of homemade Tomato-Basil Soup (page 36). Maybe it's the ambiance, or the molten cheese on a chilly day, but they always taste wonderful.

  SERVES 3 TO 4

1 8-inch (or half of a 10-inch) focaccia, cut in 3 or 4 large wedges

1/3 red onion, thinly sliced rings, cut in halves or thirds

About 3 ounces cheddar, gouda, or goat gouda cheese, thinly sliced

Extra-virgin olive oil

Use bakery-made focaccia, or make your own (page 206). Using a serrated bread knife, slice focaccia wedges horizontally to form pockets, leaving outside edge of crust as a hinge. Open each pocket, place slices of cheese on lower half, then sprinkle with red onion. Reclose "lids."

Lightly wipe frying pan, griddle, or metal baking pan with olive oil and place over low heat, preferably with a flame tamer or other heat diffuser underneath. Arrange pockets in pan and grill, turning every few minutes as needed to evenly toast both sides while melting cheese inside. Mmmm.

Salmon (or Steak) Sandwiches

Here's a glamorous way to use up leftover grilled salmon or steelhead trout (page 64) or steak. Serve open-faced salmon or steak sandwiches laced with zesty Dill-Horseradish Sauce as a simple, tasty hors d'oeuvre (using small baguette rounds), or a summertime lunch on slabs of fresh bread (or with German Potato Salad, page 48) on a salad plate of garden vegetables.

  SERVES 2 FOR LUNCH, 4 AS APPETIZER

About 1/4 pound leftover grilled salmon, steelhead trout (page 64), or beef steak, sliced in thin bite-sized pieces (*or* 3 to 4 ounces smoked salmon)

4 to 6 slabs fresh focaccia or crusty French boule or baguette, 1 inch thick
Dill-Horseradish Sauce (page 64)
Lettuce, cukes, peapods, garden tomatoes

Assemble each sandwich with enough salmon or steak to cover the bread, and top with a spoonful of Dill-Horseradish Sauce. For lunch, round out the meal with a little fresh garden lettuce (or alfalfa sprouts), ripe tomatoes, and crisp cucumbers or peapods. Beer is the beverage of choice.

ALFALFA SPROUTS

Alfalfa sprouts make a fresh, lacy garnish for a sandwich or salad, loaded with nutrition. Really, they're best—and cheapest—when grown at home on your windowsill, an easy 5-day crop.

Pour 1 1/4 to 1 1/2 tablespoons alfalfa seeds (sold at natural food stores) into a sterilized 1-quart wide-mouth mason jar and soak 8 hours or overnight in cold water. Cover the top of the jar with a doubled piece of fine nylon netting, secured with a jar ring, and drain off the water. Rinse, drain again thoroughly, and keep in a dark place for a day or so, until the seeds sprout. Once sprouted, rinse, drain, and shake the jar to spread out the seeds along the length of the jar. Keep the jar on its side near a window, in partial sunlight (or under a "grow" light if you are starting seeds), rinsing and draining the sprouts twice a day, until they are about 1 inch long and beginning to green up.

At this point the jar will be crowded with sprouts and hulls. Empty the sprouts into a large bowl of cold water and flush them gently but thoroughly, separating clumps with your fingers and freeing the sprouts from their tough brown hulls, which float conveniently to the top. Pour off the water and hulls, then rinse and repeat. Drain, then return the sprouts to their jar for a final greening. Another few hours in a sunny spot, and they'll be ready to eat. Leftover sprouts may be refrigerated in an airtight container, but be sure to eat them within the next few days while they're the most vital.

This same basic method can be used to sprout a number of other seeds—lentils, mung beans, radishes, sunflower seeds, wheat berries—which can be used in salads, sandwiches, breads, stir-fries. . .

Toasted Vegetable-Cheese Pockets

These pockets (kind of a rustic hot sub) are a favorite default for a quick light supper or lunch, or a savory hors d'oeuvre. With this in mind, we try to have at least one loaf of focaccia laid away in the freezer. Luckily, fresh authentic focaccia is usually available from local artisan bakers. Or, bake your own version of this yeasted Italian flatbread (page 206).

Focaccia is best fresh, but if frozen the porous, light-textured bread will thaw out in about 10 minutes. The loaf can then be sliced into large, meal-sized wedges (or smaller appetizer-sized ones) and each wedge sliced horizontally to form a pocket for a savory filling. Make the sautéed vegetable filling below if you have the time; otherwise just slather on a little olive oil and stuff the pockets with fresh mozzarella cheese, herbs, and raw tender vegetables (such as spinach, tomatoes, red onion, olives) to make a toasted Italian sandwich.

 SERVES 4 FOR LUNCH, 6 TO 8 AS APPETIZERS

1 loaf focaccia, plain or sprinkled with rosemary (page 206)

2 tablespoons extra-virgin olive oil

1 medium yellow onion, small crescent slices

1 clove garlic, pressed or minced

2 cups colored bell peppers (red, yellow, orange), small slices

1/2 teaspoon salt

1 cup portabella mushrooms (or 1/2 cup ripe or semi-ripe marinated olives), sliced

Fresh or dried Italian herbs to taste (basil, oregano, marjoram)

2 to 2 1/2 cups fresh spinach, washed, stemmed, and patted dry

About 3/4 pound fresh mozzarella, 1/4-inch slices

Using a serrated bread knife, cut focaccia in appetizer- or lunch-sized wedges, then slice each wedge horizontally, leaving enough outer crust to act as a "hinge," forming triangular pockets. Wash and cut vegetables into bite-sized pieces.

Sauté onion in olive oil until slightly caramelized, then add garlic and peppers (and optional mushrooms or olives), sprinkle with salt, and sauté until peppers are nicely done. Add herbs and spinach, and cook just long enough to partly deflate spinach.

Divide filling among pockets. Distribute mozzarella slices among pockets, placing cheese on top of filling. Bake in toaster oven (or near top of 375°F oven) until focaccia is lightly toasted around the edges and pockets are hot through enough to melt the mozzarella. Serve immediately.

Ploughman's Lunch

I first stumbled on this cheese-chutney combination in a remote village pub on a youthful hosteling adventure in the English Lake District. A couple decades later, as a householder with a big veggie garden, I rediscovered chutney as a perfect use for green tomatoes—and ploughman's lunch!

The open-faced sandwich is simply a slab of crusty white or whole-grain bread with ample slices of richly flavored cheddar cheese, preferably grilled. Serve with chutney, maybe some pickled onions or fresh scallions and a sprig of parsley, and ale from your favorite microbrewery (or hot tea), and you have a fine bit of lunch—or made on a smaller scale, with rounds of baguette, an hors d'oeuvre.

 SERVES 1 FOR LUNCH

1 large, thick slab white or multigrain bread (preferably boule or other rustic bread)
Several slices cheddar cheese (New England, Irish, or English cheddar; see page 135)

1 to 2 tablespoons Green Tomato Chutney
Tiny pickled onions or chopped scallions (optional)
Parsley, lettuce, or alfalfa sprouts (optional)

Arrange slices of cheese on bread. Serve sandwich cold, or toasted for a few minutes in a toaster oven, accompanied by chutney and onions, garnished with a little greenery if desired.

GREEN TOMATO CHUTNEY (MAKES 4 PINTS)

This is a noble way to put those unripened garden tomatoes, saved from the frost, to good use. Green Tomato Mincemeat (page 239) is another way. Oh, and how about fried green tomatoes, sliced, dredged in flour or cornmeal, and fried in bacon fat? a sweet-sour delicacy my Mom used to make . . .

5 cups green tomatoes, seeded, thinly sliced, then chopped
1 1/2 teaspoons salt
6 cups ripe apples, peeled, cored, and chopped
Freshly grated zest of 2 oranges
Chopped, seeded fruit of 1 orange
1 cup Thompson raisins
1 cup diced yellow onion
2 medium garlic cloves, minced

1/4 cup fresh ginger root, skinned and minced
1 small mildly hot pepper (such as Hungarian Wax or Anaheim chile)
1/2 teaspoon salt
1 3/4 cups brown sugar
1/2 cup apple cider vinegar
1 1/2 teaspoons cinnamon
1/2 teaspoon nutmeg
3/4 teaspoon ground cloves

Place all ingredients in large pot, and bring slowly to a boil over medium-high heat. Once boiling, lower heat and cook uncovered for 10 minutes, then covered for 10 minutes more, stirring occasionally; lower to minimum heat toward the end of cooking.

Meanwhile, sterilize 4 pint jars by boiling for 10 minutes. Soak 4 new lids in a pan of hot water. Ladle chutney into drained hot jars, leaving 1/2 inch headroom; wipe mouths of jars with a paper towel dipped in hot water, cap with lids and rings, and process in boiling-water bath for 10 minutes.

Chutney's flavor improves after aging for a few months. Stored in a cool, dry pantry out of direct sunlight, it should keep for several years but, like all home-canned goods, is best used in 1 to 2 years.

CRANBERRY CHUTNEY (MAKES 1 1/2 CUPS)

This spicy dried-fruit chutney, made by my creative Washburn sister-in-law Betsy Butterworth, steals the show at Thanksgiving served alongside roast turkey. It also goes nicely with rich aged cheddar—or as suggested by my Crosen sister-in-law Nancy, spread over cream cheese on crackers as an appetizer.

3/4 cup dried cranberries	1/2 cup water
1/2 cup golden raisins or sultanas	1 teaspoon fresh rosemary, chopped
1/2 cup orange juice	1 teaspoon fresh sage, chopped
1/4 teaspoon cayenne pepper	1 teaspoon fresh thyme, chopped
1/8 cup (2 tablespoons) brown sugar	3 tablespoons fresh parsley, chopped

Put first 6 ingredients in saucepan and simmer covered about 15 minutes, or until fruit plumps up. Add herbs and simmer over low heat another 5 to 10 minutes to blend flavors. Store refrigerated.

Mushroom-Cheese Baguette

This is my idea of the ultimate toasted cheese sandwich—quick, light, and satisfying. Since I mostly make it as a one-woman-sized lunch, amounts are for a single serving, but could easily be scaled up for a small lunch gathering or hors d'oeuvres. The intense flavors—savory mushrooms and garlic, sweet tarragon and sherry, sour tangy mustard—want a plain bread in the background (not sourdough). Any Dijon-type mustard will do; a nice local choice is Raye's Winter Garden, stone-ground by Raye's Mustard Mill, a century-old family-owned operation in Eastport, Maine.

 SERVES 1 FOR LUNCH, 2 AS APPETIZERS

3 to 4 baby portabella mushrooms, sliced	Grate of white pepper, dash of salt
Olive oil and butter, about 1 teaspoon each	1 large slab white/multigrain baguette or other
1/2 to 1 shallot, sliced (optional)	crusty, rustic bread (or 2 smaller rounds)
1 garlic clove, minced	Few slices Gruyère or rich cheddar cheese
1 to 2 teaspoons dry sherry	Dijon-type mustard
1/4 teaspoon dried tarragon	Handful of alfalfa sprouts (page 24, optional)

Heat oil and butter in small sauté pan, and gently sauté mushrooms (with shallots, if desired) until they begin to release their liquor, then add garlic and sauté for a moment more. Sprinkle with sherry, tarragon, salt, and pepper, sauté just long enough to cook the sherry, then turn off heat.

Meanwhile, arrange cheese on top of bread and bake/broil in toaster oven until bread is toasted around the edges and cheese begins to bubble. Spread with a little mustard, then pile mushroom mixture on open-faced sandwich. Top with fresh alfalfa sprouts if desired. Serve with hot fragrant tea, cold lager beer, or beverage of your choice.

Savory Potato Pasties

I made these as refreshments for a belated 50th. The timing hadn't worked out on my actual birthday (in late May) for a proper celebration, but heading into the new year I realized: better late than never. And what better time than the dead of winter, when we're all ready for a cabin fever reliever!

Hmm, what to serve a group of best women friends as a savory warm-up after cross-country skiing and snowshoeing through woods and snowy meadows to nearby Wight Pond? Something special I could make ahead of time and reheat . . . mmm, pasties! And with a variety of diets among us—vegetarians, meat-eaters, dairy-free—I could customize the filling by adding one of three flavorful treats: mushrooms, cheese, or sausage. Making a triple batch turned out to be quite a project, but the pasties were wonderful, just right washed down with a cold beer after our expedition in the sun and snow.

This recipe combines the featured treats—cheese and mushrooms or sausage—in two filling options. You could make some of each, using half the amounts of mushrooms and sausage. Goat gouda is a good choice for cheese, since it's less likely to melt into the filling (as cheddar would). The cheeses, butter, and milk could be left out for a dairy-free version.

You'll need one-and-a-half batches of pastry to make all of the pasties, and 1 to 2 hours cooking time. If short on time, I'd recommend baking off two-thirds of the filling with a full recipe of pastry, and refrigerating the rest to bake off later, letting it come to room temperature before assembling.

 15 PASTIES; SERVES 6 TO 8 FOR LUNCH

2 2/3 to 3 cups (3 medium) potatoes, diced

1 teaspoon salted butter

2 teaspoons olive oil

1 1/4 to 1 1/2 cups baby portabella mushrooms, coarsely chopped (or 1 to 2 Italian or fennel pork sausages, 3 to 6 ounces)

1 tablespoon dry sherry

1 1/2 tablespoons olive oil

1 medium yellow onion, chopped (2/3 cup)

3 to 4 scallions, chopped, white/green separated

2 cups savoy cabbage, shredded/coarsely chopped

1/4 teaspoon garlic powder

1/4 teaspoon nutmeg

1/8 to 1/4 teaspoon white pepper (and/or small pinch of cayenne if desired)

1/4 to 1/2 teaspoon salt

1 1/2 teaspoons dried winter savory

Few dried lovage leaves, crumbled (optional)

2/3 cup firm, flavorful cheese (such as goat gouda or Gruyère), diced

2 to 2 1/2 ounces (1/4 to 1/3 cup) Neufchatel or cream cheese

1 1/2 recipes Whole-Wheat Pastry, Double-Crust Recipe (page 238)

Cover potatoes with boiling water and cook until tender. Meanwhile, start preparing rest of ingredients for filling. When potatoes are cooked, drain water and set them aside.

Melt butter with 2 teaspoons oil in small sauté pan and gently fry mushrooms (if using) until they begin to brown up and soften. Deglaze with sherry and keep on heat just long enough to cook off alcohol, then set aside. (Or, if you are using sausage instead of mushrooms, parboil sausage in a little water, then chop. If sausage pieces are still pink, fry them a little more until well done.)

Heat 1 1/2 tablespoons olive oil in large skillet and sauté onion and white parts of scallions until translucent. Add cabbage and sauté/sweat, stirring frequently, until tender. Deglaze pan with sherry (if not already added to mushrooms), then turn off heat and stir in seasonings, potatoes, and green scallion tops. Let cool slightly before adding cheeses. (The still-warm potatoes will probably break down slightly while melting some of the cheese, but that's fine; this will help hold the filling together.) Finally, add mushrooms or sausage to filling.

To bake 10 pasties, make 1 batch Whole-Wheat Pastry, Double Crust Recipe (page 239), using olive oil in place of canola. Divide dough evenly into 10 balls 1 1/2 inches in diameter. Working one at a time on floured surface, roll out dough into ovals about 4 1/2 x 6 1/2 inches. (NOTE: This will use up 2/3 of the filling; you will need to make another half batch of pastry to bake off 5 more pasties. To bake off all of the pasties at once, make 1 1/2 batches of pastry, and divide dough into 15 balls.)

Preheat oven to 425°F. Working one freshly rolled-out pastry oval at a time, fill the front third with 1/3 cup filling (a good serving spoonful, as much as will fit without bursting at the seams), leaving 1/2 inch margin of pastry around edge of filling. Moisten around filled edge with your finger dipped in water. Fold other half of pastry over filling to line up with the moistened edge, and pat edges together to seal. Using a fork, poke three rows of holes in top of each pasty to vent steam.

Using a spatula, transfer pasties to unoiled baking sheets, 5 to a tray, keeping corners of pasties away from outside edges of pan (so pastry won't scorch). Lightly brush tops with milk. Put first tray in preheated oven to bake while you assemble second tray.

Bake for 12 to 14 minutes or until pastry is nicely golden but not overdone. Remove to cooling rack. Any leftovers can be reheated as a lunch or snack for 10 to 12 minutes in a 375° oven.

SCRAPS OF WISDOM

A simple suggestion from one of my friends made it not just a party, but a circle of women's wisdom: "What can we bring? Perhaps some words of wisdom about growing older?" This came just in time to add a P.S. to the invitations: "Bring a scrap of wisdom you have gleaned in your growing older, some touchstone to live by, handwritten on an interesting scrap of paper, to share."

After the winter outing, the pasties and visiting, we gathered in a circle and read the "scraps" one by one, and many of them resound in me still: "For every problem, there is a solution." "You gotta do what you wanna do! Seize the day!" "Whatever you wish to be doing, dream about doing, don't wait until whenever to start; do it now!" "Savor." "There is no way to happiness—happiness is the way." "The important thing is not to think much, but to love much." "Breathe." And the very question that launched the party, "Why not?"

Home-Grown Herbs

Growing, harvesting, and drying herbs takes a little more effort than buying them in bulk or in jars. Why bother? Quality—we find home-grown herbs to be much more aromatic than commercial dried herbs, even those bought in bulk from the natural food store. One key difference is that, working at the small scale of home garden, you can harvest herbs selectively, in their prime, before they bud up and bloom. Another key to flavor, I think, is drying and storing the herbs as whole leaves, to crumble with your fingers as you add them to a dish (rather than crushing them to fill the bottle); this holds the herbs' essential oils and aroma in the leaf, to be released in cooking. We store the bulk of our home-grown herbs in jars in the pantry, minimizing exposure to air and light, and refill the small bottles in our spice drawer by the stove as needed.

Most of the savory herbs are easy to harvest: snip or pinch off the leafed-out stalks or branchlets (or with sage, pick the leaves after the first frost). If the leaves grow on a large stalk (as with lovage, dill, or cilantro), it is easier to harvest the whole stalk, then snip off the small branchlets in the house. With most low-growing herbs (such as oregano, marjoram, savory, thyme), if they're at all dusty, you'll want to rinse and dry them in a salad spinner. Then spread them out in a dry, dust-free environment; with the harvests from our modest-sized garden, I simply scatter the herbs evenly over clean sheets of unbleached paper laid on wide pieces of cardboard on a dresser in our upstairs storage room, out of direct sunlight, to air-dry, which they do in less than a week. Or, you can spread them in a thin layer on clean nylon screens, or dry them in clean paper bags slashed with ventilation holes.

Basil, which has larger, fleshier leaves and stalks, needs special treatment; after experimenting with various methods of handling basil, I've settled on picking it in branchlets of 4 to 8 leaves before the plants bud up to flower, then stringing the branchlets, stem-end up, on lengths of doubled thread as you would popcorn for a Christmas tree. (I use red thread, which adds to the festivity while making the thread easier to see.) Then I drape the strings between pairs of push-pins in the driest part of our house, the storage room open to our bedroom. During the week or so it takes them to dry, they decorate our upstairs like festoons of green bats hanging upside down from the rafters.

When the basil is completely dry, I snip off the knots and slide it off its strings into a paper bag, then (in a run of dry weather) break the now-brittle leaves off the stems and into clean dry jars. As with all other leafy herbs like oregano, marjoram, savory, and thyme, sliding the dried leaves off the stems by hand lets you harvest the leaves whole and intact, preserving the essential oils and flavors.

If the herbs have dried but seem slightly damp (perhaps due to humid weather), it's wise to spread them on tinfoil (formed into shallow-sided sided trays) for a few minutes' bake in a slightly warm (not hot!) oven, with the door ajar, just to dry out any humidity, to ensure against mold. Then weed out the tough stems, and pack the herbs loosely in clean airtight jars.

NOTE: As a rule of thumb, when using dried herbs in a recipe calling for fresh herbs, use half the amount of dried herbs as you would fresh—or vice versa, twice the amount of fresh herbs as dried.

# Soups

Soup or Slumgullion?

If you have the time, there's nothing like a homemade soup stirred up from scratch—preferably a big batch, as the flavor gets fuller with each serving. Between the making and the eating, you'll be many times warmed by a pot of Pea Soup with Ham Hocks & Root Vegetables (page 43). Yet soup from scratch needn't be a production—most soups in our repertoire go together pretty quickly, especially with a soup base made ahead, as Richard often does with fish or clam chowder and a tomato soup base that can be finished off in various ways (page 35). Whether from scratch or inspired by leftovers, the soups here offer just a few of many possibilities based on pulses, vegetables, dairy, perhaps a bit of fish, fowl, or meat. And really, who needs a recipe? Some of the best *soups du jour* are made of intuition and serendipity.

Then there's the slumgullion, a seafaring stew for many made from whatever's on hand to throw in the pot. More often than not, lunch at our house is an expedient coming-together of compatible leftovers, each cook stirring their own broth, *chacun à son gout!* Whether we call it "soup" or "slumgullion" depends on the proportion of liquid and fresh ingredients that go into the pot. Come to think of it, our slumgullions are usually one-portion one-pot experiments, while soups—more of a labor of love—are made for two.

Maybe there's a leftover dinner dish, such as curry, that can be stretched into a soup with the addition of some chicken or vegetable stock—or thrown in with a quickly cooked pot of red lentils. Or some leftover cooked vegetables could be combined with stock and Italian staples like shell beans, home-made tomato sauce, basil or pesto, nuggets of bacon, ham, sausage, grated cheese. Leftover mashed potatoes, winter squash, or steamed broccoli or cauliflower can be creamed with milk or chicken stock and seasoned with sweet and savory herbs, a touch of heat or spice, garlic and onion powder (or freshly sautéed chopped onion and garlic). Or, heat leftover steamed mussels or shrimp, or the remains from a scampi or scallop dish, with a little milk or cream, shellfish stock, maybe some corn, and you have yourself a glamorous chowder or bisque. As long as you combine with discretion, staying within the same flavor family, soups inspired by leftovers are a chance to be creative while cycling things through the refrigerator.

Quick Minestrone

While Italian-style vegetable soups traditionally combine pasta, rice, and/or potatoes with beans and a mix of summer and winter vegetables, I much prefer keeping these and other brothy soups fresh and simple, without the root vegetables and redundant carbos, rounding things out instead with a slab of toast or crusty fresh bread drizzled with olive oil.

Although this summer-vegetable soup can be made entirely from scratch, a head start of leftovers and Italian staple ingredients makes for almost instant gratification, especially if you have some sautéed Summer Veggies (page 177), Rustic Tomato Sauce (page 141), or Pasta e Fagioli sauce (pages 147–48). A little Genovese Pesto (page 21) brings it all together and deepens the flavor. (I always keep a supply of homemade pesto in the freezer, frozen in small plastic containers; these green "hockey pucks" can easily be popped out and a little pesto shaved off with a knife.) An Italian cook probably wouldn't reuse leftover pasta, but a frugal Yankee could certainly add some to the pot.

For a similar quick lunch in the form of a stew, see the Tuscan One-Pot on page 145.

 SERVES 2

1/2 cup chopped onion

1 cup Tuscan kale or thinly sliced zucchini, bite-sized pieces (*or* 2/3 cup leftover sautéed summer vegetables)

2/3 cup tomato juice (from canned tomatoes)

1 cup water and/or veggie or chicken stock

Pinch (1/2 teaspoon) light brown sugar

4 canned plum tomatoes, chopped (*or* 2/3 cup leftover chunky tomato sauce)

1 to 1 1/3 cups cooked dry beans or shell beans (*or* leftover Pasta e Fagioli)

2 to 3 tablespoons pesto, fresh or frozen

1/4 cup grated/shredded Parmesan, Romano, Manchego, or smoked provolone cheese

If using fresh vegetables, briefly sauté onion in a little olive oil in small pot or saucepan, then stir in kale or zucchini and cook until al dente; otherwise put leftover sautéed veggies in pot. Add liquids, pinch of brown sugar, tomatoes (or tomato sauce), and cooked beans (or leftover Pasta e Fagioli).

Heat almost to a boil over moderate heat, adjusting liquids to make a soup of the available ingredients. When almost ready, add pesto and stir/melt into the soup.

Pour minestrone into warmed soup bowl(s), topping each serving with shredded or grated cheese. Serve with crusty bread or toast.

 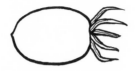

CRUSTY BOULE

To give day-old rolls or boule that just-out-of-the-oven appeal to serve with soup, put them in the oven—wrapped loosely in foil so the heat can refresh the crust—and bake at 350°F 5 to 10 minutes for rolls, 15 to 20 minutes for a boule (whole or half), or until nicely crusty and heated through. Pass the boule, so each person can tear off a hunk of steaming-hot crusty bread to butter or drizzle with oil.

Lamb & Bean Soup

Although this hearty Mediterranean-inspired soup can be made the "slow food" way, using a small lamb shank browned then cooked with the beans, the shortcut using a leftover lamb chop and precooked beans (first variation) is just as delicious. Either way, home-cooked dry beans (see pages 152 and 156) will taste better than canned beans. An even quicker shortcut might take advantage of leftover Braised Mediterranean Lamb Shanks (page 119).

  SERVES 2 TO 3

1 1/2 to 1 2/3 cup cooked cannellini or other large, plump, white beans, such as Calypso, Bumblebee, or Snowcap (2/3 cup dry beans)

1 small lamb shank

1 cup cooking liquid from beans

1 1/2 cups lamb, chicken, or vegetable stock

2 teaspoons olive oil

1/2 medium onion, chopped

2 medium cloves garlic, minced

2 tablespoons dry red wine

2 tablespoons tomato juice

2 to 3 fresh or canned plum tomatoes, seeded and chopped

1/8 teaspoon fresh rosemary, minced (1 sprig)

1/8 teaspoon thyme

Salt to taste

Few grinds multicolored pepper

Fresh lemon peel, 4 to 5 thin strips per serving, as garnish

2/3 cup fresh parsley leaves (or 1 to 1 1/2 cups fresh spinach, chard, or tender Tuscan kale, stemmed, coarsely chopped (optional)

Soak beans overnight. Drain liquid, then put beans in a pot and cover with water plus 1 inch. Cook the beans about 25 minutes, or until partly tender; then drain, reserving 1 cup cooking liquid.

Brown the lamb shank thoroughly on all sides in olive oil in Dutch oven or heavy-bottomed pot; drain grease from pan. Add browned shank to soup pot with the partly cooked beans, the reserved bean liquid, and the stock. Bring back up to a boil, then lower heat and simmer, covered, another 20 to 30 minutes, or until beans are tender and lamb is cooked through. Remove lamb from bones, cut in bite-sized pieces, and return to the pot.

While the beans are cooking, heat olive oil in Dutch oven and sauté onion until partly translucent. Add garlic and sauté a minute more. Deglaze pan with wine, tomato juice, and tomatoes; add rosemary, thyme, and pepper.

Pour contents of soup pot into Dutch oven with sautéed onions, tomatoes, and seasonings. Simmer over low heat for 1 to 2 minutes, then taste for salt and correct seasoning (less salt if using salted stock). Continue cooking for another 5 to 10 minutes.

If the beans are still mostly whole, remove a couple ladle-fuls from the pot and break them up with a hand masher; then return them to the soup, to give more body to the broth.

Bring the soup back up to heat and serve each steaming bowlful garnished with a few strips of fresh lemon peel and a handful of parsley. (Or for more of a meal, just before serving sprinkle spinach, chard, or kale over the soup and simmer for about 2 minutes, or until the greens are deflated.) Serve with toasted rustic bread drizzled with olive oil.

Variations

QUICK LAMB & BEAN SOUP: Cook soaked beans about 45 to 55 minutes, refreshing water midway, until tender; then drain, reserving 1 cup liquid. Instead of lamb shank, cut meat from 1 to 2 leftover pan-fried or broiled lamb chops in bite-sized pieces and add along with the bones (for flavor) to the soup base along with the garlic. After adding liquids and seasonings to the soup base, combine with the beans and finish soup as described above (removing bones before serving). Serve garnished with lemon and parsley.

LAMB & LENTIL SOUP: Cook brown, green, or French lentils in place of the beans (page 152). Since lentils cook more quickly than beans (about 30 minutes), use leftover roast lamb or a pan-fried loin or arm chop cut in bite-sized pieces, adding the meat to the soup base along with the garlic. After adding rest of ingredients, combine soup base with the cooked lentils and stock and simmer 10 to 15 minutes.

Tomato-Onion Soup

If you have a good crop of ripe tomatoes, this is a fine way to capture summer. A combination of plum and beefsteak tomatoes will give you a good balance of sweetness and acidity; with more of one type or the other, you will want to taste and adjust, adding a bit more or less brown sugar, or a drop of balsamic vinegar if your tomatoes are mostly sweet.

Though it's nice to have a few quarts of tomato soup base put away for a quick lunch, this recipe can easily be scaled down by one-fourth to make 1 quart of fresh tomato soup, enough for a single meal (3 or 4 servings). Lacking fresh tomatoes, you can use whole canned ones.

Although cognac is sometimes added to similar fresh cream-of-tomato soups, dry sherry is handy, less dear, and adds just the right touch of flavor and elegance.

TOMATO SOUP BASE (MAKES 4 QUARTS)

8 pounds (8 pints chopped) fresh whole plum
    tomatoes, halved, seeded, and chopped

4 cups chopped yellow onion, small dice

4 tablespoons salted butter

1/4 cup extra-virgin olive oil

1/2 cup fresh basil (optional)

1 to 1 1/4 teaspoons salt

1/4 teaspoon fresh-ground white pepper

2 tablespoons light brown sugar, lightly packed
    (more with non-vine-ripened tomatoes)

Prepare tomatoes and onions. Melt butter with oil over medium heat in large soup pot or Dutch oven, and sauté onion until translucent; do not brown. Add tomatoes, also the basil if you will be using the soup base for Tomato-Basil Soup. Add salt, pepper, and sugar to taste (more or less depending on the ripeness and sweetness of your tomatoes). Simmer for about 30 minutes.

Enjoy 1 quart of the soup fresh, finished off as Tomato-Basil Soup or Sherried Cream of Tomato Soup (page 36), and freeze or can the rest in quart containers for future use. (NOTE: Since the recipe contains oil and low-acid onions and herbs, freezing is a safer preservation method than canning.)

TOMATO-BASIL SOUP

 SERVES 3 TO 4

1 quart Tomato Soup Base

1 tablespoon dried basil, if not in soup base

1 1/4 to 1 1/2 cups low-sodium chicken stock

Add chicken stock to soup base and heat over moderate temperature. Serve with toasted focaccia or garlic toast, Potato Pancakes (page 170), or Focaccia Grilled-Cheese Sandwiches (page 23).

SHERRIED CREAM OF TOMATO SOUP

 SERVES 3 TO 4

1 quart Tomato Soup Base

2 teaspoons dried basil, if not in soup base (*or* 1/2 teaspoon dried tarragon or chervil)

1 1/2 to 2 tablespoons dry sherry

1 to 1 1/4 cups half-and-half (or equal parts milk and half-and-half)

Fresh parsley as garnish (optional)

Warm soup base in saucepan over moderate heat. Mix sherry with half-and-half, then slowly stir into warmed soup and bring up to heat (do not boil). Hopefully the half-and-half will not break, but if it does the soup will still taste delicious. Serve with crusty bread, hot rolls, or toasted focaccia.

Mussel Soup with Tomatoes

Looking for a way to use up some leftover steamed mussels and stock, Richard came up with this simple, tomato-based mussel soup rounded out with peppers, olives, and other Mediterranean flavors.

 SERVES 2

1 tablespoon olive oil

1/2 onion, finely chopped

1/3 to 1/2 green bell pepper, chopped

1 small clove garlic, minced

1/2 cup frozen corn (optional)

3 to 4 olives (green/ripe medley), sliced

3 to 4 canned plum tomatoes, chopped

2/3 cup juice drained from tomatoes

1/2 teaspoon dried Greek oregano

1 1/4 cups small steamed mussels (page 66)

1/2 cup mussel stock + 2 to 3 tablespoons water

Salt and pepper to taste

Sauté onion and peppers in olive oil, adding garlic (and corn, if desired) once peppers are sealed and al dente. Add olives, the tomatoes and their juice, oregano, mussels, and stock plus water as needed to make a nice broth. Taste for seasoning and add a pinch of brown sugar (if not using corn), salt, and a grate of pepper or dash of pepper sauce to taste. Simmer for about 5 minutes, then serve.

Crabmeat (or Shrimp) Bisque

Nothing can be finer than a shellfish bisque made from scratch, using fresh Maine crabmeat or shrimp in season (see page 70). It can be made pure and simple, or dressed up with a light touch of herbs, sherry, and paprika.

On the other hand, if you have a small amount of leftover Shrimp Scampi, Caribbean Jerk Shrimp, or Chili Scallops (pages 73, 72, 68), you have the makings of a quick (but glorious) seafood bisque. Make the same soup base, omitting seasonings, add the leftover seafood to the bisque in place of the fresh shellfish, and bring up to heat.

 SERVES 2

1 teaspoon butter
1 teaspooon olive oil
1/2 medium onion, finely chopped (*or*
    3 large shallots, minced), about 1/2 cup
Few grinds white pepper
1/2 teaspoon winter savory
1/8 teaspoon dried tarragon (optional)
1 to 2 teaspoons dry sherry (optional)
2/3 cup fresh or frozen corn (optional)

1 cup shrimp stock (page 70)
2 1/2 tablespoons flour
1 1/4 cups milk, divided
1/2 cup half-and-half
Pinch of salt to taste
3/4 to 1 cup (about 1/2 pound) fresh crab-
    meat or Maine shrimp meat (raw or
    precooked and shelled as on page 70)

Melt butter with oil in saucepan and sauté onion (or shallots) over medium-low heat for 1 to 2 minutes, until onion is translucent but not brown. Add pepper, herbs, sherry, then corn (if using) and shrimp stock, and cook 1 minute more, stirring frequently.

Meanwhile dissolve flour in 1/2 cup of the milk, smoothing out lumps. Stir wash into soup base and continue cooking over medium-low heat, stirring constantly, until thickened.

Add remaining 3/4 cup milk and half-and-half, salt to taste, and bring slowly up to heat. Add crabmeat or shrimp, and heat until shellfish is cooked through and bisque is steaming. Top each bowlful with a shaving of butter and a light sprinkle of paprika if desired. Serve with hot yeast rolls, Bakewell Cream biscuits (page 192), or crusty bread.

Creamy Potato-Cheese Soup

This can be made as a slightly chunky potato potage, or a creamier soup puréed in the blender. Either way, it's a nice way to combine leftover mashed potatoes with other staple ingredients to create a savory, satisfying soup. Leftover steamed or sautéed vegetables, if you have them, add interest (see variation).

With a couple of shortcuts, this is an easy soup to stir up in a rustic kitchen at camp or afloat. Just cream the leftover potatoes with milk at home and pour into a 1-quart container, along with the seasonings and flour (or fold them into a foil spice packet; you could even substitute a little onion powder for the minced raw onion). Pour into soup pot, add stock or bouillon, and heat until thickened, finally melting in the cheese.

 SERVES 2

1 1/2 to 2 cups Garlic Mashed Potatoes (page 170)
2 1/4 cups milk
1 to 2 tablespoons unbleached flour
1 tablespoon olive oil
1 small or 1/2 medium onion, minced (*or* 2
    scallions, thinly sliced, white and green
    parts separated)
3/4 cup vegetable or chicken stock (or bouillon)
1/2 teaspoon dried lovage (optional)

1/4 teaspoon ground coriander (*or* 1/8 teaspoon
    ground nutmeg)
1/2 teaspoon winter savory (or marjoram)
Pinch cayenne (optional)
Few grates white pepper
Salt to taste
2/3 to 3/4 cup goat gouda and/or cheddar
    (or other flavorful cheese), chopped or
    shredded

Use a fork to mash the potatoes in a small bowl, creaming in some of the milk as you smooth out lumps. Dissolve flour in remaining milk (more or less flour, depending on the consistency of the mashed potatoes; the melted cheese will also thicken the soup), then stir into creamed potatoes.

Heat oil in soup pot and sauté onion (or white scallion slices) over moderate heat until translucent. Add creamed potatoes along with stock, herbs, pepper, and salt to taste. Heat gradually over medium-low heat, stirring frequently as soup thickens. Meanwhile, chop or grate cheese.

For a chunkier soup, simply add the cheese, heat until the cheese melts, and serve. For a creamier soup, purée the potato-milk mixture in a blender, then return to the pot and stir in cheese. If the soup seems thick, add a little more stock. Bring soup back up to heat, stirring as cheese melts, and serve.

Variation

CREAM OF BROCCOLI (OR CAULIFLOWER) SOUP: Cream potatoes with milk and flour as described above. Stir-steam with the onions 2/3 to 1 1/3 cups broccoli (or cauliflower) florets, or use leftover cooked broccoli (or cauliflower). Finely chop the cooked vegetables and add to creamed potato-milk mixture. (Or purée in blender for a creamier consistency.) Add cheese, and finish soup as described above.

Butternut Bisque

Having leftover cooked winter squash on hand is a step toward any number of fragrant, simple, satisfying soups. Butternut squash cooks quickly, though, and only adds a little prep time to making the soup completely from scratch. As a rule of thumb, a 2-pound squash will yield about 4 cups diced raw squash, or 2 cups cooked and mashed.

This golden, creamy soup is subtly sweet with apple and onions, lightly spiced with ginger, coriander, and white pepper. Or try the variation seasoned with nutmeg and winter savory, two favorite companions for winter squash.

  SERVES 2 FOR LUNCH, 3 AS FIRST COURSE

2 cups raw butternut or buttercup squash, peeled, diced, and boiled till tender (1 cup mashed)

1/2 tablespoon butter

1/2 tablespoon olive oil

1 small or 1/2 large onion, minced (2/3 cup)

1/2 to 2/3 sweet apple (Empire, McIntosh, Cortland, or Golden Delicious), peeled and finely chopped (1/2 to 2/3 cup)

1/4 to 1/2 teaspoon ground ginger

1/2 to 3/4 teaspoon ground coriander

1 cup chicken broth (or vegetable stock)

1/2 cup squash stock

Freshly ground white pepper

1/2 teaspoon light brown sugar

1/4 to 1/2 teaspoon salt

1 1/2 tablespoons unbleached flour

1 1/4 cups whole milk (or equal parts 2%-fat milk and half-and-half)

Cut squash in quarters, peel, and scoop out seeds, then chop in large dice. Put in saucepan with boiling water, cover, and cook until tender. Drain squash, reserving 1/2 cup cooking liquid, then mash with a hand masher.

Melt butter with oil in saucepan and sauté onion over medium-low heat for 1 to 2 minutes. Add chopped apple, cover saucepan, and continue to cook, stirring frequently, until onion is translucent but not brown and apple is tender (add a touch of water or stock if onion starts to brown up). Stir in spices, then add the chicken stock, reserved squash stock, and mashed squash. Season with white pepper, 1/4 teaspoon light brown sugar, and 1/4 teaspoon salt. Simmer covered for about 5 minutes until the onions and apples begin to break down, then mash out remaining lumps with hand masher.

Dissolve flour in 1/2 cup of the milk (or milk plus half-and-half), smoothing out lumps. Stir this into the soup and continue cooking, stirring constantly, until soup is slightly thickened. Taste and add a little more sugar or salt as needed to round out the flavor (probably no salt if using canned chicken broth).

When ready to serve, add the remaining 3/4 cup milk (or milk plus half-and-half) and heat until soup is steaming (do not boil). Serve with toast or hot rolls.

Variation

SAVORY BUTTERNUT BISQUE: Omit apple, spices, and brown sugar, and season the soup instead with 1 teaspoon dried winter or summer savory, 1/4 teaspoon dried lovage, 1/8 to 1/4 teaspoon ground nutmeg, and a tiny pinch of cayenne for a little heat.

Curried Squash Soup with Chicken

This is one of those soups easily thrown together if you have a happy coincidence of leftover cooked winter squash, chicken stock, cooked chicken, and curry paste in the refrigerator. The best type of squash for this is any sweet, dry winter squash with rich golden-orange color, such as kabocha.

  SERVES 2

1 tablespoon olive oil	1 to 2 tablespoons flour (as needed)
1 small or 1/2 large onion, minced	3/4 teaspoon Madras (sweet) red curry paste
2 cups leftover cooked winter squash, mashed	1 cup cooked chicken, preferably dark meat,
3 cups chicken stock, preferably homemade	bite-sized pieces

Heat oil in saucepan and sauté onion over medium-low heat. Meanwhile mash squash (cooked as on page 39 or 130). Mix 1/2 cup of the chicken stock into the mashed squash, then add flour to rest of stock to help thicken the soup if the winter squash you are using is not very dry.

When onion is translucent, stir in curry paste, then add squash. Gradually stir in chicken stock, and finally the chicken. Cook over medium-low heat until soup is hot and slightly thickened. This soup goes nicely with Cranberry-Walnut Biscuits (page 192), otherwise plain biscuits or toast.

Savory Red Lentil Soup

Red lentils are a versatile soup base, quick to break down into a creamy golden purée without the fuss of a blender. Their bland, earthy flavor goes especially well with savory herbs and sweet root vegetables, as we have here, or with light curry spicing as in the following recipe. This version is nice served with Whole-Wheat Fennel Rolls (page 196) or Savory Cheese-Poppyseed Scones (page 195).

 SERVES 2 TO 3

3/4 cup red lentils, rinsed	1/2 large or 1 small celery stalk, finely chopped
2 1/4 cups water	1 small carrot, grated/shredded (*or* 2 Brussels
1 3/4 cups vegetable, lamb, or chicken stock	sprouts, slivered)
(homemade or low-sodium, 14.5-oz can)	1/2 teaspoon ground coriander
1 small bay leaf	1 teaspoon summer savory
1 tablespoon olive oil	1/2 teaspoon dried lovage
1 small (or 1/2 medium) onion, finely chopped	1/8 teaspoon thyme
1 small clove garlic, minced	Few grates white or black pepper
1/2 Empire or McIntosh apple, finely chopped	Salt to taste (minimal if using canned stock)

Wash lentils, add water plus 1 cup stock and bay leaf, and bring to a boil over medium heat. Reduce heat to low and simmer 10 to 15 minutes, partially covered.

Heat oil in non-stick skillet and sauté onion over medium-low heat until translucent. Add garlic and sauté briefly, then stir in apple, celery, and carrot (or Brussels sprouts), and sauté a minute more over reduced heat, covering pan to sweat vegetables. Add herbs and seasonings, then deglaze with remaining stock, and add mixture to lentils.

Bring soup back to heat and simmer another 10 to 15 minutes, or until apples and vegetables are tender. If still a bit chunky, use a hand masher to blend any large lumps into the soup.

Persian Red Lentil Soup

This soup, fragrant with light curry spices, was inspired by a recipe in Joanna Pruess's soup cookbook Soup for Every Body, *along with Persian soup and stew recipes in Margaret Shaida's* The Legendary Cuisine of Persia. *Though lovely as a vegetarian soup, this is a fine way to recycle the remains of Persian Lamb Shanks (page 118), as in the variation—or use up leftover roast lamb.*

 SERVES 2 TO 3

3/4 cup red lentils, rinsed	1/2 teaspoon ground coriander
2 cups water	1/4 teaspoon ground cumin
1 3/4 cups vegetable or lamb stock, preferably homemade	1/2 celery stalk, finely chopped
	1 small carrot, shredded
1 tablespoon olive oil	3 dried apricots, finely chopped, soaked in a little water
1 small (or 1/2 medium) onion, finely chopped	
1 clove garlic, minced	Few grates black pepper
1/8 teaspoon fennel seeds (12 seeds), crushed	Salt to taste (if using homemade stock)

Wash lentils in soup pot, add water and 1 cup stock, and bring to a boil over medium heat. Reduce heat and simmer lentils 10 to 15 minutes, partially covered.

Meanwhile, heat oil in non-stick skillet and sauté onion over medium-low heat until translucent. Add garlic, fennel seeds (crushed in mortar and pestle), and spices and sauté briefly. Stir in carrot and celery, and cook covered a minute more to sweat vegetables. Add apricots and remaining stock, and add mixture to lentils along with salt and pepper (minimal salt if using canned stock).

Bring soup back to heat and simmer covered for 10 to 20 minutes. Serve garnished with a little fresh parsley for greenery.

Variation
PERSIAN RED LENTIL & LAMB SOUP: Using leftovers from the Persian Lamb Shanks recipe (page 118), cut remaining meat from bones and cut in small pieces (1/2 to 2/3 cup). Place bones in small pot, cover with water, and bring to a boil, then simmer uncovered for 1 hour. Drain stock and use in place of equivalent liquid in main recipe. Make soup as described above, adding the lamb, any leftover sauce, and a little extra liquid as needed before the final simmer.

Black Bean Soup

Richard's black bean soup, creamy yet refreshingly tangy with a little hot pepper, lemon, and other Spanish/Mexican seasonings, makes a hearty bowlful. Serve hot, plain or with fresh garnishes and toasted savory bread, such as Homemade Croutons (page 57) or Olive Bread (page 202).

SERVES 3

1 cup dry black turtle beans, soaked and
    cooked till tender
1 1/2 tablespoons olive oil
1 cup chopped onion
3/4 cup green bell peppers, chopped (or
    combination hot and sweet peppers)
1 clove garlic, minced
2 1/8-inch slices lemon, minced
1 tablespoon ground cumin
1 teaspoon Greek oregano, dried

1/2 teaspoon cayenne pepper (less if using hot
    peppers)
1/2 cup canned plum tomatoes, chopped
3 to 3 1/2 cups chicken stock (homemade or
    canned low-sodium)
Salt and freshly ground black pepper to taste
1 tablespoon dry sherry (optional)
2 to 3 tablespoons fresh cilantro or green
    scallion tops, chopped (optional)
2 to 3 tablespoons sour cream (optional)

Soak black beans overnight. Drain soaking liquid, cover with fresh water plus 1 to 2 inches, and bring to a boil, then reduce heat and cook till tender. Drain.

Heat olive oil in heavy-bottomed soup pot or Dutch oven and sauté onion and peppers for about 2 minutes. Stir in garlic and lemon, then spices and herbs, just for a few seconds—long enough to quickly sauté the garlic and lemon and very lightly toast the cumin—then add tomatoes, then beans. Pour in chicken stock. Season with salt and pepper to taste. Add sherry, if desired.

Simmer soup about 10 to 15 minutes, covered, over moderate heat. Meanwhile set up blender. In a couple of batches, ladle soup into blender jar and pulse a few times until soup is partly puréed, leaving some beans a little chunky for texture.

Return soup to pot and bring back to heat. Serve plain or garnished with fresh cilantro or scallion tops and a dollop of sour cream.

Pea Soup with Ham Hocks & Root Vegetables

There are various interpretations of pea soup, ranging from stout and salty to creamy to sweet and brothy. I'll pass on a stodgy lumberjack-style "peas porridge," but always come back for more of Richard's wonderful pea soup swimming with flavorful broth, bits of "sweet earth roots" (quoting from Blossom Farm), and tender pieces of ham hock. This big batch provides enough for several lunches, plus a quart to freeze. Whole-Wheat Fennel Rolls (page 196) make a nice go-with.

SERVES 8 TO 10

2 ham hocks, washed thoroughly

5 quarts water

1 pound dry split green peas, rinsed and
    soaked in cold water

1 to 2 tablespoons olive oil

1 large yellow onion, chopped

2 medium carrots, shredded

1 to 2 parsnips, shredded (*or* 2/3 cup shredded
    rutabaga)

Freshly ground white pepper

1 teaspoon dried summer savory (*or* 1/2
    teaspoon each thyme and lovage)

Add ham hocks with water to large soup/stock pot and bring to a boil. Lower heat and simmer for 1 hour or until hocks are tender, then remove from broth to cool on a plate. Skim fat and foam from broth. When hocks have cooled, remove meat from bones and break or cut into bite-sized pieces.

Drain peas and add to stock. Bring to a boil, stirring frequently to keep peas from settling to bottom. Turn heat to low and simmer 30 minutes or until peas are tender and starting to break down.

Meanwhile chop onion, and grate carrots and parsnips or rutabaga. Sauté onion in olive oil for 1 to 2 minutes, then add vegetables and sauté/sweat them about 1 to 2 minutes more. Add to soup with a little white pepper and summer savory (or thyme and lovage) as desired. Add meat from ham hocks.

Simmer soup for 20 to 30 minutes. Serve with hot yeast rolls, crusty bread, or garlic toast.

Blossom Farm in North Penobscot

Duck Soup with Winter Vegetables

Richly flavored duck broth, combined with sweet winter vegetables and savory herbs, makes this soup a soul-satisfying lunch and a nice change from chicken soup. If you have some leftover roast duck meat and stuffing, and the stock made ahead of time (fresh or frozen), the rest of it's just. . . .

 SERVES 3 TO 4

1 quart Homemade Duck Stock (below)

1 to 1 1/2 cups cooked duck meat

1 tablespoon olive oil

1 onion, halved crescents

2 cloves garlic, minced

1 apple, cored and finely chopped, skin and all

4 to 6 fresh sweet Brussels sprouts, trimmed, cut in 5 or 6 crescent wedges

2 to 3 small sweet carrots (or parsnips), roll-cut

1/2 cup celery stalk and leaves, chopped

3 dried lovage leaves

6 dried sage leaves

1/2 teaspoon thyme

1/2 teaspoon marjoram

Salt to taste

Few grates white pepper

2/3 cup leftover stuffing (page 181) or cooked white, brown, or wild rice (optional)

In heavy-bottomed saucepan or Dutch oven, sauté onion in olive oil until tender. Add garlic and cook briefly. Add apple and celery, then the herbs, carrots, and Brussels sprouts, gently sautéing and sweating the vegetables until partly cooked. Add stock and duck meat.

If you have leftover stuffing from the roast bird (page 181), this could be added to thicken the soup; otherwise about 2/3 cup leftover cooked white, brown, or wild rice could be added if desired.

Cover and bring to a boil, then simmer 15 minutes, or until the apple gives itself to the broth.

NOTE: This same approach and seasonings work nicely with leftover roast turkey, chicken, or pork. Or use lamb stock and leftover lamb roasted with garlic and rosemary, omitting the apple and bitter herbs.

HOMEMADE DUCK STOCK

This recipe assumes you have the remains of a roast duck, having already enjoyed a sumptuous meal.

To make stock, use the whole picked carcass of the roast bird, with most of the meat removed and set aside. Break the carcass into sections and place in stockpot, along with the skin, neck, and gizzard. Cover with about 1 1/2 quarts water, or enough to cover the bones. (Alternatively, if you raise your own ducks or have a supply of necks and gizzards, a fine stock can be made from just necks and gizzards, about 6 or 7 each.) Bring to a boil, then simmer open over low heat for a couple of hours. Cool stock to allow fat to solidify on top, then skim off and reserve in refrigerator (a little duck lard adds rich flavor to biscuits or sautéed vegetables). Strain off stock and pick meat from bones, being careful to remove small bones. If the bones did not yield much meat, you may wish to supplement it with a little leftover roast duck.

NOTE: If you have a chance, by all means try free-range duck from a local farm; after sampling this dense-textured and flavorful meat, it's hard to go back to the supermarket variety. Or consider raising ducks, for their meat and delicious eggs (not to mention the entertainment; see page 215).

Salads & Dressings

Greek Winter Salad   46

Spicy Carrot Salad with Dulse   47

Come Spring Salad ~ *Tahini-Yogurt Dressing*   47

Apple-Pistachio Salad   48

German Potato Salad   48

Chicken Salad with Grapes ~ *Yogurt-Tarragon Dressing,*
   Lemon-Sour Cream Dressing   50

Curried Chicken Salad   51

Chicken Salad with Peaches & Cilantro
   ~ *Lemon/Lime Dressing*   52

Thai Rice & Pork Salad   53

Southwestern Rice & Pork Salad   53

Marinated Green Bean Salad ~ *Lemon-Cumin Dressing,*
   Lemon-Dill Dressing   54

Summer Mixed Bean Salad ~ *Red Wine Vinaigrette*   55

Marinated Cauli-Broccoflower Salad   56

Greek Festival Salad   56

Everyday Tossed Salad ~ *Balsamic Vinaigrette*   57

Spinach-Orange Salad with Red Onion, Olives & Feta
   ~ *Orange-Coriander Dressing*   58

Winter Lunchtime Salads

No matter how organic or well handled, trucked-in greens and lettuces and hothouse tomatoes and peppers just don't have the vitality and flavor of fresh local produce. Though an occasional ersatz "garden" salad is nice with dinner during the darker months, I'd almost rather hold out for fresh local produce in season and experiment with winter storage vegetables. The following three salads are variations on a theme combining sweet, crisp raw vegetables lightly dressed and tossed with a few richly flavored treats. Each has its own built-in dressing tailored to the other ingredients (although simple cabbage-carrot salads, without the treats, also go well with Tahini-Yogurt Dressing, below). I make them for lunch on sunny late-winter days, when spring seems not far around the corner and I'm satisfied just with something light and refreshing rather than hot.

Tahini-Yogurt Dressing (MAKES ABOUT 1 CUP)

1/3 cup creamy tahini (sesame butter)

3 to 4 tablespoons water

1/4 cup plain yogurt

2 tablespoons lemon juice (or orange juice)

Drop of honey (if using lemon juice)

1/8 teaspoon cumin (coriander w/ orange juice)

Few grains cayenne pepper (optional)

Few drops tamari soy sauce (optional)

Spoon tahini into small bowl or pitcher. Add water gradually, "whipping" it into the tahini with a fork until the consistency of buttercream frosting. Gradually stir in yogurt and lemon or orange juice, then remaining ingredients. Adjust consistency as desired for salad dressing, by adding a little more water or tahini. Nice with simple salads of shredded carrots, cabbage, napa, apples, and parsley.

Greek Winter Salad

There is so much more to cabbage than coleslaw. I enjoy finding chestnuts and feta in a cabbage salad together with apples and other fresh flavors and textures. An herbed Greek vinaigrette seems just right.

 SERVES 2

1 1/2 cups savoy cabbage (or a mix of savoy and
   white cabbage, or baby bok choy), shredded

1 McIntosh or Empire apple, halved thin slices

1 celery stalk, chopped or sliced

4 to 6 chestnuts, roasted and shelled (page 180),
   broken into small pieces

2 ounces feta or other crumbly, richly flavored
   cheese (such as Wensleydale or Caerphilly)

2 tablespoons raw sunflower seeds

2 teaspoon lemon juice

1/2 teaspoon apple cider vinegar

1/4 teaspoon toasted sesame oil

2 tablespoons olive oil

1/2 teaspoon dried cilantro

1/2 teaspoon dried mint

Couple grates "party" (multicolored) pepper

Combine first 4 ingredients in salad bowl. Sprinkle cheese, crumbled or chunked, over the top. Add sunflower seeds and remaining ingredients, and toss. Let stand a few minutes before serving.

Spicy Carrot Salad with Dulse

Accented with dulse (a red seaweed native to the Downeast coast, notably harvested on Grand Manan Island on the New Brunswick side of Passamaquoddy Bay), this is a somewhat heartier variation on the previous salad's juxtaposition of salty, intense cheese and sweet chestnuts, carrots, and apples.

❧ SERVES 2

2 medium carrots (the sweeter, the better), shredded

1 McIntosh or Empire apple, halved thin slices

1 1/2 cups fresh parsley sprigs (or romaine lettuce, torn in small pieces)

4 to 6 chestnuts, roasted and shelled (page 180), broken into small pieces

2 tablespoons raw sunflower seeds (*or* 1/3 cup sprouted green lentils, page 24)

A few dried dulse leaves, torn in small pieces

2 ounces crumbly, flavorful cheese (such as feta, Wensleydale, or Caerphilly, page 135)

1 teaspoon lemon juice

1 teaspoon apple cider vinegar

1 1/2 to 2 tablespoons extra-virgin olive oil

1/4 to 1/2 teaspoon tamari soy sauce

1/2 teaspoon dried mint

Tiny pinch cayenne

Combine first 6 ingredients in salad bowl. Sprinkle cheese, crumbled or chunked, over the top. Add remaining ingredients and toss. Let stand a few minutes before serving.

Come Spring Salad

Though it has nothing to do with this late-winter salad, the title of Ben Ames Williams's wonderful historical novel, based on the original settlers of Union, Maine, seems just right for a tangy fresh bowlful eaten beside a sunny window, perusing seed catalogs, in anticipation of spring.

❧ SERVES 2

2 medium sweet carrots, shredded

2 cups (about 6 leaves) napa, Chinese cabbage, baby bok choy, or other winter greens, shredded or chopped

2/3 cup fresh parsley, small sprigs

1/2 ripe avocado, bite-sized chunks

2 teaspoons fresh or dried cilantro (optional)

1/2 Valencia orange, freshly squeezed juice

1 thick slice lime, freshly squeezed juice

Dash pepper

Few grains cayenne

2 teaspoons extra-virgin olive oil

Few drops toasted sesame oil

1/8 teaspoon ground cumin and/or coriander

Dash of tamari soy sauce (optional)

Combine shredded carrot, cabbage or other greens, and parsley in individual salad bowls. Add avocado and cilantro (if you have some).

Combine remaining ingredients in a cup, drizzle over vegetables, and toss briefly. (Or for a creamier dressing, try the Tahini-Yogurt Dressing, page 46.)

Apple-Pistachio Salad

Toasted pistachios, crisp apples, sweet carrots, and buttery lettuce are a nice combination, dressed with a lightly herbed vinaigrette.

 SERVES 2

1/2 teaspoon toasted sesame oil

1/2 McIntosh or Empire apple, halved thin slices

2 small carrots (the sweeter the better), shredded

2 to 3 tablespoons lightly toasted pistachios, coarsely chopped (or raw sunflower seeds)

2 cups buttercrunch (or Bibb/red leaf) lettuce

2 teaspoons lemon juice + 1/2 teaspoon balsamic or cider vinegar

1 1/2 tablespoons extra-virgin olive oil

1 teaspoon dried marjoram or cilantro

Rub wooden salad bowl with sesame oil, and add ingredients in order listed. Toss and serve.

German Potato Salad

Many are the ways to make potato salad, including mayonnaise, sugar, hard-boiled eggs, capers, celery, gherkins. . . . Several times each summer Richard makes this classic hot German potato salad with onions and an herbed vinaigrette, and it's simply the best—and simple enough to put together even at camp, with a premixed jar of dressing. Just be sure to use new or waxy potatoes, not bakers which break down too quickly, and cook the potatoes just long enough so they don't shed their skins.

SERVES 6 TO 8

2 to 2 1/2 pounds new red-skinned, white, or fingerling potatoes, unpeeled

1 medium onion (sweet white or red), chopped

1/4 cup olive oil

1/4 cup cider vinegar

1/4 teaspoon salt (or to taste)

Half a dozen grates white pepper

Pinch of cayenne pepper

1/4 teaspoon fresh summer savory, chopped

1 to 2 teaspoons fresh dill weed, snipped

Wash potatoes, trim bad spots, and cut into bite-sized chunks. Bring a pot of water to a boil, add potatoes, and boil until knife-tender. Meanwhile, chop onions and mix remaining ingredients for dressing, and combine in a large glass bowl. (If using dried herbs, use half the amounts as for fresh.)

Drain potatoes and add immediately to the bowl, folding them gently with the dressing and onions (the hot potatoes will take the raw edge off the onions).

Can be eaten right away, but letting the potato salad rest an hour or two (or overnight in the refrigerator) will improve the flavor. Should keep up to a week refrigerated in a covered bowl.

Variation
FRENCH POTATO SALAD: Use equal parts cider vinegar and tarragon vinegar, and herb the salad with 1/2 teaspoon fresh (1/4 teaspoon dried) tarragon and 1 teaspoon fresh (1/2 teaspoon dried) summer savory.

Herbal Vinegars

Home-brewed herbal vinegars, elegantly bottled, are a nice gift—and a nice condiment to have in your own pantry. With all the culinary herbs and spices, citrus peels, garlic and shallots, and types of vinegars available, the possibilities are endless. Two simple combinations I find especially pleasing and useful in cooking are tarragon vinegar, made with fresh tarragon sprigs steeped in cider vinegar (milder than white wine vinegar); and sage vinegar, with sage leaves steeped in red wine vinegar.

Bottles can be plain or fancy, but for me the ideal bottle is a recycled dessert wine "split," which holds about a pint. I was lucky to find at a local recycling center a half dozen empty splits, graceful long-necked bottles made in France for Bartlett Fruit Wines in Gouldsboro, which I washed, sterilized, and outfitted with new corks. You could enjoy some dessert wine and recycle the bottles, or any interesting bottles in your collection. Wash them in hot soapy water with a bottlebrush, scrub off the labels, and sterilize the bottles by boiling them in a hot-water bath for 10 minutes.

For each 1-pint bottle of tarragon vinegar, use 3 sprigs of fresh French tarragon, 3 or 4 inches long; wash them thoroughly, then put in the sterilized bottle. Heat 2 cups cider vinegar to just below the boiling point (195°F) and pour it into the bottle, using a funnel. Let cool a bit, then insert a new sterile cork dipped several times in boiling water. Store in a cool dark place for 2 to 3 weeks to infuse. To make a 1-pint bottle of sage vinegar, repeat the same process, using 2 sprigs of fresh sage leaves infused in 2 cups of heated red wine vinegar.

At this point, you can strain out the spent herbs and pour the vinegar into a clean sterilized bottle with a fresh sprig of your featured herb. I've had fine results, though, skipping this step—along with the recommendation that fresh herbs be sterilized in a weak bleach solution (1/2 teaspoon bleach to 3 cups water), then thoroughly rinsed, before infusing.

To be on the safe side, flavored vinegars should be refrigerated once opened, unless you plan to use them exclusively for deglazing and sauces. More tips on safe preserving can be found on the National Center for Home Food Preservation's website, www.uga.edu/nchfp.

Tarragon vinegar can be used as part or all of the vinegar in dressings for lettuce, potato, and bean salads, or to flavor an egg salad or stuffed eggs. A few drops of sage red wine vinegar are just the thing to help deglaze the pan when browning pork for a savory stew, cassoulet, or pasta e fagioli.

If you have other fresh herbs in your garden, experiment. Chervil, summer savory, lemon balm, chives, lovage, basil, rosemary, and thyme are all likely candidates, alone or combined with peeled garlic, small chiles, multicolored peppercorns, or a spiral of fresh orange or lemon peel. Or make a fruit vinegar, using 1 1/2 to 2 cups fresh ripe raspberries or chopped peaches in place of the herbs.

Chicken Salad with Grapes

This salad came about as an offering to the Goddess at one of the Feast of Venus celebrations hosted by my soulful and creative friend Mary Weaver (Myth Weaver's Theatre) of Belfast.

Layer the ingredients as a festive salad platter garnished with dressing, or if you prefer, serve as individual portions on a bed of lettuce.

Since leftover sliced roast chicken (or turkey) breast meat tends to be dry, a nice touch is to moisten the sliced meat with a little chicken stock before serving.

 SERVES 3 TO 5

Yogurt-Tarragon Dressing (or Lemon-Sour Cream Dressing), page 51

1 large head buttercrunch (or red/green oakleaf) lettuce, torn

2 celery stalks, slant-cut

2/3 cup raw green vegetables (thinly sliced broccoli stalk or kohlrabi, or cucumbers)

3/4 pound roasted chicken (or turkey) breast, thickly sliced + broth to moisten

12 to 15 large grapes (preferably black or Ribier grapes), halved and seeded

1 to 1 1/2 cups raw peapods

1/2 cup parsley sprigs (optional)

1/3 to 1/2 cup raw almonds, halved (page 60)

Mix ingredients for dressing; chill. Wash and spin lettuce, tear into large pieces, and arrange on an oval platter. (Or, arrange lettuce and remaining ingredients as individual portions on salad plates.) Lay sliced celery and other vegetables on top of lettuce.

Cut chicken or turkey in rather thick slices (about 1/4 inch) and moisten with a little chicken broth (if not already moist), then break or slice into slender pieces. Arrange meat over vegetables, and garnish with grapes, peapods, and parsley.

When ready to serve, pour dressing over salad down length of platter (or spoon over individual salad plates), and sprinkle almond halves over the top.

REVIVING CELERY

A head of celery will stay crisp and fresh for the first week or two, but after that limpness eventually sets in. To revive rubbery celery, or as a preventive measure with each new head, slice 1/4 to 1/2 inch off the root end and stand the celery upright in a jar or pitcher in a couple inches of water, with a plastic bag over the top. (You may also need to trim some off the top to fit on your refrigerator shelf.) Be sure to use a container with a mouth large enough to give the celery some wiggle room as the stalks swell with water; otherwise the first stalk may be hard to extract. Parsley and cilantro can be revived this way, also asparagus, kale, and other greens.

Yogurt-Tarragon Dressing (MAKES 1 1/4 CUPS)

1 cup plain yogurt (or 1/4 cup sour cream + 3/4 cup yogurt)
2 tablespoons extra-virgin olive oil
1/2 teaspoon toasted sesame oil

1 tablespoon fresh lime juice (or lemon juice)
1 1/2 teaspoons fresh tarragon (or 3/4 teaspoon dried)
Few grates black pepper

Lemon-Sour Cream Dressing (MAKES 1 1/2 CUPS)

1 cup sour cream
1/4 cup plain yogurt
2 tablespoons extra-virgin olive oil
1 tablespoon fresh lemon juice

2 teaspoons honey
1 teaspoon fresh or 1/2 teaspoon dried tarragon (or 1/8 teaspoon curry powder, or 1/4 teaspoon ground cumin)

Combine ingredients in a small pitcher or pint jar and stir with fork until well blended.

Curried Chicken Salad

For those who (like me) don't care for mayonnaise, here's a curried chicken salad held together with a light, fresh-tasting sour cream-based dressing. Use leftover roast chicken, or even leftover grilled chicken if compatibly flavored (such as Grilled Lemon-Herb Chicken, page 86).

 SERVES 2

2 cups buttercrunch or oakleaf lettuce, torn
1 stalk celery, sliced
3 to 5 raw peapods, halved (optional)
2/3 to 1 cup cooked chicken, light and dark meat, small chunks

1/4 to 1/3 cup raw walnuts, broken halves (or halved almonds, page 60)
10 to 12 black or Ribier grapes, halved and seeded (or 1/2 to 2/3 cup chopped apple)
Lemon-Sour Cream Dressing, curry version

Make a bed of lettuce on each plate/bowl. Assemble the next 4 or 5 ingredients (celery through grapes) in a separate bowl, cutting them as for a chicken salad (somewhat smaller than bite-sized, with the chicken in chunks). Mix in enough curried Lemon-Sour Cream Dressing to hold the salad together. Serve on bed of lettuce.

Or if you prefer, combine the lettuce with the other ingredients and spoon a few tablespoons dressing over the top of each salad.

Variation
Tarragon Chicken Salad: Use Lemon-Sour Cream Dressing made with tarragon, as above.

Chicken Salad with Peaches & Cilantro

This summertime salad is best made with fresh fruit and lettuce in season. A delicious balance of textures and flavors—mild and assertive, sweet and tangy, smoky and hot—it's a nice way to use up leftover chicken (such as the Grilled Lemon-Herb Chicken on page 86, or Cajun Chicken, page 101). With the addition of another leftover, cooked quinoa (see variation), it becomes a satisfying lunch or light-supper meal-in-itself.

If making the salad as a single serving, go with the smaller amounts; for two, use the larger amounts.

 SERVES 1 TO 2

1/2 to 2/3 cup leftover grilled chicken, preferably dark meat

1 to 2 cups romaine, green or red oakleaf, or buttercrunch lettuce leaves, torn in pieces

1/3 to 1/2 ripe avocado, halved slices or chunks (optional)

1/2 to 1 fresh ripe juicy peach (or nectarine), bite-sized chunks

2 to 4 tablespoons fresh cilantro, coarsely chopped or whole leaves

1 to 2 scallions, chopped (*or* 1 to 3 tablespoons red onion, thinly sliced or minced)

2 to 3 tablespoons Lemon/Lime Dressing

1 to 3 tablespoons raw (or very lightly toasted) pumpkin seeds

Assemble first 6 ingredients (chicken through scallions) in salad bowl(s). Add Lemon/Lime Dressing, and toss. Sprinkle with pumpkin seeds.

Variation

CHICKEN & PEACH TABBOULEH: For each serving, add 1/2 to 2/3 cup leftover Pan-Roasted Quinoa (page 190), and toss.

LEMON/LIME DRESSING (MAKES 1/3 CUP)

3 tablespoons extra-virgin olive oil

3 tablespoons lime or lemon juice (about 2/3 large lime or lemon)

1 small garlic clove, pressed or minced

Drop of honey (1/4 teaspoon)

1/8 teaspoon ground cumin

Few grains cayenne pepper

Few drops tamari soy sauce (optional)

Combine all ingredients in an 8-ounce jar, cover with lid, and shake until well blended.

RICE SALADS

Combining grains, fresh vegetables, and dressing along the same lines as tabbouleh, this meal-in-itself lunch travels well to work or a daytime adventure. Just assemble everything in a lidded container, and you're good to go. With no lettuce or greens to wilt (unless you wish to add some at the last minute), the vegetables, meat, herbs, and dressing can get to know each other until you're ready to eat. Whether you go in a Thai or Southwestern direction, it's a nice way to use up odds and ends of leftover roasted or grilled pork (plain or cooked with compatible seasonings). Leftover cooked shrimp, chicken, flank steak, or lamb could work as well.

Thai Rice & Pork Salad

  SERVES 1 TO 2

1/2 to 2/3 cup leftover grilled pork spareribs, butt, or chops, bite-sized pieces (or leftover roast pork)

1 1/4 cups cooked brown or white basmati rice

1/2 cup European cucumber slices, roll-cut

1 1/2 tablespoons red onion, thinly sliced/chopped

1/4 cup yellow bell pepper, chopped

1 small vine-ripened tomato, bite-sized chunks

1 tablespoon chives (or scallion tops), chopped

1 tablespoon fresh-squeezed orange juice

1 teaspoon red wine vinegar

1 tablespoon extra-virgin olive oil

1 teaspoon dried mint

1 teaspoon dried basil (2 teaspoons fresh)

Tiny pinch cayenne

Salt to taste

A few fresh arugula leaves (or tatsoi, baby bok choy, or other Asian greens) (optional)

Combine all ingredients in salad bowl in order listed, reserving the arugula or greens (if desired) to add at the last minute.

Southwestern Rice & Pork Salad

  SERVES 1 TO 2

1/2 to 2/3 cup leftover grilled pork spareribs, butt, or chops, bite-sized pieces (or leftover roast pork)

1 1/4 cups cooked brown or white basmati rice (or quinoa, page 190)

1/2 cup European cucumber slices, roll-cut

1 1/2 tablespoons red onion, thinly sliced/chopped

1/4 cup yellow or orange bell pepper, chopped

2 to 3 marinated green/black olives, sliced

1 to 2 tablespoons chopped fresh cilantro

Tiny pinch ground cumin (optional)

Tiny pinch cayenne

Salt to taste

2 to 2 1/2 tablespoons Orange-Coriander Dressing (page 58)

2 to 3 tablespoons pumpkin seeds

Combine all ingredients in salad bowl in order listed. Dress, toss, and garnish with seeds.

Marinated Green Bean Salad

There is nothing like fresh green beans straight from your own (or your local market farmer's) garden. If you find yourself with an abundance of sweet, tender beans at the height of their season, this salad, dressed in a cumin-spiked or "dilly-bean" vinaigrette, is a nice way to enjoy them.

For Romanos, we love growing a prolific French pole bean called Kwintus (available from John Scheepers Kitchen Garden Seeds, www.kitchengardenseeds.com) that produces long, tender broad beans. Purple-pods are fun color chameleons (changing to green to purple to green as you blanch, freeze, and cook them), but we find tender, flavorful Jade the best variety for salads, stir-steaming, and freezing.

You can marinate leftover beans if lightly steamed, but the safest bet is to steam or blanch some specially for a salad and stop the cooking process by plunging them into ice-cold water as soon as they're al dente or "tooth tender." Easier yet, cook enough extra beans for a salad as part of the production line while blanching them for the freezer.

 SERVES 3 TO 4

3 to 4 cups fresh green beans (or purple-pods or Romanos), snapped or sliced in half

1/3 to 1/2 cup Lemon-Cumin (or Lemon-Dill) Dressing

Steam or boil beans until al dente, then plunge in ice water; drain. Add dressing as desired and toss to coat. Serve immediately, or marinate before serving. Will keep up to 2 days in the refrigerator.

LEMON-CUMIN DRESSING (MAKES 1/2 CUP)

3 tablespoons fresh-squeezed lemon juice
1 1/2 tablespoons red wine vinegar
3 1/2 tablespoons extra-virgin olive oil
1 clove garlic, pressed and minced

1/2 teaspoon light brown sugar
1/4 teaspoon ground cumin
Few grates "party" (multicolored) pepper (optional)

LEMON-DILL DRESSING (MAKES 1/2 CUP)

3 tablespoons fresh-squeezed lemon juice
1 1/2 tablespoons red wine vinegar
3 1/2 tablespoons extra-virgin olive oil
1 clove garlic, pressed and minced

1/2 teaspoon light brown sugar
Dash of ground cumin
1 tablespoon fresh dill weed, snipped
Few grates "party" pepper (optional)

Combine all ingredients in an 8-ounce jar, cover with lid, and shake until well blended.

Summer Mixed Bean Salad

The time to make this robust bean salad is at the very end of the summer, when you're savoring the last planting of beans and cherry tomatoes or fresh-sliced beefsteak tomatoes off the vine. Spiked with Lemon-Cumin Dressing or a simple Red Wine Vinaigrette and garnished with smoked provolone, pinenuts, and fresh herbs, it's a satisfying lunchtime meal-in-itself, especially with the cheese and beans together making a complete protein.

Mixing varieties of beans, both green bush beans and cooked dry beans (or freshly cooked shell beans), is not only fun and colorful but a good way to use up small amounts, perhaps combining the last pickings of your various summer beans. Although the salad is best served right away, you can combine the beans, onions, and dressing and let them chill in the refrigerator for a couple of days, leaving the tomatoes and garnishes to sprinkle fresh over each bowlful.

 SERVES 4

3/4 cup assorted dry beans (page 156), such as as chickpeas and cannellinis or other large, plump white beans (1 3/4 cups cooked)

1 quart fresh tender beans (green, purple-pods, and/or Romanos), whole or halved

1/2 medium red or yellow onion, minced

1/3 to 1/2 cup Lemon-Cumin Dressing (page 54) or Red Wine Vinaigrette (below)

2 cups whole cherry tomatoes (or 2 to 3 ripe tomatoes, large chunks)

2 to 3 tablespoons chopped fresh cilantro or basil

2 ounces smoked provolone, thinly sliced (optional, a few slices per serving)

4 tablespoons pine nuts, raw or lightly toasted (page 144), 1 tablespoon per serving

Soak dry beans overnight, drain, then cook until tender (page 152) and drain. (These can be cooked ahead of time.)

Mince onion and put in large glass or ceramic bowl. Steam green beans, or briefly cook in boiling water, until al dente; then drain and add hot to bowl with onions. Pour dressing over, add cooked dry beans, and mix to coat beans evenly with dressing.

Serve immediately in individual salad bowls, dividing tomatoes, herbs, and other garnishes among the servings; or let bean salad marinate in refrigerator up to 2 days, adding tomatoes and garnishes when ready to serve.

RED WINE VINAIGRETTE (MAKES 1/2 CUP)

1/4 cup red wine vinegar

3 tablespoons extra-virgin olive oil

1 small clove garlic, pressed and minced

1/2 teaspoon light brown sugar

Few grates "party" (multicolored) pepper

Combine all ingredients in an 8-ounce jar, cover with lid, and shake until well blended.

Marinated Cauli-Broccoflower Salad

It's a toss-up as to which of our local creative communities comprise the best cooks—the boatbuilders, the artists and publishers, or the land conservation folks. I've eaten wonderful meals at potlucks of all three. At Great Pond Mountain Conservation Trust gatherings, in the words of director Cheri Domina, you can count on finding "the people warm and the food always great—and vice versa." Among a spread of tempting dishes at a midwinter trust planning retreat, one of the stand-outs was also one of the simplest: a marinated salad made by Carol Bennatti (adapted from a recipe in The Victory Garden Cookbook)*, with contrasting subtle colors of cauliflower and pale green broccoloflower, drenched in a piquant lemon-olive oil dressing—a taste of spring in February.*

 SERVES 4 TO 6

1/2 head cauliflower, florets
1/2 head broccoflower, florets
1/3 sliced green bell pepper (optional)
1/2 to 3/4 cup olives (ripe/green medley)

2 tablespoons capers
1/3 cup extra-virgin olive oil
2 tablespoons fresh lemon juice
Salt and pepper to taste

Steam cauliflower and broccoflower florets until al dente, then plunge into cold water and drain. Add green pepper (if using) and olives. Mix remaining ingredients together, pour over vegetables, and toss. Marinate, covered, in refrigerator a few hours or overnight. Will keep up to 2 days.

Greek Festival Salad

Inspired by a Greek-style salad made by Jeanne Russell for the same lunch buffet above, this includes a few special ingredients that (unless you have them in your garden) may be a little pricey for everyday, but makes a colorful, festive salad for a special dinner or potluck. Use a combination of lettuce and mesclun, or all lettuce. Tangy sheep feta contrasts deliciously with the fruity peppers.

 SERVES 4 TO 6

8 leaves romaine, buttercrunch, or oakleaf
    lettuce, washed and torn
2 1/2 to 3 cups mesclun or other mixed tender
    salad greens, preferably including arugula
    and radicchio
1/2 European cucumber, sliced or chunks
2/3 each red and yellow bell pepper, sliced
Ripe tomato or cherry tomatoes (optional)

1/3 cup red onion, thinly sliced (*or* 2 to 3
    scallions, finely chopped)
3 to 4 ounces feta cheese, chunks
1/2 cup marinated Kalamata olives (optional)
1/2 cup Lemon-Cumin Dressing, page 54
    (*or* 1/3 cup olive oil + 3 tablespoons
    lemon juice)
1/2 to 2/3 cup coarsely chopped fresh parsley)

Combine ingredients in large wooden salad bowl in order listed. Drizzle with dressing and toss.

Everyday Tossed Salad

A basic dinner salad that can be varied with the seasons and the ingredients. Of course any salad is best with vegetables straight from the garden or farmer's market, but most of these can reliably be found year-round in the supermarket.

SERVES 2 TO 3

6 to 8 leaves romaine, oakleaf, or butter-
    crunch lettuce, washed and torn
10 to 15 leaves arugula, large pieces (optional)
1 stalk celery, sliced (*or* 2/3 cup sliced cucumber)
1 to 2 scallions, finely chopped (*or* 1/4 cup
    red onion, thinly sliced)

1/2 ripe avocado, diced
1 ripe plum tomato, chunks (optional)
1 to 2 small sweet carrots, shaved
Lemon-Cumin Dressing, Orange-Coriander
    Dressing, Balsamic Vinaigrette, or other
    favorite dressing

Combine ingredients in salad bowl in order listed, using paring knife to shave thin carrot slices over the top. (Or, make individual servings, dividing ingredients among small salad bowls.) Pass a choice of dressings at the table.

Variation

NIÇOISE SALAD: Omit avocado and carrots, and sprinkle over the salad 1 large chopped hard-boiled egg and 1/4 cup Niçoise olives. Serve with Homemade Croutons (below).

BALSAMIC VINAIGRETTE (MAKES 1/3 CUP)

3 tablespoons aged balsamic vinegar
3 tablespoons extra-virgin olive oil
1 small clove garlic, pressed and minced

1 teaspoon dried basil (*or* 2 teaspoons fresh)
Few grates "party" (multicolored) pepper

Combine all ingredients in an 8-ounce jar, cover with lid, and shake until well blended.

HOMEMADE CROUTONS

Fresh croutons made from scratch are delicious—and fun. You can use most any type of multigrain bread, plain or seasoned, preferably slightly dense and day-old or slightly stale, cut in 1/2 inch slices. (Two good choices are Onion-Walnut-Dill Bread and Three-Seed Bread, made by Morning Glory Bakery in Bar Harbor.) Brush bread slices evenly with extra-virgin olive oil, mixed with a little pressed garlic if desired. Slice into 3/4 x 1-inch or larger rectangles, and spread on lightly oiled baking sheet or metal pie plate. Bake croutons in preheated 350°F oven for 8 to 10 minutes or until golden. Serve croutons sprinkled over a tossed green salad or floated on a bowl of soup.

Spinach-Orange Salad with Red Onion, Olives & Feta

The interplay of sweet juicy orange and coriander, salty olives and feta, plus a little hot bite of red onion, make this salad a flavor treat. It's nice in the fall, when fresh lettuce and vine-ripened tomatoes are gone from the garden and those in the store seem pale by comparison. Who needs tomatoes when there are Valencia oranges in season!

❦ SERVES 2 TO 3

3 to 3 1/2 cups spinach, preferably small savoyed leaves, washed and trimmed (*or* 2 cups spinach plus 1 cup romaine, buttercrunch, or green leaf lettuce), large leaves torn into smaller pieces

1 stalk celery, sliced

1 Valencia orange, sliced, peeled, and sectioned

1/4 cup Mediterranean-style marinated olives (ripe/green medley or Niçoise), sliced

About 1/4 red onion, thinly sliced

4 ounces feta cheese, crumbled

3 to 5 tablespoons Orange-Coriander Dressing (below)

Fresh cilantro leaves (optional)

Assemble ingredients in large salad bowl in order listed. Keep cool until ready to serve. Pour dressing over salad, toss, and serve (or let people dress and toss individual servings).

Variation

SEVILLE-STYLE SPINACH-ORANGE SALAD: When making the dressing, omit the coriander and substitute 1/2 teaspoon fresh tarragon. Omit feta, and sprinkle salad with the chopped yolk of a hard-boiled egg.

ORANGE-CORIANDER DRESSING (MAKES 1/2 CUP)

3 1/2 tablespoons fresh-squeezed orange juice

1 1/2 tablespoons red wine vinegar

3 tablespoons extra-virgin olive oil

1 clove garlic, pressed and minced

1/2 teaspoon ground coriander

Few grates white pepper

Combine all ingredients in a small jar. Shake well before serving. This versatile dressing goes well with lettuce- and spinach-based salads, but can also stand up to stronger-flavored greens like arugula, baby bok choy, and cilantro (a nice combination).

Seafood Entrées

Flounder Roll-ups with Mushrooms, Spinach & Almonds

This is a light yet filling, fun-to-assemble meal, if you come across some nice fresh flounder (not previously frozen). The lime (used also in the following recipe) gives a light touch of citrus without overpowering the other more delicate flavors—and the buttery toasted almonds make the meal.

SERVES 2 TO 3

1 tablespoon olive oil

1 medium onion, crescents

4 to 6 mushrooms, sliced

1 small clove garlic, minced

Dash of salt

Few grates white pepper

Tiny pinch cayenne (optional)

1 to 1 1/2 cups fresh spinach, washed and
    stemmed, large leaves torn in two

1 thin slice of lime, minced (rind and all)

1 pound fresh flounder, 3 or 4 fillets

1 tablespoon salted butter

About 1/4 cup whole almonds, halved
    (see below)

Sauté onions in oil until halfway done. Add mushrooms, garlic, salt, and pepper. Add spinach and sauté until spinach is deflated (if using frozen spinach, thaw and drain off excess water, then add to pan and cook until heated through). Add minced lime to filling, and stir to distribute evenly.

Preheat oven to 375°F, and melt butter in small (7 x 7-inch) Corningware or Pyrex baking dish. Add almond halves and shake to coat with butter. Toast 4 to 5 minutes or until very light gold. Remove almonds and reserve.

Place a portion of the filling in the middle of each flounder fillet, and roll up, end to end. Place roll-ups in the same buttered baking dish, tail-side down. Bake for 20 to 25 minutes, or until flounder is just done (20 minutes for 4 smaller fillets, 25 minutes for 3 larger ones).

Sprinkle with toasted almonds, and serve immediately with brown or white rice, boiled new potatoes, or pesto-dressed pasta.

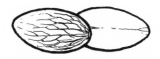

HALVING ALMONDS

There's a bit of a learning curve to splitting whole almonds in half with a paring knife, but it is worth mastering because they look beautiful and have more character than mechanically thin-sliced or slivered almonds. The knife should be non-serrated and sharp, the thinner the better. The OSHA-approved method is to hold the almond on a cutting board, seam-side up and with the rounder side down (as shown above), and cut against the board. If you hit it right, the skin will split along the seam of the nut, and the two halves will fall apart. Or, for a little more thrill of accomplishment, you can hold the almond braced between your thumbs and one index finger, while gently (also very carefully, if the knife is sharp) bearing down with the knife along the outside seam of the almond.

Fish with Lime & Garlic

Citrus, garlic, and fish are a flavor triumvirate dating way back in civilized time. Like lemons and oranges, limes are native to Southeast Asia and Indonesia, where they have been cultivated for thousands of years. A central ingredient in Persian cuisine, limes were carried west by Spanish and Portuguese traders and explorers to the Mediterranean, then across the Atlantic to the West Indies, Florida, Mexico, and Brazil. The combination of lime (or lemon) and garlic, with perhaps some cumin and cilantro or dill—common to many cuisines along this migration route—works especially well with pollock and halibut, and oily, firm pelagic fishes like swordfish and bluefish.

Fresh-caught mackerel, when they are running in late summer, as they do around Penobscot Bay, are a nice local alternative—especially when you catch them yourself on a handline and mackerel jig trailed off the stern. Grilled with a lime-garlic-cumin filling (see variation), they're a summer treat.

The rest of the year, try this combination as a stovetop "scampi" made with pollock, as in the main recipe—or baked in parchment (en papillote), sans wine, for 15 minutes in a preheated 350° oven.

 SERVES 2 TO 3

1 pound pollock (or halibut or bluefish)
1 clove garlic, minced
2 thin slices lime, minced (rind and all)
1 tablespoon olive oil
1/2 to 3/4 teaspoon ground cumin
Few grinds white pepper

Tiny pinch (less than 1/8 teaspoon) cayenne pepper
3 tablespoons dry vermouth (or white wine)
1/8 teaspoon salt
1/8 to 1/4 teaspoon dill weed (or 1/2 teaspoon fresh dill)

Cut fish in portion-sized pieces; set aside. Mince garlic and lime, and assemble spice mixture.

Heat olive oil in covered skillet over medium-low heat. Add garlic and lime and sauté over low heat for a minute or two until garlic is aromatic and light gold. Stir in cumin and pepper and sauté for 30 seconds, then deglaze pan with vermouth (or white wine). Place fish pieces on top of sauce, spooning some of the sauce and garlic/lime over each piece. Sprinkle with dill, cover, and simmer 4 to 5 minutes until fish is done through.

Serve immediately. Steamed broccoli (or other greens) and boiled or baked potatoes (gussied up with butter, white pepper, chives, or what-have-you) are fine accompaniments.

Variations

GRILLED FISH STEAKS WITH LIME-GARLIC MARINADE: Assemble the same ingredients as above, substituting 1 to 2 tablespoons fresh cilantro for the dill, and use as a marinade and/or basting sauce for an equivalent amount of halibut or swordfish steaks. Grill over medium-hot coals, spooning a little of the marinade and lime/garlic over the fish steaks as they grill.

GRILLED MACKEREL WITH LIME & GARLIC: Clean 3 to 4 freshly caught mackerel and butterfly them (hinged open), leaving the skin on. Mince the garlic and lime, adding 1 to 2 teaspoons extra-virgin olive oil (and some cumin if desired) to form a paste. Divide evenly among the fish, folding them back up so the filling is in the middle. Grill mackerel over medium coals, turning several times, until done through.

Baked Stuffed Trout

Baking is always a nice treatment for trout, whole or fillets, using the skin as a natural wrapper to keep the fish moist. A basic savory stuffing can be flavored with tangy lime and sour cream, as inspired by a recipe in A.D. Livingston's Freshwater Fish Cookbook, or with lemon and toasted almonds, as in the variation, inspired by a northern Italian recipe in Joyce Goldstein's A Mediterranean Kitchen.

A successful angler (or lucky friend) would have a fresh-caught (or frozen) Maine lake trout to bake whole; otherwise a pair of farm-raised rainbow trout fillets can stand in for a whole fish.

SERVES 3

2 rainbow or lake trout fillets (1 pound), skin on	1/3 teaspoon dried thyme
Salt and white pepper to taste	3/4 to 1 cup firm-textured rustic bread (such
1/2 tablespoon each butter and olive oil	as ciabatta), diced in small cubes
1/4 to 1/3 cup onion (or shallots), minced	1/4 cup sour cream
1 small clove garlic, minced	Juice and zest of 1/4 to 1/3 lime (or lemon)
1/4 cup celery, finely chopped	2 tablespoons water

Place one trout fillet skin-side down in center of 7 x 11-inch ovenproof baking dish greased with olive oil. Give fish a light sprinkle of salt and a few grates white pepper. Preheat oven to 350°F.

Heat butter with oil in a stainless-steel skillet and sauté onion or shallots until translucent, adding garlic and celery partway through. Sprinkle with thyme and bread and stir-fry about 1 minute, then remove from heat. Combine sour cream with lime juice and zest and stir into stuffing mixture.

Spread stuffing evenly over fillet, then top with the other fillet, skin-side up, orienting the fillets the same way, head to tail, so as to resemble a whole fish. Add 2 tablespoons water to baking dish.

Brush top of fish with olive oil and bake uncovered in center of oven for about 20 minutes. Rotate dish and bake another 8 to 10 minutes or until fish is steaming and cooked through.

Serve with spatula in wide slices, accompanied by pan-roasted white rice or wild-rice pilaf and asparagus, fiddleheads, peas or peapods, green beans, or other vegetable.

Variation
TROUT STUFFED WITH ALMONDS, LEMON & PARSLEY: Lightly toast and chop 10 to 12 almonds (as on page 74), and add with 1/4 cup chopped fresh parsley to stuffing mixture; use bread crumbs rather than cubes. In place of sour cream and lime, flavor and moisten stuffing with 1 tablespoon olive oil (or melted butter), 2 teaspoons lemon juice, and 1 to 1 1/2 tablespoons white wine or vermouth. Include 1/2 teaspoon lemon zest in the stuffing, or lay a few seeded slices of lemon over the stuffing. Bake as described above.

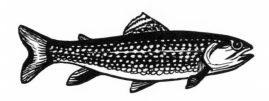

Apple-Smoked Steelhead Trout

Inspired by green twigs sprouting from an old apple tree in easy reach of our backyard "grilling station," Richard worked out this delicious way of grilling steelhead trout, using the hot-smoking process with a charcoal grill (a Weber Smoky Joe). Based on the traditional Maine method of hot-smoking alewives and herring with green alder twigs, this approach would work with any of the salmonids, including landlocked salmon, Atlantic salmon, or wild Alaskan salmon. We like steelhead trout (rainbow trout in migration), which though usually available farmed seems leaner than farmed Atlantic salmon, with a lighter, less fishy taste—especially grilled this way, permeated with the naturally sweet apple smoke. Or try green maple, beech, or alder twigs, for other pleasant flavors.

The green twigs are added not just for flavor, but to slow down the fire, so hot-smoking takes longer than normal grilling—about 25 to 30 minutes' cooking time. But the finished product, mahogany-colored on top and juicy inside, is worth the wait. Grilling the fish fillet skin-side down seals the bottom, while hot-smoking seals the top, essentially steaming the fish.

If you grill a large piece of steelhead trout, you can enjoy an elegant lunch of leftover trout alongside German Potato Salad (page 48). Or, serve leftover steelhead trout as an open-faced sandwich or appetizer (page 24), spread with the Dill-Horseradish Sauce.

 SERVES 3

1 1/4-pound steelhead trout fillet (or salmon)	Sprinkling of dried dill (optional)
Couple grinds white pepper (optional)	Dill-Horseradish Sauce (recipe follows)

Gather about 10 to 12 small green apple twigs, about 4 inches long and about the thickness of a pencil (1/4 to 3/8 inch diameter). Sprinkle the fish with white pepper and dill, if desired (no salt).

About 45 minutes before the rest of the meal will be ready, start a charcoal fire in an open grill. On top of a few dry twigs and birchbark, make a pile of 14 to 16 regular charcoal briquettes (do not use easy-light or lighter-impregnated briquettes!) and light the fire. When the coals are burning well, turn them and let them continue burning another 5 to 10 minutes or until coated with ash. Meanwhile heat the grate over the coals and scrape off any charred remains.

Reposition the coals together on one side of the grill. By now (about 15 minutes from when you started the fire) the coals should have burned down to a moderate heat, not hot enough to ignite the twigs. Pile the green twigs on top of the coals. Place the fish skin-side down on the cooler side of the grill, opposite the pile of coals and twigs, with the thicker side of the fish aimed toward the coals. Now cover the grill with the lid, with the draft (damper) almost completely shut, aligned over the salmon to slowly draw the smoke and heat up around the fish. It is this indirect "hot smoke" that will cook the salmon—not the direct heat over the coals, as with normal grilling.

Leave the grill covered, undisturbed, for about 15 minutes. By now the top surface of the fish should be sealed and turning a caramel color. Use a knife to check the color inside the fish, to

determine how far along the fish is in cooking. Depending on the size and thickness of the fillet, it may take another 10 to 15 minutes before the fish is done (light pink all the way to the skin).

When the fish is done, serve immediately. Delicious with herbed boiled potatoes, baked potatoes, or any rice dish. Fiddleheads (page 87) or asparagus (page 179) would be perfect spring vegetables.

Dill-Horseradish Sauce (makes 1/3 cup)

1 1/2 tablespoons fresh dill weed, chopped fine
1/4 cup sour cream, or plain yogurt with some
    "yogurt cream" (see Note), or combination
Tiny pinch of salt

Freshly ground white pepper to taste
1 large (or 2 small) shallots, minced (or the
    white part of 1 scallion, minced)
3/4 teaspoon prepared horseradish

Combine ingredients in small bowl. Spoon over freshly grilled fish fillets. Also delicious on grilled beef steaks, baked potatoes, or on open-faced steak or salmon sandwiches (page 24).

NOTE: "Yogurt cream," skimmed from the top of non-homogenized whole-milk yogurt, is deliciously rich, especially from yogurt made with Jersey milk. Or use yogurt sour cream if you have some (page 212).

Braised Salmon with Lemon & Tarragon

With salmon, "local versus from away" can be a dilemma. Lean wild salmon is good food, but farmed Atlantic salmon often tends to be fatty, with a strong fishy taste (and some environmental impacts). We mostly buy wild-caught Northwest salmon when affordable, otherwise farmed steelhead trout, which has nice color and moist texture whether grilled (page 63) or braised, the method used here. A Meyer lemon (page 16) is perfect with the tarragon and other light flavors, fruity without being too sour.

SERVES 2 TO 3

1 pound salmon or steelhead trout fillet, skin on
2 tablespoons olive oil (extra-virgin for drizzling)
1 tablespoon lemon peel, thinly sliced
1 1/2 to 2 tablespoons lemon juice (1/2 lemon)
Few grates of multicolored pepper

1/4 cup dry white wine
2 tablespoons (about 20) almonds, halved
1 to 1 1/2 teaspoons salted butter
2 medium shallots, slivered/crescents
1/4 teaspoon dried tarragon

The best way to make this dish is with an ovenproof skillet or baking dish, such as Corningware. Heat 2 teaspoons olive oil in skillet/baking dish and sear the fish fillet (cut in 2 to 3 portions as needed to fit the pan), skin-side down, over moderate heat for about 3 minutes, until browned around the edges. Meanwhile preheat oven to 375°F, and use a paring knife to shave about 1 tablespoon peel from the lemon, sliced into about 12 thin strips. Squeeze juice from 1/2 of the lemon.

Grate a little pepper over the fish, then drizzle with 1 teaspoon olive oil, the wine, and lemon juice, cover with lid or tent loosely with foil, and bake in preheated oven 5 to 8 minutes. While the fish is baking, halve almonds (page 60) and dry-roast in the oven in a small pan for 4 to 5 minutes, or until light gold; add butter to pan in the last minute of toasting and shake to coat almonds. Reserve as garnish. When the fish begins to flake, remove dish from oven.

In a small frying pan, sauté shallots in 1 tablespoon olive oil until translucent, then add tarragon and lemon peel and pour in liquid from baking dish. Simmer 1 to 2 minutes to reduce sauce slightly.

Spoon sauce over each portion of fish, and sprinkle with toasted almonds. Serve with rice or boiled potatoes along with steamed/stir-steamed beans, asparagus, rainbow chard, or other vegetable.

Lobster in Herbed Cream Sauce

Maybe you've come home from a clambake with a few leftover steamed lobsters. What to do with them? Lobster salad is one obvious possibility, or lobster stew. . . . Or maybe feature the lobster meat in a luxurious sauce subtly flavored with herbs from your kitchen garden.

 SERVES 3 TO 4

Meat from 3 steamed 1-pound lobsters
2 tablespoons salted butter
1 tablespoon extra-virgin olive oil
1/3 cup minced onion or shallots
3 tablespoons unbleached flour
1 1/2 cups lobster body juice
1 1/2 tablespoons dry sherry or white wine
3/4 cup light cream or half-and-half

2 teaspoons fresh tarragon leaves, chopped (*or* 1 teaspoon dried)
1 teaspoon fresh dill weed, chopped (*or* 1/2 teaspoon dried)
1 1/4 teaspoons dried cilantro (optional)
1 tablespoon fresh chives, chopped
Dash of nutmeg
5 grates white pepper

Remove lobster meat and cut any large pieces, such as the tail, into generous bite-sized chunks.

Melt butter with oil in heavy-bottomed saucepan over low heat. Briefly sauté onion or shallots, then stir in flour, browning slightly to form roux. Remove from heat and gradually add lobster body juice. Cook over low heat until sauce thickens, then add the sherry or wine, light cream, herbs, and other seasonings. Finally add lobster meat.

Let stand a little while for flavors to meld, then reheat over gentle heat (or in a casserole in a moderate oven) until hot through. Serve with brown basmati or "Saffron" rice (page 185), pennes or linguine, or warmed yeast rolls or rustic bread, along with a colorful sauté of fresh vegetables.

Variation

SPANISH SHELLFISH IN CREAM SAUCE: Replace the butter with olive oil and sauté 1 clove minced garlic along with the onions/shallots. Replace lobster juice with 1 cup shrimp and/or mussel stock (pages 66, 70) and 1/2 cup milk. Season with white pepper and dried summer savory. Replace lobster meat with 1/3 pound (2/3 cup) each of raw sea scallops; small steamed mussels (page 66); pre-cooked Maine shrimp (page 70); and chunks of monkfish, halibut, or other firm-textured fish. Serve garnished with chopped parsley.

Fish with Pine Nuts & Garlic-Wine Sauce

Pine nuts appear in a number of Spanish fish recipes, including one from Janet Mendel's Cooking from the Heart of Spain *(adapted here) featuring whole sea bass or striped bass, butterflied and braised, served with a tasty but simple garlic-wine sauce. Bass seldom appear in Maine seafood markets, but any firm-fleshed fish fillets—grouper, halibut, ocean perch, or red snapper—will do.*

SERVES 3

2 tablespoons raw pine nuts

2 tablespoons olive oil (extra-virgin for drizzling)

1 to 1 1/4 pounds sea or striped bass, grouper, halibut, or ocean perch fillets, skin on

1/3 cup dry white wine

2 medium cloves garlic, minced

1/8 teaspoon mildly hot red chile pepper flakes

2 teaspoons lemon juice

1/8 teaspoon dried thyme

1 tablespoon chopped fresh parsley or chives

The best way to make this dish is with an ovenproof skillet or baking dish, such as Corningware. Dry-roast pine nuts over low heat until light gold; remove from pan. Add 2 teaspoons olive oil to skillet/baking dish and sear the fillets, skin-side down, over moderate heat for about 3 minutes, until browned around the edges. Drizzle with 2 teaspoons olive oil and the wine, cover loosely with foil, and bake in preheated 375°F oven 5 to 8 minutes. When fish begins to flake, remove dish from oven.

In a small frying pan, briefly sauté garlic with pepper flakes in 2 teaspoons olive oil, then pour in the liquid from baking dish. Simmer 1 to 2 minutes to reduce slightly, then add lemon juice, thyme, parsley or chives, and pine nuts. Spoon a little sauce over each portion of fish. Serve with rice or couscous and steamed beans, zucchini, or other vegetable.

PICK-YOUR-OWN MUSSELS

With all the mussel growers Downeast and elsewhere, fresh farmed mussels are easily come by—in stores, roadside, maybe even from a neighbor cultivating them in a small "mussel garden." But it's just as easy—and fun—to pick some wild Maine blue mussels yourself for free, if you have shore or boat access to a nearby mussel bed in clean, well-flushed waters. (If in doubt, check with Maine's Department of Marine Resources to make sure the area is open for harvesting.)

In months with an R (when mussels tend to be at their best and safe from red tide), watch the tide tables for an extra-low tide. Arrive at the mussel bed at dead-low tide, wearing rubber boots and prepared with plastic bags/buckets and rubber gloves to insulate your fingers from the cold seawater. Pick only mussels that are closed and firmly attached to each other and the bottom. Large ones are okay (and make fine serving vessels for appetizers, as on page 12) but tend to have the most pearls.

Back home with your haul, process the mussels as soon as possible. Scrub off the "beards" and barnacles, discard any "sleepy"-looking ones, then steam the mussels in a covered stockpot in a few inches of water and/or beer. Remove the mussel meats and use in your favorite recipe, along with some of the broth. Or freeze them in some mussel broth. Thawed gradually in the refrigerator, they'll be as fresh-tasting and -textured as when just picked, ready to enjoy in those months without an R!

Mussels in Hearty Lemon-Wine Sauce

Here's a savory, intensely flavored alternative to a marinara tomato sauce for mussels. Somehow the lemon, mussels, sherry, and Romano cheese really talk to each other!

SERVES 3 TO 4

3 to 4 cups fresh Maine mussels, steamed
    (2 quarts whole mussels in shells)
5 to 6 sundried tomato halves, snipped
1/2 cup white wine
2 tablespoons dry sherry
1 1/2 tablespoons olive oil
1 large onion, sliced in crescents
2 to 3 cloves garlic, pressed
1/4 to 1/2 teaspoon minced dried hot smoked
    chile pepper (or pinch of cayenne)
1 1/2 teaspoons fresh lemon zest (1/2 lemon)

Juice of 1/2-inch slice of lemon
1/8 teaspoon lemon pepper (or white pepper)
2 teaspoons dried cilantro
2 teaspoons dried basil
1/2 teaspoon dried Greek oregano
3/4 cup fish stock made with 1/2 bouillon cube
    (*or* 1/4 cup mussel stock plus 1/2 cup water)
1 1/2 tablespoons flour
1/2 to 2/3 cup freshly grated Romano cheese
Angel hair, linguine, or fettucine (about 2
    ounces dry pasta per person)

Clean and debeard mussels, and steam in a stockpot with water and beer (see opposite). Remove mussel meats from shells and set aside; reserve stock. Soak dried tomatoes in wine and sherry.

Heat olive oil in a heavy-bottomed skillet and sauté onion over moderate heat until partly translucent; add garlic, pepper, lemon zest and juice, herbs, 1/2 cup fish or mussel stock, and the tomatoes and their soaking liquid. Let mixture come to a simmer over medium heat while you dissolve the flour in 1/4 cup fish or mussel stock, smoothing out lumps. Gradually add this to the skillet with the mussels, stirring as sauce thickens. Turn heat to very low, cover, and simmer gently while you grate the Romano and boil the pasta.

Serve mussels and sauce hot in shallow bowls over drained, oiled/buttered pasta, with a healthy sprinkle of cheese over each serving.

Variation

MUSSELS WITH RED PEPPERS: Sauté 2/3 cup chopped red bell pepper along with the onions and garlic. Omit from sauce the sherry and 1/4 cup of the stock, the tomatoes, lemon zest, and dried herbs, and use instead 1 tablespoon chopped fresh oregano. Sprinkle each serving with a gremolata (an Italian garnish; see page 73) of fresh chopped parsley, grated Romano, and a little fresh lemon zest if desired.

Chili Scallops

This is one of the easiest ways to prepare fresh Maine sea scallops, and one of the most delicious. Like shrimp, local sea scallops are best bought fresh from roadside trucks and fish markets through the winter scallop season. They freeze well, so lay in a supply in the freezer to enjoy during the rest of the year.

These sweet, succulent morsels are best cooked as little as possible. This pasta toss, inspired by a recipe in Cooking Light, *is one of our busy-night default dishes, a stovetop meal easily made at home or camp.*

Like other shellfish, scallops are quite rich, and just a few can be quite satisfying. If you have any Chili Scallops left over, they could be recycled into a scallop stew, simply by heating them up with some milk and half-and-half—or use in a bisque, as on page 37.

 SERVES 2 TO 3

1 pound fresh Maine sea scallops, whole or halved if very large	2 tablespoons shallots (or minced onion)
1 1/2 to 2 teaspoons Chili Rub (see below)	1 small clove garlic, minced (optional)
1 1/2 tablespoons olive oil	2 tablespoons dry white wine (or vermouth)
	Fresh parsley and lemon slices

Remove the "sweetmeats" (the tough hinge muscles) from the scallops and discard (or treat your cat). Slice any large scallops in half. Spread scallops in shallow bowl and dust evenly with Chili Rub.

Heat oil in pan and sauté shallots (or onion) until soft and translucent, adding garlic midway. Add scallops and cook just long enough to sear both sides. Deglaze with wine (or vermouth) and simmer over low heat just until the scallops are done (no longer translucent) in the middle.

Serve immediately over wind-y pasta (angel hair, fettucine, or linguine), garnished with parsley and lemon slices, with steamed kale or green beans alongside.

CHILI RUB (MAKES 2 TABLESPOONS)

1 small dried hot red chile pepper (amount, heat, smokiness, etc. to your taste)	1/2 teaspoon dried marjoram
1 teaspoon lemon pepper	1 teaspoon ground cumin
1/2 teaspoon dried oregano	1/2 teaspoon salt
1/2 teaspoon dried winter savory	1/2 teaspoon garlic powder
	1/2 teaspoon epazote or sage (optional)

Break up dried chile pepper, removing any stems and resistant pieces but leaving seeds as desired (the more seeds, the hotter it will be). Grind pepper in mortar and pestle, and add other herbs and spices. Store in small airtight jar.

Variation

BROILED CHILI SCALLOPS: Rather than the scampi approach above, simply place the fresh scallops in an oiled (with extra-virgin olive oil) 8 x 8-inch ovenproof casserole. Sprinkle with 1 1/2 teaspoons Chili Rub, and broil just until scallops are tender.

Lemon-Sesame Seafood Kebabs

Simple as can be are these seafood kebabs grilled in a light coating of lemon juice and toasted sesame oil. A sozzle of tamari at table rounds out the flavors. You could use all sea scallops, or a combination of scallops and swordfish, halibut, or other firm-textured fish, skewered separately.

 SERVES 3

1 pound sea scallops, swordfish, and/or halibut

Juice of 1/3 to 1/2 lemon

1/2 teaspoon toasted sesame oil

2 tablespoons toasted sesame seeds (optional)

Remove the "sweetmeats" (the tough hinge muscles) from the scallops. Place scallops in a bowl, along with fish cut in 1-inch chunks. Sprinkle lemon juice and sesame oil over seafood and turn to coat evenly. Soak 5 bamboo skewers in cold water for 20 to 30 minutes, while seafood marinates.

Start fire in charcoal grill. Thread seafood on skewers, putting scallops and fish on separate skewers (since scallops take a little less time to cook). Reserve any juice/marinade for basting kebabs.

Grill over moderate coals for about 10 to 15 minutes, turning and basting occasionally. Serve immediately with tamari and white or brown basmati rice, garnished with sesame seeds if desired.

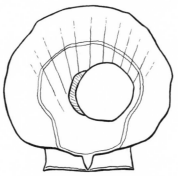

Ginger Scallops

This simple, hearty meal tastes just right on a cold night, and is a quick, flavorful way to enjoy fresh Maine sea scallops in season. There's a good balance of bright and earthy colors and flavors, between the sweet scallops and winter vegetables, the spicy garlic and ginger, the buckwheat noodles and tamari. Buckwheat in the form of baked groats, or kasha (page 189), would also go well with this dish.

SERVES 2 TO 3

1 pound Maine sea scallops

1/3 buttercup, kabocha, or other small orange
    winter squash, crescents

1 1/2 cups Brussels sprouts (or savoy cabbage)

2 teaspoons olive or canola oil

1 small to medium onion, crescents

4 to 6 scallions, chopped, white and green
    parts separated

1 teaspoon toasted sesame oil

1 clove garlic, minced

3/4-inch piece fresh ginger, skinned and minced

2 tablespoons dry sherry and/or white wine

Pinch of cayenne

1/3 to 1/2 red bell pepper, sliced

Buckwheat soba (or udon)

Tamari to taste

Remove the "sweetmeats" (the tough hinge muscles) from the scallops and discard (or call that lucky cat). Slice any large scallops in half. Set aside. Set pot of water to boil for soba.

Meanwhile, prepare vegetables: Cut skin off squash and scoop out seeds, then slice in thin crescents and place in steamer. If using fresh Brussels sprouts, trim ends and slice each sprout in halves or thirds, and set aside to add to steamer when squash is partway cooked. (If using savoy cabbage, have it sliced and ready to add around the same time.)

Time boiling the buckwheat noodles (or udon) so that they will be ready—cooked, drained, and oiled—at the same time as the steamed vegetables and the scallops.

Heat oil in skillet and sauté onion and white parts of scallions over medium heat for 1 minute; then add sesame oil, garlic, and ginger, lower heat slightly, and sauté 1 minute more. Deglaze with sherry or wine, then add cayenne, peppers, scallops, and scallion tops. Partially cover and cook just long enough so the peppers are al dente and scallops are done (no longer translucent) in the middle.

Serve in shallow bowls, spooning the scallops and pan juices over the steamed vegetables on a bed of buckwheat noodles. Season with tamari at the table.

MAINE SHRIMP

Maine (northern) shrimp, sweet and satisfying, are good food, and what could be better than some bought fresh off the boat or roadside truck, in season and close to the source? Well, and then there's the price—usually quite reasonable compared with other seafood, due to supply and market forces.

With these smaller shrimp, the key is to buy them as fresh as possible; otherwise their texture will deteriorate the longer they are kept on ice. Sample them a pound at a time as shrimp season progresses, and when they seem at their prime (fresh and firm), buy several pounds to put in the freezer.

Although it's certainly easier to buy fresh shrimp already cleaned, saving you the time and mess and disposal of the shells, it's easy enough to buy them whole and clean them yourself: Working out of a clean empty basin of your kitchen sink to contain the slurry, go through the lot, first pinching off the head, then the tail, shell, and any roe; rinse only as necessary, since it's contact with fresh water that makes shrimp mushy. Freeze in clean pint or half-pint plastic containers, or whatever amount suits your household; a rule of thumb is 1/4 pound per serving. When ready for a shrimp meal, thaw a container overnight in the refrigerator, and the shrimp will be as fresh as when you bought them.

Or better yet, buy the shrimp with heads removed (or do it yourself) and quickly boil them in the shell in salted water, adding 1 tablespoon salt per quart of water per pound of shrimp (the typical amount called for in the recipes offered here). Put a bay leaf in the pot of salted water, bring to a boil, then add the shrimp. Once the pot has come back to a boil, remove the shrimp as quickly as you can. Chill the shrimp, shells on (or freeze), until ready to use. You'll find the shrimp stay firmer this way, and the broth is delicious to use as stock in small amounts. Add these parboiled shrimp to the dish you are preparing in the last minute or so before serving.

When cooking raw shrimp, less is more—cook them just until they turn opaque, and no longer. In fact, you might turn the heat off just before they seem done, knowing they will continue cooking in the residual heat left in the pan.

You'd think with such a delicious local product we'd have no end of shrimp dishes in our repertoire, but it's actually been a challenge to think of simple, quick ways to prepare Maine shrimp that won't undermine their delicate flavor and texture. The following recipes—most of them simple stovetop meals—are house favorites, along with the occasional bisque (page 37) or flan (page 77) to use up smaller amounts of shrimp. Lobster meat could be substituted in many of the shrimp recipes.

Thai Shrimp Curry

Here's a delicious way to enjoy fresh (or frozen) Maine shrimp. The hot, astringent green curry paste, fresh ginger, tart lemon, savory garlic, and fragrant coconut milk offset the sweetness of the shrimp.

If you often cook Thai food at home, you might try making a batch of green curry paste from scratch, working from an Asian cookbook. Ingredients might include chiles, galangal or ginger, cilantro, garlic, shallots, lemongrass, lime zest, shrimp or anchovy paste, coriander, nutmeg, cumin, cloves, black pepper, fennel seeds, and peanut oil. For less frequent use, one of the authentic prepared Thai green curry pastes will do almost as well, and have a longer shelf life in the refrigerator. We're still working through a jar of green curry paste that contains galangal, rather than ginger, hence the fresh ginger in the recipe—but if your curry paste is strong on ginger, that should be enough.

SERVES 2 TO 3

1 tablespoon olive oil
1/2 tablespoon toasted sesame oil
1 clove roasted garlic, minced
1 clove raw garlic, minced
3 thin slices (1/4-inch chunk) fresh ginger, minced
1/3 cup dry vermouth (or white wine)

1 tablespoon Thai green curry paste
1/2 teaspoon freshly grated lemon zest
1/3 cup lightened coconut milk (page 115)
1 pound Maine shrimp meat, fresh (or frozen and thawed); see page 70
Pinch of salt

Heat oils in pan and lightly sauté the garlic and ginger. Deglaze with vermouth, then stir in curry paste and lemon zest. Add coconut milk and simmer over low heat for about 15 minutes.

Add shrimp, swirling pan occasionally, and cook over moderate heat just until the shrimp are opaque and done; do not overcook. Serve immediately over white basmati rice. A stir-fry of vegetables (such as baby bok choy, broccoli, onion, and carrot), garnished with lightly toasted almonds, cashews, or Old Virginia peanuts (page 262), completes the meal.

NOTE: When you open a can of coconut milk, be sure to shake or stir it before pouring off the amount needed in the recipe, to distribute the coconut "cream." Once opened, leftover coconut milk will keep up to a week in the fridge. For longer storage, freeze recipe-scaled amounts in plastic containers. (For more on coconuts, see page 249. And for a way to preserve fresh ginger if you don't use it that often, see page 115.)

Caribbean Jerk Shrimp

The jerk method of barbecue—spicing, marinating, and grilling meats and shellfish—began in the West Indies, where Spanish explorers found native Indians roasting wild pigs seasoned with allspice over coals, which they called a barbacoa. *Each of the cultures that came to the Caribbean islands— from Europe, West Africa, India—brought their own additions to the culinary melting pot, with jerk mixes evolving to combine 20 or more herbs and spices, each unique to the cook, culture, and dish.*

Like curries, their East Indian counterpart, jerk seasonings come in many forms and formulas, from dry rubs to pastes to marinades. Garlic, onion, allspice, thyme, and hot pepper are key ingredients. Jerk mixes for chicken or pork might include cinnamon, nutmeg, or cumin, crushed bay or sage, combined in a marinade with soy sauce, green onions, lime and/or orange, and rum. The dry rub featured here holds back a bit on the sweet spices, along with the onion and garlic since they are part of the dish. If using this spice rub in a barbecue/marinade, you'll want to add more onion and garlic powder.

With the jerk seasoning in a spice jar, this seasoned-scampi approach to shrimp or chicken (variation) makes a quick, easy stovetop dinner for home or wherever the winds of adventure take you.

 SERVES 2 TO 3

1 pound Maine shrimp meat, fresh (or frozen and thawed); see page 70	1/2 medium onion, finely chopped
2 to 3 teaspoons Jerk Spice Rub	1 clove garlic, minced
2 tablespoons olive oil	1/4 cup dry vermouth (or white wine)
1 tablespoon salted butter	Freshly squeezed juice of 1/3 to 1/2 lime (some zest optional)

Sprinkle jerk seasoning over shrimp (lightly coated with oil) in shallow bowl. Heat oil and butter in pan and sauté onion over medium heat until translucent, adding garlic midway. Add the seasoned shrimp and vermouth, and sauté just long enough to cook off the alcohol. Add lime juice and finish quickly; do not overcook the shrimp. Serve at once over white or brown basmati rice or couscous.

Variation

CARIBBEAN JERK CHICKEN: Dust 4 skinless chicken thighs with jerk rub and brown in olive oil, turning twice; remove to plate. Sauté onion until clear, then add to pan 4 thin lime slices (instead of juice) and fry both sides. Deglaze pan with vermouth, put lime slices on chicken, and simmer covered till done through.

JERK SPICE RUB (MAKES 5 TEASPOONS)

1/2 teaspoon dried minced onion (or powder)	1/4 teaspoon paprika
1/8 teaspoon garlic powder	1/4 teaspoon black pepper
1 1/2 teaspoons dried thyme	1/8 to 1/4 teaspoon cayenne pepper
3/4 teaspoon ground coriander (or whole seeds, crushed in mortar and pestle)	1/4 teaspoon salt
	1/4 teaspoon dried orange zest (or minced peel)
1/2 teaspoon allspice (or 1/4 teaspoon cumin)	1/8 teaspoon finely crushed bay leaf (optional)

Combine ingredients in mortar and pestle or small jar. To use as spice rub on chicken, fish, or shellfish, first coat with a little olive oil, then sprinkle with spice rub.

Shrimp Scampi

Here's another default recipe for a classic, quick, and delicious shrimp dinner. Any leftover scampi could be put to good use in a simple Shrimp Bisque (page 37) made with or without the corn. Or, make a small batch of Scampi Phyllo Tarts (page 13) as appetizers.

🅟 ⚱ SERVES 2 TO 3

About 1/2 teaspoon freshly grated lemon zest

1/4 to 1/3 cup freshly grated Romano cheese

2/3 cup fresh parsley, chopped

2 tablespoons olive oil

1 tablespoon salted butter

2 tablespoons shallots, minced

2 cloves garlic, minced

1/4 cup white wine (or dry vermouth)

1 pound Maine shrimp meat, raw (or frozen and thawed), page 70

Freshly squeezed juice of 1/4 lemon (2 to 3 teaspoons)

Combine ingredients for the garnish—an Italian "gremolata" dusting of lemon zest, grated Romano, and chopped parsley—in a separate bowl, and set aside.

Heat oil and butter in pan and sauté shallots over medium heat for 1 to 2 minutes, or until translucent. Add garlic and sauté briefly. Add wine and shrimp, and cook just long enough to cook off the alcohol. Add lemon juice and finish quickly; do not overcook the shrimp. (Or if using shrimp pre-cooked as on page 70, add them along with the lemon juice and bring up to heat.)

Serve immediately over wind-y pasta (angel hair or linguine), and garnish with the gremolata.

NOTE: Another common gremolata, for sprinkling over shell beans or pasta, combines finely chopped parsley, lemon zest, and garlic.

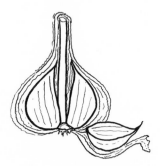

SERVE IT HOT

For those of us who like our hot food hot, warming the serving dishes makes all the difference in being able to fully enjoy a meal—not just at room temperature, but especially on a chilly night or if you are eating outdoors where heat is quickly lost. Dishes can be quickly heated in a warm oven or with hot water from the tap or teapot—or (a rough-and-ready camping shortcut) by using them as a catch basin when draining cooked pasta. Served in a warm bowl or plate, the food should stay hot long enough so you can relax and savor your meal without hurrying to finish before it gets cold.

Spanish Shrimp

The sweet flavor of Maine shrimp is nicely offset by pungent chorizo in this Spanish-style skillet dish, inspired by several classic tapas recipes (from Cooking Light *magazine, and Penelope Casas's* Tapas *cookbook). As with most tapas, this seafood medley makes a fine entrée as well as appetizer. While the dish has several ingredients in common with paella (the shellfish, chorizo, ham, and saffron), making the rice separately gives you better control over how long everything cooks, assuring al-dente shrimp and scallops, and fluffy (not gummy) rice.*

The sherry and fruity peppers complement the sweet and salty flavors of the shellfish and cured meats, while the toasted almonds add a delightful crunchy texture. Or, try the simpler variation, on the same theme but brightened up with green beans and lemon zest.

If shrimp or scallops are unavailable, chunks of monkfish or halibut would make a fair substitute. For another Spanish-inspired shellfish medley in a cream sauce, see the variation on page 65.

SERVES 2 TO 3

1/3 to 1/2 pound fresh Maine shrimp, raw or precooked with bay leaf (page 70)

1/4 to 1/3 pound fresh Maine sea scallops, halved if large

1/4 cup thick-sliced ham, bite-sized pieces (optional)

1/2 cup chorizo sausage, 1/2-inch coins

2 tablespoons "poor man's saffron" (page 185) (*or* 1/8 teaspoon saffron, dissolved in 2 tablespoons hot water)

1 to 2 tablespoons whole almonds, lightly toasted and chopped

1 recipe Pan-Roasted Rice or Rice-Noodle Pilaf (page 184)

1 tablespoon olive oil

1 small or 1/2 large onion, chopped (1/2 cup)

1/2 to 2/3 green bell pepper, lengthwise strips, halved (or combination red/green pepper)

1 large clove garlic, minced

1/8 teaspoon Chili Rub (page 68)

1/4 cup dry sherry

2 to 3 canned plum tomatoes, chopped

1/4 cup shrimp stock (page 70) or water

2 to 4 tablespoons fresh parsley, chopped

Prepare shrimp; have ready the scallops, ham, chorizo, and "poor man's saffron" (or saffron solution). Set oven to 350°F and bake almonds for 4 to 6 minutes in preheating oven until lightly toasted; chop. Pan-roast white rice, add boiling water, raise oven temperature to 375°, and bake in lidded casserole for 30 minutes.

In large skillet or Dutch oven, sauté onion in olive oil until partly translucent. Add the ham and bell peppers and sauté 2 to 3 minutes more, or until ham and peppers are just beginning to brown around the edges. Add chorizo, garlic, and Chili Rub and sauté briefly, then deglaze pan with sherry, scraping any browned bits from bottom of pan. Add tomatoes, almonds, and shrimp stock (or water) and simmer covered 1 to 2 minutes more; turn off heat.

When rice is almost cooked, sprinkle raw scallops over contents of skillet and bring up to heat. Sprinkle shrimp over the scallops, cover, and let the shellfish steam in pan juices for 1 to 2 minutes more, or until scallops and shrimp are heated through. Serve immediately over freshly cooked rice.

SPANISH SHRIMP WITH LEMON & GREEN BEANS: Omit scallops and ham, and use 1 pound shrimp and 1/3 cup chorizo. Add 2 cups tender romanos or other green beans, fresh or thawed, to the skillet along with the onions and peppers (or stir-steam the beans separately and add along with the shrimp). Double the amount of Chili Rub (1/4 teaspoon), replace saffron solution with 1 teaspoon fresh lemon zest, and use half the amount of sherry (1 to 2 tablespoons); omit tomatoes. Add shrimp and simmer covered until shrimp is heated through. Serve over Pan-Roasted Rice (page 184).

Fresh-Tomato Shrimp Scorpio

Here's a fresh take on the classic Greek combination of shrimp, feta, and tomato, usually prepared with a rich, cooked-down tomato sauce. Fresh ripe tomato added at the last minute adds color and a little flavor but doesn't overpower the shrimp. This stovetop dish makes a simple, satisfying meal for camp or camp-cruising.

 SERVES 2

1 tablespoon olive oil
1 tablespoon minced raw onion
4 scallions, white/green parts separated
1/3 to 1/2 yellow bell pepper, halved strips
1 clove garlic, slivered
2 tablespoons dry vermouth (or white wine)
Salt and white pepper

2/3 pound Maine shrimp meat, raw (or frozen and thawed), page 70
3 cups fresh spinach leaves, washed and stemmed, large pieces torn in two
1 large ripe beefsteak tomato, large dice
2/3 cup feta cheese, diced
Fresh cilantro and small lemon wedges

Heat oil in open pan over moderate heat and sauté onion (including white parts of scallions) until translucent, then add bell pepper and garlic and sauté for a minute more. Deglaze pan with vermouth, and add salt and pepper to taste.

Add shrimp to pan, cover with lid, and simmer for a minute until shrimp begins turning opaque. Distribute tomato and green onion tops over shrimp, then add spinach, cover, and simmer a couple of minutes more until spinach deflates. Sprinkle feta over spinach and turn off heat. Serve immediately over fluffy pan-roasted couscous (page 190) or rice (page 184), garnished with cilantro and lemon.

Crab Pasta Toss with Summer Veggies

*K*eep this wonderful dish in mind for a light, quick meal on a summer night. If you have summer squash, zucchini, and beans still coming in your garden, nothing's easier than picking just enough for dinner, grabbing a half-pint of fresh crabmeat at your local market—or packing these into your camp or boat cooler—and assembling the meal as fast as you can say,"Aah, the way life should be."

The critical thing (as with any pasta toss) is to time the rest of the meal to come together just before the vegetables and crabmeat are done, so that the main dish will not be waiting on other elements. This way you can enjoy your garden vegetables and succulent sweet Maine crabmeat at their best, hot through but not overcooked.

Smoked scallops (page 12) would be a nice variation for this seafood pasta toss, omitting the cheese. And salmon—fresh, grilled, or smoked—makes an elegant primavera (see variation).

 SERVES 2

1 tablespoon extra-virgin olive oil

2/3 to 3/4 medium onion, sliced in crescents

2 scallions, sliced, white/green parts separated

1 clove garlic, pressed or finely minced

1 each small (or 1/2 each medium) zucchini
    and summer squash, cut in 3/8-inch coins
    or half-moons

1 to 1 1/2 cups fresh filet beans (or young
    tender green beans), stemmed

1 to 2 ripe plum tomatoes, seeded and chopped
    (*or* 6 to 8 cherry tomatoes, halved)

1 to 2 tablespoons white wine (or water)

1 to 2 teaspoons fresh basil

1/2 to 1 teaspoon fresh summer savory

1/4 teaspoon fresh tarragon

Few grates white pepper

Dash of salt

1/2 pound (1 to 1 1/4 cups) fresh crabmeat

1/2 cup shaved Asiago or Manchego cheese

About 4 ounces dried pasta (linguine, fettucine,
    angel hair, bowties, or confetti pasta), or
    enough fresh pasta for 2 servings

Time the pasta to be cooked, drained, and dressed just when the rest of the meal is ready to serve.

Heat oil in medium to large nonstick skillet with lid, and sauté onion and white parts of scallions until partly translucent. Add garlic, zucchini, and summer squash, and sauté for a minute or so, until onion is just beginning to turn a little gold and cut edges of squash are sealed. Add beans and cook another 1 to 2 minutes or until squash and beans are al dente, keeping skillet covered and shaking pan occasionally to sweat vegetables. Before they catch on, add tomatoes and deglaze pan with wine or water; then sprinkle with herbs, salt and pepper, and simmer covered for another half minute.

Distribute lumps of crabmeat evenly around skillet over vegetables, then the green scallion tops. Cover skillet and simmer over low heat 1 minute more, just long enough to bring crabmeat up to heat and steam the scallions. Sprinkle cheese over the top, and let the dish rest for a minute. Meanwhile drain cooked pasta, dress with olive oil and a little butter, and divide between 2 shallow bowls. Serve the crab and vegetable mixture over the pasta, leaving it to each diner to toss their own.

Variation

SALMON PRIMAVERA: Omit cheese and tomatoes, and replace crabmeat with pieces of fresh poached salmon (page 10); vary vegetables with peapods, sprouting broccoli, or fresh spinach, and garnish with almond halves (page 60). Or, use leftover grilled salmon and season with Genovese Pesto (page 21).

Crabmeat Flan with Ricotta

There's nothing finer than a well-made crab roll, but how to do fresh crabmeat justice as a dinner entrée, while stretching a small container of this precious, perishable treat? This simple flan is one solution, simpler still if you omit the cheese and sauce—although their stronger flavors are a nice accent to the rest of the dish.

SERVES 3 TO 4

Caramelized Onion-Tomato Sauce (page 99)
    or Slow-Roasted Tomato-Onion Confit
    (page 176)
3 to 4 large eggs
2/3 cup ricotta
1/3 cup milk
Dash of salt
Few grates white pepper

1 tablespoon butter
2 tablespoons white or yellow cornmeal
1/2 pound (about 1 1/4 cups) fresh crabmeat
2 teaspoon fresh summer savory, chopped
1 1/2 teaspoons fresh dill weed (or 1 tablespoon
    basil, or 1/2 teaspoon tarragon), chopped
1/2 cup shredded Manchego, Muenster, or
    Monterey Jack cheese (optional)

Make Caramelized Onion-Tomato Sauce and set aside to reheat before serving (or if you have some already made, the Slow-Roasted Tomato-Onion Confit).

Beat eggs in mixing bowl, then whisk in ricotta, milk, salt, and pepper. Preheat oven to 350°F.

Butter bottom and sides of Pyrex deep-dish pie plate or other round ovenproof baking dish, and sprinkle with cornmeal. Crumble crabmeat over bottom of dish, then sprinkle with savory and dill. Pour egg mixture and smooth evenly over crabmeat. Sprinkle top with grated cheese, if desired.

Bake flan at 350° for about 30 minutes, or until eggs are set and top is nicely golden and puffed. Serve immediately, accompanying each slice with a spoonful of warmed tomato-onion sauce.

Round out the meal with yeast rolls, focaccia, or crusty bread spread with butter or olive oil, and a nice green salad tossed with balsamic or other vinaigrette.

Variation

SHRIMP FLAN: Instead of cornmeal, pat 1 1/2 cups cooked rice into buttered dish as a crust. Omit ricotta and cheese, use 1/2 cup milk, and replace crabmeat with 1/2 pound cleaned fresh shrimp. Bake as above.

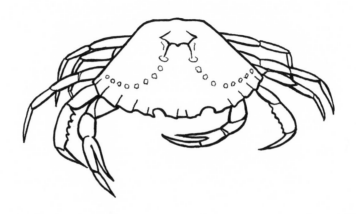

Crab (or Salmon) Frittata with Potato Crust

*H*ere is a quick, satisfying dinner to throw together on short notice. A frittata is not only a nice way to feature the luscious, sweet fresh crabmeat we are so lucky to have from local pickers (crabs being a side catch for Downeast lobstermen), but a way to stretch a small amount of this expensive delicacy into a larger meal. Another delicious approach is to combine crabmeat with zucchini and corn (page 133).

This potato-crust baked frittata, as inspired by a recipe in Cooking Light magazine, is also a good way to recycle leftover grilled salmon or Apple-Smoked Steelhead Trout (page 63). Or perhaps you have some smoked salmon from one of our local producers. Decorate the top with fresh chevre from a local farm, and you have a Downeast sampler.

 SERVES 2 TO 4

3 medium potatoes (2 3/4 cups), large dice, boiled (or leftover boiled potatoes)

2 tablespoons extra-virgin olive oil

2 to 3 shallots, minced (*or* 1/3 cup chopped onions)

2 scallions, white and green parts separated (*or* 2 tablespoons chives), chopped

Few grates white pepper

Dash of salt

1/2 pound (1 1/4 cups) fresh crabmeat (or left-over grilled salmon, or smoked salmon)

1/2 teaspoon dried dill (*or* 1 teaspoon fresh dill weed, snipped)

3 extra-large (or 4 large) eggs, beaten

3 to 4 tablespoons milk

1/3 to 1/2 cup chevre, herbed or plain (or shredded goat gouda or Manchego cheese) (optional)

Cover potatoes with boiling water and cook until tender, then drain. Use 1 tablespoon oil to grease a Pyrex deep-dish pie plate or other round ovenproof baking dish. Spread potatoes in bottom of dish and "smash" with a wooden spoon just enough to break them up a bit, so they form a crust covering the bottom of the dish.

Preheat oven to 375°F. Heat remaining 1 tablespoon oil in small skillet and sauté shallots (or onions) and white parts of scallions until slightly caramelized. Season with salt and pepper and sprinkle over potatoes. Distribute crabmeat (or salmon) evenly over onions, and sprinkle with dill (a little less if using smoked salmon) and green scallion tops (or chives).

Beat eggs, whisk in milk, and pour over crabmeat (or salmon). Gently press crabmeat into custard; otherwise let salmon stand proud. Dot chevre around top of frittata in between crab/salmon pieces (or sprinkle evenly with grated cheese), if desired.

Bake for about 10 minutes, then reduce heat to 350° and bake 20 minutes more, or until eggs are set and crust is slightly browned around edges.

Serve in large wedges, along with a green salad tossed with a balsamic vinaigrette and ripe tomatoes (page 57).

Variation
HAM FRITTATA WITH POTATO CRUST: Use 1 1/4 cups Virginia ham or smoked shoulder in place of fish.

Poultry & Meat Entrées

Chicken with Cherries & Mushrooms

This earthy, fruity stovetop chicken teriyaki is a favorite recipe from our first cookbook, We'd Like to Invite You All to Dinner . . . , *updated to include an oven variation using whole chicken thighs and braising liquid rather than marinade as the base for the sauce.*

Elegant and savory, this unusual dish makes for a special dinner. The time to make it is just over the crest of cherry season, when fresh cherries are more affordable.

SERVES 3

3 to 4 boneless chicken thighs (1 to 1 1/2 pounds), cut in bite-sized pieces
2 teaspoons olive oil
1 teaspoon butter
1 small onion, crescents
1 clove garlic, minced
6 baby portabella mushrooms, sliced
1 cup fresh cherries, halved and pitted
1 tablespoon tamari

~ MARINADE ~
3 tablespoons dry sherry
1/2 teaspoon ground ginger
Few grates black or white pepper
Few grains cayenne
1 1/2 teaspoons dried summer savory
1/2 to 1 teaspoon dried thyme
1 tablespoon tamari
5 tablespoons beer

Combine ingredients for marinade. Cut chicken in bite-sized pieces and marinate (in covered bowl or ziplock bag) for 1 hour, turning occasionally. Meanwhile, prepare other ingredients.

Heat oil and butter in skillet and sauté onion over medium heat for a couple of minutes, then add garlic and mushrooms and sauté briefly until mushrooms are lightly browned. Add chicken and marinade to skillet and cook, partially covered, for 10 minutes. Add cherries and tamari, cover, and simmer over reduced heat for another 10 minutes.

Serve with white or brown basmati rice, baked or mashed potatoes, or couscous. This dish goes well with a simple mix of stir-steamed veggies, such as summer squash and green beans (page 177).

Variation

BRAISED CHICKEN WITH CHERRIES & MUSHROOMS: Using boneless or whole chicken thighs with skin removed, dredge thighs (whole or cut in half) in a little flour seasoned with salt and pepper. Heat 1 tablespoon olive oil in skillet and brown both sides of chicken pieces over medium heat, turning several times. Place in lidded casserole dish. Deglaze pan with 2 tablespoons water, scrape up browned bits from bottom, and reserve. Preheat oven to 375°F. Wipe out skillet and sauté the onion, garlic, and mushrooms in oil with a little butter; deglaze with 3 tablespoons marsala or dry sherry, and add 1 tablespoon fresh summer savory, 1 teaspoon fresh thyme, the cherries, and 1 tablespoon tamari. Stir in reserved liquid and pour contents of skillet over chicken. Bake covered for 30 to 45 minutes.

Chicken Pockets

Plain or fancy, stuffed chicken breasts lend themselves to all kinds of delicious combinations for fillings, glazes, and sauces. We keep coming back to the classic ham-and-cheese-stuffed Chicken Cordon Bleu, stepping out with an occasional variation (these two will get you started). Whatever the ingredients, the key to tender, juicy chicken breasts is to seal the meat when browning—either with the skin on, or with the skin removed and the breasts dredged in flour, the healthier choice described here.

SERVES 2

2 chicken breasts, bone-in (or boneless thighs)	1 tablespoon olive oil (*or* 2 teaspoons oil + 1 teaspoon butter)
2 ounces thinly sliced Virginia ham or prosciutto	2 tablespoons white wine (or dry vermouth)
2 ounces cheddar or goat gouda, sliced	2 tablespoons chicken stock (or bouillon)
3 tablespoons unbleached flour + milk (or milk with yogurt) for dredging	Salt and pepper to taste

Remove skin from chicken and trim excess fat. Lay each breast bone-side-down on cutting board and, with a sharp knife, cut a horizontal slice or pocket, opening from the long, meaty axis of the breast triangle. Fill pockets with a couple slices of ham and cheese, placing the cheese on top of the ham. (If using boneless thighs, lay filling in the center of the spread-out meat, then roll up.) Secure each pocket opening with 2 toothpicks (the stronger double-pointed square ones work best).

Sprinkle flour on plate. Dip stuffed breasts in a little milk, then dredge in flour, coating all sides.

Heat oil in lidded skillet and brown chicken, starting with the bone side down. When browned, turn breast to brown the other side; then roll to brown the meaty axis side as well. Continue until all sides are nicely browned and sealed.

Deglaze pan with wine, then add stock. Cover pan, reduce heat, and simmer 15 to 20 minutes, or until chicken is done through.

The chicken can be served just with the pan juices, or the juices can be made into a sauce: Remove chicken to a plate and keep warm; then add a little more liquid if needed, along with salt and pepper to taste, a sprinkle of garlic powder, perhaps a pinch of thyme, marjoram, summer savory, and turmeric. There might already be enough flour from the dredged chicken to thicken the sauce; otherwise whisk in a little flour dissolved in stock. Return chicken to pan and bring up to heat.

Serve with rice, baked potato, fettucine, or ribbon noodles, along with steamed broccoli, asparagus, beans, or other green vegetable.

Variations

MUSHROOM-CHEESE CHICKEN POCKETS: Sauté 1/3 cup minced onion in 1 teaspoon olive oil until translucent, then add 1 teaspoon butter and 1 cup sliced baby portabella or crimini mushrooms and sauté until mushrooms are browned and tender. Deglaze pan with a little dry sherry or marsala, then add 1/4 to 1/2 teaspoon tarragon. Fill chicken pockets with mushroom filling topped with a slice or two of goat gouda or Gruyère cheese. Secure with toothpicks and cook chicken as described above, substituting sherry or marsala for wine in the sauce.

CARAMELIZED-ONION CHICKEN POCKETS: Sauté 2/3 cup thinly sliced minced onion in 1 teaspoon each of olive oil and butter until golden. Deglaze pan with a little dry sherry, marsala, or white wine, then add 1/4 teaspoon each of sage and marjoram (or thyme). Fill chicken pockets with caramelized onion filling topped with a slice or two of fontina, gouda, raclette, or other semi-soft flavorful cheese. Secure with toothpicks and cook chicken as described above.

Spanish Orange Chicken

The idea for this dish came from an appetizer in Penelope Casas's Spanish cookbook, Tapas: The Little Dishes of Spain, *of marinated boneless chicken breast meat sautéed and served with an orange-walnut sauce. Just the combination of marinade ingredients is elegantly simple, fruity and fragrant. The meat holds its juices best if grilled whole and bone-in, but a stovetop sauté of marinated boneless chicken breast (split or cut in bite-sized pieces) is delicious too.*

When peeling the orange, be sure to shave just the outer orange part of the skin (which contains the aromatic orange oil), avoiding the white pith which tastes bitter.

The proportions here can be easily scaled up by half again to serve three or four (3 or 4 chicken breasts, 3 or 4 tablespoons of sherry, orange juice, and oil).

 SERVES 2

2 split chicken breasts, whole or cut in half   Orange-Sherry Marinade

ORANGE-SHERRY MARINADE

2 tablespoons dry or semi-dry sherry   2 tablespoons olive oil
   (Amontillado, if available)   Dash of salt
Juice of 1/3 Valencia orange (2 tablespoons)   Few grinds white or multicolored pepper
   plus outer peel sliced in very thin strips

Trim fat from breasts and remove excess fatty skin. Place chicken in ziplock bag or covered bowl.

Combine marinade ingredients and pour over chicken. Marinate 6 hours or overnight. Remove strips of orange peel before cooking.

Grill chicken over medium coals, turning several times as needed, until crispy and done through (see page 121). Or, for a stovetop version, brown chicken in olive oil and simmer covered for 5 to 8 minutes, adding reserved strips of marinated orange rind and 2 slivered shallots to the pan near the end of cooking. Deglaze pan juices with a little sherry and stock, and reduce to make a simple sauce.

Serve chicken with Rice-Noodle Pilaf (page 184) or white or brown basmati rice, along with steamed green beans, sautéed summer veggies, or a green salad.

Chicken with Herbed Orange Sauce

Like many cooks before me in the orange's long culinary history (from Southeast Asia to Persia, the Mediterranean, Spain, Italy, and France, as told in John McPhee's Oranges*), I love cooking with this versatile, subtly sweet-sour fruit. Valencias—one of the most flavorful, juicy oranges—and dry sherry are natural companions, delicious just on their own (as in the previous recipe) or in a teriyaki marinade or stir-fry (Grilled Orange-Teriyaki Chicken, page 109, or Orange Beef Stir-fry, page 106). It is also nice to feature these old Spanish friends in a lighter sauce, as here, seasoned with sweet herbs.*

Any leftover chicken and sauce can be recycled into a filling for Chicken Ployes (page 94).

℗ SERVES 3 TO 4

4 chicken thighs, bone-in or boneless	1/2 teaspoon dried marjoram
1 to 1 1/2 tablespoons olive oil	1/4 teaspoon dried basil
2 to 3 large scallions, white/green parts	1/8 teaspoon white pepper
separated	Pinch of cayenne pepper
1/2 onion, crescents	1/2 teaspoon salt
1 clove garlic, minced	1/3 cup chicken stock
1/4 to 1/3 cup dry sherry	Freshly squeezed juice of 1 Valencia orange
3/4 teaspoon dried chervil	2 Valencia orange slices, halved

Trim skin and fat from chicken thighs. Heat 1/2 tablespoon olive oil in lidded skillet and brown chicken thighs. Meanwhile prepare other ingredients.

Transfer browned chicken to plate and drain excess fat. Add 1/2 to 1 tablespoon olive oil and sauté onion and white parts of scallion over medium-low heat until partway done. Add garlic and sauté for a minute more. Deglaze with sherry and use spatula to scrape fond from bottom of pan. Add herbs, salt and pepper, then stock and about 2/3 of the orange juice, and return chicken to the pan. Spoon some of the sauce over the chicken and simmer covered for about 5 minutes until sauce is slightly reduced and chicken is done through.

Place orange slices on top of thighs and sprinkle green scallion tops over all, then cover and simmer partly covered another 1 to 2 minutes. Turn off heat and let the flavors marry while you prepare the rest of the meal, then reheat to serve. Serve with brown rice and steamed asparagus, sautéed zucchini or greens, or a green salad.

Variations

CHICKEN WITH ORANGE & CORIANDER: Add 1 teaspoon whole coriander seeds to the sautéed onions and garlic in place of the dried herbs. Also sprinkle 1/2 cup chopped fresh cilantro (the green part of the coriander plant) over the chicken along with the scallion tops.

CHICKEN WITH ORANGE & FENNEL: Add 1/4 teaspoon crushed fennel seeds to the sautéed onions and garlic in place of the herbs. Garnish with about 1/3 cup chopped fresh flat-leaf parsley.

CHICKEN WITH ORANGE & TARRAGON: Add 1 teaspoon fresh tarragon (or 1/2 teaspoon dried) to the sautéed onions and garlic in place of the other herbs. (The tarragon is subtle here so as not to overpower the orange; but if you really like tarragon, by all means add more.)

Greek Lemon Chicken

The next best thing to a trip to the Aegean, this festive, colorful dish makes a fine focus for a midwinter dinner party, a delicious combination of sweet and intense Mediterranean flavors. Sautéing mellows the the lemon slices. Meyer lemons, if available (usually between October and February), are a nice choice, being sweet and fruity, rind and all; otherwise, choose a juicy, thin-skinned, deep yellow organic lemon.

SERVES 6

1 whole frying chicken, about 3 1/2 to 4 pounds
    (*or* combination breasts/thighs, 6 portions)
1/2 cup sundried tomatoes
1/4 cup white wine
2 tablespoons chicken stock (or water)
1 1/2 tablespoons olive oil
1 onion, crescents
1 to 2 cloves garlic, minced
6 marinated olives (green/ripe medley), sliced

1/2 teaspoon cinnamon (*or* 1/2 to 1
    cinnamon stick, split lengthwise)
1 teaspoon honey
1/2 teaspoon dried Greek oregano
Few grates black or multicolored pepper
1/2 to 2/3 cup chicken stock, homemade (*or*
    14-ounce can low-sodium chicken broth)
1 small to medium organic or Meyer lemon,
    thinly sliced and seeded

If using a whole bird, cut chicken into similar-sized pieces, and remove excess skin, leaving just the thinner skin over the meat. Place neck and gizzard in small saucepan, cover with water, and bring to a boil, then simmer to make stock while you prepare the rest of the dish. (If you are using precut chicken parts and canned broth, wash chicken and pat dry, and remove excess skin.)

Snip tomato halves into 4 or 5 strips and "plump" them in wine and chicken stock (or water).

Heat 1/2 tablespoon olive oil in skillet and brown chicken pieces on all sides, starting with the bone (or interior) side down. Transfer to plate.

Drain chicken fat from skillet, add remaining 1 tablespoon olive oil, and sauté onion until partway done, then add garlic and sauté briefly. Add the soaked tomatoes, olives, cinnamon, honey, oregano, pepper, and chicken stock.

Grains such as pan-roasted quinoa or white rice go nicely with this dish and can bake in the oven along with the chicken. Preheat oven to 375°F, prepare grains (pages 184, 190), and put in oven to bake, giving either grain about 5 minutes' lead time in the oven before adding the chicken.

Warm a 10 x 12-inch casserole in preheating oven. Transfer chicken pieces to dish, bone-side down, and pour sauce over chicken. Cover with foil and bake for 10 to 15 minutes.

Meanwhile, wash and slice lemon, and remove seeds. Sauté lemon slices in a little olive oil, turning once. Remove chicken from oven, baste with sauce, then place lemon slices on top of chicken pieces. Taste sauce and add salt if needed (probably little to none if you are using canned stock). Add a dash more cinnamon to the sauce if desired.

Bake, uncovered, another 5 to 10 minutes, or until chicken is done through. Serve with hot cooked grains, along with a salad or stir-steamed vegetables (green beans, summer squash, zucchini).

Chicken with Olives & Lemon

This dish combines the fundamental Mediterranean flavors of olives, onions and garlic, herbs, and lemon. If you're in a more exotic mood, the cooking method and basic ingredients suggest a tagine, *with the addition of a few fragrant spices (see second variation). Moroccan tagines (named for the earthenware dish they are stewed in) are usually slow-cooked using a whole chicken, but either version of this simple stovetop dish is a delicious shortcut—instant gratification and a taste of warmer climes on a busy cold-weather night.*

 SERVES 2 TO 3

2 tablespoons olive oil

3 to 4 chicken thighs, skin removed

1 medium (1/2 large) onion, coarsely chopped

2 to 3 thin slices lemon, finely minced
   (1 1/2 tablespoons)

1 large clove garlic, minced

1 1/2 tablespoons marsala (or white wine)

5 to 6 marinated green olives (or green/
   semi-ripe medley), thinly sliced or minced

1/2 teaspoon dried summer savory

1/2 teaspoon dried marjoram (or oregano)

Freshly grated white pepper

1/3 cup chicken stock

Salt to taste

Heat 1 tablespoon olive oil in stainless-steel skillet and brown chicken pieces on both sides, turning twice. Remove to plate.

Add second tablespoon olive oil to pan and sauté onion until translucent and beginning to caramelize. Reduce heat, add lemon and garlic, and sauté a half minute, then deglaze pan with marsala. Add olives, herbs, and a few grinds fresh pepper.

Return chicken to pan and add 1/3 cup chicken stock and a dash of salt (less if using canned broth). Simmer covered 15 to 20 minutes, uncovered for the last 5 minutes to slightly reduce sauce.

Serve with pan-roasted rice (page 184), couscous, or quinoa (page 190), along with a cooked vegetable or salad.

Variations

PORK WITH OLIVES & LEMON: Replace chicken with about 8 ounces pork butt or fresh ham steak, cut in bite-sized pieces and browned in olive oil; or use an equivalent amount (about 1 1/4 cups) leftover roast pork shoulder, cut in pieces, adding to the sauté pan along with the garlic. Otherwise, finish the dish as in main recipe.

CHICKEN TAGINE WITH OLIVES & LEMON: To replace the herbs and spices in the main recipe, mince 1/2 teaspoon (1 to 2 thin slices) fresh ginger, and combine 1/8 teaspoon ground cumin, 1/8 teaspoon cinnamon (or piece of cinnamon bark), and a dash each of turmeric and cayenne pepper. After briefly sautéing the lemon and garlic with the onions, stir in the ginger and spices, and cook about 5 seconds. Deglaze pan with the marsala or white wine; add the olives, chicken stock, and salt to taste, and finish dish as described above, adding a little chopped fresh cilantro or parsley in the last few minutes of cooking.

Grilled Lemon-Herb Chicken (or Pork)

This simple approach to lemon chicken could be considered a "campfire chicken piccata." The fresh-flavored marinade, lightly herbed, is a nice complement to either chicken breast or thigh meat. Or to consolidate grilling for a camp menu, you could marinate two chicken thighs together with a couple of butterflied pork medallions (see first variation) in a "mixed grill," using the pork in a subsequent meal.

 SERVES 4

1/2 frying chicken, cut in 4 or 5 pieces (*or* 2 split chicken breasts or 4 thighs; *or* 4 butterflied

pork tenderloin medallions, first variation)
Lemon-Herb Marinade

LEMON-HERB MARINADE

1/2 small to medium lemon, washed
1/4 teaspoon honey
1/4 cup white wine (or dry vermouth)
1 tablespoon olive oil
1 small to medium clove garlic, pressed

1/2 teaspoon fresh marjoram or oregano
1/2 teaspoon fresh thyme
1/2 teaspoon fresh summer savory
Dash of salt
6 to 8 grates "party" (multicolored) pepper

Cut chicken (or pork) into parts of a more or less uniform size, for even grilling times. If using chicken, trim fat and remove excess fatty skin. Place in ziplock bag or covered bowl.

To make marinade: Cut 3 thin slices from cut end of lemon half; then halve slices, place in small bowl, and drizzle with honey. Squeeze juice from remaining lemon and add to bowl along with wine, olive oil, and garlic. Chop fresh herbs (or crumble dried herbs, using half the amounts listed for fresh) and add to marinade, and season with salt and pepper to taste. Pour marinade over chicken (or pork) in bag or bowl, and let marinate from 2 hours to 2 days.

Before grilling chicken, pull skin away from meat on each piece just enough to tuck 1 or 2 lemon slices under the skin. Grill over medium coals (page 121), turning several times as needed, until crispy and done through. (With pork, or if there is not enough chicken skin to hold the lemon slices, reserve them to put on the grill 5 to 8 minutes before meat will be done; grill over moderate heat, carefully turning them once or twice with tongs, and serve as a garnish on top of the meat.)

Serve with couscous, quinoa, pasta, or rice, along with summer veggies (page 177) or a salad.

Variations

GREEK LEMON-HERB PORK: Cut 1/2 to 2/3 of a medium-sized pork tenderloin into 4 butterflied (hinged) medallions, each slice 5/8 to 3/4 inch thick. Grill and serve as above, or use in a Pork Primavera (page 87), a quinoa or rice lunch salad (pages 52, 53), or sandwiches.

GREEK LEMON-HERB CHICKEN (OR PORK): For herbs, use just 1 tablespoon chopped fresh oregano in the marinade, along with pepper and 1/4 teaspoon ground cumin. Marinate and grill as described above.

GRILLED LEMON CHICKEN (OR PORK) MARSALA: Omit honey, and replace wine with marsala. Marinate and grill chicken or pork as described above.

Pork Primavera with Fiddleheads

Synonymous with "pasta primavera," "pasta toss" is a handy term for a bowl of sautéed fresh tender vegetables combined with a small amount of meat or fish, tossed with pasta—all cooked to al-dente doneness—and sprinkled with aged Parmesan, toasted pine nuts, or other flavorful garnish. This pasta toss is truly a pasta primavera, featuring fiddleheads and other delicate green harbingers of spring.

*Here in Maine, fiddleheads—the tightly curled emerging fronds of the ostrich fern—are a springtime treat, picked along streams and rivers from about Bangor north. Their price, when they appear in supermarkets, reflects their status as an ephemeral wild delicacy—expensive enough to enjoy only a few times a season. I would love to be able to pick them wild locally, but they're rarely found along the Downeast coast; I guess that's part of the allure of spring fishing and canoe-camping trips further north! But you might be able to cultivate some of these native perennials (*Matteuccia struthiopteris*) near a backyard stream.*

Later in the season, a summertime pasta toss could include sautéed zucchini, sprouting broccoli, or green beans, and a garnish of toasted pine nuts. A sprinkling of aged Parmesan, accented with lemon zest, brings these simple ingredients—leftover pork, pasta, tender greens, onion and garlic—together.

  SERVES 2

1 1/2 cups fresh fiddleheads (or asparagus stalks)	2 to 4 tablespoons chicken stock
1 full cup (6 ounces) leftover roast pork shoulder, (or grilled pork tenderloin, page 86), sliced 1/4 to 3/8 inch thick, bite-sized pieces	Few grates white or multicolored pepper
	Salt to taste
2 to 3 teaspoons olive oil	2 scallions, chopped
1/2 medium onion, crescents	1/2 to 1 teaspoon lemon juice
1 clove garlic, minced	1/2 teaspoon freshly grated lemon zest
1 to 2 tablespoons marsala	1/4 cup grated Parmesan (and/or pine nuts)
	4 ounces dry artichoke linguine (or other pasta)

Wash fiddleheads thoroughly in cold water, drain, and trim off stem ends. (Or, if using asparagus stalks, snap off ends and break stalks in two.) Cut pork in bite-sized pieces.

Heat olive oil in skillet or heavy-bottomed saucepan and sauté onions until just beginning to turn gold, then add garlic and pork and sauté for a half a minute. Deglaze with marsala, then stir in stock and season with pepper and salt. Sprinkle with scallions and lemon juice, cover, and remove from heat until the pasta and fiddleheads have been cooked and drained and are ready to serve.

Put fiddleheads in a saucepan with more than enough hot water to cover them. Bring up to heat and boil for about 3 minutes, or until fiddleheads release enough tannin to turn cooking water brown. Drain, replace water with fresh hot or boiling water, and cook another 2 minutes or so, just until fiddleheads are tender. Drain, except for 1 tablespoon or so water. (Or, if using asparagus, plunge stalks in boiling water and cook until al dente.) Grate lemon zest and cheese for garnish.

Boil pasta, drain, and dress with olive oil and butter. Bring pork-and-onion mixture back up to heat, cooking covered for about 1 minute more. Quickly bring fiddleheads (or asparagus) up to heat.

Serve pasta in 2 shallow bowls. Divide pork-and-onion mixture and fiddleheads (or asparagus) between the bowls. Sprinkle Parmesan-lemon mixture over each serving, and toss at table.

Chicken Sausage with Green Beans, Feta & Dried Tomatoes

This tangy meal-in-itself, a simple dish of pasta and fresh green beans spiked with intense Greek flavorings, is a favorite among our camp menu repertoire. Most grocery stores carry one or more lines of nicely seasoned chicken sausage sold fully precooked, a healthy and practical choice if you are away from reliable refrigeration. (Check the label; not all chicken sausage is precooked.) Head out on your adventure with the sausage frozen, and it will help cool the rest of your food as it thaws.

Island Acres, in Stonington, Maine, makes wonderful organic chicken sausage; their lemon-pepper sausage is perfect for this meal. If you are unable to find some, or the price is beyond your budget, a lesser brand of Italian-herbed or roasted-garlic chicken sausage, accented with a little extra lemon zest and grated pepper, will work fine—or use pork sausage if you prefer.

 SERVES 2

2 (6 ounces) precooked chicken sausages, preferably lemon-pepper (or sweet Italian chicken sausage)

1 tablespoon olive oil

2/3 to 1 medium onion, crescents

1 clove garlic, minced

2 to 2 1/4 cups fresh green beans, stemmed, large ones cut or snapped in half (or 2 1/2 to 3 cups fresh spinach, washed and stemmed)

5 to 6 sundried tomato halves, snipped and soaked in a little wine or water

1/4 teaspoon lemon zest (1/2 teaspoon if not using lemon-pepper sausage)

Few grates white or black pepper (if not using lemon-pepper sausage)

3 ounces feta cheese, small chunks

4 ounces dry whole-wheat rotini (or other chunky pasta)

Slice sausage in 1/2-inch coins, and set aside. (If sausage has been frozen and is not completely thawed, parboil in water, then slice.) Set covered pot of water to boil for pasta.

Heat oil in (preferably) nonstick skillet or sauté pan, and sauté onion over medium-low heat until translucent. Add garlic and sausage slices, and sauté for 1 minute more, then add beans. (If using spinach instead of beans, wait until the last few minutes of cooking to add, and steam just long enough to deflate.) Cover, reduce heat to low, and continue cooking for 1 to 2 minutes, stirring or shaking pan occasionally, until beans are nearly al dente. Add a little water if onions start to catch on.

Meanwhile cook pasta till al dente; drain half of cooking water, keeping pasta hot in remaining water for a minute or two until the rest of the meal is ready to serve.

Add dried tomatoes and their soaking liquid to the skillet, along with lemon zest and pepper (if not using lemon-pepper sausage). Simmer covered 1 minute longer, while you drain the pasta and dress it with a little olive oil and/or butter.

Serve pasta into 2 bowls, then divide sausage-vegetable mixture between the bowls, served over the pasta. Crumble feta over top of each.

NOTE: The feta, served as a garnish, will be warmed to almost molten by the hot vegetables and pasta; but feel free to sprinkle it into the skillet at the last minute if you like your cheese fully melted.

Chicken Sausage (or Linguiça) with Summer Veggies

Richard and I discovered linguiça while we were backpacking in Baxter State Park, before we switched to a much more luxurious mode of backcountry travel: canoe-camping where you can carry a cooler and things too perishable to keep very long in a pack. We still talk about the couple we passed on upper Telos Lake, on our way to Webster Lake, settling in for their canoe-camping vacation with a cooler full of champagne on ice!

Portuguese linguiça is a cured pork product that, like most chicken sausage, is usually sold precooked (check the label to be sure), so there's less concern about keeping raw meat sufficiently cold. Both products are richly flavored treats that, combined with sautéed fresh summer vegetables, make for a satisfying, healthy, and comforting meal with a minimum of cooking and pot sullying—just what you want in a rustic kitchen.

For more on camp kitchens, ashore and afloat, food planning and packing, and strategies for keeping things cool, see the Camp Kitchen section starting on page 281.

 SERVES 2

2 (6 ounces) precooked roasted-garlic chicken sausages (*or* 1/2 coil linguiça sausage)

1 tablespoon olive oil

2/3 to 1 medium onion, crescents

1 clove garlic, minced

1 small zucchini, 3/8-inch half-moons

1 small summer squash, 3/8-inch half-moons

1 to 1 1/2 cups fresh green beans (Romano, filet, or young tender purple or jade beans), stemmed, large ones cut or snapped in half

2 to 3 ripe plum tomatoes, seeded and chopped (*or* 6 to 8 cherry tomatoes)

1/2 to 1 teaspoon fresh summer savory, chopped

1 to 2 tablespoons fresh basil, chopped

Dash salt

Few grates multicolored pepper (optional)

4 ounces dry confetti, farfalle (bowties), or other chunky tri-colored pasta

1/3 to 1/2 cup grated Manchego or smoked provolone cheese (optional)

Slice sausage in 1/2-inch coins, and set aside. (If using linguiça, parboil in water if desired, to release some of the fat; cool to lukewarm, then slice.) Set covered pot of water to boil for pasta.

Heat oil in (preferably non-stick) skillet, and sauté onion over medium-low heat until translucent. Add garlic and sausage slices, and sauté for 1 minute more, then add zucchini, squash, and, after 1/2 minute or so, the green beans (and/or cooked shell beans; see Note.) Cover, reduce heat to low, and continue cooking for 1 to 2 minutes, stirring or shaking pan occasionally, until beans are nearly tender; add a little water if onions start to catch on. Finally, add tomatoes.

Meanwhile, cook pasta till al dente. Sprinkle fresh herbs over stew, add salt and pepper to taste, and simmer covered 1 minute longer while you drain the pasta and dress with olive oil and/or butter.

Serve pasta into 2 bowls, then divide sausage-vegetable mixture between the bowls, served over the pasta. Sprinkle a little grated cheese over each serving if desired.

NOTE: If you happen to have any leftover cooked shell beans on hand (pages 146), add them as well to round out this summer stew.

Pennes Alfredo with Grilled Chicken

Like the following recipe, this stovetop dish miraculously recycles leftovers into a whole new meal, and can be quickly thrown together in a camp or galley kitchen. Make the sauce ahead, zip 3 or 4 chicken breasts into a freezer bag with a light marinade (such as Grilled Lemon-Herb Chicken, page 86), don't forget the pasta, broccoli crowns, and cheese, and you have the makings for two dinners. As with all pasta tosses, timing is everything—so make the sauce first, so it's waiting on the other ingredients.

 SERVES 2

Light Alfredo Sauce (below)
1 to 2 leftover grilled chicken breasts (whole, split, or boneless)
1/4 cup grated aged Parmesan or Romano cheese

3 cups cooked plain or whole-wheat pennes, about 4 ounces uncooked pasta
1 1/2 cups broccoli florets, lightly stir-steamed (page 177)

Make sauce; remove from heat until the rest of the dish is ready. Remove grilled chicken from bones (if not boneless breasts) and cut into smaller pieces. Set water to boil for pasta. Grate cheese.

While the pasta is cooking, stir-steam the broccoli. When both are al dente, drain all but about 1 tablespoon water from pot of pasta and add chicken pieces, broccoli, and a drizzle of olive oil, then quickly bring up to heat while reheating sauce over low heat. (Or if you are not quite sure of the timing, heat chicken and broccoli in 1 tablespoon water in separate saucepan just before serving.)

Divide pennes, chicken, and broccoli between 2 pasta bowls, and pour half of the sauce (about 2/3 cup) over each serving. Sprinkle 2 tablespoons grated cheese over each serving.

LIGHT ALFREDO SAUCE (MAKES 1 1/3 CUPS)

2 teaspoons olive oil
2 large shallots (*or* 1/2 small onion), minced
1 tablespoon salted butter
3 tablespoons flour
1/4 cup dry white wine
3/4 cup chicken stock (or vegetable stock)
1/3 cup half-and-half

1/2 cup grated aged Parmesan, Romano, Manchego, or Asiago (or combination)
1/4 teaspoon dried marjoram
1/4 teaspoon dried summer savory
Salt to taste (omit if using canned stock)
Few grates white or multicolored pepper
1/4 teaspoon lemon zest

Heat oil in a small saucepan and sauté shallots (or onions) over gentle heat until translucent. Melt butter into shallots (or onions), then stir in flour and cook roux for about 30 seconds. Remove from heat and gradually add wine, then stock, whisking until smooth after each addition. Cook over moderate heat, stirring constantly, until sauce is thickened. Whisk in half-and-half.

Add cheese and stir until melted (or reserve some to sprinkle over servings). Then add herbs, salt, and pepper, and cook over low heat for 1 minute more. Sauce will seem fairly thin, but the consistency will be just right poured over the pasta. Stir in lemon zest, remove sauce from heat, and let the flavors get to know each other while you prepare the rest of the meal. When ready to serve, gently bring sauce back up to heat (do not let it boil). Serve with freshly cooked, drained pasta.

Turkey (or Chicken) Tetrazzini

What to do with all that leftover turkey (or roast chicken), especially the white meat which is so often dry? After Pot Pie (page 96), there's Tetrazzini. The herbed cheese sauce moistens the meat and creates an entirely different meal after you've finished up the stuffing, gravy, and other fixin's. The stovetop version is easy enough to prepare in a rustic kitchen: Pack a container of made-ahead sauce, along with the leftover turkey meat sealed in a ziplock bag. Or with a little more effort, the dish can be finished off in the oven as a casserole topped with aged Italian cheese.

 SERVES 2 TO 3

2 cups cooked turkey, mostly white meat
Savory Cheese Sauce (or Light Alfredo Sauce)

4 to 6 ounces dry pasta (garlic & parsley angel hair, tagliatelle, or linguine)

Cut turkey into large bite-sized pieces; set aside. Put pasta water on to boil. Meanwhile, make the cheese sauce as on page 90 or 135, either with white wine in the sauce or reserving lemon zest or juice to add just before serving. Add turkey and simmer uncovered over low heat for about 15 minutes, stirring occasionally, to allow meat to absorb sauce, while you cook the pasta and vegetables.

When nearly ready to serve, add lemon zest or juice (if using) to the sauce and remove from heat. Serve over freshly cooked pasta, alongside a colorful mix of stir-steamed (sautéed and sweated) vegetables such as broccoli or green beans with onions, herbs, and red bell pepper.

Or, as a casserole, fill an oiled baking dish with drained pasta cooked al dente, then make a well in the center and pour in turkey and sauce. Sprinkle with 1/2 to 2/3 cup grated Romano or Parmesan cheese and bake at 375°F for 15 minutes, or until cheese is golden. Serve with spoon and pasta tongs.

Skillet Bistro Chicken

Another of Richard's elegantly simple "Wayside Bistro" inventions, this stovetop chicken with reduced herbed wine sauce has much the same crispness and piquancy as marinated grilled chicken.

 SERVES 2

2 chicken thighs, bone-in
1 tablespoon olive oil
1 clove garlic, minced

1/2 cup dry (white) vermouth
2 tablespoons fresh summer savory, chopped
Few grates white pepper

Trim excess fatty skin from chicken. Heat oil in stainless-steel skillet and brown both sides, starting bone-side down, then frying the skin side to a rich golden brown. Turn thighs skin-side up and briefly sauté garlic, then deglaze pan with half of vermouth and scrape browned bits from bottom. Add savory and rest of vermouth and simmer until slightly reduced, then cover and simmer a few minutes more. Serve with summer veggies and corn, boiled new potatoes, or seasoned oven fries.

Hunter's Chicken

Recipes abound for Chicken Chausseur and Cacciatore, "chicken in the style of hunters." In France and Italy, the basic ingredients evolved from the way hunters cooked their venison, tenderized with wine (or vinegary wine) and simply seasoned with rosemary and garlic. With time and cultural exchange, "hunter's style" has become more a way of preparing chicken, usually with rosemary and other herbs, tomatoes, and wine; sometimes accented with lemon juice or wine vinegar, mushrooms, peppers, capers, or even anchovies. Here, the chicken is complemented by an herbed ratatouille of tomatoes, zucchini, and eggplant—or use small summer squash, shallots, small leeks, whatever's fresh and in season.

Any way you make it, this stovetop dish is nice to have in your delicious-but-quick repertoire, an easy and economical dinner for home or camp/cruising. Leftovers could recycle nicely into a Shepherd's Pie (page 154) or Quick Minestrone (page 33).

 SERVES 2

2 tablespoons olive oil

2 to 3 boneless chicken thighs, bite-sized
    pieces

1 medium onion, halved crescents

1 1/2 cups zucchini, 3/8-inch half-moons

1/3 to 1/2 eggplant, peeled and cubed (1 cup)

1 clove garlic, minced

1/2 teaspoon fresh rosemary, minced

1/4 teaspoon dried sage (1/2 teaspoon fresh)

1/4 teaspoon dried oregano (1/2 teaspoon fresh)

1/4 cup white wine (or dry vermouth, or white
    wine with 1/4 teaspoon sage wine vinegar)

2 to 3 fresh plum tomatoes

Salt and pepper to taste

Heat 1 tablespoon olive oil in skillet and brown chicken pieces; remove to plate. Add remaining oil (as needed) and sauté onion until partway cooked, then add zucchini and eggplant and sauté/sweat vegetables for about 2 minutes, then briefly add garlic and herbs. Return chicken to pan and deglaze with wine (or vermouth), cover, and simmer another 2 minutes, then add tomatoes, salt and pepper, and simmer covered 5 to 6 minutes more.

Serve with Party Polenta (page 183), Rice-Noodle Pilaf, or tagliatelle or other pasta.

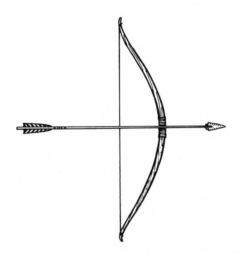

Oven-Fried Chicken

Without question, fried chicken is an ultimate comfort food, whether you're north or south of the Mason-Dixon Line. Between the smell and the sizzle, home-made oven-fried chicken warms heart and soul, while bringing an economical and healthful meal to the table. Make plenty—leftover drumsticks reheat well, or can be served cold as a picnic item or with an on-the-go lunch salad.

SERVES 4

8 chicken drumsticks
1/2 cup unbleached flour
1/8 teaspoon garlic powder (couple shakes)
1/4 teaspoon dried marjoram (or Greek oregano)
1/8 teaspoon dried thyme

1/8 teaspoon dried summer savory
1/4 to 1/2 teaspoon turmeric
1/4 teaspoon salt (or to taste)
6 grates white pepper (1/8 to 1/4 teaspoon)
1/2 cup milk + yogurt (or buttermilk)
Olive oil

Wash drumsticks in cold water; pat dry with paper towels. Trim fat and excess skin (see Note).

Combine seasoned flour mixture (flour through pepper) on plate. Pour milk or buttermilk into shallow bowl or pan. Liberally oil a baking sheet (preferably a rectangular one with sides) with olive oil. Preheat oven to 375°F.

One at a time, roll drumsticks in milk, then dredge in seasoned flour, and lay them in 2 rows on baking sheet, with the meaty ends of the drumsticks facing the edge of the pan. Bake 20 minutes, until bottom side is crispy and ready to turn. If you have an oil sprayer filled with olive oil, spray tops with oil before turning.

Loosen drumsticks with spatula and flip to other side. Raise heat to 400°, and bake for 20 minutes more, then turn heat off and continue baking another 5 minutes or until meat is done through (no longer pink). Serve with Garlic Mashed Potatoes (page 170) and a green salad.

NOTE: To skin or not to skin the drumsticks? 'Tis nobler to remove the fatty chicken skin, but this crisp wrapper helps hold in meat juices, has rich flavor, and makes it "fried chicken." We compromise and trim off the looser, fatty skin. Use the freshest drumsticks available (check the date) and wash the chicken thoroughly, then pat dry, before using. If you would prefer to remove the skin entirely, use the more traditional breading technique described in the variation.

Variation

SOUTHERN OVEN-FRIED CHICKEN: Rather than seasoning the flour, make a seasoned crumb or cornmeal mixture for the outer coating using 1 cup fresh fine breadcrumbs, cracker crumbs, or cornmeal enriched with a little olive oil. Mix 1/2 cup buttermilk with 2 teaspoons olive oil for dipping. Having removed the skin and excess fat from the drumsticks, dredge them first in plain unbleached flour, then roll in buttermilk mixture, then coat in seasoned crumb mixture. (Keep a wet hand and a dry hand.) Bake drumsticks as described in the main recipe.

Chicken Ployes (or Crêpes)

Although this light but filling supper dish can be made from scratch, it's more quickly made using leftover roast chicken, gravy, and stock—and a good way to use them up. Or you can recycle leftover chicken pieces cooked with compatible flavorings, such as Chicken with Herbed Orange Sauce (page 83), Spanish Orange Chicken (page 82), or your favorite version of chicken marsala or tarragon chicken. Lacking one of these shortcuts, brown a couple of boneless chicken thighs (whole, or cut in bite-sized pieces) and proceed from there as described in the recipe.

Acadian buckwheat ployes are a healthy, satisfying wrapper for a savory chicken filling—or a vegetarian one, as on page 134. If you'd prefer a traditional egg crêpe, the recipe opposite makes the same amount of crêpes as ployes (6 thin pancakes about 6 to 7 inches in diameter).

 SERVES 2 TO 3

1 1/2 cups Light Chicken Sauce (*or* leftover gravy thinned with stock and wine)

1 1/3 cups leftover cooked or grilled chicken, white and/or dark meat (*or* 2 browned chicken thighs), bite-sized strips/pieces

1 tablespoon olive oil

1 small (*or* 1/2 medium) onion, thin crescents

1 large clove garlic, minced

1 teaspoon fresh chervil (*or* 1/2 teaspoon tarragon)

1 teaspoon fresh summer or winter savory

Dash of salt

Few grates white pepper

2 tablespoons freshly squeezed orange (*or* tangerine or clementine) juice

2 tablespoons water

1 cup ployes mix combined with 1 1/3 cups water (*or* Crêpes, page 95)

2/3 cup fresh parsley, coarsely chopped

LIGHT CHICKEN SAUCE (MAKES 1 1/2 CUPS)

2 teaspoons olive oil

2 shallots, minced (*or* 1/2 small onion, minced)

1 tablespoon butter

3 tablespoons unbleached flour

3 tablespoons white wine (*or* wine + dry sherry)

1 1/3 cups chicken stock, homemade or canned

Salt to taste (less if using canned broth)

Few grates white pepper

If not using thinned leftover gravy, make the chicken sauce: Heat oil and gently sauté shallots (or onion). Melt butter into shallots, then stir in flour and cook roux for about 1 minute. Remove from heat and gradually add wine (or equal parts wine and sherry) and stock, whisking until smooth after each addition. Season to taste, then cook over low heat, stirring constantly, until thickened.

If using leftover chicken, break the meat into bite-sized pieces; otherwise brown boneless chicken pieces from scratch. Set aside while you make the rest of the filling: Heat oil in skillet and sauté onions until translucent. Add garlic, herbs, salt and pepper, and cook briefly; then deglaze pan with orange juice and water. Add chicken (along with any sauce if recycling a leftover chicken dish). Combine filling with the chicken sauce, bring up to heat, cover, and keep warm.

Combine ployes mix with water and let stand 5 minutes. Fry ployes one at a time in a hot, lightly oiled crêpe pan. Use 1/6 of the batter (2 serving-spoonfuls) for each ploye, using the back of the spoon to smooth batter into a 6- to 7-inch circle. Start with the pan good and hot to prevent sticking, then lower heat to medium; fry 1/2 to 1 minute on one side only, until lightly browned. (Or make and fry 1 recipe of Crêpes.) You can fry all of the ploye/crêpes and keep them in a warm oven while you bring the filling back up to heat, then fill the ploye/crêpes and serve them all at once. Or you can assemble them a serving at a time (2 ploye/crêpes per person) and serve as you go.

To assemble ploye, spoon about 1/6 of the filling along the middle of each ploye (or crêpe), then roll up and set on plate seam-side down. Spoon a little extra sauce over each serving, then sprinkle with parsley. Round out the meal with steamed green beans or zucchini, or stir-steamed (page 177) broccoli or cauliflower florets, onions, garlic, and mushrooms or red pepper, herbed with marjoram.

CRÊPES

1 extra-large egg
1/4 cup + 2 tablespoons milk
1/3 cup whole-wheat pastry flour
1/3 cup unbleached flour
1 teaspoon baking powder

1/4 teaspoon salt
1/4 cup water
2 teaspoons olive or canola oil
1 teaspoon butter

Beat egg with fork or small whisk in batter bowl, then whisk in milk. Melt butter and oil over low heat in crêpe or omelette pan, and add to liquid mixture. Combine dry ingredients and whisk in, smoothing out lumps. Whisk in water. Batter may seem a little thin, but that's what you want for a nice, thin crêpe. Let the batter rest for 10 to 20 minutes.

Fry the crêpes one at a time in a moderately hot, lightly oiled crêpe pan or stainless-steel skillet, using 1/6 of the batter (about 2 1/2 tablespoons) for each crêpe, swirling it around in the pan to 6 or so inches diameter. Wipe pan with a little oil and/or butter between crêpes, allowing about 30 seconds frying time for the first side, less for the flip side.

PLOYES

Ployes are light-buckwheat pancakes traditionally made by French Acadians in Maine and New Brunswick. An authentic Acadian ploye mix produced in Maine by the Bouchard family is available in most Maine supermarkets (or from the Bouchard Family Farm in Fort Kent, Maine, www.ployes.com). The mix contains buckwheat flour, wheat flour, baking powder, and salt; all you add is water. Plain light buckwheat flour is also sold on its own as "Acadian buckwheat flour."

Ployes are a heart-healthy alternative to crêpes: light, satisfying, dairy- and cholesterol free, and virtually fat free. Though it's not necessary to grease the cooking surface if using a hot seasoned skillet, it helps to brush a pad of paper towel soaked in oil over the bottom of the pan between ployes.

You can serve ployes as breakfast pancakes or crêpes rolled around fresh or stewed fruit (page 216), as a layered fresh-fruit torte with whipped cream, as main-dish crêpes with a savory filling—or simply on their own as a bread accompaniment to meals, rolled with butter, as the Acadians do.

Pot Pie with Root Vegetables

Homemade pot pie has got to be one of the most soul-satisfying meals, especially on a chilly raw night when hovering around the stove feels like the place to be. The hot, savory pie will warm you inside too. Although Pot Pie can be made using fresh meat, this economical wintertime dish is the perfect way to use leftover roast turkey or chicken, lamb, beef, or pork. Hopefully you also have some leftover gravy that can be stretched into a sauce with good-quality stock (preferably homemade). Generously sauced with gravy and sweet root vegetables, and topped with crusty whole-wheat biscuits (or pastry, as in the Acadian tourtière-inspired variation), it's a one-dish meal.

Leftover Pot Pie tastes even better the second time around; just reheat it in a way that keeps the biscuits (or crust) from getting soggy, with perhaps a little extra liquid to keep the filling from drying out. Cover with foil and bake 10 minutes in 375° oven, then remove foil and bake until hot through.

 SERVES 2 TO 3

1/2 to 2/3 pound leftover roast chicken, turkey, beef, or lamb (1 1/2 cups meat), bite-sized pieces (or an equivalent amount of fresh meat, preferably tender cuts of chicken, beef, or lamb)

1 tablespoon olive oil

1/2 large yellow onion (1/2 to 2/3 cup), halved crescents

2 carrots and/or parsnips, cut into chunks

3 to 4 Brussels sprouts, trimmed and quartered, or 3/4 cup sliced raw rutabaga (or 1/2 cup frozen peas)

1/2 clove garlic, minced (optional)

2 1/2 to 3 1/4 cups homemade chicken, beef, or lamb stock, including leftover gravy, if available (or low-sodium canned stock)

1 tablespoon unbleached flour, or as needed to thicken stock slightly

1 to 2 potatoes (1 to 1 1/3 cups), chunks (or leftover boiled/roasted fingerlings)

1 teaspoon potpourri of savory herbs: thyme, marjoram, winter or summer savory, lovage, sage (with chicken or turkey), rosemary (with lamb)

Salt and white/black pepper to taste

Whole-Wheat Biscuit Crust (or Pastry Crust)

Cut up leftover roast meat, and set aside. Or, instead of using leftovers, cut about 2/3 pound fresh meat (such as boneless chicken thighs, or tender cuts of beef or lamb) into bite-sized pieces. Brown meat pieces in olive oil on three sides, and remove to plate.

The proportions here for both filling and crust fit well in a 1 1/2-quart casserole 8 x 8 inches square and 2 inches deep. If using Corningware, the sweet root vegetables can be sautéed right in the baking dish, otherwise in a lidded skillet, over moderate heat, starting with the onion. When the onion is beginning to turn translucent, add carrots and/or parsnips and Brussels sprouts (or rutabaga), along with the garlic, and sauté 2 minutes, until vegetables are sealed and their sweetness slightly caramelized; then add potatoes, seasonings, and 1/2 cup of the stock. Simmer covered a few minutes more until potatoes are nearly tender. (If using cooked fingerlings and/or frozen peas, add them now.)

If using leftover gravy, thin with enough stock to make 2 to 2 3/4 cups light gravy. Dissolve 1 1/2 tablespoons flour in 1/2 cup of this liquid, then add it back to the gravy, stirring continually over low heat until thickened. (Or to make a light gravy from scratch, add 2 to 2 3/4 cups chicken stock plus dissolved flour to the sautéed vegetables along with the potatoes and 1/2 cup stock, and cook over moderate heat, stirring constantly until gravy has thickened.)

Preheat oven to 425°F. If you have been making the filling in a skillet, transfer to warmed baking dish. Distribute meat over vegetables and pour gravy over. Keep warm.

Meanwhile, make dough for Whole-Wheat Biscuit Crust (or Pastry Crust), following recipe below. Place a sheet of aluminum foil on bottom rack of oven to guard against spills.

With Biscuit Crust, turn dough out onto floured surface, shape into a flattened ball and turn to coat with flour, then pat out into a square about 5/8 inch thick and slightly smaller than the baking dish. With floured knife, cut in tic-tac-toe pattern, creating 9 squares. Transfer biscuits to top of casserole. (With Pastry Crust, turn dough out onto floured surface, fold it over on itself once or twice to make it easier to handle, then roll out into a square slightly larger than the baking dish. Carefully move pastry to casserole, centering it on top of filling. Make a few slashes in the top to vent steam.)

Bake for 6 to 8 minutes at 425° until topping has puffed up a bit and is beginning to brown, then turn heat down to 375° and bake about 20 minutes or until the pie is gently bubbling and the topping nicely browned.

Variation

ACADIAN PORK POT PIE: Using 1/2 pound fresh pork shoulder and/or loin, cut pork in bite-sized pieces and brown in a little olive oil on three sides, then deglaze bottom of skillet (or baking dish) with 1 1/2 to 2 tablespoons white or red wine. (Or if using leftover roast pork, add the wine to the sautéed root vegetables before adding the potatoes and stock.) Make gravy and vegetables as described above, seasoning with 1/4 teaspoon thyme, 1/2 teaspoon winter or summer savory, and 1/4 teaspoon allspice. Top pie with Pastry Crust and bake as described in main recipe.

WHOLE-WHEAT BISCUIT CRUST

1 1/2 cups whole-wheat pastry flour	1/4 teaspoon baking soda
1/2 cup oat flour	3 tablespoons chilled salted butter, diced
1/4 teaspoon salt	2 tablespoons olive oil
1 tablespoon baking powder	2/3 cup cold milk mixed with a little yogurt

Toss dry ingredients in mixing bowl. Rub butter into flours with fingers until evenly distributed, then sprinkle oil over and stir to combine. Add milk mixed with a little plain yogurt (or buttermilk) all at once and stir briefly to bring dough together. Form biscuits as described above.

WHOLE-WHEAT PASTRY CRUST

1/2 cup whole-wheat pastry flour	1/2 teaspoon baking powder
1/2 cup unbleached flour	1 1/2 tablespoons chilled salted butter, diced
1/4 cup oat flour	2 tablespoons canola and/or light olive oil
1/4 teaspoon salt	3 1/2 tablespoons ice water

Toss dry ingredients in mixing bowl. Rub butter into flours with fingers until evenly distributed, then sprinkle oil over and stir to combine. Sprinkle with ice water, a tablespoon at a time, as needed to bring dough together into a ball. Form pastry as described above.

Apple-Herb Meatloaf

This fall-flavored meatloaf (which can be made as croquettes or burgers) is missing the egg and breadcrumbs typical of most meatloaf recipes; they may have found their way into American cookbooks during leaner times as a way to stretch a small amount of meat, but there's really no need for these cloggy binders. The meatloaf holds together fine without them and is much fresher tasting, and plenty juicy with the addition of grated vegetables, apple, and a little liquid.

SERVES 3

1 1/2 pounds ground turkey (or equal parts ground turkey and ground pork)

1 whole apple, cored and grated

1 small sweet carrot, grated (optional)

1/2 medium onion, grated or finely minced

1/4 teaspoon dried lovage

1 teaspoon dried thyme

1/2 teaspoon sage

1 teaspoon dried summer or winter savory (or equal parts savory and marjoram)

1/4 teaspoon salt

1/2 teaspoon white pepper

2 tablespoons apple cider (or equal parts water and dry sherry)

Preheat oven to 375°F. Assemble ingredients in medium-sized mixing bowl in order listed. Mix thoroughly, using hands to distribute vegetables and seasonings evenly through the meat. Pat mixture into a 7 x 7-inch Corningware baking dish or 4 1/2 x 8 1/2-inch Pyrex loaf pan.

Bake for about 30 minutes, or until meatloaf is browned around the edges and done through. Meanwhile, make Sherried Mushroom Sauce.

Serve meatloaf in squares or slices with a generous helping of sauce. Baked or mashed potatoes and steamed green beans go especially well with this meal.

SHERRIED MUSHROOM SAUCE

5 ounces baby portabella mushrooms, sliced

1 tablespoon butter

2 tablespoons olive oil

1 clove garlic, minced

Small pinch (1/4 teaspoon) dried tarragon

Few grates white pepper

3 tablespoons dry sherry

1/2 cup chicken stock (or bouillon)

1/2 cup milk

3 tablespoons unbleached flour

Melt half the butter and oil in a small saucepan and sauté the mushrooms, then add garlic. Add seasonings, and deglaze with sherry. Pour mushroom mixture into separate bowl.

Using the same saucepan, melt remaining butter and oil, stir in flour, and cook over low heat for 1 to 2 minutes. Remove from heat and gradually whisk in stock or bouillon, then milk, being careful to prevent lumps. Add mushroom mixture and simmer gently 5 minutes.

Variation

TURKEY LOZENGES OR BURGERS: Form meat mixture into oval lozenges 1 1/2 x 2 x 1 inch thick; fry in olive oil, and serve with pan juices deglazed with a little wine and Worcestershire. Or form into 3 burgers 3/4 inch thick, and grill over a medium-hot charcoal fire (page 121). Serve with your favorite sauce.

Herbed Pork Lozenges

This lightly herbed, fruity, savory variation on meatballs is a favorite easy dinner at our house. As with the other ground-meat dishes offered here, no egg or breadcrumbs are called for; the meat holds together just fine without any binders, seasoned with a little grated onion, apple, lemon, and herbs to accent the pork. If you combine the seasonings with the meat ahead of time, the flavors will get to know each other that much better. Though the lozenges have plenty of flavor on their own, serving them in a sauce of caramelized onions and tomatoes, sweetened with a little marsala, brings the meal together. This same sauce makes a fine topping for crostini (page 20).

SERVES 3

1 pound fresh ground pork (or combination of ground pork and turkey)

1/4 cup minced fresh onion

1/2 apple, grated (without skin)

1/2 teaspoon dried thyme

1/4 teaspoon dried summer savory

1 teaspoon dried marjoram

1/8 teaspoon Cajun Rub, page 101 (optional)

1/8 teaspoon garlic powder

1 to 1 1/4 teaspoons freshly grated lemon zest

1/2 teaspoon lemon juice

1 tablespoon dry sherry

Salt and pepper to taste

1 tablespoons olive oil (for frying)

2 tablespoons + 2 teaspoons marsala

2 tablespoons water

CARAMELIZED ONION-TOMATO SAUCE

1 tablespoon olive oil

1 medium onion, halved thin crescents

3 to 4 fresh ripe plum tomatoes, seeded and diced

2 tablespoons marsala (add only if making sauce separately as crostini topping)

1/2 to 1 teaspoon fresh summer savory or basil (optional, if making as crostini topping)

Combine ground meat with onion, apple, and seasonings (thyme through salt and pepper) in a bowl and mix well with hands. Let mixture rest at room temperature (or covered in refrigerator, if longer than 15 or 20 minutes) until ready to make dinner.

Form seasoned meat mixture into 8 or 9 lozenges (ovals 3/4 to 1 inch thick) and set on plate. Heat 1 tablespoon olive oil and fry lozenges over moderate to low heat in one or two batches in large stainless-steel skillet, turning as needed to brown evenly on all sides. Remove to plate. Deglaze pan with 2 tablespoons marsala and scrape fond from bottom of pan with spatula. Pour over lozenges.

To make Caramelized Onion-Tomato Sauce, add 1 tablespoon olive oil to deglazed pan and sauté onions over low heat until a light golden brown. Add diced tomatoes and sauté 3 to 5 minutes over medium-low heat until tomatoes are tender. (NOTE: If making Caramelized Onion-Tomato Sauce separately as a topping for crostini, without the deglazed pan drippings from frying the pork, add 2 tablespoons marsala and one of the optional herbs to the pan along with the diced tomatoes.)

Return lozenges to the pan, along with their liquid. Rinse plate with 2 tablespoons water and add to sauce. Spoon some of the tomato-onion mixture over the lozenges, and sprinkle with additional 2 teaspoons marsala. Simmer in covered pan 2 to 3 minutes over low heat.

Serve over freshly drained pasta with a salad, steamed green beans or greens, or other vegetable.

Pork Chops with Apples & Onions

What could be nicer on a cold night than thick pork chops pan-fried with onions, apples, and savory herbs? Especially in early fall, with fresh local cider and cooking apples on hand (we use Wolf Rivers, otherwise Empires). Baked sweet potatoes (or brown rice) and stir-steamed Brussels sprouts go just right. For chops with best flavor and texture, choose "all-natural" rather than "lean" or "self-basting" pork.

SERVES 2

1 tablespoon olive oil	1/2 teaspoon dried thyme
2 thick center-cut or loin pork chops, bone-in	1/2 teaspoon dried sage (or summer savory)
1 medium onion, crescents	Few grinds white or black pepper
1 firm, flavorful apple (such as Empire), sliced	2 tablespoons dry vermouth (or stock)
1 small clove garlic, minced (optional)	1 to 2 tablespoons cider (or water)

Heat 1/2 tablespoon oil in skillet and brown chops on both sides, turning twice. Remove to plate.

Drain fat from pan, add remaining oil, and sauté onion 1 minute. Add apples and sauté another minute or two, until apples and onions begin to brown up. Briefly add garlic, then herbs and pepper. Deglaze pan with vermouth and scrape up browned bits with spatula. Return chops to pan, piling apples on top. Add cider and simmer covered 5 to 10 minutes or until chops are done through.

Chicken Marsala with Bacon & Sage

This classic stovetop dish is another easy, satisfying fall-back on a fall night, combining chicken and pork with sweet wine and savory herbs. It's wonderful served with Garlic Mashed Potatoes and a stir-steam of savoy cabbage, onions, and winter savory.

 SERVES 3 TO 4

4 chicken thighs, bone-in, skin removed	1/4 cup marsala + 1/3 cup chicken stock
2 strips thick lean bacon, bite-sized pieces	1 teaspoon dried summer savory
1 to 1 1/2 tablespoons olive oil	1/2 teaspoon dried sage (2 small leaves)
1/2 to 2/3 yellow onion, crescents	1/4 teaspoon dried thyme

Trim fat from chicken thighs; cut each in 2 pieces lengthwise, at the joint. Fry bacon in skillet or Dutch oven; remove to paper towel to drain. Drain excess fat from pan, add a little oil, and brown chicken pieces on all sides; remove to shallow bowl. Add remaining oil and sauté onion until translucent, then deglaze pan with marsala, scraping up browned bits with spatula.

Return chicken pieces to the pan, along with the bacon, herbs, chicken stock, and salt and pepper to taste (less salt if using canned broth). Simmer partly covered over medium-low heat for 5 to 10 minutes, stirring occasionally, until chicken is done through and sauce is slightly reduced.

Cajun Chicken with Sautéed Fruit

This light, satisfying dinner for two can easily be scaled up to serve a larger group. Make a batch of Cajun Rub ahead of time, and the rest of the meal is quick to assemble at home or in more rustic cooking conditions. Cleanup is simple—no bones, and probably no leftovers! The sautéed fruit garnish is a colorful, tasty complement to the subtly hot and spicy chicken.

 SERVES 2

2 tablespoons raw onion, very finely minced
1 clove garlic, minced
2 tablespoons olive oil
1 1/4 teaspoons Cajun Rub (see below)
1 to 2 boneless chicken breasts or 2 thighs,
    (2/3 to 3/4 pound), sliced lengthwise
1 to 2 tablespoons chicken stock

~ SAUTÉED FRUIT ~
1/2 small onion, thin (1/8 inch) crescents
1/3 medium apple, cored, peeled, thinly sliced
1/3 Valencia, Minneola, clementine, or other
    juicy orange, cut in halves or thirds
6 to 8 black grapes, halved

Combine minced onion, garlic, 1 tablespoon olive oil, and Cajun Rub on a plate. Trim fat from chicken pieces and cut in strips lengthwise. Coat chicken pieces evenly with seasoning mixture.

Slice onion and prepare fruit; remove seeds and any tough membranes from orange sections.

Heat 1/2 tablespoon oil in sauté pan and fry meat over moderate heat, turning twice to brown both sides of meat (hopefully browning but not burning the minced onion). Transfer to clean plate.

Add remaining 1/2 tablespoon oil to pan and sauté onion until partly cooked, then add fruit; stir fruit as it begins to sweat and deglaze pan. Sauté up to 1 minute more, just until fruit is hot through and onion is translucent but not browned.

Return chicken pieces to the pan, and deglaze with a tablespoon or two of chicken stock. Spoon fruit garnish over top, bring up to heat, and cook for another minute. Serve with pan-roasted quinoa, couscous, or bulghur (roasted pumpkin seeds or pistachios make a nice garnish) along with a green salad or steamed vegetable.

CAJUN RUB (MAKES 5 TEASPOONS)

1/2 teaspoon fennel seeds, crushed
1/4 teaspoon dried sage
1/4 teaspoon dried lovage
1/2 teaspoon dried thyme
1/2 teaspoon dried winter (or summer) savory

1/4 teaspoon dried oregano
1/2 teaspoon salt
1/4 teaspoon cayenne pepper
8 grates ground black pepper (1/8 teaspoon)
1/2 teaspoon garlic powder

Crush fennel in mortar and pestle, then add remaining ingredients, crushing the dried herbs as you measure them. Mill mixture with a few grinds of the pestle, then store in an airtight jar.

NOTE: This mixture includes a modest amount of garlic powder, assuming the spice rub will be used in recipes calling for garlic in various forms—powder, pressed, or minced. Otherwise, you could add another 1/2 teaspoon to the mix.

Chicken (Beef) Enchiladas with Salsa Verde

What's special about this dish is not just the colorful spicy filling, but the intriguingly fruity, savory Salsa Verde made with tomatillos and mild chiles. This pale green sauce, bursting with summer flavors, has become a staple in our wintertime pantry—well worth an 8-pint run, using the proportions on page 103 (enough for three meals) scaled up by 4. We based the salsa on a recipe from James McNair's Chicken cookbook (shared by friend and neighbor Cara Guerrieri), adapted to our garden and taste.

With the salsa prepared ahead of time, the rest of the dish is quick to assemble. Best made with freshly cooked chicken (or beef sirloin), it's also a great way to use leftover chicken dark meat or pork. The black beans add interest and complete protein to the dish, but the filling is just as delicious without them. If omitting the beans, you can bulk out the filling by using more pepper and corn.

 SERVES 3

1 1/2 tablespoons olive oil	1/2 teaspoon Greek oregano
2 to 3 chicken thighs/drumsticks, or 1/2 to 2/3 pound beef sirloin (or 1 1/2 cups leftover cooked chicken or pork)	1/2 teaspoon cayenne pepper
	2/3 cup frozen corn
	1 cup cooked black beans (optional; see Note)
1/2 medium onion, minced	1/4 cup cooking liquid from beans
1 clove garlic, minced	1/4 to 1/3 cup chicken stock or tomato juice
1/2 red bell pepper, strips (or combination of red and green pepper)	1 1/3 cups Tomatillo Salsa Verde
	1 1/4 to 1 1/2 cups shredded smoked provolone, Manchego, and/or Monterey Jack
2 teaspoons ground cumin	
1 1/2 teaspoons ground coriander	1 tablespoon olive oil
Small pinch epazote (optional, page 158)	6 white corn tortillas, 6-inch diameter

If using whole chicken drumsticks or thighs, remove skin and trim fat. Heat 2 teaspoons olive oil in skillet and brown chicken pieces on all sides; add a little water to the pan and continue cooking over low heat until meat is cooked through. Remove meat from bones, break into bite-sized pieces, and reserve on plate. If using boneless chicken thighs (or beef sirloin), cut into lengthwise strips and brown in olive oil; remove to plate. Prepare vegetables, and assemble herbs and spices.

Add remaining oil to pan and sauté onion until partway cooked, then add garlic and red pepper and sauté another 1 to 2 minutes over medium-low heat, until pepper is sealed. Add seasonings and sauté 1/2 to 1 minute more, just long enough to toast the spices. Add corn, beans plus 1/4 cup cooking liquid, and stock or juice. Simmer another 2 minutes; meanwhile grate cheese.

Preheat oven to 375°F. Fill tortillas one at a time, holding sides of tortillas upright, curled side-by-side (like tacos) in 7 x 11-inch ovenproof baking dish: Divide meat and peppers evenly among tortillas, then distribute remaining filling. Spoon Salsa Verde over filling (about 3 tablespoons per enchilada). Tent loosely with foil and bake 10 minutes, then sprinkle cheese over the top and bake uncovered another 20 minutes until enchiladas are heated through and cheese browns up.

Serve with a salad of lettuce and arugula, ripe tomatoes, and avocado, garnished with cilantro.

NOTE: To cook dry beans, soak 1/2 cup black beans overnight. Rinse and drain, then cover with water and bring to a boil. Lower heat and cook covered 35 to 45 minutes or until beans are tender.

TOMATILLOS

Although tomatillos are sometimes available in supermarkets, fresh-picked ripe ones are superior in flavor—and nothing could be easier than growing your own tomatillo jungle at home. The husked green fruits are prolific and fun to pick. Though edible while still green (and often used this way), tomatillos become much fuller and mellower in flavor the more they ripen; wait until the husks begin to turn a papery light gold, and the fruits are more of a khaki-sage green.

Tomatillo fruits have a natural coating of saponin, a soapy bitter substance which you'll need to rinse off thoroughly by washing them with hot water, and then boiling and draining.

Salsa Verde, as mild green chile sauce is known in the Southwest, is one of the best ways to use tomatillos. So if you grow a bumper crop, or can buy a quantity while they're in season, make a double or quadruple batch of sauce for your wintertime larder—just the thing to warm up a Northeastern night. It will brighten up many Southwestern dishes, from enchiladas to omelets and chiles rellenos.

TOMATILLO SALSA VERDE (MAKES 2 PINTS)

2 pounds (about 10) fresh tomatillos (2 cups chopped), husked, rinsed with hot water
1 to 1 1/2 tablespoons olive oil
3/4 to 1 cup chopped onions
1 large clove garlic (2 teaspoons minced)
3/4 to 1 cup mild green fresh chile peppers, seeded and coarsely chopped (or 2:1 combination of mild peppers such as Ancho chiles and green bell peppers, and hot peppers such as jalapeño or Hungarian Hot Wax)

3/4 to 1 cup chicken stock, homemade or canned
1 tablespoon fresh Greek oregano, chopped (1 1/2 teaspoons dried)
2 tablespoons fresh cilantro, chopped
1 tablespoon freshly squeezed lime juice
1 teaspoon light brown or organic sugar
1/4 teaspoon salt (reduce or omit if using canned chicken broth)
1 small bay leaf

Place husked, rinsed whole tomatillos in saucepan or pot, cover with water, and bring to boil. Cook over medium-high heat about 5 minutes, or until translucent and soft. Drain off cooking liquid, rinse with hot water, and drain (or if tomatillos are mostly ripe and soft, remove with slotted spoon). Let cool, then chop tomatillos; they will be messy, so use a large cutting board.

Chop onions, chiles/peppers, and tomatillos finely enough for a fairly smooth, chunky sauce without puréeing. Heat oil in saucepan or Dutch oven and sauté onions until nearly translucent, then add garlic and peppers and sauté another 1 or 2 minutes. Add chicken stock, then tomatillos. (If a smoother sauce is desired, transfer sautéed vegetables to blender along with the tomatillos and half the chicken stock, and pulse until mixture is puréed, then return to saucepan.)

Add herbs, lime juice, sugar, salt (to taste), and bay leaf to sauce and bring to a boil, then reduce heat, cover, and simmer over low heat for 25 to 30 minutes, or until sauce is slightly thickened and creamy. Remove bay leaf before serving or storing. Salsa should keep refrigerated for 1 to 2 weeks.

Since the acidity of tomatillos varies depending on ripeness, and the sauce contains oil and low-acid onions, peppers, and herbs, freezing is the safest preservation method for future use. (We have, however, safely enjoyed many batches of Salsa Verde processed in pint jars for 20 minutes in a boiling-water bath.) For more information on preserving low-acid foods, visit www.uga.edu/nchfp.

Spicy Moroccan Beef (or Lamb)

This quick stovetop sauté is just one of many possibilities using harissa, a Moroccan hot red pepper–spice paste. Beef, lamb, and chickpeas are traditional focal points for a warmly exotic couscous dish.

 SERVES 2

2/3 pound sirloin beef tips, bite-sized pieces
(or lamb chops, leg steak, or stew meat)
1/2 yellow onion, halved crescents
1/4 large red onion, halved crescents
1 tablespoon extra-virgin olive oil

1 small to medium clove garlic
1 1/2 to 2 teaspoons harissa red chile paste
Dash each of allspice, cumin, and cinnamon
1/2 teaspoon fresh lemon peel, finely minced
1 teaspoon lemon juice + 2 tablespoons water

Heat oil in lidded skillet and brown beef (or lamb) on both sides. Remove to shallow bowl. Add onions to pan and sauté until translucent, then briefly add garlic. Stir in harissa, allspice and cumin (1/8 teaspoon each), then the meat and its juices, using spatula to scrape browned bits from bottom of pan. Add lemon peel and juice + 2 tablespoons water (or vermouth) and a light dusting of cinnamon.

Stir, simmer 2 minutes with pan partly covered, then turn off heat and keep warm until the rest of the meal is ready. Bring up to heat and serve with hot fluffy couscous and steamed or stir-steamed green beans (or a colorful combination of vegetables including bell pepper strips).

Moorish Lemon Pork Kebabs

Adapted from a recipe in Sarah Woodward's Classic Mediterranean Cookbook, *this is a deliciously different way to enjoy pork. The ideal cut, flavorful and juicy, is thick-sliced fresh (uncured) ham—not always available, but keep an eye out in the meat department just after Easter. Let the pork marinate for 2 to 3 days, then skewer, set up the grill, and celebrate the start of grilling season!*

 SERVES 3

1 pound fresh ham steak (or pork loin),
thick-sliced (1 to 1 1/4 inches)
2 1/2 to 3 tablespoons extra-virgin olive oil
2 tablespoons fresh-squeezed lemon juice
1/2 to 3/4 teaspoon ground cumin

1/8 teaspoon garlic powder
1/3 teaspoon dried thyme, crushed
3/4 teaspoon paprika
1/8 teaspoon cayenne pepper (or to taste)
Fresh lemon slices or wedges

Cut meat in 1- to 1 1/4-inch cubes. Combine ingredients for marinade and pour over pork in ziplock bag, "massaging" bag until meat is coated evenly. Marinate in refrigerator 1 to 3 days.

Pre-soak 5 bamboo skewers for 20 minutes, then thread meat on skewers. Grill over medium-hot coals, turning to brown all sides, for about 10 minutes or until meat is cooked through.

Serve garnished with lemon slices, along with pan-roasted quinoa, couscous, or white rice.

Lemon Pork (or Chicken) Stir-fry

Dark, flavorful cuts of these "white" meats make all the difference in this colorful stir-fry finished off with a citrus-based teriyaki sauce. Rich-tasting pork butt (or fresh shoulder) is the cut of choice, but leaner chicken or turkey thigh meat is just as delicious. Thanks to Glenn and Nancy Crosen for the bottled-sauce inspiration!

SERVES 2

1/2 to 3/4 pound trimmed pork butt steak, about 3/4 inch thick, sliced into thin strips (*or* 2/3 to 3/4 pound boneless chicken or turkey thighs, lengthwise pieces or slices)

2 tablespoons olive or canola oil

1/2 yellow onion, crescents

1 to 2 small garden leeks (or 4 scallions), sliced julienne, white/green parts separated

1 clove garlic, minced

1 teaspoon sesame oil

1/2 to 3/4 red bell pepper, seeded, cut in strips

1/4 savoy cabbage (2 to 2 1/2 cups), coarsely sliced or shredded (or bok choy or collards, or combination of greens)

2 small sweet carrots, thinly sliced julienne

5 tablespoons Lemon-Garlic Finishing Sauce

Fresh cilantro leaves

Toasted sesame seeds (optional)

If using pork butt, trim and cut meat into thin slices (about 1/4 to 3/8 inch thick). If using chicken or turkey, section or slice meat into pieces about 3/4 x 1 1/2 x 3 inches. Heat 1 tablespoon of the oil in large skillet or Dutch oven, add meat, and quickly sear both sides; set aside on a plate.

Prep vegetables and organize in order listed, according to cooking time. Make finishing sauce; reserve half of the sauce (5 tablespoons) for use in this dish, and refrigerate the rest for another meal.

Add a little more oil to pan as needed and sauté onion and white parts of leek or scallions, reserving the green tops to add at the end. Stir in garlic, sesame oil, then pepper and cabbage, stir-frying briefly until vegetables are sealed and partly cooked.

Return meat to pan and bring back up to heat, then quickly pour finishing sauce over meat to deglaze, using spatula to scrape up browned bits from bottom of pan. Stir in carrots and green scallion or leek tops, cover pan, and simmer another minute or two until carrots are hot through but still firm.

Sprinkle cilantro over stir-fry and serve over hot, drained buckwheat noodles/soba or brown basmati rice in shallow bowls. Garnish at table with sesame seeds if desired.

LEMON-GARLIC FINISHING SAUCE (MAKES 2/3 CUP)

2 tablespoons lemon juice (*or* 3 thin slices Meyer lemon, peel and all, minced)

2 1/2 tablespoons tamari soy sauce

2 tablespoons canola oil

1 teaspoon sesame oil

1/2 teaspoon garlic powder (*or* 1 large clove pressed fresh garlic)

3 tablespoons dry sherry

1/4 teaspoon balsamic or rice wine vinegar

Pinch of cayenne

Combine ingredients in small bowl or jar. Use as a finishing sauce for a stir-fry, to deglaze the pan and add an intensely flavorful coating to the meat. Makes enough for 2 stir-fries; shake jar of sauce or stir vigorously just before adding. Keeps refrigerated for up to 1 week.

Orange Beef Stir-fry

Stir-fries are usually best starting with fresh uncooked meat, but this works equally well with leftover grilled steak if on the rare side. In fact, this is one of the more interesting ways we've found to feature leftover steak in a second meal. Orange, fresh ginger, and other teriyaki ingredients combine in an aromatic finishing sauce, added, as the name implies, in the last minute or so of cooking, so the flavors stay intense, not diluted.

 SERVES 2

1/2 to 3/4 pound trimmed beef sirloin tips, chuck, or flank steak, about 1 inch thick, sliced into thin strips (either raw, or leftover meat grilled or broiled medium-rare)

1 1/2 tablespoons olive, canola, or peanut oil

1 small yellow onion, crescents

2 scallions (or small leeks), sliced julienne, white/green parts separated

1 clove garlic, minced

1 teaspoon sesame oil

1/2 to 3/4 red or green bell pepper, seeded, cut in strips

1 head broccoli, small spears or florets, plus trimmed/sliced stalk (or Brussels sprouts, Tuscan kale, collards, savoy cabbage)

2 small sweet carrots, thinly sliced julienne (or thinly sliced rutabaga, or combination)

5 tablespoons Orange-Ginger Finishing Sauce

Fresh cilantro leaves (optional)

Lightly toasted Virginia peanuts or cashews

If using raw steak, trim and cut meat into thin slices (about 1/4 to 3/8 inch thick). Heat 1 tablespoon of the oil in large skillet or Dutch oven, add meat strips, and quickly sear both sides; remove from pan and set aside on a plate. If using leftover steak, cut in thin slices and set aside.

Prep vegetables and organize in order listed, according to cooking time. Make finishing sauce; reserve half of the sauce (5 tablespoons) for use in this dish, and refrigerate the rest for another meal.

Add a little more oil to pan as needed and sauté onion and white parts of scallions (or leeks), reserving the green parts to add at the end. Stir in garlic, sesame oil, then pepper and broccoli (or Brussels sprouts or other brassicas), stir-frying briefly until vegetables are sealed and partly cooked.

Return meat strips to pan and bring back up to heat, then quickly pour finishing sauce over meat to deglaze, using spatula to scrape up browned bits from bottom of pan. Stir in carrots (and/or rutabaga) and green scallion or leek tops, cover pan, and simmer another minute or two until carrots are hot through but still firm.

Sprinkle cilantro over stir-fry and serve in shallow bowls over hot, drained buckwheat noodles/soba, brown basmati rice, or pan-roasted white rice (page 184). Garnish at table with lightly toasted Old Virginia peanuts (page 262) or cashews if desired.

Variation

PINEAPPLE BEEF STIR-FRY: Make finishing sauce using 1/4 cup pineapple juice in place of orange juice and peel; omit Five Spice Powder. Include 1 cup fresh pineapple chunks in stir-fry, adding them to the pan along with the peppers and broccoli.

ORANGE-GINGER FINISHING SAUCE (MAKES 2/3 CUP)

2 tablespoons fresh orange or tangerine juice

1/2 teaspoon orange peel, finely minced

2 to 3 thin slices (or 1/8- to 1/4-inch chunk) ginger root, skinned and finely minced

2 1/2 tablespoons tamari soy sauce

2 tablespoons canola oil

1 teaspoon sesame oil

1/2 teaspoon garlic powder (*or* 1 large clove pressed garlic)

2 1/2 tablespoons dry sherry

Pinch of cayenne

Tiny pinch fresh Five-Spice Powder (page 110)

Combine ingredients in small bowl or jar. Use as a finishing sauce for a stir-fry, to deglaze the pan and add an intensely flavorful coating to the meat. Makes enough for 2 stir-fries; shake jar of sauce or stir vigorously just before adding. Keeps refrigerated for up to 1 week.

Orange-Ginger Pork Spareribs

These spareribs in a tangy citrus basting sauce—orange, or lime as on the next page—are delicious braised or grilled. For summertime grilling, combine the same ingredients in a marinade. Let the spareribs marinate from 4 hours to 2 days for stronger flavor, then cook on a charcoal grill (page 121).

Any leftover spareribs, cut in bite-sized pieces, can be savored in a rice salad (page 53) or wrap sandwiches, or added to Oven-Fried Egg Rolls (page 114), stir-fries, or Baked Beans (page 157).

 SERVES 4

1 1/2 to 1 3/4 pounds country-style all-natural pork spareribs

1 teaspoon olive oil

1/2 to 1 teaspoon toasted sesame oil

1/4 cup fresh-squeezed orange/clementine juice

1/2-inch piece fresh ginger root, finely minced

1 large (or 2 small) garlic cloves, pressed or minced (about 2 teaspoons)

1 tablespoon tamari soy sauce

1/4 teaspoon cayenne pepper

1/4 cup dry sherry

1 to 2 tablespoons water

Preheat oven to 375°F. If making brown rice (page 187) to serve with the spareribs (a good combination, baked at the same temperature and time), put in the oven to bake in lidded casserole.

Heat oil in skillet and brown spareribs on all sides. Meanwhile, combine orange juice, ginger, garlic, tamari, and cayenne in small cup. Place the seared pork in an 8 x 8-inch Corningware or other lidded ovenproof baking dish. Deglaze skillet with sherry, then add remaining ingredients (rinsing cup with water) and pour basting liquid over pork.

Bake spareribs, covered, for 40 minutes, basting once (add a little more water if dish seems dry). Meanwhile, prepare a vegetable stir-fry to serve with the spareribs: half an onion, sliced in crescents; 1 1/2 cups sliced savoy cabbage, broccoli florets, or quartered Brussels sprouts; 2 chopped scallions; and a slivered carrot. When the veggies are close to tender, pour in 2 to 3 tablespoons liquid from the spareribs and cover for the last minute of cooking. Serve the spareribs and vegetables with hot rice.

Lime-Horseradish Pork Spareribs

Here, as in the previous recipe, the spareribs can be baked and basted, or marinated and cooked on the grill—a delicious menu variation (with recyclable leftovers) on camp or waterborne adventures.

SERVES 4

1 1/2 to 1 3/4 pounds country-style all-natural
    pork spareribs
2 teaspoons olive oil
1 1/2 to 2 tablespoons fresh lime juice (1/3 lime)
3/4 teaspoon Dijon-type mustard (such as
    Raye's Winter Garden)
1 teaspoon prepared horseradish

1 teaspoon honey
1/8 teaspoon garlic powder (*or* 1 medium
    garlic clove, pressed or minced)
Pinch of cayenne
Few grates white pepper
2 tablespoons dry white wine (or vermouth)
1 tablespoon water

Preheat oven to 375°F. Heat oil in skillet and brown spareribs. Meanwhile, combine lime juice and seasonings in cup. Place seared pork in 8 x 8-inch lidded ovenproof baking dish. Deglaze skillet with wine or vermouth, then add lime mixture (rinsing cup with water) and pour basting liquid over pork. Bake spareribs, covered, for 40 minutes, basting once. Or, marinate and grill as in the variation.

Variation

GRILLED LIME-CUMIN PORK SPARERIBS: Omit mustard, horseradish, and honey, and combine the olive oil, lime juice, and garlic with 1/8 teaspoon cayenne, 1/2 teaspoon cumin, 1/2 teaspoon toasted sesame oil, and 2 tablespoons dry sherry. Marinate 4 hours to 2 days, then grill over a charcoal fire (page 121).

PURE PORK

Although leaner (as most commercially raised pork is now bred to be) is supposedly better, pork spareribs of the "lean" persuasion can be dry and tough. Bone-in spareribs are often better than boneless ("the nigher the bone, the sweeter the meat")—but if you're after juicy, flavorful pork, go for "all-natural" and avoid anything "self-basting" (packaged in briny water, which dries the meat). Another option is to raise your own pork (challenging, but doable) or buy some from a local farmer.

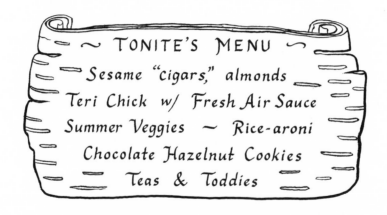

~ TONITE'S MENU ~
Sesame "cigars," almonds
Teri Chick w/ Fresh Air Sauce
Summer Veggies ~ Rice-aroni
Chocolate Hazelnut Cookies
Teas & Toddies

Grilled Orange-Teriyaki Chicken (or Steak)

If I had to choose one favorite summertime meal, it would have to be this one—a regular on our camp menu, as delicious as it is versatile. Ah, the savor of "teri chick" wafting from a charcoal fire! As Richard suggests in a scribbled comment among our earlier camp-cooking notes, "best served with fresh air sauce."

Though the stores carry a dazzling array of bottled marinades, nothing beats a teriyaki marinade made from scratch, using all fresh ingredients. The combination of fresh orange juice, ginger, sherry, garlic, tamari, and cayenne works especially well with darker, richer cuts of poultry: chicken, turkey, or even duck. These flavors are also a nice complement to beef chuck, sirloin, or flank steak (see variation).

Make plenty, and plan to use leftover grilled chicken (or steak) in sandwiches, perhaps wrapped in a flour tortilla along with some fresh arugula, or in a rice salad (page 53). Or recycle leftover grilled meat into a stir-fry or filling for Oven-Fried Egg Rolls (page 114).

 SERVES 4

1/2 frying chicken (3 1/2 to 4 pounds whole), cut in 4 or 5 pieces (*or* 4 chicken thighs)

Orange-Teriyaki Marinade

ORANGE-TERIYAKI MARINADE

Freshly squeezed juice of 1/3 Valencia orange (2 to 2 1/2 tablespoons)

1 large clove garlic, pressed or minced (*or* 1/4 teaspoon garlic powder)

1/4-inch piece fresh ginger root, skinned, thinly sliced, and minced

2 to 3 teaspoons tamari soy sauce

2 1/2 to 3 tablespoons dry sherry

1/2 teaspoon toasted sesame oil

2 teaspoons peanut or canola oil

1/8 teaspoon cayenne pepper (or to taste)

1/8 to 1/4 teaspoon coriander (optional)

Cut chicken into parts of a more or less uniform size, for even grilling times. Trim fat and remove excess fatty skin. Place chicken in ziplock bag or covered bowl.

Squeeze orange juice into small bowl. Add garlic, ginger, and remaining ingredients, and mix well. Pour marinade over chicken in bag or bowl, and let marinate from 2 hours to 3 days.

Grill chicken over medium coals, turning several times as needed, until crispy and done through (page 121). Serve with white or brown rice, Rice-Noodle Pilaf (page 184), brown rice fettucine, or udon, along with sautéed summer veggies such as squash, beans, or broccoli.

Variations

GRILLED ORANGE-TERIYAKI STEAK: Replace chicken with about 1 1/2 pounds beef chuck, flank steak, or sirloin tips, whole or cut into wide strips. Marinate, grill, and serve as above.

GRILLED PINEAPPLE-TERIYAKI CHICKEN: Replace orange juice with an equivalent amount of pineapple juice, and omit coriander. Serve with a stir-fry of onions, peppers, broccoli, and chunks of fresh pineapple.

SIMPLE TERIYAKI STEAK: Combine 2 1/2 tablespoons each tamari and dry sherry, and 1/4 to 1/2 teaspoon each garlic powder and ground ginger. Pour marinade over 1 1/2 pounds beef chuck, flank steak, or sirloin tips, whole or cut into wide strips. Marinate, grill, and serve as above.

Apple-Smoked Chinese Chicken

Applying the same hot-smoking technique we enjoy with Apple-Smoked Steelhead Trout (page 63), Richard came up with this recipe for apple-smoked chicken thighs steeped in a Chinese-flavored marinade. The blend of flavors in the marinade is subtle, letting the sweet apple smoke be the dominant aroma. Hot-smoking with fragrant green twigs is a bit more effort and takes longer than direct grilling (page 121), but the results are worth it. Since bone-in chicken thighs are thicker than a fish fillet, they need a slightly hotter fire and more cooking time than the trout.

Make a big enough batch so you can enjoy leftover chicken served hot or cold. Arugula and baby bok choy pair nicely with the sweet-smoky chicken in a salad or a wrap sandwich. The subtle smoky flavor also works well in the Chicken Salad with Peaches & Cilantro (page 52).

 SERVES 3 TO 5

4 to 5 chicken thighs, skin removed   Chinese Marinade

CHINESE MARINADE

3 thin slices fresh ginger, skinned and minced
  (*or* 1/8 teaspoon ground ginger)
1 small clove garlic, minced (*or* 1/8 teaspoon
  garlic powder)
1/8 teaspoon fresh Chinese Five Spice Powder
  (*or* fresh-ground spice mix of equal parts
  star anise, fennel, cinnamon, cloves, and
  Szechuan peppercorns)
1/8 teaspoon ground allspice
Dash of salt

3 tablespoons tamari soy suace
1 teaspoon toasted sesame oil
1/2 to 1 teaspoon fresh tangerine peel, very
  thinly sliced (*or* 1/8 to 1/4 teaspoon dried
  peel, or 2 to 3 drops pure orange or
  tangerine oil)
4 grinds black pepper
1/2 cup dry sherry
1/2 teaspoon chipotle sauce (*or* 1/8 teaspoon
  ground chipotle pepper, or to taste)

Remove the skin from the chicken and trim fat. Combine ingredients for marinade and pour over chicken pieces in large ziplock bag. Marinate for 2 to 4 hours or longer (up to 2 days).

Gather about 24 small green apple twigs, about 3 to 4 inches long and about the thickness of a pencil (1/4 to 3/8 inch diameter). About 45 minutes before the rest of the meal will be ready to serve, start a charcoal fire in a kettle grill or hibachi (we use a Weber's Smoky Joe) with lid. On top of a few dry twigs and birchbark, make a pile of about 16 or 17 regular charcoal briquettes (do not use easy-light or lighter-fluid-impregnated briquettes!), and light the fire. When the coals are burning well, turn them and let burn a few minutes more until the coals are lightly coated with ash. Heat the grate over the coals and scrape off any charred remains.

Reposition the coals together on one side of the grill to line up opposite the draft on the hibachi lid or grill cover. By now (about 10 to 12 minutes from when you started the fire) the coals should have burned down to a moderate heat, not hot enough to ignite the twigs. Pile half of the green twigs on top of the coals. Place the marinated chicken thighs bone-side down on the cooler side of the grill, opposite the pile of coals and twigs, aiming the thicker side of the meat toward the coals. Now cover the grill with the lid, with the draft (damper) aligned over the chicken but almost completely shut, to slowly draw heat up while creating smoke inside the grill. It is this indirect "hot smoke" that will cook the chicken—not the direct heat over the coals, as with normal grilling.

Leave the grill covered, undisturbed, for 6 to 8 minutes. Then turn the chicken pieces, and drizzle with a little of the marinade. If the first batch of twigs have burned completely and given up their smoke, add the rest of the twigs; otherwise wait until next time you turn the chicken, in another 7 to 8 minutes.

By now (having turned the meat twice) the top surface of the chicken should be sealed and beginning to turn a caramel color. Let the meat smoke another 7 to 8 minutes, then turn a third time. Use a knife to check for doneness. Depending on size and thickness of the thighs, it will probably take another 7 to 8 minutes before the chicken is cooked through, a total cooking time of about 30 minutes.

When the chicken is done, serve immediately with freshly cooked or steamed white or brown rice and mixed steamed or sautéed vegetables. Any leftover chicken is delicious cold.

Red-Stewed Chicken, Duck, or Pork

A completely different cooking method using nearly the same ingredients as in the previous recipe produces this intensely flavored stewed meat. Both dishes were inspired by several traditional Chinese recipes in The Regional Cooking of China, *by Margaret Gin and Alfred E. Castle.*

SERVES 3 TO 4

4 chicken thighs, skin and fat removed (*or* 3 to 4 duck thighs; or 3 to 4 pork spareribs)

Red-Stewing Broth

RED-STEWING BROTH

2 cups water	1-inch piece soaked dried tangerine peel, sliced
1 1/2 tablespoons honey	1/2-inch chunk fresh ginger root, sliced
1/2 tablespoon Szechuan peppercorns, crushed	1/4 cup dry sherry
1 to 2 whole star anise pods	1/2 cup tamari soy sauce
1/2 teaspoon fresh Five-Spice Powder (page 110)	1 to 2 teaspoons toasted sesame oil (optional)

Combine first 9 ingredients in large saucepan or Dutch oven and bring to a boil. Lower heat, add tamari, and simmer 15 minutes.

Add pieces of chicken (or duck, or pork), turning to coat both sides in broth, and simmer 10 minutes on one side; then turn and simmer 10 minutes more, or until meat is done through. Let stand in broth about 20 minutes. Then remove meat and coat with oil. Spoon a few tablespoons of broth over the stewed meat and serve with hot white or brown rice and a mix of stir-steamed veggies (page 177). Any leftover meat would be a delicious addition to Oven-Fried Egg Rolls (page 114).

Vonuo's Pork Egg Rolls (or Spring Rolls)

These are flavorful, crisply satisfying egg rolls, made from scratch with fresh ingredients. Our sister-in-law Vonuo Washburn, a gifted cook with a knack and know-how for various Asian cuisines, says, "My egg rolls and spring rolls are cooked according to what I feel like eating or what's available in the fridge. It's never the same." This is her basic recipe, with a filling of sautéed ground pork seasoned with oyster sauce, fresh cilantro, ginger, tamari, and a variety of fresh vegetables with different textures.

The egg rolls as made here were the centerpiece of a family cooking lesson and festive lunch one cold winter day, with several of us taking a hand with the filling, then rolling and shallow-frying the egg rolls one at a time in a small saucepan. They can also be served as spring rolls, wrapped but not fried, as a snack or appetizer.

SERVES 4 TO 6 FOR LUNCH, 12 TO 14 APPETIZERS

3 tablespoons canola or peanut oil (total)

1-inch piece fresh ginger root, skinned and grated

3 cloves of garlic, minced

1 pound lean ground pork

4 scallions, chopped, white/green parts separated

1 cup napa or bok choy (or mung bean sprouts)

1 carrot, grated

1/2 cup water chestnuts (optional)

1 tablespoon fresh cilantro

2 tablespoons oyster sauce

1 tablespoon tamari or soy sauce

2/3 to 1 cup bean thread noodles (optional)

1 package egg roll wrappers (13 to 14 wrappers), room temperature (or 2 packages rice wrappers for spring rolls)

Canola oil for frying

Heat 1 tablespoon of the oil and add ginger, then garlic. After sautéing 30 seconds, add the pork and stir-fry until meat is done. Remove stir-fried mixture to a separate dish. Clean the pan, heat remaining 2 tablespoons oil, then add vegetables in the order listed and stir-fry, adding the green scallion tops and cilantro last. Once the vegetables are cooked, return pork mixture to pan and season with oyster sauce and soy sauce. Let cool.

If using bean thread noodles, place them in a bowl, cover with boiling water, and soak 5 minutes, then drain and cut in 1-inch lengths. Add to cooled vegetable-meat mixture.

Orient egg roll wrappers diagonally on clean surface, and place a spoonful of filling (1/4 cup or less) in the center lower third of wrapper. Fold bottom point up over filling, then fold sides in and roll up from bottom. Set tail-side down on a tray or plate. (NOTE: Don't open the wrappers until you are ready to assemble the egg rolls; once opened, cover the package with a damp towel to keep the wrappers from drying out, otherwise they'll be difficult to work with.)

When all the egg rolls have been wrapped, preheat oven to "warm" and place a baking sheet in upper third of oven. Cover a dinner plate with a couple of paper towels.

Heat oil for frying in a small (about 6-inch) saucepan, about 1 1/2 inches deep. When the oil is hot, add the first egg roll and fry for 1 to 2 minutes, turning with tongs to lightly brown all sides. Drain briefly on paper towels, then transfer to baking sheet to keep warm. Continue frying the rest of the egg rolls one at a time, piling them on the baking sheet to keep warm until ready to serve.

For fresh spring rolls, use rice wrappers. They tear easily, so Vonuo recommends a double layer of wrappers, 2 per roll, and assembling them one at a time: Fill a large bowl with warm water, and soak 2 rice wrappers at a time for about 10 seconds. Dry them on a clean kitchen towel, spoon in the filling, and wrap them just as you would egg rolls.

Serve with Dipping Sauce, steamed rice, and stir-fried veggies.

Variation

SHRIMP EGG ROLLS (OR SPRING ROLLS): Replace pork with an equivalent amount (or slightly less) of Maine shrimp, pre-cooked as on page 70.

DIPPING SAUCE (MAKES 2/3 CUP)

1/4 cup tamari soy sauce

1/4 cup rice vinegar

1/4 teaspoon honey or organic sugar

1 clove garlic, minced

1 to 2 thin slices fresh ginger, minced (or
    1/2 tablespoon chives, snipped) (optional)

1 teaspoon toasted sesame oil

1 teaspoon peanut oil (or hot chili oil)

Dissolve honey or sugar in tamari and vinegar. Stir in garlic, optional ginger (or chives), and oils. Serve in a small bowl.

PLUM DUCK SAUCE

When the height of summer brings red plums that are plentiful, ripe, relatively local, and cheap, we put up a batch of this dipping sauce to enjoy with homemade egg rolls—especially the vegetarian, chicken, or pork Oven-Fried Egg Rolls on page 114—as a fruity counterpoint to a hot mustard sauce. Any time of year, hovering over this beautiful, aromatic, deep-red plum sauce as it simmers is good therapy. It's fine to omit the shallots, scallions, or chives, for a fruitier sauce.

MAKES 6 HALF-PINTS

20 red plums, fully ripe, pitted and sliced into
    small pieces

1 1/3 cups water

4 good-sized shallots (1/4 cup), thinly sliced
    (or 1/4 cup scallions or fresh chives)

2 cloves garlic, minced

5 tablespoons honey

5 tablespoons brown sugar

2 tablespoons + 2 teaspoons cider vinegar

2 tablespoons tamari soy sauce

Place plums in heavy, flat-bottomed enameled or stainless-steel pot. Add water and simmer covered over moderate heat, stirring frequently to prevent plums from sticking on, until fruit softens enough to make a rich red sauce. Meanwhile, slice shallots (or chives, or scallions) and mince garlic and add to the sauce; cook 5 minutes. Add honey and brown sugar, vinegar, and tamari, stir well, and simmer gently 5 minutes more. Meanwhile heat water in canning kettle. Wash 6 half-pint jars.

Ladle the hot sauce into clean jars, leaving 1/2 inch headroom. Wipe jar mouths and cap with new lids soaked in hot water; secure with rings, and process for 20 minutes in boiling-water bath.

Oven-Fried Egg Rolls

It was a revelation to discover (in an article in Harrowsmith *magazine) that egg rolls don't need to be deep-fried. Just lay the filled egg rolls on a lightly oiled baking sheet, brush them with oil, and bake at high heat until crisply golden. They're just as tasty, with less fat and a cleaner kitchen. (Although, after sampling my sister-in-law Vonuo's delicious Pork Egg Rolls—shallow-fried in oil one at a time in a small saucepan as in the previous recipe, avoiding the production of a deep-fryer—I have to say that frying homemade egg rolls need not involve a lot of fuss, and the crispness is wonderful.)*

Freshly stir-fried vegetables, such as the combination suggested here, can be your basic filling, but as you roll 'em up you might add some tofu slices or precooked shrimp, small pieces of leftover Grilled Orange-Teriyaki Chicken (page 109) or Orange-Ginger Pork Spareribs (page 107), Red-Stewed Chicken, Duck, or Pork (page 111), or most any leftover meat with compatible Asian spicing.

For tangy, colorful dipping sauces, warmed homemade Plum Duck Sauce (page 113) and hot mustard sauce are a good place to start. Round things out with white or brown basmati rice and tamari, a pot of fragrant tea, maybe some fortune cookies, and you have a satisfying, healthful meal that's fun and really quite easy to put together.

 SERVES 3 TO 4

1 package egg roll wrappers (13 to 14 wrappers), room temperature (keep wrapped)

2 teaspoons toasted sesame oil

2 tablespoons canola or peanut oil

1 large onion, crescents

1-inch chunk fresh ginger root, skinned and minced (about 2 tablespoons)

1 large clove garlic, minced

1/4 medium head savoy cabbage, shredded

1 good-sized carrot, cut in half and thinly sliced julienne

1 stalk celery, thinly sliced julienne (*or* 6 to 8 peapods, or 3/4 cup mung bean sprouts)

1/3 cup sliced water chestnuts (optional)

2 teaspoons tamari

1/8 teaspoon cayenne pepper

2 tablespoons cilantro or fresh parsley, chopped

1 teaspoon chervil (optional)

4 to 6 fresh mushrooms, sliced (optional)

1/2 pound firm tofu, small slices (*or* 1/2 pound shrimp, raw or precooked as on page 70; or leftover cooked chicken or pork)

Wash and chop veggies. Heat oil in Dutch oven or wok and, beginning with the onions, stir-fry vegetables and other ingredients, adding in the order listed. Give ginger and garlic only a few seconds alone in the pan before adding vegetables, so the garlic won't become bitter. Preheat oven to 425°F.

Spoon about 1/3 cup filling into bottom third of each wrapper and roll once, then fold sides up and roll to end of wrapper. Lay egg rolls on lightly oiled baking sheet, seam-side down. (NOTE: Don't open the wrappers until you are ready to assemble the egg rolls; once opened, cover the package with a damp towel to keep the wrappers from drying out, otherwise they'll be difficult to work with.) Brush lightly with oil, and bake in preheated 425°F oven for 15 to 20 minutes. (Or, fry them if you wish, as described in the previous recipe.)

Serve at once with white or brown rice, and a choice of dipping sauces served in small bowls: Plum Duck Sauce (page 113) and hot mustard sauce (powdered Chinese hot mustard, mixed with water to the consistency of cream).

Thai Green Chicken Curry

Vonuo introduced us to this aromatic, simply prepared chicken curry, made with Thai green curry paste. (The same recipe can be followed using Thai red curry paste.)

Prepared green curry pastes keep well for many months refrigerated. The one we use is made of chile, lemongrass, garlic, galangal, salt, onion, pepper, lime, and peanut oil. We add a little fresh ginger, skinned and minced, to balance the flavors in the curry paste. If you use a green curry paste that includes ginger, either prepared or home-made, feel free to omit the fresh ginger from the recipe.

Although full-fat coconut milk brings richer flavor and more body to the sauce, we prefer the lightened coconut milk with 60 percent less fat. Coconut milk is more economical in larger cans, but it doesn't keep well once opened, so it's a good idea to freeze meal-sized batches in plastic containers. Nor is it "homogenized" in the sense of regular milk—so be sure shake or stir the coconut milk before using, to distribute the coconut "cream."

SERVES 2 TO 4

4 chicken thighs, whole or boned and cut in smaller/bite-sized pieces (*or* 2 boneless chicken breasts, cut in pieces)

2 tablespoons oil (1 tablespoon each canola and peanut oil; or 1 1/2 tablespoons canola oil + 1/2 tablespoon toasted sesame oil)

1/2 onion, chopped or sliced

2 cloves garlic, minced

1/4-inch chunk fresh ginger, sliced and minced

1 to 1 1/2 tablespoons green curry paste

4 to 6 ounces (1/2 to 2/3 cup) coconut milk

1/2 cup fresh cilantro, chopped

Heat half of the oil in a large skillet with lid, and brown chicken pieces on all sides. Remove from pan. Add remaining oil, and sauté onion until translucent, then add garlic and ginger and cook gently for a minute more. Stir in the curry paste and cook for about a minute, then add coconut milk, cover, and simmer for 3 to 5 minutes.

Return chicken to pan with sauce, and simmer, covered, 10 to 12 minutes or until chicken is done through. Sprinkle fresh cilantro over the curry just before serving, if desired. Serve the curry over fresh hot basmati rice. A few lightly toasted cashews make a nice garnish.

Ginger Keeper

A piece of fresh ginger root at large in the fridge will eventually become tough, dried-out, and not very enticing. Having had several pieces of ginger get away from us and turn into wizened "monkey's paws," we were glad to come across a tip for keeping ginger in a jar with enough white wine or dry sherry to cover. The wine or sherry (a frequent companion in marinades and sauces) keeps the ginger fresh, moist, and easy to slice, nicely preserving it for several months in the refrigerator.

Chicken (or Lamb) in Simmer Sauce

Although the name of this sauce is spelled "simmer," it could just as well be "summer" as it's a good way to preserve a late-summer bounty of ripe tomatoes and apples. We're blessed with a Wolf River tree loaded with plump cooking apples every other year (if we get to them before the fall winds, frost, and deer). When a good Wolf River year coincides with a good tomato year, we make Simmer Sauce!

Make a batch of this fragrant, tomato-based curry sauce, and it will last you for a good many hurry-up dinners, at home or at camp. Simply brown chicken pieces or lamb stew meat, add sauce, and simmer for a few minutes. Any leftovers could be added to a lentil soup

 SERVES 3 TO 4

1 tablespoon olive oil
4 chicken thighs, bone-in (or lamb leg steaks)

1 pint Simmer Sauce
Banana-Date Chutney (or toasted coconut)

Remove skin and excess fat from chicken (or trim lamb and cut in bite-sized pieces, or use stew meat). Heat oil in sauté pan over medium heat and brown pieces of chicken (or lamb) on all sides. Add Simmer Sauce, cover, and simmer for 8 to 10 minutes or until meat is done through.

Serve with white or brown basmati rice, sautéed or steamed veggies, and Banana-Date Chutney (or shredded dried coconut, lightly toasted as on page 250).

SIMMER SAUCE (MAKES 6 TO 7 PINTS)

3 1/2 cups cooking apples, peeled, cored, grated
11 cups vine-ripened beefsteak or sauce tomatoes, seeded and chopped
2 tablespoons olive oil
3/4 to 1 cup raw onion, chopped
2 small mildly hot peppers, such as Hungarian Hot Wax (about 1/3 cup), finely chopped
4 teaspoons garlic, minced
1 1/2 teaspoons fresh ginger root, minced

2 to 3 tablespoons apple cider vinegar (use 3 to 3 1/2 tablespoons if tomatoes are fully ripe and sweet)
4 teaspoons mild red curry paste (featuring cilantro and cumin)
1 teaspoon ground coriander
3/4 teaspoon ground cloves
1/2 teaspoon cinnamon
1/2 teaspoon cayenne pepper + salt to taste

Prepare apples, tomatoes, and vegetables. Heat oil and sauté onion until translucent, then add peppers and sauté for a couple of minutes. Add garlic and ginger and sauté briefly, then add vinegar, tomatoes, and apples, and simmer uncovered over medium-low heat for 8 to 10 minutes. (Vinegar and juice from tomatoes should be sufficient to deglaze pan; otherwise, add 1 to 2 tablespoons water as needed.) Stir in curry paste and spices, cayenne pepper, and salt to taste (1/2 to 1 teaspoon). Simmer for another 10 to 12 minutes, or until you have a rich, fragrant sauce.

Since the sauce contains oil and low-acid peppers, onion, and ginger root, freezing is the safest preservation method. For water-bath processing, ladle sauce into 7 hot clean pint jars, leaving 1/2 inch headroom. Wipe jar mouths, top with new lids soaked in hot water, secure with rings, and process in rapidly boiling water bath for 20 minutes. Let cool, check seals, then store in cool, dry place. For more information on preserving low-acid foods, visit www.uga.edu/nchfp.

Banana-Date Chutney

I first met this combination of banana and onion, served as a simple fresh chutney with an Indonesian curry dinner, while living at the Findhorn Community in Scotland. I loved the light, fresh taste and natural sweetness—so different than the more intensely sweet, vinegary cooked chutneys. Over many years of serving this fresh chutney at home, I've embellished the recipe with lemon juice (to keep the banana from browning), dates (for sweetness), and coriander (for its subtle fragrance). It doesn't keep well, but don't worry about having any left over—this chutney (really a fresh-fruit salsa) is the perfect counterpoint to curry, especially chicken or lamb. Ripe pears can stand in for bananas, in a pinch.

SERVES 3 TO 4

1 1/2 medium ripe bananas, diced
1/2 medium onion, finely minced
3 to 4 Medjool dates, chopped

1/2 teaspoon ground coriander
Juice of 1/3 organic or Meyer lemon
(1 to 1 1/2 tablespoons)

Combine ingredients in small bowl, and stir with fork just enough to bring chutney together. Serve immediately.

Local Organic Lamb, Etc.

There is a world of difference between supermarket lamb and locally raised grass-fed organic lamb, not least of which is flavor—plus organic lamb's health advantages of being leaner and "chem-free," having lived the good life. Once you've tasted the difference, you may want to consider ordering lamb from a local organic farmer. You can buy it by the piece at many Maine natural food coops and stores or from the farmers themselves, but buying a whole or half lamb is a more economical way to enjoy "real lamb." It also helps sustain the local market farming economy, and fills your freezer with the makings for delicious lamb dinners to carry you through the winter and coming year.

For a number of years we've been ordering lamb from our North Penobscot neighbor King Hill Farm, just up the road from us on Route 199, at 29 Faerie Kingdom Road (kinghillfarm@gwi.net, 207–326–9701). Dennis King and his partner Jo Barrett keep a customer list and mail out order forms in early fall. We fill out the form with cutting instructions, and then pick up our order, usually in November after the lamb comes back from a nearby slaughterhouse, with the lamb cut, packaged and labeled, frozen and ready for the freezer. In addition to lamb (and side products including a knockout spicy sheep sausage), King Hill Farm raises free-range turkeys and chickens, pork, and grass-fed beef. They also offer free-range eggs, fall storage vegetables, and seasonal produce.

And they are just one of many organic farms alive and well throughout Maine, raising organic meats along with eggs, fruits, and vegetables, available at natural food stores, farmer's markets, or straight from the farm (on a walk-in, pre-order, or community-supported-agriculture basis). A complete, interactive database of Maine organic farms by county, with contact information and product listings for each farm, is posted on the MOFGA website, www.mofga.com.

Persian Lamb Shanks

*F*or inspiration on delicious ways to cook and serve lamb, one need only look to the Near and Middle East. One nice, and very simple, way to cook lamb shanks involves a Persian spice rub called an advieh. The delicate, fragrant spice mixture featured here (based on a recipe in Margaret Shaida's The Legendary Cuisine of Persia) is one used in the Persian Gulf in hearty, everyday dishes.

Lamb shanks are a reasonably priced cut of lamb, and appealing for a small household—sort of a miniature leg of lamb with all the culinary possibilities but fewer leftovers. A lamb leg it is not, however, in terms of juiciness and texture of the meat; those who don't like the gumminess characteristic of pot roast will be happier with leg roasts or steaks and leg or arm chops. But if you like the sample here, the advieh spice rub treatment will work its same magic on a whole lamb leg. As the centerpiece of an exotic but festive dinner party, a boned leg of lamb can be rolled around an advieh-seasoned stuffing of sautéed onion, dried apricots, and almonds, tied and browned, and roasted, and served with the pan drippings alongside fluffy basmati rice. Or use a touch of advieh for a light curry treatment with a simple lamb-and-onion stew.

With larger lamb shanks, each shank should yield two dinner portions; with smaller shanks, plan on serving one shank per person. If cooking for two, this makes enough for dinner plus a follow-up meal using the stock and trimmings, such as a lentil stew or soup (page 41).

℗ SERVES 3 TO 4

2 to 3 lamb shanks, 3/4 to 1 1/4 pounds each
1 tablespoon olive oil
3/4 to 1 teaspoon Advieh (Persian Spice Rub)
1 cup boiling water (or chicken or lamb stock)
1 medium onion, halved crescents

2 teaspoons olive oil
4 to 5 dried apricot halves, soaked in water
    and sliced (optional)
1 1/2 teaspoons fresh-squeezed lemon juice
    (1/2 teaspoon if using apricots)

Preheat oven to 375°F. Wash lamb shanks, pat dry, and trim off excess fat and skin. In skillet over moderate heat, lightly brown outside of shanks, turning often enough to brown all sides—not easy, with this ungainly cut of beast!

Transfer shanks to a small roasting pan with lid and rub the Advieh (recipe follows) all over their browned surfaces. Lightly sprinkle with salt, pour water or stock around the lamb shanks, and roast covered in preheated oven for 15 to 20 minutes.

If you are serving the lamb with white basmati rice, now is the time to put it on to cook. An efficient way to make plain rice is to place the rice in a covered casserole, 2 cups boiling water to 1 cup rice, and bake it in the oven while the lamb finishes roasting (about 30 minutes). Or for a special dinner, "Saffron" Rice (page 185) would go nicely with this dish.

With the rice in the oven, sauté onion till partly translucent, then add the soaked apricots (if desired) and lemon juice. Spoon into roasting pan, and baste shanks with pan juices.

The rice and lamb should be done at about the same time (45 to 50 minutes for the lamb). Serve with steamed green beans or vegetable(s) of your choice. Sliced or halved almonds, lightly toasted dry or in a little butter and/or oil (page 60), make a nice garnish for both the beans and rice.

ADVIEH (PERSIAN SPICE RUB)

1 teaspoon cumin seeds, whole or ground

1/2 teaspoon cardamom seeds (contents of pods)

1/2 teaspoon black peppercorns

1/2 teaspoon cloves, whole or ground

2 1/2 teaspoons ground cinnamon

1 1/2 teaspoons turmeric

Use mortar and pestle to grind any spices that are whole, then add ground spices. Mix and keep in an airtight jar. (NOTE: This advieh traditionally includes caraway, but we prefer to omit it.)

Braised Mediterranean Lamb Shanks

Recipes for lamb shanks often lean toward a reduced sauce robustly flavored with beef stock, tomatoes, and red wine. Here the lamb shanks are sauced with a lighter hand, complementing their deep gamy flavor and dense texture with fragrant Mediterranean spices and herbs, balancing sweetness and acidity with wine, lemon, honey, and tomatoes. This dish takes about 2 hours to cook, but the oven does most of the work, and the results are delicious. If you have any left over, meat and sauce would be a fine addition to a Lamb & Bean Soup (page 34) or Lamb & Lentil Soup (page 35).

SERVES 3 TO 4

2 cloves garlic, each sliced into 5 or 6 slivers

1 1/2 to 2 tablespoons olive oil

2 lamb shanks, 3/4 to 1 1/4 pounds each

1/2 large (or 1 small) onion, thin crescents

1/4 cup red or white wine

2/3 cup water or stock (vegetable or lamb)

1/2 teaspoon ground cinnamon

1/4 teaspoon allspice

1 to 1 1/2 teaspoons honey

4 canned plum tomatoes, pieces (3/4 cup)

1/2 cup tomato juice

1 1/2 tablespoons fresh-squeezed lemon juice

1 tablespoon dried Greek oregano

1 teaspoon dried mint

1/4 teaspoon salt

6 grates black or multicolored peppercorns

Slice garlic into slivers. Cut an equal number of slits, about 1/2 inch deep, in surface of shanks and insert garlic slivers. Preheat oven to 425°F.

Heat 1 tablespoon oil in 8 x 8-inch Corningware or other lidded ovenproof casserole, and brown lamb shanks on all sides. Add a little more oil and onions during final few minutes of cooking, and sauté with shanks until onion is partway done. Deglaze with the wine (carefully avoiding hot steam). Place casserole uncovered in oven and roast at 425° for 15 minutes. Meanwhile, combine remaining ingredients in a separate bowl or 2-cup measuring cup.

Remove casserole from oven and pour braising liquid over lamb shanks and onions. Lower oven temperature to 350°, cover casserole, and bake uncovered for about 20 minutes. Turn shanks and baste with pan juices, and bake uncovered 20 to 25 minutes more, basting occasionally, until lamb is done and tender and sauce is somewhat reduced.

Serve over white or brown basmati rice, with steamed spinach or chard, green beans, or broccoli.

GREEK LAMB STEW: Use 1 1/3 pounds lamb leg or stew meat cut into medallions or bite-sized pieces. Heat 1 tablespoon olive oil in Dutch oven and brown meat on three sides in two batches. Drain excess fat, leaving fond in bottom of pan; add a little more oil and sauté onion. Return lamb to pan and pour braising liquid over (the wine, stock, and remaining ingredients in lamb shanks recipe, or the Greek Tomato Sauce ingredients on page 164). Simmer covered for 20 minutes, then simmer open another 15 minutes until lamb is tender and sauce somewhat reduced. Crumble 1 to 2 tablespoons feta over each serving if desired.

Mediterranean Lamb Kebabs

Salivating for some nice lamb kebabs to grill at camp, I consulted several Mediterranean and Middle Eastern cookbooks (including a Time-Life favorite of Grandma's) and let the various approaches "marinate," then settled on these time-tested Eastern Mediterranean accompaniments for lamb. With lemon, garlic, onion, oregano, and mint, you can't go wrong! This is a good way to deal with lamb that (due to weather or schedules) you won't be able to grill for a few days; the marinade will help hold the meat's freshness, flavor, and color, while adding complementary flavors.

  SERVES 3

1 to 1 1/4 pounds lamb leg steaks or stew meat, trimmed and cut in bite-sized pieces

~ MARINADE ~

1/2 medium onion, grated or sliced in 1/8-inch rings (*or* 1/4 teaspoon onion powder)

1/8 teaspoon garlic powder (*or* 1 clove, pressed)

3 tablespoons fresh-squeezed lemon juice (*or* equal parts lemon juice and white wine)

1 1/2 tablespoons olive oil

1 tablespoon fresh oregano, finely chopped

2 teaspoons fresh mint, finely chopped

Pinch of salt, few grates black pepper

Trim fat from lamb and cut in 1- to 1 1/2-inch pieces for skewering. Grate or slice onion and combine with remaining ingredients for marinade. Pour over lamb in bowl and cover with plate; or put lamb in ziplock bag with marinade, and massage package so the marinade evenly surrounds meat. Marinate lamb in the refrigerator (or camp cooler) for 4 hours to 2 days, until you're ready to grill.

Pre-soak 4 bamboo skewers (8 inches long) in cold water for 10 to 20 minutes, then thread on chunks of lamb, dividing them evenly among the skewers. Grill over moderate coals, turning several times and basting occasionally with a little of the marinade, until lamb is browned, tender, but still juicy on the inside. Serve with brown, pan-roasted white, or "Saffron" rice (page 185).

Variation

SPICY GRILLED LAMB: Double the garlic, and replace the herbs with 1/2 teaspoon allspice, 1/4 teaspoon paprika or cinnamon, and a dash cayenne. Replace 1 tablespoon of the lemon juice with balsamic vinegar.

Greek Lamb-burgers

If you're heading off into the wild blue (or green), this burger mixture is easy to put together at home, pack into a ziplock, and chill in the cooler till you're ready to grill.

SERVES 2 TO 3

1 pound ground lamb
1 small apple, cored, peeled, and grated (*or* 1 small sweet carrot, grated, or combination)
1 clove garlic, minced
1/2 small onion, minced

1 1/2 teaspoons dried mint leaves, crushed
3/4 teaspoon dried Greek oregano
1/8 teaspoon salt
1/4 to 1/2 teaspoon white or black pepper
1/4 cup beer, apple cider, or other liquid

Assemble ingredients in order listed. Mix thoroughly, using hands to distribute vegetables and seasonings evenly through the meat. Form into 2 to 3 oval patties about 3/4 inch thick.

Grill over medium-hot charcoal fire, turning a couple of times, until both sides are evenly browned. Serve with rice, couscous, or Greek-Style Oven Fries (page 174).

CHARCOAL GRILLING

For all the convenience of gas grills, there's nothing so satisfying as cooking on a charcoal grill—and savoring the results. For us in rural Maine, part of the satisfaction comes from living within easy reach of birchbark scraps and dry twigs to use as kindling for charcoal fires, more woodsy and aromatic than lighter fluid—the ambiance of a campfire and a pot-bellied stove, contained in a kettle grill.

Working with the variables of wind, draft, fuel, and flame, there's an art to charcoal grilling, and men seem to have all the right instincts for it. It also takes someone dedicated to the task, with that sense of timing that comes from experience. And so our usual division of labor finds Richard tending grill, and me doing what women are so good at—multitasking, getting the rest of the meal together.

Yet there are times, at camp, when I'm on my own and only grilling will do. So I've been paying more attention grillside, gradually catching on to the ways of successful grilling. (Not as easy as it looks, especially if it's just you scurrying between stove and grill—talk about multitasking!)

Prepare the grill 30 to 40 minutes before you plan to serve. First, lay a good foundation—several Lincoln-log layers of dry twigs, 6 to 8 inches long, stacked over a few pieces of birchbark, fire watch (water jug) at the ready. On these, build a pyramid of traditional charcoal briquets. For a medium-hot fire to grill 2 or 3 portions of steak, burgers, chops, kebabs or chicken, 15 to 19 briquets is about right; for 4 to 6 portions, go with 20 to 24 briquets. Use more for a larger, hotter, or longer-lasting fire.

Light the fire, set cooking grate in place, and wait 8 to 10 minutes until the charcoal is burning well, then use tongs to rearrange the coals in one-and-a-half layers. (You can favor one side with the second layer, making this the hotter side.) Meanwhile the heat will have charred any cooking grate residue, which you can scrape or wire-brush into the coals. Giving the grate a swipe with an oil-soaked pad will help keep food from sticking.

When the coals are lightly coated with ash, check the heat. If you can hold your hand above the grate for 3 to 4 seconds, your fire is medium-hot, just right. Put the food on the grill, well spaced.

With bone-in chicken, start with the bone side down, placing the meat on the hotter side of the grill; partially cover with the lid, leaving the draft open over the opposite side, to draw heat up and around the meat. If you have left some skin on, cook the bone side for 4 or 5 minutes before turning, to lessen the chance of conflagration from fat dripping into the fire. Cook the skin side for less time.

Once the meat or fish is sealed on both sides, continue grilling over moderate heat, turning the pieces every few minutes, perhaps basting, until browned and done to your liking and juices run clear.

There are many more fine points and techniques to grilling, such as wrapping food in foil packets to steam it; using the vents to quicken or slow the fire; using green hardwood twigs (pages 63 and 110) or soaked hardwood chips for flavorful smoke. Another option is using real hardwood charcoal, avoiding the chemicals and binders used in briquets. Hardwood charcoal burns hotter and faster than briquets. You can even make your own "cowboy charcoal," as Richard's brother Jon does, by dumping hardwood ashes from a wood furnace/stove outside, then collecting the rain-washed unburned coals.

Baked Kibbeh

This Middle East–style meatloaf of ground lamb and finely crushed soaked bulghur is traditionally served either raw or baked with a savory filling in the form of egg-shaped balls or baklava-like "trays." I like exotic dishes but draw the line at eating raw meat or undercooked grain (the bulghur available here is a coarse cracked wheat, not as finely ground as the crushed burgul of the Middle East)—so baking kibbeh (or kibbi) seems a good way to go, using precooked bulghur (or leftover pilaf, page 187).

Kibbeh is delicious but quite rich, so you'll want to serve it in smallish portions along with a salad or colorful side dish of sautéed vegetables. A good combination might be Romanos, favas, or shell beans (page 146) with onions, spinach or Tuscan kale, tomatoes, basil, oregano, and marjoram.

  SERVES 4 TO 6

1 cup raw bulghur (cracked wheat) cooked in
    2 cups water (or 2 to 2 1/4 cups leftover
    cooked bulghur or Bulghur Pilaf, page 187)
1/2 tablespoon butter
1 tablespoon extra-virgin olive oil
1 large onion, chopped
1/4 cup pine nuts (or sunflower seeds, or a
    combination)
1/2 cup fresh parsley, chopped

1/2 teaspoon dried mint leaves
1 pound ground lamb (the leaner, the better)
1 small onion, finely minced
3/4 teaspoon ground allspice
1/4 teaspoon cinnamon
1 teaspoon salt
1/4 teaspoon ground black pepper
1/3 cup ice water
Extra-virgin olive oil

To precook bulghur, pour boiling water over grains and simmer over very low heat for 15 to 20 minutes, then let cool to lukewarm—or use leftover Bulghur Pilaf (page 187).

To make the filling, sauté onion in butter and olive oil. Stir in pine nuts and/or sunflower seeds, and sauté briefly; add parsley and mint, and remove from heat.

Place ground lamb in large bowl. Add minced raw onion, spices, salt and pepper, then gradually work in ice water with your hands. Finally mix in the bulghur.

Preheat oven to 375°F. Oil an 8 x 8-inch casserole dish. Pat half of lamb mixture into bottom of dish. Spoon filling onto lamb layer and spread evenly, then smooth remaining lamb mixture over filling. (Or, if you prefer, combine filling with lamb mixture.) Traditionally a little olive oil is spread over the top of the kibbeh. With a wet knife, score a diamond pattern in the top surface.

Bake until the lamb is no longer pink—about 45 to 50 minutes. Cut the kibbeh in squares or rectangles and serve warm.

Spanish Beef with Olives

This skillet dish is a flavorful compromise between steak and stew, simple enough to make in a camp/cruising kitchen and a good alternative in weather too inclement to grill. Preparation is as easy as bringing along some salsa, olives, herbs, and red wine—things you'd likely have on hand anyway.

If using store-bought or homemade salsa (page 19) in lieu of peppers, choose some that is generous with the peppers or chiles, which bring flavor to the dish. Or if using fresh market peppers (or growing your own), choose one of the more flavorful varieties like Lipsticks, poblano chiles, or Romanian frying peppers.

 SERVES 2 TO 3

1 pound beef chuck steak, cut into mini-steaks
    or bite-sized pieces (or beef chuck for stew)
Dash of Worcestershire sauce
1 tablespoon olive oil
1 onion, thin crescents
1 clove garlic, minced
1 to 1 1/2 green bell peppers, large pieces
    (*or 2 tablespoons tomato-chile salsa*)

1/4 to 1/3 cup red wine
1 to 2 canned plum tomatoes, chopped
3 to 6 marinated olives (mixed green/ripe
    medley), sliced
1/2 teaspoon dried oregano
1/4 teaspoon dried thyme
1/4 teaspoon salt or to taste
Few grates black or multicolored pepper

Cut beef into mini-steaks or bite-sized pieces. Heat 1 1/2 teaspoons oil in Dutch oven or skillet and brown beef on three sides. Set aside in shallow bowl, "wooshed" with a squirt of Worcestershire.

Drain fat, leaving fond in bottom of pan, add another 1 1/2 teaspoons oil, and sauté onion for a minute, then add peppers and sauté until both are partway done. (Remove peppers at this point if you prefer them al dente; otherwise leave them in the pot.) Add garlic and briefly sauté; then deglaze with wine and tomatoes. Add olives, seasonings, tomato-chile salsa (if you are not using peppers), and steak. Cover and simmer for another 10 to 15 minutes.

Serve with pan-roasted quinoa (page 190), Garlic Mashed Potatoes (page 170), Rice-Noodle Pilaf (page 184), or plain rice, along with a green salad tossed with a Parmesan vinaigrette (or other piquant dressing). And Spanish red wine, of course!

Beef Stroganoff

Here is how Richard makes this classic dish, with the creative-cook's caveat: "but I never make it the same way twice." Rather than break out the variations, we've listed the ingredients that vary (mushrooms, horseradish) as options. The constants that make it Stroganoff are bacon, onion, red wine, and sour cream—and the main attraction, the beef. Beef chuck is the key to a delicious Stroganoff, being a reliably flavorful and tender cut (the bovine equivalent to pork butt). Tender sirloin or tips also make a nice Stroganoff, or a simple summertime beef bourguignon with fresh tomatoes and savory (see variation).

SERVES 3 TO 4

1 1/4 to 1 3/4 pounds beef chuck, steak or roast

1 1/2 slices bacon

1/2 teaspoon Worcestershire sauce

1 to 2 tablespoons olive oil

1 cup chopped yellow or red onion

8 to 10 baby portabella or other firm, flavorful
  mushrooms, thick slices (optional)

1/4 teaspoon dried thyme

1 to 1 1/2 teaspoons horseradish (optional)

1/4 to 1/3 cup red wine

3/4 cup chicken or beef stock

1/8 teaspoon garlic powder (*or* 1 clove, pressed)

1/4 to 1/2 teaspoon salt (or to taste)

Few grates black pepper

2 tablespoons unbleached flour

2 tablespoons sour cream + 2 tablespoons
  plain yogurt

Artichoke or egg ribbon noodles

Trim fat from meat, and cut in bite-sized pieces. Cut bacon in small pieces. In lidded skillet or Dutch oven, fry bacon over moderate heat; remove bacon, and drain fat. Add olive oil to skillet as needed and brown meat on three sides (leaving fourth side open to absorb liquids and flavors of the sauce). Remove meat to shallow bowl or plate, and douse with a couple squirts Worcestershire.

Add olive oil to pan and sauté onion over medium-low heat until translucent, then push to side of pan and add mushroom slices (if using), cut-side down. Reduce heat to low and cook mushrooms, turning to brown both sides. Add thyme and (optional) horseradish, then deglaze pan with wine. Pour in stock, then return beef to pan, along with meat juices plus a little water (1 to 2 tablespoons) to rinse remaining juices from bowl or plate. Add garlic, salt, and pepper to taste.

Sprinkle flour over top and quickly stir flour into the pan juices, keeping heat low to prevent lumps. Then continue cooking over medium heat, stirring frequently, until sauce thickens.

Combine sour cream and yogurt in cup, smoothing out any lumps. When almost ready to serve, spoon a little of the sauce into the sour cream mixture (to warm it), then stir this back into the sauce. (Hopefully this will prevent the sauce from breaking, caused by a combination of heat and acidity.) Let Stroganoff rest or keep warm over minimal heat for a few more minutes to let flavors mingle.

Serve over buttered artichoke or egg ribbon noodles, along with steamed broccoli or green beans.

Variation

SUMMER BEEF STEW: Prepare beef, bacon, and onion as above, finishing with a douse of Worcestershire. Deglaze pan with wine and 1/4 cup water or stock, and add 1 tablespoon fresh summer savory, the garlic, salt, and pepper. Return beef and bacon to pan and lay 8 to 10 halved cherry tomatoes over top of stew. Simmer partially covered for 5 to 10 minutes, then serve over noodles with sautéed summer veggies.

Deglazing

Deglazing is a technique for freeing the browned bits from the bottom of a sauté pan while adding deliciously complex flavors to a meat or fish entrée or sauce. Vinegars (page 30) and wines (page 126) work especially well, as their acidity (helped by a few scrapes of a metal spatula) releases the cooked-on sugars, proteins, and oils, cleaning the pan. Stock, water, beer, cider, citrus, tomato, or other juice can be used as well. Just be sure, if browning or searing meat in a hot pan, to lower the heat first before adding deglazing liquid, to avoid getting a face-ful of hot steam.

Rouladen (Beef Birds in Sauce)

This special-occasion dish of stuffed beef rolls in sauce involves a little more preparation than a braised bottom round, but oh my, it is worth it! Bottom round is one of the most flavorful cuts, but tends to be tough; pounding and braising make it more tender. Be sure to have your butcher cut the meat on a slicer, as it is difficult to get uniformly thin slices by hand. Once the "birds" are filled and rolled, they simmer in a rich sauce fragrant with mushrooms and wine. The sauce can be served "au jus" or thickened—or taken in a Stroganoff direction with a little horseradish and sour cream.

Rouladen means "roll-ups" in Germany where this dish originated. After sampling it at the table of my mother-in-law, Dolly Washburn, I begged Richard to make it at home—hence this recipe.

SERVES 3 TO 4

2 pounds beef bottom round, sliced across
    the grain, 3/16-inch slices

~ FILLING ~
7 to 8 baby portabella mushrooms, cleaned
1/2 medium onion, finely chopped
2 1/2 to 3 strips thick bacon, 1/4 inch pieces
1 1/2 to 2 tablespoons olive oil (total)
1/8 teaspoon thyme
1/8 teaspoon summer savory
3 to 4 grinds white or black pepper
1/4 cup dry vermouth

~ SAUCE ~
1/2 medium onion, coarsely chopped
1/4 teaspoon thyme or summer savory
Salt and pepper to taste
1/3 cup dry red wine
1/4 cup beef stock (*or* 1/2 portion/cube beef
    bouillon dissolved in 1/4 cup hot water)
1/4 cup water
1/2 teaspoon prepared horseradish (optional)
1 tablespoon unbleached flour
2 tablespoons sour cream (optional)

Trim fat from meat, and, one at a time, pound slices all across on one side with a meat hammer (preferably a maple mallet) to an even thickness, about 1/8 inch. Set aside while you make the filling.

Chop mushroom stems along with 2 of the caps. Slice remaining caps in half, and set aside. Fry bacon pieces in Dutch oven over moderate heat; remove to drain on paper towels. Drain fat from pan (leaving the fond), then add 2 teaspoons olive oil and sauté minced onion and mushrooms until they start to brown up. Sprinkle with seasonings and deglaze with vermouth. Transfer filling to shallow bowl. Leave Dutch oven (still with some fond as a base for the sauce) on back of stove to cool.

Divide filling among meat slices, spooning 1 tablespoon or so at wide end of each slice. Starting there, roll up slices to form "birds," securing each (tail-end down) with 1 to 2 toothpicks. Set aside.

Add another 2 teaspoons olive oil to Dutch oven and, over moderate heat, brown the "birds" on three sides, turning as each side browns up. As they finish browning, remove to shallow bowl.

Add oil to pan if needed and begin sautéing coarsely chopped onion over medium heat, then add reserved halved mushroom caps, cut-side down. Gently fry/sweat vegetables, lowering the heat to prevent over-browning the fond in the pan. Add thyme or savory, salt, and pepper, then deglaze pan with red wine. Remove mushrooms and reserve as garnish. Add beef stock (or bouillon), then the browned beef birds; rinse shallow bowl with 1/4 cup water and add to sauce, along with horseradish if desired. Cover and simmer over low heat for 15 to 20 minutes (or longer).

Sprinkle/stir flour into sauce and cook over low heat, stirring constantly, until sauce thickens slightly. Sauce can be thickened further with sour cream (as on page 124) for a Stroganoff touch.

Serve over hot, drained, oiled/buttered egg or artichoke ribbon noodles, or with rice or potatoes.

COOKING WITH WINES

Not everyone likes to cook with wine, but a little wine, dry vermouth, sherry, or marsala adds a lot to meat and fish dishes, whether in a marinade, braising liquid, or to deglaze pan drippings as the base for a sauce. The complex sugars and acidity of wines not only enhance the food, but act as a preservative in a marinade. Our wine cupboard usually holds at least one bottle of red or white wine available for cooking (any disappointing table wine being a candidate), white vermouth (an herbed fortified wine), dry sherry, and marsala, which appear in many of the meat and seafood recipes. (The alcohol "cooks off" or evaporates in the cooking process, but if you'd prefer not to use wine called for in a recipe, feel free to substitute stock, water, citrus or tomato juice, or cider.)

And then there's wine to accompany the meal—a world of possibilities, from wineries near and far. Full-bodied, floral, crisp, oaky, toasty, "big," buttery, or bright, wine has a way of complementing the flavors of food, especially savory dishes. Thank heavens for those keywords on the labels—cherry, pepper, spice, vanilla, peach, pear—that help increase the odds of choosing a palate-pleasing wine. Since vintages and vintners come and go and everyone's tastes are different (and changing), I'll stop short of making recommendations, other than to sample and enjoy, and find out what you like.

Egg, Bean & Cheese
Entrées (with Meat Options)

Vegetarian, Mostly

I chose to follow a vegetarian diet in my late teens, affected by the opening scene of *2001: A Space Odyssey* (a graphic portrayal of cave-people devouring fresh-killed meat, ew!). Surrounded at college by alternative choices including yoga and Eastern religions, it seemed a natural step to explore a gentler lifestyle and a wider culinary world of bean-, grain-, and dairy-based food traditions.

Back then life was not so easy for would-be vegetarians, with slim pickin's at most restaurants and college cafeterias, and mixed reactions at family tables—plenty of questions, but a vegetarian meal mostly meant doing without the main course, unless you were lucky enough to have an adventurous, accommodating mom or chef, or live in a place with ethnic or vegetarian restaurants. Otherwise, if you wanted a healthy, delicious, protein-balanced vegetarian meal, you generally had to make it yourself.

And so, as soon as I had access to a kitchen, I started learning to cook with lentils and beans, eggs and cheese, nuts and seeds, whole grains, herbs, dried fruits and natural sugars—things we had never eaten much at home. Guided by several pioneering vegetarian cookbooks (*The New York Times Natural Foods Cookbook*, *Diet for a Small Planet*, Tassajara and Moosewood), I started experimenting with whole ingredients and ethnic dishes. It didn't take me long to realize that a vegetarian diet was a passport to a round-the-world cook's tour of different cultures and ways of eating.

Living in Scotland at the vegetarian Findhorn Community in my early twenties gave me an education in all kinds of things, including cooking in a group kitchen. Imagine the opportunities: a well-stocked natural-foods larder, a congenial kitchen crew, and 150 hungry people expecting delicious vegetarian meals cooked for them twice a day! I cooked part-time for most of my three-year stay, and loved it—especially one memorable week at Findhorn's beach-side retreat house, Traigh Bhan, on the isle of Iona, when I really had a chance to spread my wings as a cook. The other members of our house party were more interested in exploring the island than the kitchen, so I happily took on the role of kitchen genie, concocting creative dishes for an appreciative group.

After returning to Maine, I stuck with a vegetarian diet for quite a while. But changing circumstances have a way of shaping choices. By the time I was in my late twenties, settling in on the Blue Hill Peninsula, close to the source of all kinds of fresh seafood and surrounded by creative cooks, I began eating fish and poultry again. And then I got hitched up with a meat eater . . . and the last of the diet parameters fell away. How could I resist tempting dishes offered up by a good-hearted, live-in, good cook? One with restaurant experience no less, without whom my life and this book would no doubt have been a lot less interesting.

But I still love meals centered around beans and eggs and cheese, uplifted by interesting herbs and spices, and though Richard and I eat meat and fish fairly regularly for dinner, I'll often make a vegetarian lunch. And many of our dinner entrées include smaller portions of meat, a few flavorful gobbets as a treat, with beans or dairy as the main event in company with vegetables and grains or pastas (as with many ethnic dishes that evolved to include a small amount of meat because that's all that was available). This chapter includes various "company dishes" that we'll make purely vegetarian for vegetarian friends, but might include a little meat if cooking just for ourselves. Though mostly entrées, many of these dishes can be served as lunch, a light supper, or hearty appetizer.

About half the recipes in this chapter are bona fide vegetarian. The others lend themselves to optional meat additions. Since we (and probably other folks) make such dishes either way, with or without meat, it seemed to make sense, rather than have a separate vegetarian chapter, to present these bean, egg, cheese, and vegetable-oriented entrées—many of them from regional and ethnic cuisines—with meat options, which vegetarians will understandably wish to ignore. Here and in other non-baking chapters, wherever you see the "vegetarian" recipe icon (page 7), it indicates a vegetarian recipe or one that would be just as satisfying without the meat.

Being a former vegetarian myself, I hope that vegetarians reading these recipes will not be offended by the meat options, but simply follow these basically vegetarian recipes as you wish, omitting any meat or substituting whatever vegetarian ingredient appeals to you.

Onion-Asparagus Quiche

This savory custard pie is delicious just with onions and cheese, or with bacon (Quiche Lorraine)—or a featured tender vegetable, as here. Since keeping the bottom crust crisp makes all the difference, I favor a belt-and-suspenders approach of sealing it two ways: with egg white and a layer of cheese.

 SERVES 3 TO 4

2 teaspoons olive oil

1 teaspoon butter or bacon fat

2/3 onion (*or* 1 cup leeks or green onions), sliced

Oaty Piecrust, made with olive oil (page 242)

1 1/4 cups shredded Gruyère or smoked provolone

1 tablespoon unbleached flour

1/2 teaspoon dried tarragon and/or savory

1 1/2 cups tender asparagus stalks, tough ends snapped off (or sliced tender leek tops)

3 extra-large (or 4 medium) eggs, 1 separated

1 1/4 cups milk + half-and-half (combination)

1/4 teaspoon salt or to taste

1/8 teaspoon nutmeg

Pinch cayenne (or few grates white pepper)

Heat oil and butter or bacon fat in skillet and sauté onions until translucent. Remove from heat.

Line 9-inch deep-dish pie plate with Oaty Piecrust; crimp edges. Separate 1 egg and brush some white over bottom of crust. Cut asparagus stalks (or leek greens) in pieces and steam until al dente.

Toss unbleached flour with 3/4 cup grated cheese (reserving 1/2 cup to sprinkle over top) and spread over bottom crust. (Or, use all of the cheese in filling.) Cover with the cooled onions. Distribute asparagus (or leek greens) evenly over onion mixture, and sprinkle with tarragon/savory.

Preheat oven to 425°F. Beat eggs (including remaining egg white), and whisk in milk, half-and-half, and seasonings. Pour over onion-cheese layer. Sprinkle remaining cheese over the top.

Bake for 5 minutes at 425°, then reduce heat to 350° and bake 35 to 40 minutes until puffed and golden on top and knife inserted in center comes out clean. Let quiche rest 5 minutes before serving.

Variation

MUSHROOM-ONION QUICHE: Omit asparagus. Sprinkle tarragon over onion-cheese filling, and top custard mixture with 2 cups sliced baby portabella mushrooms, briefly sautéed in olive oil and butter, sprinkling 2 teaspoons dry sherry to deglaze pan. Otherwise, assemble and bake quiche as described above.

Autumn Pie

This sweetly savory quiche is great for a dinner party or potluck, since you can make it ahead—in fact, it's better that way, giving the flavors a chance to come together. Somehow the combination of nutmeg and winter savory, with a touch of cayenne, is just right with the squash filling, encased by a golden crust and cheesy top. Scallions, leeks, or late-garden onion tops add some tender green.

Winter squash can be cooked various ways: peeled, cut in chunks, and boiled; sliced in 1-inch crescents and steamed; or (easiest) halved, seeded, and baked (in a foil-covered pan) with a little water in a 375°F oven until tender, and then scooped out of the skin and mashed with a fork or masher. Prepare the squash ahead of time, and the pie will be that much easier to assemble.

 SERVES 4

1 1/2 to 2 cups butternut or other flavorful
    winter squash, cooked and mashed
Wheat-Corn Crust (below)
2 tablespoons olive oil
6 scallions + 1 small onion (*or* 2 leeks or green
    onions), sliced, white/green parts separated
1 clove garlic, minced (optional)
1/4 teaspoon nutmeg

1 1/2 teaspoons winter savory
1/2 teaspoon salt
Pinch of cayenne
Several grates white pepper
3/4 cup ricotta, part-skim
3 large eggs, beaten
3/4 cup shredded New England cheddar (or
    Asiago or Italian cheddar cheese)

Prepare squash, or use leftover mashed squash if available. Make crust (good way to pass the time while squash is cooking) and roll out or pat into 10-inch deep-dish Pyrex (or ceramic or stoneware) pie plate. Crimp edges, or leave crust with smooth edge. Prepare onions or leeks.

Preheat oven to 375°F. Meanwhile, make filling: Sauté white parts of onions (or leeks), then add garlic and green onion (or leek) tops, and stir in seasonings. Remove from heat and let cool a little; then stir in ricotta, mashed squash, and eggs. Scrape filling into prepared crust, smoothing surface with spoon or spatula.

Bake pie at 375° for 10 minutes; remove from oven to sprinkle cheese over top, and return to oven to bake at 350° for another 35 to 45 minutes or until set and top is nicely golden (opt for the shorter baking time if you are making it ahead to reheat). Let stand a few minutes before serving.

If there is some left over, it's even better the second time around. Simply reheat wedges in a metal pie plate at 350° until hot through.

WHEAT-CORN CRUST

1/2 cup corn flour
1/4 cup oat flour
1/4 cup unbleached flour
1/3 cup whole-wheat pastry flour

1/4 teaspoon salt
2 tablespoons chilled salted butter, diced
2 tablespoons olive oil
3 1/2 to 4 tablespoons ice water

Toss flours together with salt and rub in chilled butter with fingers. Stir in oil until evenly distributed, then enough ice water to bring dough together into a ball.

Broccoli Mini-Quiches

These simple little quiches are a festive offering for a potluck, quick to make and guaranteed to disappear! Serve whole as single lunch portions (easily reheated if leftover), or serve halved or quartered as appetizers.

  8 LUNCH SERVINGS, 16 TO 32 APPETIZERS

1 tablespoon olive oil

1/2 onion, sliced in small thin crescents (*or* 3 scallions, thinly sliced)

1 to 1 1/2 cups broccoli florets (or leftover lightly steamed broccoli)

1/2 clove garlic, minced (*or* 1/8 teaspoon garlic powder)

1/2 teaspoon dried basil

1/4 teaspoon dried summer savory

1/4 teaspoon salt

Few grates white pepper

Whole-Wheat Pastry, Double Crust Recipe (page 239)

1 cup part-skim ricotta

3 large eggs, beaten

1/4 teaspoon ground nutmeg

12 cherry tomatoes, halved; or 8 plum tomato slices, seeded (*or* 16 to 24 small strips of red bell pepper)

2/3 to 1 cup shredded or thinly sliced cheese (smoked mozzarella or provolone, cheddar, or Gruyère, or a combination)

Sauté onion (or white parts of scallions) in olive oil until partly translucent, then add broccoli and stir-steam until al dente, adding garlic near the end. Season with herbs, salt, and pepper.

Make pastry and divide evenly into 8 balls of dough. For a batch of mini-quiches, you'll need 8 non-stick tart pans about 4 inches in diameter. Roll out tart crusts one at a time, or pat into place in tart pans, forming a slight lip around the top; crimp, alternating thumbs and index fingers.

Beat eggs into ricotta in small bowl. Season with nutmeg. Preheat oven to 375°F.

Distribute seasoned vegetables among tart crusts, then pour the egg-ricotta mixture over filling. Arrange 3 cherry tomato halves, a tomato slice, or 2 to 3 slices of red bell pepper around the top of each quiche. Sprinkle cheese evenly over the tops.

Arrange mini-quiches on a large rectangular baking sheet (8 should just fit) for ease in handling, and bake 20 to 25 minutes or until set and lightly browned. Serve immediately, or cool and reheat.

FRITTATAS

Although frittatas are traditionally made like an omelet, in a frying pan or cast-iron skillet, we like the low-maintenance approach of layering the components—grains, pasta, breadcrumbs, potatoes, or corn; seasoned sautéed vegetables; eggs and ricotta; cheese, bacon, smoked fish, or shellfish—and baking the frittata in the oven, like a savory cheesecake or quiche (or, more properly in Italian, a torta). This way there's no risk of scorching the bottom, no skillful flipping required. Just assemble, sit back, and enjoy the aroma as your creation bakes.

For, yes, frittatas are an opportunity to get creative with leftovers, a perfect way to use up cooked carbos and sautéed or steamed veggies, along with odds and ends of cheese and whatever other treats you can twitch out of the freezer or pantry. Garnish the top with a mandala of colored peppers or sliced seeded tomatoes, or serve with a tomato-onion sauce (pages 99 and 176) for a little pizzazz. The following recipes and variations are just a few of many possibilities, vegetarian or tucked with a little bacon or crab (see also the crabmeat flan on page 77).

Baked Vegetable Frittata

 SERVES 3 TO 4

1 tablespoon olive oil

2/3 medium or 1/2 large onion, thin crescents

2 cups broccoli florets (or equal parts broccoli and cauliflower florets)

1 small clove garlic, minced

1/2 teaspoon dried marjoram

1/4 teaspoon dried summer or winter savory (or 1/8 teaspoon dried thyme)

1/4 teaspoon salt

Few grates white pepper (*or* pinch of cayenne)

1 teaspoon butter

1 1/2 cups leftover cooked brown rice (or whole-wheat breadcrumbs)

2/3 to 3/4 cup part-skim ricotta

3 extra-large eggs

1/3 cup milk

1/8 to 1/4 teaspoon ground nutmeg or coriander

2/3 red or orange bell pepper, cut in strips

3/4 to 1 cup shredded or thinly sliced cheese (Gruyère, cheddar, goat gouda, Manchego)

Heat olive oil in sauté pan and fry onion over medium-low heat until translucent. Add broccoli (florets or sprouts, or a combination of broccoli and cauliflower) and sauté 1 to 2 minutes to seal, then add garlic and stir-steam (page 177) a minute more. Stir in seasonings, and remove from heat.

Preheat oven to 375°F. Butter 9-inch Pyrex, stoneware, or other deep-dish pie plate. Spread rice (or breadcrumbs) evenly over bottom and up sides of baking dish. Spoon filling evenly over bottom.

Put ricotta in small batter bowl and beat in eggs one at a time, then milk. Stir in nutmeg or coriander (if desired), then scrape into pie plate and smooth evenly over filling.

Decorate top with sliced red or orange pepper, then sprinkle with cheese. Bake in top third of oven for 40 to 45 minutes or until frittata is nicely puffed and golden, and a knife inserted in the middle comes out clean. Serve immediately.

Zucchini-Corn Frittata

SERVES 3 TO 4

1 1/3 to 1 1/2 cups sweet kernel corn, fresh or
    frozen, preferably shoepeg (*or* 1 1/4 cups
    breadcrumbs or diced slightly stale bread)
2 slices bacon, chopped in 1/2-inch pieces
    (optional)
1 teaspoon butter
1 tablespoon olive oil
2/3 medium or 1/2 large onion, thin crescents
1 medium (8-inch) zucchini (or combination
    zucchini and summer squash), shredded or
    thinly sliced half-moons, about 1 1/2 cups
1/2 clove garlic, minced (*or* pinch garlic powder)

1/2 teaspoon dried basil
1/4 teaspoon dried summer savory
1/4 teaspoon salt
Few grates white pepper
2/3 to 3/4 cup part-skim ricotta
1/4 cup milk
3 extra-large eggs
1/4 teaspoon ground nutmeg (optional)
3/4 to 1 cup shredded or thinly sliced cheese
    (cheddar, Asiago, Manchego, smoked
    mozzarella or provolone, Gruyère, or
    combination)

If corn is frozen, thaw in bowl in slightly warm oven. Meanwhile fry bacon (if desired) until lightly browned; remove from pan and drain on paper towel. Drain excess fat.

Butter 10-inch Pyrex, stoneware, or other deep-dish pie plate. Spread corn kernels (or breadcrumbs) evenly over bottom and up sides of baking dish.

Heat olive oil in skillet or sauté pan and fry onion over medium-low heat until translucent. Add zucchini (or zucchini and summer squash) and sauté a couple of minutes, then add garlic and sauté 1 minute more. Stir in herbs, salt, and pepper, and remove from heat. Preheat oven to 375°F.

Put ricotta in small batter bowl and beat in eggs one at a time, then add milk and nutmeg (if desired). Stir eggs and ricotta into cooled vegetable mixture.

Spoon about half of vegetable filling over the corn (or breadcrumbs). Sprinkle about 1/3 of the (optional) bacon and cheese over the first layer, then spoon in remaining filling and smooth evenly. Sprinkle with remaining cheese and bacon.

Bake 40 to 45 minutes or until frittata is nicely puffed and golden, and a knife inserted in the middle comes out clean. Serve immediately along with a salad or steamed spinach or other greens.

Variations

CRAB-ZUCCHINI FRITTATA: Omit bacon, and combine corn with sautéed vegetables as bottom layer in pie plate. Season with savory and a little basil or tarragon. Sprinkle 1/2 pound (1 pint) fresh crabmeat over vegetables, then scrape ricotta-egg mixture (omitting nutmeg) over filling and spread evenly. Decorate with thin slices of seeded fresh tomato, sprinkle cheese evenly over the top, and bake as described above.

POLENTA-SPINACH FRITTATA: Instead of corn, make 1/2 recipe Party Polenta (page 183), cool slightly, and spread over bottom and 3/4 inch up sides of buttered deep-dish pie plate. Make filling of sautéed onion, zucchini, garlic, and herbs as described above; add 2 to 2 1/2 cups washed fresh spinach to pan and cook long enough to deflate. Spread filling over polenta layer, and pour egg-ricotta mixture over all (or spread filling in two layers with egg-ricotta mixture in between). Decorate with thin slices of seeded fresh tomato, sprinkle cheese evenly over the top, and bake as described above.

Acadian Veggie Roll-ups

Ployes are an Acadian tradition still popular in northern Maine's Upper St. John Valley, where many of the French colonists of Acadia, on the Bay of Fundy—the original "Cajuns"—resettled after being deported from their homes by the British in the mid-1700s. Featuring light buckwheat flour milled in Maine (page 95), ployes are a heart-healthy alternative to crêpes: cholesterol free (no egg is added to the batter), and virtually fat free. If you have a seasoned iron griddle or skillet, you needn't grease the cooking surface; otherwise simply brush a piece of paper towel lightly soaked in oil over the hot surface. (If you are unable to find ployes mix, the delicate eggy Crêpes on page 95 are a nice alternative.)

With herbed sautéed vegetables and a tangy cheddar sauce, ployes make a light, satisfying meal. If you have some leftover lightly stir-steamed (page 177) broccoli, cauliflower, or other vegetables, they could be added to the pan with the onions and mushrooms in lieu of cooking everything from scratch.

 SERVES 2 TO 3

Savory Cheese Sauce (page 135)
1 cup ployes mix + 1 1/3 cups water (*or* Crêpes)
1 tablespoon olive oil
1 small onion, thin crescents (2/3 cup)
1/2 tablespoon butter
2 cups (8 to 10) baby portabella or other
    flavorful mushrooms, thick slices

1 clove garlic, minced
1 tablespoon white wine (or vegetable stock)
1 cup cauliflower, bite-sized florets
1/2 medium carrot, julienne (1/2 cup)
1/2 teaspoon dried summer savory (or basil)
3 cups spinach, washed and torn up (*or*
    1 cup broccoli florets)

Make sauce and set aside. Combine ployes mix with water in small bowl, smoothing out lumps.

Prepare vegetables. Heat olive oil in non-stick pan and sauté onion until translucent. Add butter and mushrooms and cook for a minute or two, then stir in garlic. Deglaze with wine (or stock). Add cauliflower (and broccoli if using in place of spinach) and cook until florets are almost cooked through, then add carrots. Finally add savory (or basil) and spinach, cover, and turn off heat.

Fry ployes as described on page 95, making 6 ployes about 7 inches in diameter; keep on plate in warm oven. When ready to serve, reheat both filling and sauce over low heat. Spoon about 1/2 cup filling in center of each ploye and roll up. Ladle cheese sauce over each serving.

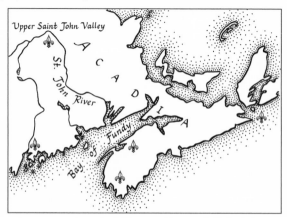

"L'Acadie," the area settled by 17th-century Acadians

SAVORY CHEESE SAUCE (MAKES 1 1/2 CUPS)

1 tablespoon butter
2 teaspoons olive oil
4 tablespoons flour
1/2 cup milk
1 cup vegetable stock (or chicken stock)
1 cup (4 ounces) cheddar cheese, sliced and
 crumbled or shredded

1 1/4 teaspoons dried marjoram
1/4 teaspoon dried summer savory
A little salt and garlic powder to taste
 (about 1/8 teaspoon each)
Few grates of "party" (multicolored) pepper
1/2 teaspoon freshly grated lemon zest or juice
 (or 2 tablespoons white wine)

In small saucepan, make a roux of the butter, oil, and flour. Remove from heat and gradually add milk, whisking until smooth after each addition. Whisk in stock and cook over moderate heat, stirring constantly, until thickened. Add cheese and stir until melted. Add marjoram and savory (double the amounts if using fresh herbs), salt, garlic powder, and pepper. If using white wine, add it now and simmer sauce a minute more; otherwise reserve lemon zest or juice to add just before serving.

CHEESES FOR COOKING

Everyone has favorite cheeses kept on hand for cooking. In recipes in this chapter and others, you'll encounter a number of old friends from our "cheese palette," introduced here with notes on their flavor, storage, and uses. Although most of these cheeses are still produced in their country of origin, some are produced domestically, in dairies large and small. Aged, imported, and artisan cheeses tend to be more expensive but worth their weight in golden flavor, so a little usually goes a long way.

PARMIGIANO-REGGIANO, OR PARMESAN (a nutty Italian cow's milk grating cheese, aged mellow like butterscotch)—use freshly grated as a garnish for soups, salads, and pasta dishes.

PECORINO ROMANO (a piquant aged Italian sheep's milk grating cheese, salty and sharp in flavor, with a hint of lamb tallow)—use freshly grated or shaved as a garnish for hearty soups, pasta dishes, and bean/vegetable stews; combine with lemon zest and fresh parsley as a "gremolata."

MANCHEGO (an aged Spanish sheep's milk cheese, somewhat milder and less salty than Romano)— use coarsely grated as a garnish for chilis and bean-vegetable soups and stews, or as a casserole topping.

MONTEREY JACK (a mild melting cheese)—use grated as a garnish for Southwestern/Mexican dishes.

ASIAGO (an aged sharp golden Italian cheddar with pungent flavor)—use shaved or coarsely grated as a garnish for pasta dishes, in sauces, or as a casserole topping.

CHEDDAR (a sharp, rich, flavorful aged melting cheese made throughout New England and the northern U.S.)—use in soups, sauces, sandwiches, on casseroles.

CHESHIRE, WENSLEYDALE, and CAERPHILLY (rich, crumbly, pale or golden English cheddars)—use crumbled over a salad, in sandwiches, or as a garnish for soup; delicious cheesecake-like flavor when paired with dried fruit.

GOAT GOUDA (a sweet, nutty, dense cheddar-like goat's milk cheese that holds its shape when heated)—use in savory fillings, toasted sandwiches, as an appetizer, or paired with fruit for dessert.

GRUYÈRE (an aged, solid Swiss cow's milk cheese, rich, sweet, and nutty)—use grated as a garnish for soups, as a casserole topping, or in toasted sandwiches.

EMMENTHALER (an aged Swiss cheese, milder and less rich than Gruyère) and JARLSBERG (a mild, semisoft Norwegian cheese)—less-expensive, yet nutty-tasting cheeses that can stand in for Gruyère.

MORBIER and RACLETTE (pungent, nutty French semisoft cheeses)—serve alone or with crackers or fruit as an appetizer or dessert; or as a flavor accent melted in sandwiches, appetizers, or over potatoes.

TALEGGIO (a rich, pungent, spreadable semisoft Italian cheese with a crust, similar to French BRIE or CAMEMBERT)—serve with fruit or crudités, or spread on bread as an appetizer or sandwich.

FONTINA (a mellow, nutty Italian melting cheese)—use in egg and pasta dishes, and on casseroles.

PROVOLONE (an Italian cow's milk melting cheese, sometimes aged, sometimes smoked; apple-smoked is particularly sweet and mellow)—use coarsely grated as a topping for casseroles, pizzas, sprinkled over stews and pasta dishes.

MOZZARELLA (a mild Italian cow's milk or buffalo milk melting cheese, stringy when cooked; apple-smoked especially flavorful)—use as a topping for casseroles, pizzas, pasta dishes.

FRESH MOZZARELLA (a mild, white, fresh-tasting cheese that melts in your mouth or anywhere warm; highly perishable, often sold in enzyme brine)—use in sandwiches, omelettes/frittatas, appetizers.

FETA (a salty, intense, crumbly white Greek cheese made from cow's milk or traditionally sheep's milk; French feta is creamier and less salty; perishable, keeps best in salted brine)—use crumbled in salads, melted on top of stews or sauces, in fillings.

CHEVRE (a tangy, white, crumbly or creamy fresh goat cheese, highly perishable)—use as a flavor accent in frittatas and casseroles, plain or herbed as a spread for sandwiches, appetizers.

RICOTTA (a mild, creamy white fresh cow's milk cheese, highly perishable)—use in flans and frittatas, as a pasta or omelette filling, a pizza topping, or in cheesecakes and other desserts.

Upscale Mac & Cheese

Ah, good ol' mac & cheese, the ultimate comfort food! Made plain or fancy, it always hits the spot. The key components of a good mac & cheese are plenty of sauce, made from scratch; fresh ingredients; complementary seasonings; and a crisp golden gratin topping, perhaps with a little fresh tomato for color, or bacon or goat cheese for interest (see variations). I love the subtly tangy combination of cumin, marjoram, pepper, and lemon zest in this hearty cheese sauce, but if your taste buds prefer something plainer, go with what you like. Make plenty—leftover mac & cheese is delicious reheated for lunch.

 SERVES 4

3 1/2 to 4 cups cooked chioccciole (large elbows) or pennes, about 6 ounces dry pasta

~ SAUCE ~

1 tablespoon olive oil

1 small (or 1/2 medium) onion, minced

2 teaspoons salted butter

3 tablespoons unbleached flour

1 1/2 cups milk

1/2 cup chicken or turkey stock (or water or vegetable stock)

1 teaspoon marjoram

1/4 teaspoon white pepper + tiny pinch cayenne

1/4 teaspoon salt

1/4 teaspoon cumin (optional)

1 2/3 cups shredded Manchego, cheddar, or Italian cheddar cheese (or combination)

~ GRATIN TOPPING ~

2/3 to 3/4 cup dry breadcrumbs (1 to 2 slices bread, or 4 to 5 crushed breadsticks)

2 teaspoons olive oil

3 teaspoons grated Romano (or Parmesan)

1/2 teaspoon lemon zest (optional)

Set pot of pasta water to boil and have ready about 6 ounces dry pasta.

Heat oil in medium saucepan and sauté onion until translucent. Melt butter into onions, then simultaneously sprinkle and stir in flour, and cook over low heat for about 1 minute. Remove from heat and gradually whisk in about half of the milk, stirring constantly to smooth out flour lumps. Return to heat and gradually whisk in remaining milk and stock. Add seasonings, and cook over low heat for another minute or so, stirring constantly, until sauce is thickened. Melt in the cheese, then remove sauce from heat.

Boil pasta until tender, then drain in colander and spread in 8 x 8-inch ovenproof casserole. Pour cheese sauce over pasta and stir to distribute evenly. Preheat oven to 375°F.

While pasta is cooking, prepare gratin topping: On a large piece of waxed paper, grate bread or crush breadsticks (see "Golden Gratin"). Sprinkle olive oil over crumbs and toss with fingers to work in evenly. Add grated Romano and lemon zest. Sprinkle gratin topping over the sauced pasta.

Bake 15 minutes at 375°, then another 20 to 30 minutes at 350°, or until pasta is hot through and bubbling and gratin topping is nicely golden. Serve with steamed green vegetables or a salad.

Variations

MAC & CHEESE WITH CHEVRE: Use 1 1/4 cups grated cheese in the sauce. Before sprinkling with gratin topping, dot top of sauced pasta with small knobs of plain chevre (about 5/8 cup fresh goat cheese), gently pressing them into the sauce. Then sprinkle gratin topping over all and bake as described above.

MAC & CHEESE WITH BACON: Cut 2 slices bacon in 3/4-inch pieces and fry gently, "trying out" most of the fat. Drain on paper towels. Before sprinkling gratin topping, arrange bacon on top of sauced pasta. Then sprinkle gratin topping over all and bake as described above.

MAC & CHEESE WITH TOMATOES: Omit cumin from sauce. Slice 1 or 2 seeded tomatoes (beefsteak or plum; the riper and more flavorful, the better) and arrange slices on top of sauced pasta. Scatter a little crushed dried basil over the tomatoes, then sprinkle gratin topping over all and bake as described above.

GOLDEN GRATIN

I always thought au gratin meant "with cheese," but it actually refers to the grated crumbs and/or cheese gilding the casserole, sprinkled on top and browned. Whether you use sesame breadsticks or crackers (as we do) crushed with a rolling pin, or breadcrumbs grated from dry bread, adding a little olive oil to gratin crumbs helps them crisp up nicely. For seasoned crumbs, add a little grated Parmesan, Asiago, or other cheese, along with some dried herbs.

If you use crackers or breadsticks, be sure they are fairly fresh; if in doubt, taste them first to make sure the oils haven't turned rancid. Break them in sections and place in a plastic bag or between folds of a sheet of waxed paper, then crush with a rolling pin. If using bread, it will grate a little easier if you lightly toast it, sliced, in a slow oven, then let it cool before grating.

Homemade Pizza

Next to the instant gratification of store or parlor pizza, making pizzas at home from scratch takes a commitment of time and effort . . . but it's also a fun and creative collaboration, and the taste beyond compare. Maybe it's the chunky homemade sauce, the light crisp multigrain crust, or the colorful combination of toppings all just "As You Like It" (the name of my favorite pizza at Blue Hill's former eatery, Pie in the Sky, and its predecessor Petty's Pizza, which inspired this recipe). . . . In any case, fresh pizza made from scratch, generously loaded with good stuff, is a very fine thing. Finer yet are leftovers reheated the next day (be prepared for plate envy at work). This recipe makes two 12-inch deep-dish pizzas, more than enough for two to share for dinner, leaving the second one to look forward to for lunch.

The combination of flours makes for a crispy crust with good flavor and texture. King Arthur's unbleached bread flour and semolina (pasta) flour, both milled from hard wheat, produce an easy-handling dough.

The best pizza sauce is simple, but it's nice if there's a little more to the sauce than just puréed tomatoes and paste. The simmered sauce is worth the few extra minutes it takes to sauté onion and garlic and marry the flavors a bit. But if you're pressed for time, go the quick route (see page 139).

For a vegetarian pizza, baby portabella mushrooms, sliced or briefly sautéed in olive oil with a little pressed garlic, would be a flavorful replacement for sausage.

 SERVES 3 TO 4

1 recipe Pizza Crust (below)

3 cups Simmered Pizza Sauce (page 139)

3 to 4 cups fresh spinach leaves, washed, stemmed, and patted dry

1/2 green bell pepper, seeds and membranes removed, sliced in 1/8-inch rings

1/2 yellow or orange bell pepper, seeds and membranes removed, 1/8-inch rings

1 to 1 1/3 cups part-skim ricotta

1/2 red, yellow, or Vidalia onion, thinly sliced and separated into rings

2 to 2 1/3 cups shredded smoked provolone or mozzarella cheese (or combination of smoked provolone and Manchego)

2 (6 ounces) Italian or fennel sausages, coins (or 4 to 5 ounces sliced summer sausage or linguiça; or 2 cups baby portabella mushrooms, 1/4-inch slices)

PIZZA CRUST

1 package rapid-rise dry yeast

1 cup very warm water

1/2 teaspoon organic or white sugar

1 tablespoon extra-virgin olive oil

1 1/2 cups whole-wheat bread flour

1/4 cup yellow corn flour or cornmeal

1/4 cup fine semolina (pasta) flour

1 cup unbleached bread flour (reserve 1/4 cup for kneading)

1/4 teaspoon salt

2 to 3 tablespoons coarse cornmeal or semolina flour

Sprinkle yeast over warm water in large ceramic mixing bowl. Stir in sugar and proof 5 minutes while you assemble dry ingredients (flours through salt) in separate bowl. Add olive oil to yeast mixture, then add flour mixture and stir with wooden spoon until dough comes together.

Turn pizza dough out onto floured surface and knead for 6 to 8 minutes, or until dough is elastic.

Clean and rinse bowl, oil liberally with olive oil, and roll ball of dough around to coat. Cover with damp dishtowel and let rise in warm, draft-free place 30 to 40 minutes, or until doubled.

While dough is rising, make Simmered Pizza Sauce and prepare vegetable toppings: Pat spinach dry between clean towels, and tear large leaves in half. Slice peppers, removing seeds and membranes. Grate cheese. Prick sausages with knife and parboil in a little water to release some fat; drain, cool, and slice in 1/4- to 3/8-inch coins. (Or if using mushrooms, cut in thick slices and have ready to put on pizza, either raw or very briefly sautéed in garlicky oil.)

Sprinkle coarse cornmeal or semolina flour evenly over 2 round 12-inch pizza pans, to prevent scorching bottom of crust. (Or, use a pizza stone under each pan to even out the heat.)

Punch dough down and knead briefly on lightly floured surface. Divide in half and, one at a time, roll each ball of dough out to 12 to 13 inches diameter. Transfer dough to pizza pan by wrapping it around rolling pin, then unfurling across the pan. Adjust dough as needed to cover pan and form a lip around the edge. Repeat with other crust.

Preheat oven to 425°F, setting 2 racks near top of oven. (Depending on the size of your oven, both pans may not fit on the top rack, in which case you'll need to juggle them back and forth a couple of times for even baking.) While the oven is preheating, assemble the pizzas: Fill center of each pizza crust with sauce, swirling with ladle out to edge. Then layer pizza toppings in the order listed, beginning with the spinach and peppers; dot spoonfuls of ricotta between pepper rings. Top with onion (and mushrooms, if using in place of sausage). Sprinkle cheese evenly over the pizzas, then distribute sausage coins over the cheese.

Bake pizzas, one pan to each side of oven, for about 6 minutes; then rotate pans and positions on racks. Continue baking for another 6 minutes, then swap again. Reduce heat to 400°, bake another 6 minutes, and swap again. From here on, watch the pizzas like a hawk, checking the underside of the crust every few minutes to see whether it is beginning to brown up (gently lift edge to check for doneness), for a total baking time of 20 to 25 minutes. Do not overbake.

Serve immediately, cutting each pizza into 6 wedges. If your pans are non-stick, you can work a steel spatula and serrated knife together like scissors to cut the pizza without scratching the pan.

SIMMERED PIZZA SAUCE (MAKES 3 1/2 CUPS)

2 to 3 teaspoons olive oil	1 to 2 teaspoons dried oregano
1/2 onion, minced	1 teaspoon dried basil
1 clove garlic, minced	1 teaspoon dried marjoram
1 28-ounce can crushed tomatoes	Sugar, salt, pepper, balsamic vinegar to taste

Sauté onion in olive oil, then add garlic briefly. Pour in tomatoes and add herbs. (For a quicker sauce, replace onion with 1/4 teaspoon onion powder and raw garlic with 1/4 teaspoon garlic powder.) Sample a little of the tomato juice and adjust flavor to taste by adding a pinch of sugar, a shake of salt, and/or a few grinds of pepper. Bring sauce up to heat and simmer for 5 to 8 minutes before ladling onto pizza crust. Any leftover sauce can be used in a soup, stew, or pasta dish.

Ricotta-Stuffed Shells

Festive and fun to make, this is also one of the quickest dinners in our repertoire. When it's just us, and a batch of stuffed shells will make enough for a second meal, we keep the sauce simple and serve a separate vegetable, either sautéed, steamed, or in a salad. But if making this as a vegetarian main-dish casserole, you could add a mix of summer vegetables—Romano beans, eggplant, summer squash or zucchini, lightly sautéed with extra onion and garlic—to the sauce in place of the sausages.

 SERVES 4

3 cups Rustic Tomato Sauce (opposite)
2 sweet Italian or fennel sausages (optional)
16 to 20 jumbo pasta shells
1 1/3 to 1 1/2 cups ricotta cheese, part-skim

1 extra-large egg
1/2 teaspoon lemon zest (optional)
1 to 1 1/4 cups shredded provolone or smoked
    mozzarella (preferably apple-smoked)

Make tomato sauce and let simmer. Meanwhile, prick sausage (if using) and parboil in separate pot in 1/2 inch of water to reduce fat; drain on paper towel. When cool, slice sausage into 5/8-inch chunks or coins and add to sauce.

For the pasta shells, bring a large pot of water to boil. Meanwhile, combine ricotta, egg, and lemon zest in separate bowl, and grate the cheese. Plop shells one at a time into boiling water and cook, stirring occasionally, until al dente; then pour off hot water and cover shells with cool water.

Preheat oven to 375°F. Ladle sauce into 7 x 11- or 8 x 12-inch casserole. Fill shells with ricotta mixture and set on top of sauce. (NOTE: Like a good Maine harbormaster, you'll want to have all your "boats" pointing into the wind, oriented diagonally in their harbor of sauce.) Sprinkle evenly with cheese and bake 30 to 40 minutes, or until cheese is golden. Let stand a few minutes before serving.

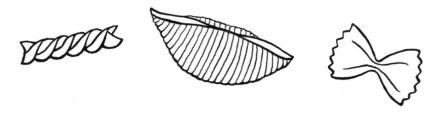

DOCTORING TOMATOES

Not all tomatoes are created equal. I often wondered about tomato sauce recipes calling for sugar or balsamic vinegar until, after comparing our home-canned ripe tomatoes to commercially canned ones, I realized why: Since commercially canned tomatoes usually have added salt and citric acid (as preservatives), they can often taste too salty or sour. For this reason, when making tomato sauce from canned plum tomatoes, many cooks see fit to adjust the acid/sugar balance to taste. The same goes with hothouse-grown plum or "cluster" tomatoes, which more often than not lack the full, ripe flavor of garden-ripe tomatoes. The judicious addition of a few drops of balsamic or red wine sage vinegar, or a pinch of light brown sugar—or both—can greatly improve the flavor of your sauce.

RUSTIC TOMATO SAUCE

There are plenty of "rustic" jarred sauces you can buy (for a price!), but there's nothing as rustic—or economical—as your own kitchen, and your own garden herbs and vegetables. Actually, you can have the best of both worlds, if you have a bumper crop of plum tomatoes, by putting up batches of homemade sauce—a very nice thing to have in the freezer or on your pantry shelf.

The proportions here are scaled to a single meal, such as Ricotta-Stuffed Shells (opposite) or Eggplant Parmesan (page 142)—or simply add a couple of sweet and/or hot Italian sausages, parboiled and sliced in chunks or coins, with perhaps some sautéed green bell peppers, for a quick spaghetti supper for two. Any leftover sauce could be the making of a Quick Minestrone (page 33).

MAKES 3 CUPS

1 large onion, sliced into crescents
1 1/2 tablespoons olive oil
2 cloves garlic, minced or pressed
2 teaspoons oregano
2 teaspoons basil
1/4 teaspoon crushed fennel seeds (*or* 1/2 teaspoon thyme)

1 teaspoon marjoram
1 1/2 pints (16-ounce can) Italian plum tomatoes (drain off any watery juice)
1/2 teaspoon balsamic vinegar (optional)
Pinch of salt (as needed)
1/2 teaspoon light brown sugar (as needed)
Freshly grated "party" (multicolored) pepper

To make tomato sauce, sauté onion in oil. Lower heat to moderate and add garlic, then herbs, then tomatoes, vinegar, and other seasonings. (Add sugar only if canned tomatoes taste a little sour.) Simmer uncovered for 15 to 20 minutes, so that it cooks down to a rich sauce.

NOTE: For two other tomato sauces with more complex flavors, to be served more as a condiment, see the Caramelized Onion-Tomato Sauce (page 99) and Slow-Roasted Tomato-Onion Confit (page 176).

PASTA TRANSLATIONS

Intrigued by all the pasta names and shapes? Wandering through a couple of dictionaries (Italian and English), I came up with rough literal translations of some of the more common pasta shapes:

agnoletti = priests' caps	fettuccine = narrow ribbons	radiatore = radiators
bucatelli = pierced, bored	fusilli = spindles	ravioli = little turnips
cannelloni = pipes	gemelli = twins, cufflinks	rigatoni = striped
capellini = fine hair	gnocchi = dumplings	rotini = little twirls
cappelletti = little hats	lasagna = noodle dish	spaghetti = cords, strings
cavatappi = corkscrews	linguine = thin strips, tongues	tagliatelle = cut strips
chiocciole = snails	manicotti = muffs	tortellini = little pies
chitarra = guitar strings	orecchiette = little ears	tubetti = little tubes
conchiglie = shells	orzo = barley	vermicelli = little worms
farfalle = butterflies	penne = penpoints	ziti = bride's macaroni

Eggplant Parmesan

This classic southern Italian dish is traditionally quite rich, with the eggplant breaded and fried until crisp in olive oil, layered with sauce and cheese. The simpler approach of baking the eggplant in a little olive oil until tender makes for a lot less fuss, fewer dishes, and fewer calories. The fresh light flavors of eggplant and ricotta, spiked with a little lemon zest and laced with a generously herbed tomato sauce, combine in a satisfying dish rich in calcium and flavor.

The proportions here are general, meant to be scaled to the size of the eggplant and number of servings desired. Including green vegetables in the casserole makes it a meal-in-itself, otherwise serve them separately, sautéed or in a tossed salad.

 SERVES 3 TO 4

1 medium to large eggplant, peeled, 1/4-inch slices (rounds or halved lengthwise slices)

2 tablespoons olive oil

2 to 3 cups Rustic Tomato Sauce (page 141)

1 1/2 cups Romano beans, fresh or frozen, halved (*or* 1 1/2 to 2 cups fresh spinach) (optional)

1 1/4 to 1 1/3 cups ricotta, part-skim

1 large egg

1 teaspoon lemon zest (optional)

Few grates "party" (multicolored) pepper

3 ounces mozzarella, "string cheese" or braided, pulled in thin strips + 1/3 cup grated Romano or Parmesan (*or* 1 to 1 1/2 cups shredded smoked provolone or mozzarella)

Preheat oven to 350°F. Peel and slice eggplant and arrange slices on a baking sheet greased with 1 tablespoon olive oil. Bake until eggplant begins to steam, then flip to other side and bake until tender. Take from oven and let cool on baking sheet, and turn off oven. (Or if you prefer the traditional breaded-and-fried eggplant, coat both sides of each eggplant slice in herbed bread crumbs or unbleached flour seasoned with a little salt and black pepper, then in beaten egg, then again in flour. Heat 2 to 3 tablespoons olive oil, as needed, in skillet and brown eggplant on both sides; set aside to drain on a paper towel.)

Meanwhile, prepare Rustic Tomato Sauce (page 141). If you want to include Romanos, add them to the sauce and simmer 1 to 2 minutes; the beans needn't be cooked through. (If using spinach, wash, trim, pat dry, and tear large leaves into smaller pieces; set aside.)

Spoon about half of the sauce into the bottom of an 8 x 8-inch or 7 x 11-inch casserole. Sort eggplant slices into even-sized pairs. Arrange half of the eggplant slices on top of sauce.

Preheat oven to 375°F. Beat together ricotta, egg, zest, and pepper, and spoon evenly over eggplant slices. Top with remaining eggplant. Finally spoon remaining sauce over eggplant. If using spinach, distribute leaves over top and press into sauce. Decorate top of casserole with 4-inch thin strips of unsmoked mozzarella "string cheese" laid in lattice pattern, then sprinkle with grated Romano or Parmesan. (Or, sprinkle casserole evenly with shredded smoked provolone or mozzarella.)

Bake, loosely covered with foil, for about 15 minutes, then bake another 15 to 20 minutes uncovered until cheese is nicely browned.

Florentine Eggplant Roll-ups

The combination of spinach or chard, garlic, pine nuts, and raisins or currants, sometimes with cured pork or ricotta and cheese, is an ancient one, still popular in central Italy. In American and French cuisine this combination of ingredients, particularly with spinach, is often labeled "Florentine"—perhaps more as a culinary term, though, than as indicating a dish made in Florence.

And yet, I did come across a recipe in The New Romagnolis' Table *for a Florentine-style pasta roll filled with spinach and ricotta and served with tomato-basil sauce—an appetizer rather similar to one I sampled at the former Turriglio's Ristorante in Ellsworth. There, instead of fresh pasta, the spinach-ricotta filling was sprinkled with pine nuts and rolled in tender slices of baked eggplant, and served with a simple tomato sauce. As the center of a delicious light meal with pasta, it was memorable enough to try and re-create at home, hence this recipe.*

Whether authentically Florentine or not, dishes like this bring on a Botticelli-inspired reverie of Renaissance Italy, timeless villages, and the enjoyment of life's finer pleasures.

 SERVES 2 AS MAIN COURSE, 4 AS APPETIZER

1 large eggplant, skinned and sliced lengthwise
    (1/4- to 3/8-inch slabs)
1 tablespoon olive oil
1 cup ricotta, part-skim
1 large egg
Dash of salt
2 teaspoons olive oil
1/2 medium onion, chopped
1/2 clove garlic, minced (*or* 1/8 teaspoon
    garlic powder)

2 to 2 1/2 cups fresh spinach, washed, stemmed,
    coarsely chopped
1 tablespoon fresh basil (1 1/2 teaspoons dried)
1/4 teaspoon dried marjoram
1/4 cup pine nuts, raw or very lightly toasted
    (page 144)
2 tablespoons dried currants
1 3/4 to 2 cups Simmered Pizza Sauce (page
    139), about 1/2 recipe (or other tomato
    sauce)

Preheat oven to 350°F. Peel and slice eggplant and arrange slices on baking sheet greased with olive oil. Bake until eggplant begins to steam, then flip to other side and bake until tender. Take from oven and let cool on baking sheet.

Meanwhile, mix ricotta with egg and set aside. To make filling, heat oil in non-stick skillet and sauté onion until translucent, then add garlic and sauté for a minute more. Add spinach, partly cover, and cook over medium-low heat until spinach is deflated. Add herbs.

Lightly toast pine nuts (page 144) if desired. Make or reheat 1/2 recipe Simmered Pizza Sauce, and ladle about two-thirds of sauce (1 1/4 cups) into 8 x 8-inch ovenproof baking dish.

Divide ricotta mixture evenly among eggplant slices, and spread thinly over each slice, favoring the wide end, letting it run out toward the tail end. Sprinkle with pine nuts and currants. Distribute spinach filling evenly over slices. Roll up eggplant, starting with the wide end; hold with toothpick if necessary. Place roll-ups tail-down in dish, and spoon remaining sauce over the tops.

Bake at 350° for about 20 to 25 minutes, or until roll-ups are hot through and ricotta filling is set.

Serve with white or brown basmati rice, linguine or angel hair pasta, or warmed focaccia or crusty bread (page 33) drizzled with olive oil.

Pasta Romagna

A delicious balance of Renaissance flavors, combining ingredients popular in Romagna and other parts of central Italy, this simple one-pot pasta toss is quick to assemble and makes a satisfying lunch dish. Artichoke linguine or fettucine makes a simple backdrop for the colorful sauté, but use whatever shape of pasta you fancy.

For a vegetarian version, omit the pork and garnish with smoked provolone cheese. Or, try one of the Pasta e Fagoli recipes (pages 147–48), which combine similar ingredients with shell beans.

 SERVES 2

1 tablespoon olive oil
1/2 large onion, sliced in crescents
1 clove garlic, minced
2 fresh plum tomatoes, seeded, chunks
2 tablespoons dried currants (or sultanas)
2/3 to 3/4 cup leftover roast or pan-fried pork butt (shoulder) or pancetta, thinly sliced (*or* 1/2 cup smoked provolone), optional

2 cups fresh spinach leaves, washed, stemmed, large leaves torn into pieces (or Tuscan kale or Swiss chard, stemmed and chopped)
1 to 2 tablespoons Genovese Pesto (page 21)
Few grates black pepper
Salt to taste
4 ounces dry pasta, boiled and drained
2 tablespoons pine nuts, very lightly toasted

Set pot of water to boil for pasta. Meanwhile, prepare vegetables and other ingredients.

Heat olive oil in non-stick skillet or heavy-bottomed saucepan and sauté onion until just beginning to turn gold, then add garlic. (If using kale or chard, add to the pot and sauté/sweat along with the onion and garlic.) Add chopped tomato, currants, and pork or pancetta (if desired). If using spinach, add to pot and cook briefly over moderate heat, stirring occasionally, until the greens have deflated. Stir in pesto. Taste for seasonings and add a little salt or pepper as needed; remove from heat. Set water to boil for pasta; toast pine nuts (see below).

Boil pasta, drain, and drizzle with a little olive oil and butter. When ready to serve, quickly bring vegetable mixture back up to heat, then divide between individual portions of pasta served in shallow bowls. (For vegetarian version, top each serving with smoked provolone.) Serve immediately, leaving it to each diner to toss vegetable mixture with pasta.

PINE NUTS

Pine nuts (pignoli) are a favored ingredient not just in Italian dishes, but in cuisines throughout the Mediterranean and Middle East where these edible-nut pines thrive. In North America, several species of piñon pines grow throughout the Southwest, from the Rockies to New Mexico, California, and into Mexico, where the nuts (harvested from the pine cones) have long been an important food source for native peoples. Their rich, sweet, resinous flavor gives a unique accent to many dishes.

To bring out their full flavor, toast pine nuts in a preheated 325°F oven for just 2 to 3 minutes, shaking the pan frequently, until they begin turning a very light gold. Or, pan-roast them in a heavy-bottomed skillet over low heat—dry or in a little olive oil—stirring constantly, until lightly toasted. It only takes a minute, so give them your undivided attention; too brown, and they'll taste bitter.

Tuscan One-Pot

Here's one of my favorite one-woman workday lunches, combining all your basic Italian "food groups" in a simple one-pot meal. If no fresh or frozen shell beans (page 146) are at hand, leftover cooked dry beans (such as Bumblebee, cannellini, cranberry, or horticultural beans, page 156) will do just fine. With pesto in the freezer and the other staple ingredients, it's quick to stir up, satisfying, and rich in vitamins and calcium—especially the ricotta variation (kind of a stovetop lasagna). Toast rounds out the meal, otherwise a bit of leftover cooked pasta, such as bowties or spirals, could be added to the pot.

SERVES 1

1 tablespoon olive oil

1/4 onion, minced

1 to 1 1/3 cups Tuscan (lacinato) kale, about
    3 medium leaves (or savoyed spinach or
    rainbow Swiss chard), stems removed, cut or
    torn in bite-sized pieces

Dash of garlic powder (less than 1/8 teaspoon)

1 to 2 fresh or canned plum tomatoes, chopped
    (or 2 to 3 sundried tomato halves, snipped
    and soaked in a little water or marsala)

1/2 to 2/3 cup fresh/frozen shell beans, boiled
    till tender (or leftover cooked dry beans)

1/2 to 1 tablespoon fresh or frozen pesto (or
    1 teaspoon dried basil)

Salt and "party" (multicolored) pepper to taste

2 tablespoons shaved or thinly sliced aged
    Parmesan, Romano, Manchego, or smoked
    provolone cheese

1 tablespoon pine nuts, raw or very lightly
    toasted (page 144)

Heat oil in small heavy-bottomed pot or non-stick saucepan, and sauté onion over medium-low heat. Add kale (or spinach or chard) and stir-fry until leaves begin to deflate. Sprinkle with garlic powder, and toss in tomatoes, and stir-fry for another half minute; then add shell beans, pesto or basil, salt and pepper. Sprinkle in a little more water if needed to keep things from catching on.

Partly cover pot, reduce heat, and cook a minute more until vegetables are tender. Sprinkle with cheese and cook covered over very low heat 1 to 2 minutes more, just long enough to melt the cheese. Serve sprinkled with pine nuts, accompanied by toast drizzled with extra-virgin olive oil.

Variation

RICOTTA ONE-POT: Use dried tomatoes; and instead of the shell beans, stir 3/4 cup cooked pasta in with the sautéed, seasoned vegetables. When hot through, add 1/2 cup part-skim ricotta to the pot, dropping 4 or 5 small spoonfuls around the top. Sprinkle with cheese, cover, and cook over very low heat 1 to 2 minutes more, just long enough to warm the ricotta and melt the cheese. Serve sprinkled with pine nuts.

SHELL BEANS

I must have a Tuscan farmwife's soul, because there's nothing I love better for a quick, simple dinner than a pasta dish featuring shell beans. The following pasta e fagioli variations are two favorites. Buttery shell beans, boiled till tender, are satisfying even just tossed with a little pressed garlic, olive oil, and summer savory, rosemary, or thyme. Or, compatible with any Italian ingredients you desire— pine nuts, basil, fresh or sundried tomatoes, summer squashes, Tuscan kale, bacon, pork or sausage, cheese—they can be the center of a healthy, colorful, well-balanced meal . . . and a quick one, too, if you have some in your freezer. Unlike dry beans, which need thinking ahead to soak and precook, with shell beans all you need for lead time is the 10 or 15 minutes it takes to boil them.

They'll probably need to be home-grown, though, or from an ethnic or local farmer's market, because for whatever reason, shell beans (other than edamame) haven't really caught on in Maine as a commercial product. We've grown them from seed marketed specifically for shell beans—such as Tongue of Fire and other varieties of French horticultural beans—but have also had steady success with dry bean varieties like Bumblebee (page 156), harvesting them a little early while the bean skins are still tender. Really most any plump, relatively thin-skinned dry bean will do, or even a broad pole bean like Kwintus (page 54) let go to the shell-bean stage; just harvest them before the pods turn brown and dry. You want to catch them when there is a little color to the developing beans, but while they are at their height of plump, buttery freshness, before they begin to harden up.

It is pleasant work to shell them, sitting outside in the late-afternoon sun, a glass of wine at hand, crickets humming in the field, maybe some Celtic reels . . . Your bounty of freshly shelled beans can then be refrigerated for a few hours or a day or two until you are ready to blanch and freeze them, or use them fresh in a meal. Either way, they are the essence of late summer.

To blanch, bring water to boil in a large lidded pot. Throw batches of the shelled beans into the pot, a quart of beans at a time, replace the lid, and cook in boiling water for about 20 to 30 seconds, until their tourmaline colors (green, rose, pinkish-tan) brighten and the outside of the bean looks translucent—just long enough to zap the enzymes in the skin. Plunge them into ice water (a pot or large bowl of water chilled with ice cubes) for a few minutes, then drain and put in freezer bags.

When ready to cook a meal with shell beans, take them from the freezer and parboil until tender (8 to 12 minutes); do not overcook, as they will continue cooking once added to the rest of the dish.

 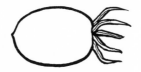

DRYING TOMATOES

Drying your own home-grown tomatoes is a fine home economy. Principe Borghesi, an Italian heirloom sold by Fedco Seeds and John Scheepers Kitchen Garden Seeds, is a small plum tomato perfect for drying, having fewer seeds and the intense flavor you expect from a sundried tomato. But you can dry saladettes (like Juliet) or other small, meaty, full-flavored plum tomatoes. Cut them in half, core and seed, and arrange skin-side down on nonreactive screens or racks in a dehydrator, solar dryer or hot greenhouse, or 120–140°F gas oven. Dry for 10 to 20 hours, spreading them open as they curl, until dry and leathery with no tacky spots (finish off in oven if necessary). Store in airtight bags.

Pasta e Fagioli with Pine Nuts & Dried Tomatoes

This classic Italian dish celebrates late summer's vine-ripened vegetables, fresh herbs, and bright flavors. But with sundried tomatoes and blanched shell beans laid by in the freezer (page 146), you can enjoy a taste of summer any time of year.

Roman-style pasta e fagioli, made as a soup or stew, traditionally includes bacon, pancetta, or salt pork, onion, garlic, and savory herbs, as in the following heartier version with kale or the White Beans & Bacon on page 149. Here the golden richness of toasted pine nuts and molten aged cheese take the place of pork.

Dried tomatoes are wonderful to cook with in this type of summer vegetable stew, adding bright, intense notes of flavor without giving themselves to the sauce; this lets the vegetables hold their own distinct flavors and sweet juices. But if you have a bounty of vine-ripe plum tomatoes, by all means substitute them for the dried tomatoes. With this or any of the rustic Italian bean dishes, any leftovers can be the makings of a Quick Minestrone (page 33).

 SERVES 4

2 1/2 to 3 cups fresh or frozen shell beans, par-boiled until al dente (or cooked cannellini or other large, plump white beans, most of the liquid drained)

1/2 to 2/3 cup sundried tomatoes (*or* 2 cups ripe plum tomatoes, seeded and chopped)

1/2 cup white wine and/or vegetable broth

2 tablespoons extra-virgin olive oil

1 large onion, sliced in crescents

4 cloves garlic, pressed or finely minced

2 small to medium zucchini and/or summer squash, coins or half-moons

1 tablespoon dried basil

1 1/2 teaspoons dried Greek oregano

Few grates black or multicolored pepper

Dash of salt

About 8 ounces dried pasta (linguine or fettucine, whole-wheat or handmade), or enough fresh pasta for 4 servings

1 to 1 1/2 cups shaved Manchego, Asiago, or smoked provolone cheese

1/3 cup pine nuts, very lightly toasted (page 144)

Boil shell beans (or soaked dry beans) until tender or a little al dente (page 146 or 152); drain off most of the cooking liquid, and set aside. Snip sundried tomatoes into bite-sized strips and soak in wine or broth in a small cup. (Or, seed and chop fresh plum tomatoes.)

Heat oil in large skillet or Dutch oven and sauté onion until translucent. Add garlic and zucchini and/or squash and sauté for a minute or two; cover skillet for the last minute to sweat the squash. Add basil and oregano (twice as much if using fresh herbs), salt and pepper, then stir in the tomatoes with their liquid and finally the beans. Simmer, covered, over low heat for about 5 minutes. Then remove from heat and prepare the rest of the meal, and bring back up to heat when ready to serve.

Serve over freshly cooked, drained, oiled and/or buttered pasta, generously sprinkled with the cheese and the pine nuts. Round out the meal with a fresh tossed salad dressed with vinaigrette, and a warmed crusty boule (page 33) or multigrain garlic bread.

Pasta e Fagioli with Pork & Plum Tomatoes

Pork and fennel lovers will enjoy this robust variation on the theme of Mediterranean "pork & beans," a rustic stew of ingredients that travel well and come together easily in a single cookpot. The rich-flavored pork and sweet fennel stand up to the strong flavors of Tuscan (lacinato) kale and aged cheese—all a good foil for shell beans, if you have some (page 146); otherwise, use soaked and cooked dried beans (pages 152, 156). Any leftovers would be a fine addition to a Quick Minestrone (page 33).

 SERVES 4

2 1/2 to 3 cups fresh or frozen shell beans, par-boiled until al dente (or cooked cannellini or other large, plump white beans, most of the liquid drained)

2 (6 ounces) sweet Italian sausages (or 1/2 to 2/3 pound pork butt or thick bacon, cut in bite-sized pieces, or leftover cooked pork)

1 tablespoon extra-virgin olive oil

1 large onion, sliced in crescents

2 to 4 cloves garlic, pressed or finely minced

1 1/2 to 2 cups chopped fresh or canned plum tomatoes

1/4 to 1/2 cup bean stock, tomato juice, or wine

1 1/2 tablespoons fresh basil (2 teaspoons dried)

2 teaspoons fresh oregano (1 teaspoon dried)

1/4 teaspoon thyme

1/8 teaspoon fennel seeds, crushed in mortar and pestle (or 1 small sprig rosemary)

1/2 teaspoon summer savory

Few grates black or multicolored pepper

Dash of salt

2 cups tender Tuscan kale (or spinach)

1 to 1 1/2 cups shaved Manchego, Asiago, or smoked provolone cheese

About 8 ounces dried pasta (linguine or fettucine, whole-wheat or handmade), or enough fresh pasta for 4 servings

Boil shell beans (or soaked dry beans) until tender or a little al dente; drain off most of the cooking liquid, and set aside. Parboil sausage to release some of the fat; when cooled, cut in bite-sized coins or half-moons. Or, if using bacon or pork butt, cut in bite-sized pieces and brown in large saucepan or Dutch oven; drain fat from pan. (If using leftover cooked pork, cut in bite-sized pieces.)

Add olive oil to pan and sauté onion until translucent. Then add garlic and sauté over low heat for a minute. Return meat to pan and add tomatoes, 1/4 to 1/2 cup liquid (bean stock, tomato juice, wine, or a combination), the herbs, salt and pepper, and finally the beans. Simmer, covered, over low heat for about 5 minutes. (If using canned or hothouse tomatoes, add a pinch of brown sugar and a few drops of balsamic or red wine vinegar to correct the flavor balance; see page 140.) Then remove from heat and prepare the rest of the meal, giving the flavors a chance to get to know each other.

Wash kale (or spinach), discard tough stems, and coarsely chop. When ready to serve, distribute kale over the top and bring the stew back up to heat, cooking just long enough to deflate the leaves. Serve over freshly cooked oiled/buttered pasta, and sprinkle with shaved cheese.

Variation

SHELL BEANS WITH LAMB: Use leftover lamb roasted with garlic and rosemary, or leftover Mediterranean Lamb Shanks (page 119), cut in bite-sized pieces, in place of the pork. Omit fennel, and use 1 to 2 cloves garlic. Serve over whole-wheat pasta or rice. Sprinkle with a little coarsely grated Manchego or Romano cheese, if desired. Leftover stew could be stretched into a soup (pages 33–35).

White Beans & Bacon (Cassoulet)

This Mediterranean "pork & beans" has ancient roots in northern Italy, where it takes the form of a very simple dish, and in southern France as the much more elaborate "cassoulet" involving layers of beans and rich viands and hours of slow cooking in the oven. We lean toward the stovetop approach of Tuscany, with the emphasis on the beans, savory herbs, and a small amount of tomatoes and bacon or pork for flavor. (A generous sprinkling of apple-smoked provolone would carry that smoky flavor in a vegetarian version, making a complete protein with the beans.)

Although the cooking time is short, making the stew a little ahead will give the flavors a chance to meld. Any leftovers could be recycled into a Quick Minestrone (page 33) or other soup; with this in mind, you might want to reserve more of the cooking liquid from the beans.

The stew can be finished off in the oven as a pork or lamb cassoulet (see variations), less meat-rich than the classic layering of sausage, bacon, pork, and duck confit among a background of beans.

Although traditional recipes call for cannellini (white kidney beans) or the smaller Great Northern beans, we like to use one of the meatier local heirloom varieties such as Bumblebee, Snowcap, or Big-Eye Yelloweye (all grown by The Beanery, page 156).

℞ SERVES 3 TO 4

1 1/4 cups large dry white or speckled beans, such as cannellini, Bumblebee, Big-Eye Yelloweye, or Snowcap (2 3/4 cups cooked beans)

1 bay leaf

1/3 cup cooking liquid from beans

1 tablespoon olive oil

2 to 3 slices slab/thick bacon or pancetta, 1/2-inch pieces (*or* 2 sweet Italian sausages, parboiled and sliced in coins; *or* pan-fried pork, see variation)

1 medium onion, crescents

2 cloves garlic, minced

1/2 to 1 teaspoon red wine sage vinegar (page 49)

1/2 cup chicken or vegetable stock

2 to 3 fresh or canned plum tomatoes, chopped

1/4 cup juice from tomatoes

1/2 to 3/4 teaspoon dried sage (*or* 1 to 1 1/2 teaspoons fresh)

1/4 teaspoon fresh rosemary, minced (1 small sprig)

1/2 to 3/4 teaspoon dried thyme

1/2 teaspoon salt (or to taste)

Few grinds black or multicolored pepper

2/3 to 3/4 cup smoked provolone/mozzarella or Manchego, shredded or thinly sliced (optional)

Soak beans all day or overnight. Cover with plenty of fresh water, and bring to a boil. Add bay leaf, reduce heat, and cook about 45 minutes or until beans are tender but not beginning to break up. Drain cooking liquid, reserving 1/3 cup (more if you plan to make a soup), and set on back of stove.

Heat a little of the oil in Dutch oven and add the sliced bacon. Fry bacon over moderate heat for about 1 minute, drain excess fat (reserving some for flavor), then add remaining oil and onion, and sauté until bacon and onion are cooked. (If using sausage, sauté onion in oil for about 1 minute, then add sausage coins and sauté with onions until both are cooked.) Add garlic and sauté a minute more, then deglaze with vinegar and stock, tomatoes, and juice. Add seasonings and beans with reserved liquid. Simmer over low heat for 10 to 15 minutes.

When almost ready to serve, remove bay leaf and sprinkle with cheese (if desired). Turn off heat, cover, and let sit a minute or two until the cheese is melted.

Serve with steamed spinach or zucchini or a tossed salad, along with brown rice, chunky pasta, or crusty bread drizzled with olive oil.

Variations

WHITE BEANS & PORK CASSOULET: Instead of bacon, brown 1/2 to 3/4 pound pork butt or boneless spareribs, trimmed and cut in bite-sized pieces; remove from pan, drain fat, sauté onions, and return meat to pan. Pour stew into 9 x 9-inch casserole dish and place in preheating oven set to 375°F. Brush several slices of French or Italian bread with extra-virgin olive oil (removing thick or darkened crusts), then cut into large cubes. Arrange bread over top of casserole, pressing into top. Cover loosely with foil and bake 20 minutes. Remove foil, raise heat to 400°, and bake another 5 to 8 minutes or until croutons are golden.

WHITE BEANS & LAMB CASSOULET: Instead of bacon, brown 1/2 to 3/4 pound lamb arm chops, trimmed and cut in bite-sized pieces; remove from pan, drain fat, sauté onions, and return meat to pan. Add remaining ingredients in main recipe, omitting the sage and sage vinegar, and doubling the amount of rosemary. Pour stew into 9 x 9-inch casserole dish and place in preheating oven set to 375°F. Toss 1 1/2 cups homemade breadcrumbs, grated from dry bread, with about 1 1/2 tablespoons extra-virgin olive oil and a dash of salt, and sprinkle evenly over the top. Cover loosely with foil and bake 20 minutes. Remove foil, raise oven temperature to 400°, and bake another 5 to 8 minutes or until crumbs are golden.

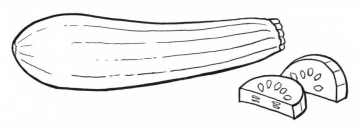

Stuffed Squash

Stuffed with a seasoned rice filling and cheese, summer or winter squash can be a special side dish or a vegetarian entrée. The simple Mediterranean-style filling for zucchini is just one of many possibilities using grains; see also the Bulghur Pilaf (page 187). Or try Delicata or Sweet Dumpling squash filled with savory Brown Rice Pilaf (page 186) or one with Thanksgiving flavors of sage and toasted hazels.

 SERVES 2

1 medium zucchini, sliced in half lengthwise
Rice Filling (page 164) (or 2 to 2 1/2 cups
   other seasoned grain pilaf with nuts)

Extra-virgin olive oil
3/4 cup shredded Manchego (or Romano,
   firm feta, goat gouda, or Parmesan)

Prepare squash, scooping out enough of seed area to create a hollow for filling. Arrange squash halves in baking pan filled with 1/2 inch hot water. Brush with oil, cover with foil, and bake at 375°F for 30 to 35 minutes, or until somewhat tender; meanwhile make the Rice Filling or other pilaf.

Remove foil and brush again with olive oil, then stuff with Rice Filling, rounding filling slightly across top of squash. Sprinkle with cheese and return squash to oven, uncovered, to bake for another 10 to 15 minutes, or until cheese is golden and squash is tender. Serve with tomato sauce if desired.

Quick Risotto

Genuine risotto made the time-honored way—first pan-roasting the grains, then incrementally adding broth, wine, or other flavored liquids, as in the Butternut Risotto on page 184—is a creamy, melt-in-your-mouth dish. For those of us who are pressed for time but crave an Italian one-pot feast, I offer this lunchtime risotto with shortcuts—and at least three nice variations.

Basically what we have here is an Italian stir-fry with all the right stuff—olive oil, onion, garlic, basil, pine nuts, cheese, tomatoes, summer veggies—brought together with leftover cooked brown or white rice. (Pan-Roasted Rice, page 184, works best since the sealed grains are less likely to stick on.) Lunch in less than 15 minutes, I promise—at home, camp, cruising, or anywhere you need a one-pot meal in a hurry.

 SERVES 2

3 to 4 sundried tomato halves soaked in 2 to 3 teaspoons marsala, water, or white wine (*or* ripe cherry or saladette plum tomatoes)

1 tablespoon olive oil

1 small onion (*or* 2 shallots), thin crescents or minced

2/3 cup zucchini or summer squash, thinly sliced

1 1/2 cups Tuscan kale (or spinach, or chard)

Dash of garlic powder (1/8 teaspoon)

2 1/2 to 3 cups leftover cooked brown or white rice (preferably Pan-Roasted, page 184)

1 1/2 teaspoons dried basil (1 tablespoon fresh)

Salt and "party" (multicolored) pepper to taste

1/3 to 1/2 cup Parmesan, Romano, Manchego, or smoked provolone cheese, coarsely grated/shredded or thinly sliced

2 tablespoons pine nuts, raw or very lightly toasted (page 144)

If using sundried tomato halves, snip each into 4 or 5 pieces and soak in marsala (or water or white wine) while you prepare the other ingredients (or ahead of time). If using fresh tomatoes, cut small plum tomatoes in half or thirds, and shake out loose seeds; cherry tomatoes can be halved or left whole. Remove stems from kale (or spinach or chard) and cut or tear leaves into large pieces.

Heat oil in small heavy-bottomed pot or saucepan, and sauté onion (or shallots) and zucchini or squash over medium-low heat until translucent. Stir in greens and sauté/sweat briefly, until leaves deflate. Sprinkle with garlic powder and toss in dried tomatoes with soaking liquid (or fresh tomatoes), and stir-fry for another half minute; then sprinkle rice over vegetables, along with basil, salt, and pepper. Add a little water (1 tablespoon) only if needed to keep vegetables from catching on. Reduce heat, and cook covered for 1 to 2 minutes more until rice comes up to heat, shaking pot occasionally.

When vegetable-rice mixture is hot through, sprinkle cheese over the top, turn off heat, and allow cheese to melt and flavors to blend. Serve hot sprinkled with pine nuts.

Variations

QUICK CREAMY RISOTTO: Use sundried tomatoes rather than fresh, and dial back on the grated cheese, using 2 to 3 tablespoons aged grated or thinly sliced Parmesan, Romano, or Manchego. Just before serving, add cheese plus 2/3 to 3/4 cup part-skim ricotta to the pot, dropping the ricotta in spoonfuls around the top of the sautéed vegetable-rice mixture. Cover and simmer over low heat 1 to 2 minutes more, gently shaking or stirring pot a couple times, just long enough to warm the ricotta and melt the cheese.

QUICK RISOTTO WITH PESTO: Hold the garlic powder and basil, and add 2 tablespoons fresh or frozen Genovese Pesto (page 21) to the pot with the tomatoes. Finish risotto as described in the main recipe.

LEMON-MUSHROOM RISOTTO: Omit the greens and tomatoes, and sauté 1 cup baby portabella mushrooms, stemmed and quartered, with the onions (or shallots) along with 1 teaspoon butter and a shake of garlic powder. Deglaze with a splash of white wine, sherry, or marsala, then add the leftover cooked rice and 1/2 teaspoon lemon zest, salt, and pepper. Cook as described in the main recipe. When rice is hot through, stir in 1/4 to 1/3 cup grated aged Parmesan or Romano cheese, and serve.

COOKING BEANS & LENTILS

Although it's easy to pick up a can of beans in a pinch, the flavor of beans or lentils soaked and simmered at home is so much better, well worth the thinking ahead. Plus you have the pleasure of choosing from a much wider variety, including local and heirloom beans and lentils (page 156), than are available canned—and sorting these colorful jewels into jars, then selecting combinations to soak for, say, a mixed-bean chili (page 158).

Soaking and cooking dry beans and lentils is no more difficult than measuring the amount called for in a recipe (generally one-third to half as much dry for the volume cooked), rinsing to remove any grit or bits of hull, and soaking in twice their volume of cold water for 4 to 6 hours or overnight. Drain off the soaking liquid, place the beans or lentils in a covered pot, cover with water (to about 1 1/2 to 2 inches over the surface of the soaked beans), and bring to a boil; then reduce heat to medium-low or low and simmer, partially covered, until tender. (We like to add a bay leaf to the pot for its fragrance, which goes so well with beans.)

Some cooks swear by the shortcut method of soaking beans: Rinse dry beans, cover with plenty of cold water, bring to a boil and cook for 2 to 3 minutes; then remove from heat and leave the covered pot to soak for about 1 hour. Then finish cooking as described above.

Cooking time varies with the size, type, and age of beans or lentils (old beans take longer to cook), so watch them carefully to make sure the beans do not boil over, run dry, or begin to break up. Also the yield varies with the size of bean (generally 2 to 3 cups cooked beans to 1 cup dried). The conventional wisdom is to not add salt until you season the dish itself; adding salt to the beans would likely toughen the skin and delay cooking.

Drain most of the cooking liquid from the cooked beans, reserving enough to cover the cooked beans in the refrigerator, or to use as part of the liquid in the dish you plan to make.

Leftover plain cooked beans, stored with some of their cooking liquid in a closed plastic container, will keep several days in the refrigerator, but it is best to use them up fairly quickly, perhaps in a soup. Once acids (tomatoes, wine, lemon juice, vinegar) have been added as part of a dish, the beans will tend to keep longer.

Hoppin' John

Though Hoppin' John has Southern roots, it goes right along with Yankee thrift as a way to recombine leftovers with a whole new twist—especially if made with cavatappi or other twirly pasta, and spiked with a little mustard, thyme, and hot pepper sauce (as called for in the Cooking Light *recipe that inspired us). This interpretation is a little spicier than your basic Carolina hoppin' John combining ham hocks or bacon and cooked black-eyed peas with onions, seasonings, and brown or white rice, garnished with chopped scallions and fresh tomatoes. We've made this dish using our own home-grown shell beans (page 146) in place of the black-eyed peas. French horticultural beans, such as Tongue of Fire, are a good choice, whether freshly shelled or dried, soaked, and cooked.*

Although traditionally some kind of richly flavored pork, ham, or bacon provides the smoky flavor, you could make a vegetarian Hoppin' John using smoked provolone or other smoked cheese and chipotle Tabasco sauce in place of the green pepper sauce.

This economical "bowl of soul" is good to keep in mind for camping or camp-cruising: It not only uses up likely leftovers (such as rice or pasta), but can also recycle leftover pork in practically any form—grilled spareribs (pages 107–8) or cutlets, pork butt or tenderloin, roast pork, ham or bacon—as long as the marinade or other flavorings are compatible. The other ingredients are probably already in your camp/galley kitchen or food box.

  SERVES 2 TO 3

1 pork butt steak or 2 slices thick bacon (or
    leftover grilled pork spareribs or chops)
6 sundried tomato halves, snipped (1/4 cup)
1/4 cup white/red wine or water
1 1/2 to 1 3/4 cups fresh or frozen black-eyed
    peas or horticultural shell beans, boiled
    (or 2/3 to 3/4 cup dry beans, soaked and
    cooked till tender)
1 bay leaf
1 tablespoon olive oil
1 small onion, crescents, sliced in half
1 clove garlic, minced
1/2 to 3/4 cup fresh/frozen green bell peppers
    (or 2 tablespoons fresh/canned chiles)

1/3 to 2/3 cup cooking liquid from beans
1/2 teaspoon dried thyme
1 teaspoon Dijon-type mustard (such as
    Raye's Winter Garden)
1 1/2 teaspoons Tabasco green pepper
    hot sauce (or chipotle Tabasco if
    not using pork)
Salt to taste
2 1/2 to 3 1/2 cups hot cooked cavatappi,
    rotini, or fusilli (or brown or white
    basmati rice)
2 scallions (green onions), chopped
1/2 to 2/3 cup fresh cilantro or parsley,
    chopped

Cut pork butt or bacon in bite-sized pieces and fry until browned but not overcooked; drain off fat. If using leftover pork, cut in bite-sized pieces. Snip tomatoes in pieces and soak in wine or water.

Put black-eyed peas or shell beans in a pot with enough water to cover, add bay leaf, and bring to a boil. Simmer 10 to 15 minutes, or until tender yet slightly al dente. (Or, if using soaked dried beans, cook until tender/al dente.) Drain, reserving about 2/3 cup cooking liquid.

If cooking a fresh batch of rice or pasta, time things so that the hot rice or drained pasta will be ready by the time you finish cooking the rest of the dish. If using leftover pasta, reheat just before serving in a separate pot, with a little hot water to keep it from sticking. Leftover rice can be reheated in the oven (page 190), in a saucepan with a little water, or in a steamer (sprinkle grains in layers to allow steam to heat evenly).

Heat oil in skillet or Dutch oven and sauté onion, then add garlic and peppers and sauté a couple minutes more, until peppers are tender. Then add tomatoes with their soaking liquid. Add the pork or bacon, then the drained beans along with 1/3 to 2/3 cup cooking liquid (enough for a little sauce). Add thyme, mustard, hot pepper sauce, and salt to taste and mix well.

When ready to serve, put the hot rice or pasta in a large, warmed serving bowl and top with the hot seasoned bean mixture; toss to combine. Or serve the rice or pasta in individual shallow bowls, top with bean mixture, and let diners toss their own. If making a vegetarian Hoppin' John, sprinkle smoked cheese over top of each serving. Garnish with chopped scallions and fresh cilantro or parsley.

Variation
HOPPIN' JOHN WITH HAM: In place of pork, wash 2 ham hocks thoroughly, cover with water, and simmer for 1 hour or until the meat is tender. Remove meat from bones and cut into bite-sized pieces. (Or use leftover baked ham, or prosciutto.) Use ham stock as cooking liquid for the peas/beans and in the sauce.

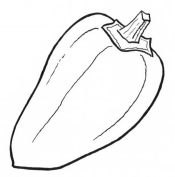

Shepherd's Pie with Bell Peppers

A truly heartwarming supper on a cold night is this time-honored casserole of peppery, savory lentils topped with fluffy mashed potatoes, piping hot. It reheats with even fuller flavor, so you might as well make plenty for a second meal. Although there are several components to the dish, it goes together quickly if you have leftovers to work with. When we find green pepper, Garlic Mashed Potatoes, and maybe some leftover lamb and stock together in the refrigerator, the light goes on: Shepherd's Pie!

Made as a vegetarian dish (as in the main recipe), Shepherd's Pie is plenty satisfying. We often add a small amount of meat, though: if not lamb, then chunks of Italian sausage (see variations).

If you have a set of Corningware, the recipe makes enough to fill an 8 x 8-inch square casserole plus a 7 x 7-inch one for a second meal. Or use a single 8 x 12 or 10 x 12-inch casserole.

White pepper—piquant, skunky, and gently hot—is a sensational potato spice. The amount called for may seem a bit much, but that's what it takes.

If you're growing peppers in the Northeast, you can't go wrong with Lipsticks, an early sweet, well-fleshed pepper with excellent flavor. Given enough time and the right weather, they'll ripen to a deep red. A bumper crop is easy to blanch and freeze, in assorted colors, for winter cooking.

1 1/4 cups dried French, green, or brown lentils
    (2 1/2 cups cooked)
2 3/4 cups water (or water + lamb/vegetable stock)
1 tablespoon olive oil
1 large onion, crescents
1 clove garlic, minced
3/4 cup fresh/frozen green bell pepper, large dice
2 teaspoons dried summer savory
1/4 teaspoon dried thyme
1 teaspoon dried marjoram
1 teaspoon dried basil
Salt to taste
Freshly ground white or multicolored pepper

4 to 6 plum tomatoes (canned or fresh), bite-sized chunks

~ TOPPING ~

2 to 3 cups leftover Garlic Mashed Potatoes page 170) + 1 large egg, *or:*
3 to 4 large potatoes, scrubbed and diced
1 tablespoon butter + 2 teaspoons olive oil
Dash of garlic powder
1/3 cup milk (or half-and-half)
1/2 to 3/4 teaspoon ground white pepper
1/4 teaspoon salt
1 large egg
Paprika

Rinse and pick over lentils, cover with 2 3/4 cups of water (or water plus stock), and bring to a boil; then turn to low heat and simmer until tender (about 30 to 40 minutes). Pre-cook meat, if desired (see variations). Do not drain. (If you think ahead, soak the lentils for several hours or overnight in cold water; they'll cook more quickly.)

If using leftover mashed potatoes, take from refrigerator. If making topping from scratch, put potatoes in pot with boiling water and cook until tender.

In large pot or Dutch oven, begin sautéing onion in olive oil. When partly translucent, add garlic and green pepper, and cook covered for a minute or so. Add herbs, the lentils and their cooking liquid, salt and pepper to taste, and tomatoes. Simmer for another minute or two, then remove from heat.

When potatoes are tender, drain off liquid and mash. Stir in butter and oil, garlic powder, and enough milk or half-and-half for a fluffy consistency. Add white pepper and salt. Beat in egg.

Fill 8 x 12- or 10 x 12-inch casserole with lentil mixture; it should be about half full. (Allow for about 1/2 inch headroom after potato topping has been spread on casserole; any less, and you'll want to lay a sheet of foil on a lower oven rack to catch any drips.) Spread potato mixture over top, and fluff up surface with fork. Dust with paprika.

Bake at 375°F for 25 to 30 minutes, until pie is bubbling and potato topping is golden. Serve with steamed Romano beans, broccoli, or greens.

Variations

SHEPHERD'S PIE WITH LAMB: Cook the lentils in a combination of water and lamb stock, if you have some, and add to the filling 1 to 1 1/4 cups leftover roast lamb, cut in bite-sized pieces. (Or, trim fat from about 1/2 pound fresh lamb stew meat and cut in bite-sized pieces. Brown meat in olive oil. Drain excess fat, deglaze pan with a little water, and add lamb with liquid to vegetable mixture.) Add a pinch of fresh chopped rosemary in place of basil. Assemble and bake as described above.

SHEPHERD'S PIE WITH SAUSAGE: Add to the filling 1/2 pound Italian sausage, pricked and parboiled to release some fat, cut in bite-sized chunks. Assemble and bake as described above.

Heirloom Beans

Most natural-foods coops and supermarkets carry a fairly diverse selection of dry beans, but nothing compares to the array of local, organic, and heirloom beans stocked by John Edwards Market in Ellsworth. It had been a while since I'd shopped there for pulses, and when I happened by their bean selection I gaped in awe, bedazzled by beans. Their four shelves include 17 local varieties (mostly New England/Maritime heirlooms) grown by Patti Qua, in Exeter, Maine, at The Beanery (207–278–3572). Here are some of the most useful varieties, with notes about their characteristics and uses:

MARFAX (a medium-large, plump golden-brown pea bean), SWEDISH (similar color, but a bit larger and kidney-shaped)—richly flavored, good baked bean varieties.

SOLDIER (a white kidney-shaped bean with a red-brown "soldier" silhouetted along one side), MAINE YELLOWEYE (a smaller, plump, rounded Soldier with a gold "eye"), BIG-EYE YELLOWEYE (a large, plump gold-and-white bean)—New England heirlooms, all good for baked beans, vegetable stews, or cassoulets.

BUMBLEBEE (a large plump Yelloweye-type bean, white with a black "eye"), CALYPSO (a plump black-and-white bean similar to Bumblebee but with yin-and-yang markings), CANNELLINI (large white kidney-shaped bean)—all mild-tasting beans with creamy texture, good in vegetable stews, cassoulets, pasta e fagioli, and as shell beans.

GARBANZO, aka CHICKPEA (a large round, tan bean)—an ancient Near Eastern legume, adopted by many Mediterranean cuisines; used in soups, stews, salads, and falafel; also puréed into a spread or dip.

BLACK TURTLE (a small, firm black bean)—South American heirloom, used in Mexican and Caribbean dishes; nice in combination with other beans (although the inky broth will stain lighter ingredients).

FRENCH FLAGEOLET (a small, light green bean)—firm, flavorful shell beans, for stews and salads.

VERMONT CRANBERRY (a small, speckled maroon-and-brick-red bean)—New England heirloom, good in soups, stews, and baking; nice in combination with other varieties; also a fine shell bean.

LOWE'S CHAMPION (a medium-large, deep burgundy bean), RED KIDNEY (a large red bean), KING OF THE EARLY (a medium-large mottled reddish-brown kidney-type bean)—flavorful varieties for chili, vegetable stew, or baked beans.

JACOB'S CATTLE (a red-and-white speckled bean)—a New England heirloom dry bean, good in soups and vegetable stews but tends to break down when overcooked; also good as shell bean.

SNOWCAP (a large, plump, half white, half pink-and-brown-speckled bean)—good in vegetable stews, chili, and cassoulets; a meaty, buttery bean that holds its shape without breaking down. We've found this a good replacement for ANDREW KENT, a large pink-and-brown speckled Scottish heirloom that we grew for many years but is no longer available from local seed catalogs.

I would add to this list TONGUE OF FIRE, a plump, tan-and-maroon-speckled horticultural bean with creamy texture that is traditionally grown as a shell bean, but can also be dried and used in soups and vegetable stews. Similar varieties include FRENCH DWARF HORTICULTURAL and ITALIAN ROSE.

A good source for these and other varieties is Fedco Seeds in Waterville, Maine, www.fedcoseeds.com, 207–873–7333. The Vermont Bean Seed Co. is another longtime seller of New England and other heirloom bean seeds (www.vermontbean.com, 800–349–1071). Or try using saved seeds, or locally grown heirloom beans—we've found The Beanery's dry beans germinate quite reliably.

And these are just the more common varieties. These multicolored, patterned gems are pretty enough to collect. Fellow bean connoisseurs might check out the amazing display of bean diversity in the Exhibition Hall at the Common Ground Fair in Unity, where I counted 130 different heirloom beans, most of them grown by bean aficionado Herbert (Sam) Birch in Coopers Mills, Maine.

Baked Beans

Maine-grown beans and Raye's mustard make this a down-home treat. We usually go with a combination of two of the meatier beans, such as Bumblebee, Soldier or Yelloweye, Snowcap, King of the Early. Maybe it's the sozzle of sauce or some other secret ingredient, but Richard's baked beans are always delicious. A fine meal (some people even have them for breakfast!) just on their own, they also combine well with leftover pork, such as Orange-Ginger Pork Spareribs (page 107). For vegetarian baked beans, leave out the bacon or pork and double up on the chipotle.

 SERVES 4 TO 6

1 pound dry beans (all same variety or a combination; see varieties recommended for baked beans on page 156)

2 1/2 to 3 1/2 teaspoons Dijon-type mustard (such as Raye's Winter Garden or Old-Fashioned)

5 tablespoons unsulphured Barbados molasses

Dash of Worcestershire and/or chipotle sauce (optional)

1 small to medium onion

1 tablespoon light brown sugar

1/2 slice thick bacon (*or* 1- to 2-inch chunk salt pork) (optional)

1/2 to 3/4 teaspoon salt (optional)

Soak beans overnight, then drain and cover with fresh water in large pot. Bring to a boil, then reduce heat and cook about 1 hour or until beans are nearly tender. Drain, reserving cooking liquid.

Fill 1 1/2-quart lidded bean pot (or casserole) about 1/4 to 1/3 full of cooked beans. Add mustard, 3 tablespoons molasses, and a dash of sauce as desired. Peel onion, cut an X in root end, and place root-end down in bottom layer of beans. Fill pot with about 1/3 more beans, to the top of the onion. Add 2 tablespoons more molasses plus the sugar, along with the bacon or salt pork, and salt if desired, then top up the pot with the rest of the beans (or as many beans as will fit). Pour enough bean liquid into the pot to cover the beans, leaving just a little headroom (1/4 inch).

Put foil on floor of oven to protect against spills, or put bean pot on a baking sheet, and place covered pot in bottom third or half of oven. Bake beans at 350° to 375°F for about 1 hour (perhaps along with dinner makings); then check liquid level, adding a bit more water if necessary. Lower heat to 325° to 350° and let beans continue to bake 1 hour more, then turn oven off and leave beans in covered pot overnight to finish baking in residual heat.

Richard's Chili

Despite his English-German-American roots, Richard has a Latin way with chili. Maybe it's the authentic ingredients, including epazote (a licorice-flavored herb traditional in Mexican cooking), cumin, hot peppers, and freshly cooked beans—nothing out of a can, except maybe the tomatoes. A good chili, he says, balances the sharp and bitter flavors of the herbs and spices, the piquant hot peppers and sweet tomatoes, against the bland, savory background flavors of beef, onions, and beans.

Another key ingredient, as with many soups and stews, is making the chili a day ahead, giving the flavors a chance to mingle. And though you can use ground cayenne or bottled hot sauce in a pinch, fresh peppers—mild or hot to suit your taste and heat tolerance—will give the chili a whole lot more character. Sautéing them first helps seal in their juice and flavor. A wide range of chiles and other peppers can be found in most supermarkets and farmer's markets—or better yet, grow your own, choosing from the many varieties listed in Johnny's and other seed catalogs.

And have fun with the beans. Rather than the standard pintos or kidney beans, use a colorful assortment of cranberry beans, black beans, Bumblebees, Calypsos, or any of the solid or speckled beans on the shelves of your natural food store (page 156)—or grow them yourself.

If you are, as we were, intrigued about trying epazote but unable to find any in stores, Johnny's to the rescue! (Johnny's Selected Seeds in Winslow, Maine, www.johnnyseeds.com, 877–564–6697). Epazote is an interesting plant, with fresh leaves smelling and tasting strongly of . . . well, shoe polish, but the flavor quickly grows on you to the point where it just ain't chili without it. In one summer you can easily grow and dry enough epazote to last several years.

There is plenty here to tingle the taste buds so that a meatless version, sprinkled with Manchego or other cheese, would not seem wanting in rich flavor.

Chili is one of those things worth making in a big batch. Serve half as a main course with Hearty Cornbread (page 194) and kale, leaving enough for a supper of Enchiladas (page 159)—or to serve for lunch as chili or thinned into a soup with a little water, stock, and tomato juice.

ℛ SERVES 4 TO 6

1 1/2 to 2 cups dry beans, assorted

2 to 3 tablespoons olive oil

1 pound ground beef chuck

1 to 2 teaspoons Worcestershire sauce

1 large onion, chopped

1 to 2 cloves garlic, minced

2 to 3 teaspoons ground cumin

1 teaspoon dried oregano (2 teaspoons fresh)

1 teaspoon dried epazote (2 teaspoons fresh)

1/2 teaspoon dried sage (1 teaspoon fresh)

1 teaspoon summer savory (optional)

2 to 3 fresh green jalapeño peppers (or Anaheim or other mildly hot chiles), membranes and seeds removed, coarsely chopped (or 1/4 to 1/2 teaspoon cayenne plus some chipotle pepper sauce)

12 to 16 ounces canned plum tomatoes plus juice (1/3 to 1/2 of 35-ounce can)

Bean broth and water as needed

Soak beans overnight; drain, cover with water, and bring to a boil; then lower heat and cook until tender. (Refresh cooking water midway through if desired.) Drain about 2/3 of the cooking liquid from the beans, reserving the rest.

In Dutch oven, cook ground beef in batches: Using a little olive oil, quickly brown small clumps of the ground meat, then use spatula to remove to separate bowl. When the last of the meat is browned, squirt a little Worcestershire over the top, and set aside.

Assemble chili seasonings, chop peppers, and use your fingers to break tomatoes into large pieces.

Drain beef fat from Dutch oven, leaving the fond in the bottom of the pan, and add a little olive oil as needed to sauté onion until halfway cooked. Add peppers and continue cooking until onion is translucent. Then briefly add garlic, cumin, and herbs. Deglaze with juice and tomatoes from 1/3 to 1/2 of the can, then add the beef, and the beans and their liquid. Rinse the beef juices into the pot with a little water (about 2 tablespoons). There should be plenty of liquid in the chili; some of the beans will give themselves to the broth as the chili cooks, making a nice, loose sauce.

Once all the ingredients are together in the pot, simmer the chili for about 1/2 hour or until the beans are just starting to break down. Remove from heat, and allow chili to cool and take up the flavors. The flavor will be much fuller the next day.

Enchiladas

This is one of the easiest, most satisfying dinners in the Southwest or the Northeast, assuming you made the chili a day or two ahead. It's also an occasion for teamwork, with one person spooning the chili and salsa, and the other grating the cheese and holding the tortillas open. Let the oven work its magic while you make the salad . . . and relax. For a sautéed chili vegetable filling featuring chicken, corn, peppers, and black beans, try the Chicken Enchiladas with Salsa Verde (page 102).

 SERVES 3 TO 4

4 to 5 cups Richard's Chili (page 158)
    or vegetarian version
6 to 7 white corn tortillas, 6 inches diameter,
    fresh or frozen

1/2 to 2/3 cup Salsa Verde, page 102 (optional)
2 tablespoons sliced marinated green/ripe
    olives or raw pumpkin seeds (optional)
1 to 1 1/2 cups shredded smoked provolone

Heat chili in saucepan over moderate heat. Preheat oven to 375°. If using frozen tortillas, pry them apart using a knife and let thaw at room temperature. Grate the cheese.

When chili is hot, spoon into thawed tortillas, curled upright side by side in a 7 x 11-inch Pyrex or other ovenproof casserole. Fill each tortilla with about 3/4 cup chili; spoon any remaining sauce lengthwise along edges of tortillas. If desired, spoon a stripe of Salsa Verde down the middle of the row of enchiladas. (Or, sprinkle with sliced olives or pumpkin seeds.) Sprinkle cheese evenly over the top.

Bake at 375°F for 20 to 30 minutes, or until sauce is bubbling and cheese is nicely browned.

If serving as a main dish, plan on 1 1/2 to 2 enchiladas per person. Serve with a fresh green salad (with some ripe avocado if available), along with a little rice or quinoa to round out the meal.

Spanish Black Bean Stew

The flavors of orange, sherry, cumin, and chorizo combine wonderfully in this fragrant Spanish-inspired dish. For a vegetarian option, omit the chorizo and sprinkle each serving with shaved Manchego cheese.

SERVES 4

1 1/2 cups dry black turtle beans (3 cups cooked)

2 tablespoons olive oil

1 large onion, crescents

2 cloves garlic, minced

1/2 coil (about 1/2 pound) chorizo sausage, sliced in 1/2-inch coins or half-moons

1/4 to 1/3 cup mildly hot fresh green peppers (or combination bell and hot peppers, like Lipstick and Hungarian Hot Wax), chopped fine

1 teaspoon ground cumin

1/2 to 1 teaspoon fresh sweet orange peel, finely minced

1 teaspoon dried Greek oregano

1/2 teaspoon winter savory

1/4 cup dry sherry

1/2 to 3/4 cup chicken stock or water

4 to 5 tablespoons Tomato Soup Base, page 35 (or any simple tomato-onion sauce)

Few grinds multicolored pepper

1/2 cup shaved Manchego cheese (optional)

Soak beans overnight in twice their volume of cold water. Drain, cover with fresh water, and bring to boil in covered saucepan. Lower heat and simmer 40 to 50 minutes or until beans are tender. Drain.

In large pot or Dutch oven, heat oil and sauté onion over medium heat until partly translucent. Add garlic and sauté very briefly, then add chorizo, peppers, seasonings and herbs, and sauté a minute more. (If you like the flavor of toasted cumin, add it now; otherwise add it later.) Deglaze with sherry, scraping browned bits from bottom of pan. Add stock or water, Tomato Soup Base or sauce, and the cooked black beans. Bring up to heat, then simmer partially covered, stirring occasionally, for 10 to 15 minutes.

Serve with white basmati rice, along with broccoli or other cooked green vegetable. Sprinkle each serving with shaved Manchego cheese if desired.

NOTE: Portuguese chouriço, available in most Northeastern supermarkets, can be used interchangeably with Spanish chorizo in this and other recipes.

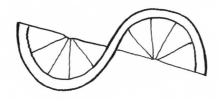

Caribbean Black Beans

Made with or without rice and vegetables (onions, scallions, green peppers or ancho chiles), Caribbean black beans can be eaten as a vegetarian main dish, or as a side dish alongside chicken, pork, fish or shellfish. The version here was served by our friend Heather Spangler as part of a vegetarian Caribbean dinner to warm up a blustery winter night along Eggemoggin Reach. Based on a recipe from Wild Oats natural foods, this combination of black beans with sweet-sour orange, pungent cilantro, golden garlic, and warming cayenne is melt-in-your-mouth delicious. Heather served the beans with lime-cilantro brown rice, ripe avocado wedges, and underripe bananas fried in butter with a hint of brown sugar and cinnamon—four simple dishes whose flavors and textures complemented each other sublimely (and the proteins, too).

As a side dish with meat or fish, Caribbean Black Beans go well with Caribbean Jerk Chicken or Shrimp (page 72), or Grilled Fish Steaks with Lime & Garlic (page 61).

Using precooked or canned beans, this would be an easy stovetop meal at camp or afloat. Leftovers could be puréed into a soup (see also the Black Bean Soup on page 42).

 SERVES 4

1 cup dry black turtle beans (2 1/4 cups cooked)	1/2 cup freshly squeezed orange juice (1 1/2 oranges)
1 tablespoon olive oil	1/4 to 1/2 teaspoon salt
2 cloves garlic, pressed	1/3 cup fresh cilantro, chopped
1/4 teaspoon cayenne pepper	

Soak beans overnight in twice their volume of cold water. Drain, cover with fresh water, and bring to boil in covered saucepan. Lower heat and simmer 40 to 50 minutes or until beans are tender. Drain, reserving about 1/4 to 1/3 cup cooking liquid to include with the beans.

Have all ingredients prepared before you begin cooking, to avoid over-browning the garlic. In small saucepan, sauté garlic in olive oil very briefly (half a minute) over medium-low heat until just beginning to turn gold. Immediately add the beans and remaining ingredients. Bring up to heat, then simmer partially covered, stirring occasionally, for 10 to 15 minutes or until juices are somewhat reduced.

Serve with brown basmati rice; a nice touch is to cook the rice with fresh lime juice (1 lime per cup of raw rice) and chopped cilantro.

Chickpea Rolls in Phyllo

The contrast between the crisp buttery phyllo pastry, the soft bland chickpeas (aka garbanzo beans), and the piquant seasonings in the filling make this an unusual and delicious treat. We've adapted this authentic Greek flavor combination from Jack Santa Maria's Greek Vegetarian Cookery.

The paper-thin leaves of phyllo ("leaf" in Greek) are delicate and call for patient, careful handling. Be sure to keep the roll of pastry covered with a plastic wrapper or bag and damp towel between lay-ups to prevent drying out and cracking.

Though the fussy phyllo makes them a little more labor-intensive than you might feel up for on a work night, a batch of Chickpea Rolls will go two meals for two (dinner plus lunch); a double batch makes for a festive dinner with friends. It helps to make the filling ahead of time—and if you precook the chickpeas the day before, all the better. It is well worth the effort of soaking and cooking dried chickpeas, which taste so much better than canned ones.

 SERVES 4 (8 ROLLS)

2 cups cooked, drained chickpeas (2/3 cup dried), mashed

1 small bay leaf

1/4 cup cooking liquid from chickpeas (or vegetable stock)

1 medium onion, chopped

1 tablespoon olive oil

1 canned or fresh plum tomato, chopped

Few grates black pepper

1 clove garlic, minced

2 tablespoons chopped fresh cilantro (*or* 1 tablespoon dried)

1 egg, beaten

1/4 teaspoon salt (less if using very salty feta)

1/2 cup feta cheese, diced

1/4 to 1/2 teaspoon fresh lemon zest

2 1/2 to 3 tablespoons butter, melted

1/4 cup extra-virgin olive oil

16 sheets (about 5 ounces) frozen 9 x 14-inch phyllo (fillo) pastry, thawed

Soak 2/3 cup chickpeas overnight, then drain, cover with water, and bring to a boil. A small bay leaf added to the pot gives a nice fragrance to the beans. Cook 45 minutes to an hour or until tender and drain, reserving 1/4 cup stock. Mash with a fork or hand masher, leaving a few lumps for texture.

In a large skillet or sauté pan, sauté onion in oil till translucent, then add tomato, pepper, garlic, and cooking liquid from chickpeas. Cover and cook gently for 5 minutes. Then add cilantro, beaten egg, mashed chickpeas, and salt. Mix together well and cook briefly over low heat until egg is set, then remove from heat and stir in feta and lemon zest. Melt butter with oil in a small metal bowl.

On a clean counter with plenty of elbowroom, lay up (a boatbuilding term for laminating) 4 sheets of phyllo at a time, brushing between layers with the warm butter/oil mixture. Cut each stack in half, making 2 rectangles, each 7 x 9 inches. Preheat oven to 375°F.

Spoon 1/8 of the filling along the narrow end of the first pastry rectangle, leaving 1 inch margin of pastry at bottom and sides. Fold the bottom margin of pastry up, then fold right and left margins over toward the center and roll to end. Repeat with 3 more stacks of phyllo and remaining filling, making a total of 8 chickpea rolls. Spread them out, seam-side down, on 1 or 2 lightly oiled baking sheets. Brush tops with remaining butter/oil. Bake at 375° for 15 to 20 minutes, or until nicely browned. Serve hot with white or brown rice or couscous, and a salad or leafy green vegetable.

NOTE: If using a 16-ounce box of frozen phyllo, packaged in 2 furls of dough, each with 24 or 25 sheets of pastry, you'll use two-thirds of a roll in making a single batch of Chickpea Rolls. To use up the remaining 8 or 9 sheets, you might make a half batch of Spanakópitas (page 14).

Chickpea Stew with Feta

This Greek-inspired stew is one of our favorite meals any time of year, plenty flavorful and satisfying with or without sausage. Cooking the beans a day ahead speeds the supper-making—and as with any savory stew, this is better the next day after the flavors have had a chance to get to know each other.

SERVES 4

3 1/2 to 3 3/4 cups cooked garbanzo beans/
    chickpeas (1 to 1 1/4 cups dried)
1 bay leaf
1/2 cup cooking liquid from chickpeas
2 (6 ounces) sweet Italian or fennel pork
    sausages, simmered, drained of fat, and
    sliced (optional)
1 tablespoon or so olive oil
1 onion, sliced in crescents
1 to 2 cloves garlic, minced
1/2 to 2/3 cup tomato juice

2 cups canned whole tomatoes, coarsely
    chopped or broken by hand
1/4 to 1/2 teaspoon dried thyme
1/4 to 1/2 teaspoon dried winter (or summer)
    savory
1 teaspoon dried oregano
1 teaspoon dried marjoram
Salt and pepper to taste
3/4 cup feta cheese, chunks (about 3 table-
    spoons per serving)
2/3 cup chopped fresh parsley

Soak chickpeas all day or overnight. Drain, cover with plenty of fresh water, and simmer with bay leaf 45 minutes or until tender. Drain off broth and hulls, reserving about 1/2 cup of the stock.

If using Italian sausage, simmer in shallow pan of water, drain off fat, and let cool. Slice sausage into bite-sized pieces (1/2-inch coins).

Sauté onion in olive oil, adding garlic for last minute or so. Deglaze with a little of the tomato juice, then add tomatoes, herbs, and sausage. Add reserved chickpea stock and enough tomato juice for a nice stew. Cover and simmer over moderate to low heat for 10 to 20 minutes.

Serve hot in shallow bowls over rice, couscous, or bulghur, with feta and parsley for garnish. Sprinkled over each individual serving, the feta will soon become molten. Brown rice and lightly steamed spinach or kale go especially well with this dish.

Variation
CHICKPEA STEW WITH CILANTRO & LEMON: Use Island Acres' lemon-pepper chicken sausage (page 88), or add 1/2 teaspoon lemon zest along with Italian sausage. For herbs, use 1 teaspoon fresh Greek oregano, and sprinkle 1/2 cup chopped fresh cilantro over top of stew before serving. (If using dried herbs, add 1 teaspoon each oregano and cilantro along with the tomatoes.) Serve with a half slice of lemon.

Vegetarian Moussaka

Greek moussaka, made the traditional way (second variation) with lamb and a top layer of béchamel sauce, though rich in flavor, can also be quite rich with saturated fat and cholesterol. Here are two somewhat lighter, vegetarian interpretations drawing from various Greek moussaka and sauce recipes. As in the other eggplant dishes, eggplant roasted in the oven soaks up less oil, and the first variation goes even further, layering slices of lean tofu with sauce and feta, omitting the béchamel. And yet, with the rich-tasting eggplant, spicy tomato sauce, and intense feta, none of the variations stints on flavor.

❧ SERVES 4 TO 6

3 to 4 tablespoons olive oil, total
1 large (or 2 small) eggplant, skinned and
    sliced lengthwise (1/4- to 3/8-inch slabs)
Greek Tomato Sauce

Rice Filling
2/3 cup feta cheese (3 1/2 ounces), diced
Béchamel Sauce

GREEK TOMATO SAUCE

1 medium onion, crescents
2 cloves garlic, minced or pressed
1 1/2 teaspoons red wine vinegar (1/2 to 1
    teaspoon if using canned tomatoes)
3 cups fresh or canned plum tomatoes, chopped,
    plus 2/3 to 3/4 cup water + juice

1 1/2 teaspoons dried basil
1 small bay leaf
2 to 3 teaspoons dried Greek oregano
1 teaspoon dried marjoram
1/2 teaspoon cinnamon
1/2 teaspoon allspice

RICE FILLING

1/2 medium onion, chopped
1 small clove garlic, minced
3 tablespoons pine nuts or raw sunflower
    seeds, or combination
1 tablespoon dried currants

1 1/2 cups cooked brown rice (page 187)
1/4 cup chopped fresh parsley
1 teaspoon dried Greek oregano
Salt to taste
Few grates black or multicolored pepper

BÉCHAMEL SAUCE WITH FETA

1/3 cup unbleached flour
1 tablespoon salted butter
2 tablespoons olive oil
2 cups milk, warm or room temperature
1/2 cup (2 1/2 ounces) feta cheese, diced

Few grates black pepper
Small pinch nutmeg (1/8 teaspoon)
1/4 teaspoon salt (or to taste)
1 large egg + 1 yolk

Preheat oven to 350°F. Peel and slice eggplant and arrange slices on baking sheet(s) generously greased with olive oil. Bake about 10 minutes until eggplant begins to steam, then flip to other side and bake another 10 minutes or until tender.

Meanwhile, make Greek Tomato Sauce: Heat 1 tablespoon oil in heavy-bottomed Dutch oven or saucepan and sauté onion, adding garlic for the last minute or so (avoid browning the garlic which makes it bitter). Deglaze pan with red wine vinegar and add tomatoes, juice (or a combination of juice and water), and herbs. (If using canned tomatoes that taste a little sour, cut back on the vinegar or add a pinch of light brown sugar.) Let sauce simmer for a few minutes while you prepare feta. Add cinnamon and allspice to sauce and simmer over low heat, covered, while you make filling.

For the filling, sauté chopped onion in olive oil till translucent, then briefly add garlic, pine nuts, seeds, and currants. Sprinkle in cooked rice, then herbs, salt, and pepper to taste.

To make Béchamel Sauce with Feta, combine flour, butter, and olive oil in small saucepan and heat over low heat about 1 minute, stirring constantly, to form roux. Remove from heat and gradually stir in milk, smoothing out lumps before adding more liquid. Return sauce to heat and bring to a simmer, stirring constantly, until sauce has thickened. Remove from heat and let sauce cool slightly. Add feta, pepper, and nutmeg; then beat in egg and yolk. Wait a few minutes for feta to melt into sauce, then season with salt to taste.

To assemble, lightly grease a 7 x 11-inch, 9 x 9-inch, or (ideally) 8 x 12-inch ovenproof casserole with olive oil. (The two smaller sizes are just big enough; 8 x 12 is the best fit.) Remove bay leaf from tomato sauce and layer the moussaka ingredients twice, beginning with a little sauce and ending with sauce and feta: sauce, eggplant, rice filling; sauce, feta, eggplant, rice filling; sauce, feta. Smooth Béchamel Sauce over top of casserole.

Bake in center of oven at 350° for 40 to 50 minutes, or until sauce has formed a golden skin. Let moussaka rest 5 minutes before serving. Serve with steamed spinach, green beans, or other vegetable.

Note: This is one of those dishes that, made ahead, only improves in flavor. To reheat, give the moussaka 1 to 2 hours to come to room temperature. Cut in portion-sized squares, add 2 to 3 tablespoons water, and bake, covered with foil, at 350°F for 25 minutes; then remove foil and bake another 20 minutes or until hot through.

Variations

Tofu Moussaka: Use 12 to 14 ounces firm tofu, sliced (1/4 to 3/8 inch thick), between layers in place of rice filling. Omit Béchamel Sauce, using a generous 2/3 cup feta, and bake at 350° for 40 to 45 minutes. Serve with long-grained or basmati brown rice, along with steamed spinach or other green vegetable.

Traditional Lamb Moussaka: In place of the tomato sauce and rice filling, make Greek Lamb Stew as on page 120, using lamb leg or stew meat chopped fine, or ground lamb. Assemble casserole in 5 layers, alternating between stew and eggplant, ending with stew. Top casserole with Béchamel Sauce or crumbled feta, and bake as described above.

Eggplant Kookoo

This recipe is based on a traditional Persian dish called Kookoo Bademjan, which I came across in a Persian cookbook. A kookoo (also spelled coucou) *is an omelette. This one, really more of a soufflé, is nice served with fluffy white basmati rice and steamed spinach, broccoli, or other greens.*

SERVES 4

1 medium eggplant, peeled and cubed
1 small onion, minced
1 tablespoon tamari soy sauce
3 tablespoons chicken or vegetable stock
   (*or* 1/4 cube bouillon dissolved in water)
1 1/2 teaspoons dried cilantro (or 1 tablespoon
   fresh cilantro)
1 teaspoon ground coriander
1/2 teaspoon nutmeg
4 large eggs, separated
1/2 tablespoon butter + 1/2 tablespoon olive oil

4 ounces shredded Gruyère or cheddar cheese
   (*or* 3 tablespoons pecans, lightly toasted
   and chopped)
1 fresh ripe tomato, seeded and chopped
   (optional)
~ WHITE SAUCE ~
2 tablespoons salted butter for roux
4 tablespoons flour (2 tablespoons unbleached
   + 2 tablespoons whole-wheat pastry flour)
1/2 cup milk
2 tablespoons chicken or vegetable stock

Boil eggplant (in enough water to cover) till tender; drain and mash. Add onion, tamari, 3 tablespoons stock, and seasonings, then egg yolks. Grate cheese and chop tomato, and set aside.

To make white sauce, melt butter, add flour, and stir to make a very lightly browned roux. Remove from heat and gradually add milk, whisking after each addition to avoid lumps. Whisk in stock and cook over low heat, stirring constantly, until thickened.

Preheat oven to 350°F. In separate bowl, beat egg whites until fairly stiff. Using flexible spatula or wooden utensil with curved front edge, fold white sauce into egg whites, then fold this into the eggplant mixture.

Warm 1/2 tablespoon each butter and oil and grease a 7 x 11- or 8 x 12-inch ovenproof casserole. Pour in half the soufflé filling, sprinkle with the tomatoes and a little of the cheese (if using), and top with remaining filling. Sprinkle remaining cheese (or pecans) over the top, and bake about 40 minutes or until set and golden.

Variation
ZUCCHINI KOOKOO: Substitute shredded zucchini for the eggplant; instead of boiling, quickly sauté the zucchini with the onions in a little olive oil. Otherwise, assemble the kookoo as described above.

Cooking Together

Preparing food together is a natural way to enjoy one-on-one time with someone—whether it's a friend or sister-in-law, your spouse or housemate, a visiting niece or other houseguest. And if it's a multi-component recipe like many in this chapter—Homemade Pizza, Ricotta-Stuffed Shells, Enchiladas, or Moussaka (pages 138, 140, 159, and 164)—where four hands are definitely better than two, collaboration makes cooking a festive meal fun, and a lot quicker for sharing the work.

With guests: I probably wouldn't have thought to invite houseguests to pitch in before meeting my in-laws, who readily take a hand in whatever needs doing in a large family. When I was growing up, my mother's kitchen was too close for much collaboration, and (other than setting me with small tasks, and letting me take charge of dinner once a week as a teen) she seemed to prefer the creative autonomy of cooking for our four-person household (and creative she was, producing many a Down-east feast). I can certainly understand—it's much easier to concentrate on trying a new recipe, or measuring ingredients, without the distraction of carrying on a conversation or directing a helper.

But I've come to realize that putting a guest to work in the kitchen, if they'd like to join in, is not an imposition, but a welcome invitation to feel like part of the household. Plus it's a way to share culinary experience and ideas, a casual "cooking class," along with good conversation. Just make sure everyone has a comfortable place to work, and allow a little more time and patience if cooking with someone less experienced or unfamiliar with your kitchen.

For several years we made a Crosen family tradition of having our preteen niece Kelsey, and then Megan, come for a few days' visit over April vacation, for a little grown-up adventure away from home and some time to get to know them one-on-one. Also our end-of-the-road homestead and rural community gave them a chance to see some different ways of doing things, closer to the land and shore than in their more suburban setting at home. In place of a disposal, dishwasher, and clothes dryer, here they'd find a compost bucket, kitchen sink, and clothesline. Here they could try exotic food items like artichokes, pumpkin seeds, avocados, feta cheese, "free-range" venison.

Rather than let our girl lounge as a pampered princess while we cooked, we'd include her in the dinner preparations—pulling carrots and onions from the garden, making salad, and (with a bit less enthusiasm) washing dishes. We'd make fun foods like pizza, seasoned croutons and French fries, stuffed shells, muffins and cookies. Food-related adventures outside the kitchen would include planting and watering seedlings for the garden, gathering duck eggs, measuring out grains and flours at the Blue Hill Co-op, picking mussels for supper at the shore.

Now they're on to college, and homes of their own, but I hope next time they (and their sister Molly, a budding cook) come visit, they'll feel right at home in our kitchen.

With family: Gathering with the Washburns several times a year at my mother-in-law's in Harrison, Maine, the tables are turned, and we are the willing recruits—the potato peelers, the turkey carvers and gravy sauciers. Happily I married into a family of cooks, all eager to share their favorite dishes and be part of what's happening in the kitchen. Good thing, since there are often 12 or more of us around Dolly's table (where the conversation inevitably drifts to other meals, other recipes).

With a large group together for a weekend or longer, it's almost essential to invite a comfortable collaboration to spread the load of meal preparation and cleanup, so that everyone has a share in the work and the fun. I remember doing the same at my family's camp on Beech Hill Pond in Otis, with me and my Mom, and whoever else was willing, helping Grandma turn out amazing meals from the Old Cabin's tiny kitchen, handing dishes through its little window to the porch, to serve family style around the big pine table (as you can see in the pictures opposite page 280). There's still plenty of mealtime synergy happening there, with serendipitous potlucks and menu sharing between the now three cabins.

At Dolly's, sometimes she has the menus planned and anyone with a spare hand pitches in to help, but as the family has grown we've been doing more with collaborative menus or potluck, each of us making a special hors d'oeuvre, brunch dish, prize dessert, or fruit salad, prepped at home and assembled in Dolly's kitchen . . . or in sister-in-law Vonuo's kitchen next door, where one time we had a class on how to make her Pork Egg Rolls (page 112), the feature of that day's lunch. At summer cookouts, cooks and servers shuttle merrily back and forth between both kitchens and backyards.

With spouse: Richard and I practice much of that same collaboration at home when making dinner, each of us taking on parts of the meal ("You make the sauce and brown the meat, Honey; I'll make the filling, grate the cheese, and put it together"). We trade off in menu planning and shopping, coming up with ideas and adaptations, then helping each other carry them out. Although we'll confer on main-dish ingredients (as one friend jokingly puts it, "cooking by consensus"), Richard, a former line cook, usually mans the skillet and saucepan while I share in the prep work and take care of vegetables, salad, casserole toppings, breads and desserts. There are plenty of other chances—breakfasts, lunches, the occasional solo supper at home or camp—where we can each experiment or fix a favorite dish the other isn't wild about.

Not all couples are compatible in the kitchen, and not all kitchens are set up so that two cooks can comfortably share the territory. But, with two roomy workstations, we manage to stay out of each other's way pretty well; sometimes it's almost a dance. Cooking dinner together is our happy hour, our chance to swap stories of the day . . . and with both of us working, it makes dinner happen at a reasonable time. I like being queen of the kitchen now and then, but wouldn't want it as a full-time job. The reasons for cooking together go beyond sexual equality; we do it because it's collegial, creative, and fun.

Opposite, at home in Penobscot (top to bottom): Test kitchen at work; Kelsey and Aunt Jane with stuffed shells in the oven; pulling green onions for supper; backyard duck rodeo; herbal vinegars and drying summer savory; Richard making salsa.

Overleaf, Washburns gathering around food (counterclockwise): Vonuo and Nicole making Indian flatbread in Dolly's kitchen; summertime lobster feed at Dolly's; mingling with the cooks, good eating, and dinnertime fun at Art and Dot's in Penobscot.

On the Side

Garlic Mashed Potatoes

This all-American staple hardly needs a recipe—every cook has a favorite formula—but since it's a component of several recipes in the book, here's how we do the mashed potato.

We always make more than we can eat at one sitting, since leftover mashed potatoes tend to inspire other meals: as a topping for a Shepherd's Pie (page 154), lofted with beaten egg; as the base for a Creamy Potato-Cheese Soup (page 38); herbed and fried or baked as Potato Pancakes or Puffs. . . .

℗ SERVES 3 TO 4

5 medium Yukon Gold, white, or red-skinned
    potatoes, skins on
1 1/2 tablespoons salted butter
1 tablespoon extra-virgin olive oil
1/4 teaspoon salt
1/4 teaspoon white pepper, freshly ground

1/4 teaspoon garlic powder (*or* 3 to 4 cloves
    roasted garlic; see Note)
1/2 cup milk (with yogurt or half-and-half)
2 tablespoons fresh chives or scallion tops,
    finely chopped (*or* 1 teaspoon fresh or
    dried summer savory)

Scrub potatoes, leaving skins on if thin and presentable; cut off any dark spots, then dice. Add to pot of boiling water and cook until tender. Remove from heat, and add butter, oil, and seasonings. Mash slightly with hand masher, then add milk, milk with yogurt, or half-and-half (plus a little more as needed for creamier potatoes) and continue mashing until as lumpy or smooth as desired. Stir in chives or scallions (or savory) right before serving, or sprinkle on top.

NOTE: To roast garlic, brush whole cloves or head of garlic with a little olive oil, leaving skins on. Wrap garlic in aluminum foil and bake in 375°F oven for 15 to 20 minutes, or until tender. Peel cloves, mash or chop, and add to potatoes (or other dish).

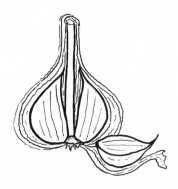

Potato Pancakes

Latkes these are not, but as a way to use up leftover mashed potatoes while rounding out a meal, they are mighty fine. The keys to success are a hot pan, sufficient frying oil, and patience: wait until the bottom is crisp before flipping, and you'll have food fit for a king (otherwise, a sticky mess). For a baked no-fuss alternative, see the following recipe.

1 3/4 to 2 cups leftover Garlic Mashed Potatoes
1 large egg
1 to 2 tablespoons sour cream, buttermilk, or
    yogurt, or half-and-half (optional)
Few grates white pepper, dash of salt

1/8 teaspoon onion powder (*or* 1 tablespoon
    minced scallions, white parts)
1/2 teaspoon summer or winter savory
    (*or* 1/4 teaspoon dill weed)
1 to 2 tablespoons olive oil

Put mashed potatoes in bowl and beat in other ingredients in order listed, adding a little sour cream, buttermilk, yogurt, or half-and-half as needed for a fairly stiff but spreadable batter.

Heat half of oil in stainless-steel sauté pan (or non-stick skillet) over medium heat, and when just beginning to smoke add three spoonfuls of potato mixture, spreading them out to about 3/8 inch thickness. Lower heat to medium-low and fry for about 1 minute until brown around the edges, then turn with spatula. Repeat with remaining oil and potato mixture. Serve hot.

Potato Puffs

Filling a similar niche as the Potato Pancakes above, but a bit more dressed-up, are these tart puffs, presentable for a special dinner. Baking gives you the same golden crispness with more certain success (no artful flipping required!), and you could even assemble the Potato Puffs in their pans ahead of time to bake at the last minute, perhaps along with the main course if already in the oven.

 SERVES 3 TO 4

3 to 3 1/2 cups Garlic Mashed Potatoes
    (page 170)
1 scallion, thinly sliced
1 large egg
3 tablespoons grated Romano cheese

2 tablespoons plain yogurt
Few grates white pepper, dash of salt
1/2 teaspoon summer or winter savory
1 to 2 tablespoons olive oil
Paprika

Preheat oven to 375°F, and preheat a baking sheet with sides. Put mashed potatoes in bowl, and stir in the scallion, egg, and 1 tablespoon of the grated cheese. Mix in yogurt, salt and pepper, and savory (if not already in the mashed potatoes).

Liberally grease 6 non-stick tart pans with olive oil and place on preheated baking sheet (remember, it's hot!). Spoon potato mixture evenly among tart pans, leaving surface slightly peaked (rather than smooth) for browning. Sprinkle remaining 2 tablespoons cheese over the tops, and lightly dust with paprika.

Bake puffs at 375° for 12 to 15 minutes, then boost heat to 400° and bake for another 10 to 12 minutes, or until tops are nicely browned and puffs are crisp around the sides. To serve, remove puffs from pans, using a fork or bamboo skewer to free sides if necessary.

Scalloped Potatoes

This is the ultimate comfort food—creamy potatoes, savory onions, sweet milk, and the subtle bite of white pepper (ripe peppercorns) which goes so perfectly with potatoes. Nothing compares to real-thing scalloped potatoes, slow-baked in milk, letting the starch of the potatoes thicken the sauce—what I consider the Downeast way of making them (learned from my Mom, Joyce Hancock Crosen). Slightly caramelized around the edges, this dish is melt-in-your mouth delicious, well worth the wait—and only tastes richer on reheating.

SERVES 4 TO 5

3 to 3 1/2 cups milk (whole or 2% butterfat), scalded (or enough to cover the layered potatoes and onions)

1 teaspoon butter (to grease dish)

1 large onion, thinly sliced

6 to 7 medium Yukon Gold, russet, red-skinned, Kennebec (or other Maine white) potatoes, skins left on, thinly sliced (3/16 inch thick)

Salt and white pepper to taste

2 teaspoons salted butter, diced (for top)

Preheat oven to 350°F. Heat milk in saucepan to scalding point and remove from heat. Butter an 8 x 8-inch lidded ovenproof baking dish. Starting with onions, place alternating layers of potato and onion in baking dish; season between layers with salt and a few grates of pepper, and a few small dots of butter. (NOTE: If using redskins with less starch, sprinkle with 2 teaspoons flour.) Cover potatoes with scalded milk. Set in top third of oven, laying a piece of foil on a lower rack to catch any spills.

Bake covered for about 10 minutes. Gently turn or fold top layer of potatoes over into lower layers, and continue baking uncovered until a skin starts to form on the top. Repeat every 15 to 20 minutes until potatoes are tender and beginning to break down, about 6 times. Let skin form one last time, then turn off heat and let finish baking in warm oven (1 1/4 to 1 1/2 hours total baking time).

TIMING IS EVERYTHING

As my Mom always used to say, the biggest challenge with any meal is getting the different components—entree, carbo, vegetable—to come together in perfect doneness all at the same time (and getting the diners to sit down and partake at that optimum moment). What makes it happen is a combination of planning, experience, intuition, maybe an extra pair of hands (see page 167).

Nicely browned, al dente, cooked through but tender . . . The idea is to have dishes that are more forgiving, like grains, sauces, stews, and casseroles, waiting on those that are more ephemeral, like stir-steamed vegetables, pasta tosses, shellfish, grilled meats. Keeping watch on the various parts of the meal (using your eyes, ears, and nose), you can slow things down by reducing the heat or giving a fast-cooking dish a time-out. For the not-so-intuitive or easily distracted, timers are a big help. And if part of the meal—casserole, salad, dessert—can be made ahead and brought out or reheated, that's one less thing to keep track of (some things are even better that way).

Praised be the cooks with that tuned-in sense of timing who get it all together, done to a turn!

Sweet Potato Oven Fries

If you've sampled sweet potato fries in restaurants, you'll know that deep-frying makes for heavenly, crispy results. Oven-frying, which works so well with white potatoes (see the following recipe), involves less fuss, mess, and fats but is more of a challenge with sweet potatoes because of their denser, moist texture and high sugar content. The key is soaking the cut potatoes in an ice-water bath to remove sugars that would otherwise stick to the pan and scorch (dusting with rice or semolina flour helps prevent this also). If possible, use the drier golden sweet potatoes, rather than the damper orange-garnet ones.

These hot-and-sweet fries are especially good with pork chops or chicken thighs cooked simply with herbs and onions.

SERVES 4

2 large golden sweet potatoes, skins on bad spots trimmed	Half dozen grates white pepper
4 tablespoons olive oil	Dash of cayenne pepper
1/4 teaspoon garlic powder	Few dashes salt
1/4 teaspoon onion powder	About 1 1/2 teaspoons rice flour (or semolina flour)

Wash sweet potatoes and trim off stem ends and any bad spots, leaving rest of skin intact. Cut each potato in half crosswise, then lengthwise. Lay flat side of each quarter section on cutting board and, using a large sharp knife, slice into sticks about 1/4 to 3/8 inch square and about 3 1/2 inches long. Soak them in an ice-water bath for 5 minutes while you combine the olive oil and seasonings in a mixing bowl. Preheat oven to 425°F.

Stir potatoes around in ice water, then drain off soaking liquid, which will have become cloudy with dissolved starches. Rinse in cold water, drain, and spread potatoes out on a clean, dry dishtowel; pat dry.

Coat 2 baking sheets with olive oil and dust lightly with rice or semolina flour.

Transfer potato sticks to the mixing bowl with seasoned oil and turn them around in the oil until evenly coated. Divide potatoes between the baking sheets, spreading them out in a single layer.

Bake near top of oven about 10 to 12 minutes until potatoes are just beginning to brown on the bottom, then turn with spatula. Bake for another 10 to 12 minutes or until potatoes are done through, crispy on the outside, and tender in the middle. Bake a few minutes longer in turned-off oven.

Seasoned Oven Fries

These are a regular at our house, usually accompanied by steak and salad or green beans, or grilled burgers and salsa. We alternate between "fish & chips" style (with vinegar and paprika, as in the main recipe) and two variations, golden Greek-style fries tart with lemon, and spicy Cajun-dusted fries.

You can use most any type of potato, even fingerlings, but red-skinned potatoes, with the skins left on, are best, cooking quickly and crisply and staying moist and sweet (not mealy) in the middle. Yukon Golds or yellow potatoes, with mellow sweet flavor, "eat just as good." If using one of the varieties that contain more sweet starch, which can tend to stick to the pan and scorch, you may want to take the same precaution used in the previous recipe with sweet potatoes, and give the cut potatoes a quick soak in ice water before roasting.

Starting out at a higher temperature crisps the outside, while reducing the heat midway helps them cook through. They're prime sizzling hot fresh out of the oven, but any leftover oven fries can be reheated.

SERVES 3

4 or 5 medium to large potatoes, preferably red-skinned	1/2 to 1 teaspoon dried Greek oregano
4 tablespoons extra-virgin olive oil	1/8 to 1/4 teaspoon paprika
2 tablespoons apple cider vinegar	6 to 8 grates (about 1/4 teaspoon) white or "party" (multicolored) pepper
1/4 teaspoon garlic powder	1/4 to 1/2 teaspoon salt

Wash potatoes and trim off bad spots, leaving rest of skin intact. Slice into sticks and wedges about 1/2 inch square by 3 to 4 inches long.

Preheat oven to 450°F. Place sliced potatoes in large mixing bowl, or on 1 or 2 baking sheets with sides. Combine oil, vinegar, and seasonings and drizzle over potatoes. Turn potatoes until evenly coated with seasoned oil. Spread out in single layer on baking sheet(s).

Bake near top of oven for about 20 minutes, turning with spatula every 5 to 7 minutes. Turn heat down to 375–400° and bake another 15 to 20 minutes, or until fries are crispy on the outside and tender through. Serve hot.

These will probably disappear at the first sitting, but any leftovers will reheat nicely in a 375° oven in an open pan.

Variations

GREEK-STYLE OVEN FRIES: Replace vinegar with 2 tablespoons fresh-squeezed lemon juice. Instead of paprika, add a small pinch of turmeric (1/8 teaspoon or less) for color.

CAJUN OVEN FRIES: Replace pepper and paprika with 1/2 teaspoon Cajun Rub (page 101).

Roasted Fingerling Potatoes

Although fingerlings came on the scene fairly recently, they've quickly become a staple, treasured for their nutty dense texture and quick roasting time. Indeed, roasting is one of the best ways to enjoy them, simply with a little olive oil or mingled with a sprig of rosemary and head of garlic, as Richard's brother Art Washburn does them. Leftover roasted fingerlings can be sliced and fried as hash browns.

As a variation on roasting, try using fingerlings for Seasoned Oven Fries (page 174), sliced lengthwise. Although they're not good bakers, fingerlings will make decent boiled or chunky mashed potatoes. As with other potatoes, leftover boiled fingerlings can be recycled into a crust for a frittata (page 78) or added to a pot pie (page 96).

Thanks to Kim Ridley and Tom Curry for introducing us to these versatile gold nuggets!

 SERVES 3 TO 4

1 tablespoon olive oil	1 to 2 heads of garlic (optional)
24 to 30 fingerling potatoes	1 sprig fresh rosemary (optional)

Preheat oven to 425°F. Oil roasting pan with olive oil.

Scrub potatoes, leaving skins on, and remove any sprouts or blemishes. Prick each potato once with paring knife and add to pan; shake pan to coat potatoes evenly with oil. If fingerlings are unevenly sized, cut larger ones in half so they'll all roast in the same amount of time.

Place in top third of oven and roast 15 to 20 minutes, shaking pan occasionally. Potatoes will start to whistle and hiss as they bake.

To roast garlic and rosemary along with fingerlings, brush garlic head with a little olive oil and place in roasting pan with the potatoes along with a sprig of rosemary. Reduce heat to 375° and roast about 15 minutes more. Check garlic for doneness; if tender and starting to turn gold, remove from pan while potatoes finish roasting, to avoid scorching the garlic. (Or, if you prefer, wrap head of garlic in foil and roast separately, page 170.)

Potatoes are done when a paring knife cuts easily through the middle. Serve immediately.

GROWING FINGERLINGS

Classed as gourmet heirlooms, fingerlings are usually sold at a premium, whether as a market vegetable (at farmer's markets, natural food stores, and some supermarkets) or as seed potatoes (although Fedco Seeds' Moose Tubers division offers a good selection at a reasonable price). Once we discovered the thrift of letting a portion of last summer's crop sprout as seed potatoes, we've had no problem keeping them in circulation—not just in our own larder, but shared back and forth with Art. Swedish Peanut and Rose Finn Apple are two of our favorite varieties.

Fingerlings are among the more forgiving and prolific potatoes to cultivate, usually yielding up to a dozen tubers per plant. And, because of their small size, they're an early harvest, giving you new potatoes by as early as midsummer. Try some, and enjoy!

Slow-Roasted Tomato-Onion Confit

If you have an abundance of cherry tomatoes—and I mean buckets of them, a likely predicament anytime you grow this prolific plant, or its cluster-tomato relative the saladette plum tomato—this slow-roasted tomato sauce is an easy and delicious way to deal with them. Inspired by a cluster of recipes shared by my Penobscot friend and neighbor Kathy Turok (from The New Legal Sea Foods Cookbook *and Sally Schneider's* The New Way to Cook*), the confit can be elegantly simple with just the caramelized onions and tomatoes roasted in olive oil, or brightened with a little rosemary, bay, or thyme, garlic, and balsamic vinegar. Serve it as a condiment with grilled or roasted meats, grilled, broiled, or pan-fried fish, egg-and-cheese dishes, or as a spread for crostini toasts (page 20).*

Garden-ripe tomatoes need only a little encouragement to bring out their sweet intensity, but you can use this same treatment to transform off-season plum tomatoes, with a pinch of light brown sugar and a little more balsamic vinegar. For a stovetop tomato confit sweetened with marsala, see page 99.

MAKES 1 1/2 PINTS; SERVES 4 TO 5 AS CONDIMENT

2 tablespoons extra-virgin olive oil

1 small to medium yellow onion, thin crescents

1 1/4 quarts cherry or saladette plum tomatoes, halved or cut in thirds, gently seeded (enough tomatoes to fill baking dish in 1 1/2 layers)

1 medium clove garlic, slivered

2 to 3 small sprigs fresh rosemary (*or* 2 small bay leaves, *or* 1 teaspoon fresh thyme)

Salt and fresh-ground multicolored pepper

1 teaspoon balsamic vinegar

Preheat oven to 325°F. Oil a 10 x 12-inch ovenproof baking dish and spread onions over the bottom. Cover with tomatoes cut in halves or thirds, cut-side up, shaking out and discarding loose seeds. Distribute herbs and garlic evenly among the tomatoes; sprinkle with salt and pepper to taste.

Set dish in top third of oven, and roast for 30 minutes, moving tomatoes around from time to time with a spoon or spatula so they roast evenly. Sprinkle with balsamic vinegar, reduce heat to 300°, and continue baking, stirring occasionally, for 1 hour, or until juices are reduced and onions and tomatoes are semi-caramelized into a rich, chunky sauce.

Serve as a condiment or store in the refrigerator, where it will keep for up to a week.

NOTE: If seriously inundated with garden cherry tomatoes, try Richard's expedient way of dealing with them: Using a food mill, press them into bright tomato juice or soup, cook briefly, then freeze—or add a touch of balsamic vinegar to boost acidity and can in pint jars.

Summer Veggies

A celebration of fresh garden vegetables, this sauté goes well with most anything you might want to throw on the grill on a summer evening. Add some bite-sized pieces of leftover grilled chicken or steak, lamb or pork, shell beans and/or corn, and you have a summertime stew.

SERVES 2

1 to 2 tablespoons extra-virgin olive oil

1/2 onion, crescents

1/2 summer squash, roll-cut or half-moons

1/2 zucchini, roll-cut or half-moons

1 pint green beans, whole or halved, stemmed

1 clove garlic, minced (*or dash garlic powder*)

2/3 pint cherry or saladette plum tomatoes, whole or halved

2 tablespoons fresh basil (or pesto)

1 to 2 tablespoons pine nuts, lightly toasted

Heat oil in non-stick pan and sauté onion, about 1 minute. Add squash and sauté briefly, then add beans and garlic and sauté over medium heat for 3 minutes, stirring frequently, otherwise leaving pan covered to sweat vegetables. (If the onions begin to turn gold, sprinkle a little water into pan.)

When beans are al dente (almost tender), stir one last time, add tomatoes, cover pan, and turn off heat; give residual heat a couple of minutes to heat the tomatoes through. Garnish with chopped fresh basil and pine nuts (or top each serving with a spoonful of Genovese Pesto, page 21).

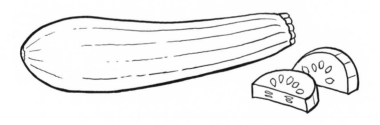

STIR-STEAMED VEGGIES

This simple technique is nothing more than vegetables sautéed and sweated, with the help of a little water to deglaze the pan and keep things from catching on. It works especially well with firm but succulent vegetables that benefit from a quick coating of oil and heat, then a slow steam until tender, such as summer squash, zucchini, peppers, peapods, and green beans; leeks, cauliflower, broccoli, collards, and bok choy; kale, rainbow chard, baby beets, and other greens. Pan-roasting with onions really brings out the sweetness of storage vegetables like carrots, parsnips, rutabaga, savoy cabbage, and Brussels sprouts. Starchy vegetables (peas, beets, winter squash) do better in the steamer.

As in stir-fries, in a stir-steam there's a certain Zen of judging when to add each vegetable, in order of density and thickness, so that each will be at its best. The idea is to seal and slightly caramelize the onions and vegetables, then deglaze the pan (page 125) with just enough water to release the flavorful fond. Start the sauté over moderate heat with a little olive oil and about a half cup of onion, sliced in thin crescents; then add the vegetables in order of cooking time, intermittently stir-frying and covering the pan to sweat moisture from the vegetables. At the first sign of their catching on, sprinkle water as needed; replace lid and let the veggies finish steaming over low heat until al dente.

Cauliflower with Indian Spices

*W*ho said cauliflower needed to be bland and blah? Stir-steamed with colorful fresh vegetables and fragrant Indian spices, it's a feast for the eyes and palate, a sure cure for a white supper!

   This dish was inspired by a recipe in Madhur Jaffrey's classic Delhi-style Indian cookbook, An Invitation to Indian Cooking. *She started the sauté with a bit of fresh ginger paste, and included fresh cilantro leaves with the vegetables—two other options for genuine Indian flavor.*

SERVES 2 TO 3

1/2 head cauliflower, spears or florets (about 2 cups)

1 small or 1/2 large onion, crescents

1 small clove garlic, minced

2/3 red bell pepper, sliced in strips

1 to 1 1/2 cups green beans, whole or cut in half (optional)

1/2 teaspoon ground coriander

1/8 teaspoon ground cumin

1/8 teaspoon turmeric

1 to 2 cardamom seeds (not pods), ground in mortar and pestle (optional)

Few grates black or multicolored peppercorns

Dash of salt

1 tablespoon olive oil

1 to 1 1/2 teaspoons fresh-squeezed lemon juice

About 1/4 cup fresh cilantro leaves, chopped

Wash cauliflower and separate stalks into spears or florets about 3/4 to 1 inch wide by 2 inches long. Prep other vegetables. Assemble spices on a small piece of waxed paper.

   If cauliflower florets are fairly large or dense, it's best to give them a couple minutes' head start in the steamer before joining the vegetable sauté, to avoid overcooking the other vegetables; otherwise you can add them to the skillet along with the garlic, peppers, and optional beans.

   Heat olive oil in large skillet and sauté onion about 1 minute over moderate heat. Briefly stir in spices, then add garlic, pepper strips, cauliflower florets (raw if small, partially steamed if large), and green beans (if desired). Stir to coat cauliflower evenly with spices, and sauté 1 to 2 minutes more, stirring occasionally while keeping pan covered to sweat vegetables. Sprinkle in lemon juice plus 1 to 2 teaspoons water as needed to keep veggies from browning.

   When vegetables are al dente, sprinkle with cilantro, then turn heat off and let vegetables steam briefly in the fragrant juices, covered. Serve immediately.

CORIANDER AND CILANTRO

*N*ot everyone realizes that coriander and cilantro are actually two parts of the same plant, *Coriandrum sativum.* No wonder they go together so well! Cilantro (aka Chinese parsley) is the pungent leaf, at its most flavorful when first picked around the base of the plant. Coriander comes from the seeds, dried and ground into a spice with the subtle sweet fragrance of lemon or orange. Coriander seeds are seldom available as a whole spice, but you can easily grow your own coriander "berries" by letting a row of cilantro flower and go to seed; store the light brown dried seeds in a jar, and sprinkle them whole into savory dishes in lieu of ground coriander.

Asparagus with Orange-Cilantro Cream

Thinking what might dress up some steamed asparagus alongside a dinner of Chili Scallops (page 68) and rice, I remembered how well orange and cilantro go together in a simple herbed butter for fish—and why not asparagus? To make enough for just two servings, though, the eggbeater method of whipping cream seemed too much trouble. Then I remembered the shake-jar method of churning butter, learned way back in Brownies. Whipping the ingredients this way into a thick flavored cream takes a bit longer than with an eggbeater, but is fun and sparing of dishes.

Whichever method, you could keep "churning" the cream until it warms and turns to butter, then drain off the whey. I prefer it as a thickened cream, the orange zest turning the cream a subtle gold.

This simple side dish would go equally well with simply prepared or leftover roast chicken breast. Or spoon a little of the cream as a sauce over scallops, halibut, salmon, or some other firm flavorful fish, grilled or broiled.

2 TO 3 SERVINGS

2/3 bunch fresh asparagus (2/3 to 3/4 pound)   Orange-Cilantro Cream

ORANGE-CILANTRO CREAM

1/3 cup heavy/whipping cream, chilled
1/4 teaspoon freshly grated orange zest
1 teaspoon freshly squeezed orange juice
1 tablespoon fresh cilantro, finely chopped

1 teaspoon fresh chives, snipped (optional)
Few grates white pepper
Few grains salt

Snap pale stem ends off asparagus; snap stalks in half or leave whole. Trim off any tough bracts.

Place ingredients for Orange-Cilantro Cream together in a lidded 8-ounce jar, chilled to keep the cream cold (if the cream warms, it will make butter). Shake jar continually for 5 to 10 minutes, or until cream has thickened to a whipped cream. (Or if you prefer, whip the cream with a whisk or eggbeater, then add the other ingredients.) The flavored cream can be made up to 2 hours ahead.

Steam asparagus until bright green and tender through. Serve immediately.

Variation

LIME-CILANTRO CREAM: Use a little minced or grated lime rind along with fresh lime juice in place of the orange zest and juice.

Brussels Sprouts with Chestnuts, Fennel & Orange

Here's a nice way to serve Brussels sprouts, a little dressed up for a special dinner or holiday meal— also a nice way to celebrate chestnut season. The tender "little cabbages" (petits chous in French) and chestnut meats soaked in the sweetly savory drizzling sauce would go especially well alongside roast beef, pork, or duck.

If you like chestnuts as much as we do, you'll probably want to roast a couple dozen while you're at it, sample a few fresh-roasted ones, and save the rest (shelled and refrigerated) to use in other dishes (see Greek Winter Salad, page 46, and Brown Rice Pilaf with Chestnuts, page 186).

SERVES 4 TO 6

6 to 8 Spanish chestnuts

2 to 3 cups raw Brussels sprouts

1 tablespoon salted butter

2 tablespoons extra-virgin olive oil

1/4 teaspoon whole fennel seeds, ground in mortar and pestle

1/4 teaspoon salt (*or* 1 to 2 teaspoons tamari soy sauce)

1/4 teaspoon onion powder

Pinch of cayenne

1/4 cup freshly squeezed orange juice (about 1/2 orange)

Preheat oven to 350°F. With a sharp paring knife, cut crosses in tops of chestnuts (important, to prevent explosion!) and roast in a metal pan for 15 to 20 minutes, or until hulls open up where cut and chestnuts give when squeezed. Remove chestnuts from oven and test one for doneness; if tender, immediately shell them all, peeling off hulls and inner skin (which has an acrid taste). Wrap them in a towel to hold their heat as you shell them (don't wait; chestnuts are much harder to shell once cooled). Discard any off-smelling or moldy sections. Break nutmeats into 2 to 4 pieces and set aside.

While chestnuts are roasting, prepare the Brussels sprouts: If large, trim and halve them; otherwise if small, leave them whole and cut an X in the bottom.

Also prepare the drizzling liquid: Heat butter and oil in small metal bowl in oven; once butter has melted, add fennel seeds and other seasonings (all except for orange juice). Remove from oven and keep warm on back of stove.

Steam Brussels sprouts until tender all the way through but not overdone, and place in saucepan. Add chestnuts. Squeeze orange and add juice to drizzling liquid, then pour over vegetable mixture and toss. Let stand while you assemble the rest of the meal.

When ready to serve, quickly bring vegetables back up to heat and put in warmed serving bowl.

Orange-Herb Stuffing

The key to this stuffing is having on hand (fresh or in the freezer) a loaf of Onion Walnut Dill Bread, made by Morning Glory Bakery of Bar Harbor. A few slices of this light-textured, walnut-studded, mildly savory bread, diced and tossed with herbs and moistened with a little butter, oil, and orange, makes an easy, delicious stuffing for turkey, chicken, or especially duck, whether roasted whole or in parts. Lacking this particular bread, substitute any porous, light wheat bread (such as Pane Pugliese), plus a handful of lightly toasted walnuts. Leftover stuffing can help thicken a Duck Soup (page 44).

℗ SERVES 4 TO 6

1 medium yellow onion, diced (1/2 to 2/3 cup)

2 tablespoons olive oil

1 tablespoon butter

About 3 large (or 4 medium) slices Onion Walnut Dill Bread (or similar), cut in large cubes

1/2 teaspoon dried lovage (*or* 1/4 cup chopped celery stalk)

1/4 teaspoon marjoram

1/4 teaspoon thyme

1/2 teaspoon sage

1/4 teaspoon summer savory

1/2 teaspoon salt

Few grates each white and black pepper

1 to 2 teaspoons freshly grated orange zest

Flesh of 1 medium Valencia orange, peeled, sliced, seeded, and chopped

1/4 cup walnuts, lightly toasted (page 269)

3 to 4 tablespoons chicken, turkey, or duck broth, as needed (or cider)

Heat oil and lightly sauté onion (and celery, if using instead of lovage), adding butter as onion starts to clarify. Turn off heat and add bread and seasonings. Chop orange pulp and add to stuffing mixture. Toast walnuts for a few minutes at 325°F (double the amount of nuts if using an alternate bread), chop coarsely, and toss to combine. Add broth as needed to bring stuffing loosely together.

Stuff cavity if roasting whole bird (duck, chicken, turkey); otherwise, if roasting parts of the bird, pile a portion of stuffing under each thigh, breast, or other part, and roast.

CHESTNUTS

I discovered chestnuts on one of many visits to Kew Gardens while spending the fall semester of my junior year at Richmond College in London. There, under an ancient chestnut tree near the Thames, I came upon a family scrabbling around in the fallen leaves, gathering up the shiny brown nuts that had rolled out of their spiny husks. The people were glad to tell me how to oven-roast chestnuts, and eager to try some I picked up a batch and roasted them in the college dorm kitchen. Mmmmm . . .

Thanks to recent efforts to restore the American chestnut (decimated by wood harvesting and blight in the last century), maybe someday we'll again have healthy chestnut trees in Maine big enough to produce local nuts; till then, I'll keep looking forward to the brief season each fall when imported Spanish chestnuts are available in supermarkets. (Get them early on, as they tend to develop acrid moldy spots later in the winter.) Their sweet, spicy flavor and texture makes a nice complement to onions and savory herbs, cabbage, and other brassicas.

Hazelnut Spoon Bread

Deliciously sweet and nutty, this soufflé-like side dish has a few more steps and ingredients than your basic spoon bread, but is well worth the effort. Some steps (such as preparing the corn and nuts) can be done ahead. Based on a recipe from Betty Fussell's wonderfully eclectic and creative cookbook Crazy for Corn, *it combines fresh corn off the cob with toasted hazelnuts, flavors just made for each other.*

The key to the sweet flavor is using corn straight from your garden or local farm stand, preferably bicolor sweet and at its prime (not too mature). Lacking fresh or frozen local corn, commercially frozen shoepeg or gold & white corn should be nearly as sweet. If using frozen corn, give it time to thaw before adding. Also it's best to bake the soufflé in a dish with a good thermal mass—we use a curved 2-quart stoneware pottery casserole made by Brooksville potter (and old Findhorn friend) Scott Goldberg.

With fresh corn, the closer to home you find it, and the less time between harvest and cooking, the better. Just-picked sweet corn stands head and shoulders above most "native" supermarket corn in texture and flavor, so take advantage of a good harvest by blanching and freezing a supply while it's in season. It will bring sunshine into your cooking all winter long.

SERVES 6

1/4 to 1/3 cup raw hazelnuts	1 tablespoon salted butter
2 cups raw fresh corn kernels (2 to 3 ears)	1 tablespoon olive oil
1 cup yellow cornmeal	1 tablespoon white or organic sugar
2 cups boiling water	(or less if using very sweet corn)
1 1/4 cups milk	1/2 teaspoon salt
3 large eggs, separated	2 teaspoons baking powder

In preheating oven set to 350°F, lightly toast hazelnuts in baking pan for 6 to 8 minutes or until skins loosen. Place on towel and rub off skins, then chop nuts.

If using fresh corn, husk corn and slice off kernels with sharp knife, being careful not to include cob. Scrape off any corn "germ" remaining on cob with back of knife. If using frozen corn, prethaw or soak well-sealed bag of corn in a bowl of warm water to hasten thawing. When thawed, put corn in a strainer to drain off the corn "milk" thoroughly; discard or reserve liquid for another use.

Measure cornmeal into large mixing bowl and gradually stir in boiling water. Let stand while you assemble the other ingredients, keeping oven set to 350°.

Put 1 cup of the corn kernels in a blender and purée, then add milk and egg yolks, and pulse until blended. Stir into cornmeal mixture. Meanwhile, melt butter with oil in 2-quart ovenproof casserole or baking dish in oven (this also greases and preheats the dish). Stir the warm melted shortening into cornmeal mixture along with hazelnuts, sugar, salt, baking powder, and remaining corn kernels.

Beat egg whites until moderately stiff and fold thoroughly into soufflé batter. Spread butter/oil residue around bottom and sides of baking dish, then pour/scrape batter into dish. Bake in center of 350° oven for 50 minutes, then turn off heat and bake another 5 to 10 minutes in residual heat until soufflé is puffed up and nicely browned on top. Serve at once.

The spoon bread is a nice complement to ham, pork shoulder, or a shell bean–vegetable stew.

Party Polenta

The "party" comes from the colorful peppers in this seasoned polenta. If you can find them at a farmer's market or in your own garden, Romanian frying peppers are a good choice, or mildly hot colored peppers in place of the sweet bell peppers and cayenne. Italian herbs and cheeses round out the flavor.

One of the quickest side dishes to make, this melt-in-your-mouth polenta (inspired by a recipe in Cooking Light *magazine) can be served alongside eggs, steak, burgers, chops, chili—or spread in a Pyrex or stoneware deep-dish pie plate as the bottom layer of a vegetable frittata (page 133).*

℗ SERVES 3 TO 4

1 cup Italian-style polenta (or coarse cornmeal)

3 1/4 cups water

1/2 teaspoon salt

2 teaspoons dried basil

1 teaspoon dried marjoram or oregano

1/8 teaspoon cayenne

1/2 cup bell peppers (combination red/orange and green/yellow), seeded and chopped

1/3 cup grated Romano and/or Parmesan cheese

1/4 teaspoon paprika (optional, if no red peppers available)

Pumpkin seeds, lightly toasted (optional)

Put polenta and cold water in saucepan and bring to boil over medium heat, stirring constantly with spoon or whisk. As polenta begins to thicken, add seasonings and chopped peppers; stir frequently to keep from sticking on.

Cover and continue cooking over low heat for 10 to 15 minutes more, stirring occasionally. Stir in cheese, turn off heat, and let rest, covered, until ready to serve, reheating if necessary. Serve as a side dish, garnished with pumpkin seeds if desired.

Rice-Noodle Pilaf

So simple it hardly needs a recipe, this quick rice pilaf (based on an old Armenian tradition) has a mellow flavor and nice texture, especially when baked in the oven. A fun change from plain old white rice, it's one of our favorite carbos to make at home and camp. All you need is rice and a few straws of uncooked angel-hair pasta or linguine—in fact, here's a good way to use up the short, broken pieces.

Pan-roasted white basmati rice, just by itself, is another nice variation from regular cooked rice. Lightly roasting the grains in a little oil seals and separates them, yielding fluffier rice that reheats well in a stir-steamed dish like Quick Risotto (page 151). For a traditional risotto, read on.

 SERVES 4

1/4 cup angel hair, linguine, or other fine pasta, broken into 5/8-inch pieces

2 to 3 teaspoons olive oil

1 cup white basmati rice

2 to 2 1/4 cups boiling water (or water + chicken or vegetable stock)

For baked Rice-Noodle Pilaf, preheat oven to 375°F. Break pasta into short pieces. Heat oil in small (7 x 7-inch) lidded Corningware or other ovenproof baking dish. Add rice and pan-roast over low-moderate heat for 1 to 2 minutes, stirring constantly to prevent scorching. Add pasta pieces, and pan-roast with rice about a minute more, until evenly a very light gold. Add boiling water (or water plus stock), and cover with lid. Bake for 30 minutes (oven may be turned off after 25 minutes).

To cook on top of the stove, pan-roast grains and pasta the same way, over low heat, then place covered pot on a flame-tamer heat diffuser to keep the bottom from catching on. Cook 25 minutes.

Variation

PAN-ROASTED RICE: Omit the pasta, and add 2 cups boiling water to the pan-roasted rice.

Butternut Risotto

This savory risotto, golden with winter squash, makes a nice side dish for chicken or pork. Thanks to Betsy Washburn Butterworth and Judith Barrett (author of a lovely vegetarian cookbook, In an Italian Garden*) for the inspiration.*

SERVES 4

1 tablespoon butter

2 tablespoons olive oil

1/4 cup chopped onion

1 to 1 1/2 cups shredded butternut squash

1 cup arborio or Carolina golden rice

1/4 cup white wine

1 3/4 cups boiling water

1 1/2 cups chicken or vegetable stock

Few grates white pepper

1/4 teaspoon sage

1/4 teaspoon winter savory

1/4 cup grated Parmigiano-Reggiano cheese

Heat half of butter and oil in skillet and briefly sauté squash over medium-low heat, until tender. Transfer to bowl to cool. Clean pan and sauté onion in remaining butter and oil till translucent; add rice and pan-fry another 1 to 2 minutes. Add wine and stir to deglaze pan and cook off alcohol.

Stir in 3/4 cup water and simmer, covered, until liquid is mostly absorbed. Stir in another 3/4 cup water and simmer. Repeat with 3/4 cup stock, adding pepper and herbs; then stir in the remaining stock and squash. Simmer over low heat, until rice is al dente, adding last 1/4 cup water as needed to keep risotto from sticking. Stir in cheese, turn off heat, and let risotto rest 5 minutes before serving.

"Saffron" Rice

This golden "saffron" rice is one reason to grow calendulas in your garden—Calendula officinalis, an old kitchen garden favorite nicknamed "poor man's saffron." Though edible fresh (sprinkled over stews and salads), the bright yellow-gold-orange flower heads can also be snipped in full bloom and air-dried, then stored in an airtight jar in your pantry. The petals will hold their color for several years, lending it to rice dishes—especially welcome when you are serving what would otherwise be a "white dinner" (as with haddock or scallops). This stand-in saffron rice (or the simpler petal-sprinkled variation) is just right with Middle Eastern dishes like Persian Lamb Shanks (page 118).

Genuine saffron (the stigma of a certain crocus flower) is literally worth its weight in gold, but if you are have some, by all means use it in place of the calendula petals and turmeric.

SERVES 4 TO 6

1 tablespoon olive oil	Tiny pinch (less than 1/8 teaspoon) turmeric
1 cup white basmati rice	2 teaspoons salted butter
2 cups boiling water	2 teaspoons olive oil
2 tablespoons calendula petals, fresh or dried	1/2 teaspoon salt
1 1/2 tablespoons boiling water	1/4 cup lightly roasted pistachios, cut in half

Preheat oven to 375°F. In 8 x 8-inch square Corningware or other ovenproof casserole, heat oil and pan-roast rice over moderate heat, stirring constantly—not long enough to brown, but to coat grains and heat until light gold and glistening. Add 2 cups boiling water, cover, and bake 1/2 hour.

While rice is baking, remove petals from calendula flowers and place in cup. Pour 1 1/2 tablespoons boiling water over petals. Steep 10 minutes, then squeeze out extract. Prepare pistachios.

Melt 2 teaspoons each butter and oil in small saucepan or stainless-steel bowl, then add turmeric and calendula extract. When rice is done, remove from oven and drizzle with "saffron" liquid. Sprinkle nuts over rice and lightly fluff contents of casserole with fork or knife. Serve immediately.

Variation
QUICK "SAFFRON" RICE: Simply sprinkle 1 tablespoon calendula petals over rice before adding boiling water. The golden dried flowers on top will add color as well as a subtle fragrance.

Brown Rice Pilaf with Chestnuts

Serve this pilaf as a side dish or stuffing for a roast chicken, capon, or turkey. Or stretch it into a simple, savory meal-in-itself, with double the amount of sausage, accompanied by sautéed onions and savoy cabbage.

SERVES 4 TO 6 AS SIDE DISH, 3 AS MAIN DISH

8 to 10 Spanish chestnuts (page 181)

1 cup brown basmati rice

2 cups boiling water

3 to 4 ounces fennel/sweet Italian pork sausage (or spicy lamb/sheep sausage made with pepper and allspice, such as King Hill Farm's) (optional)

2 teaspoons olive oil

1 small or 1/2 large onion, chopped (1/2 cup)

1 teaspoon butter

1/3 to 1/2 cup chopped celery (or 1 teaspoon dried lovage)

1 small clove garlic, minced (or 1/8 teaspoon garlic powder)

1/2 teaspoon winter or summer savory

1/8 teaspoon thyme

1/4 to 1/2 teaspoon dried marjoram (optional)

1/4 teaspoon salt

Few grates "party" (multicolored) pepper

1/4 cup chicken or vegetable stock

Preheat oven to 350°F. With a sharp paring knife, cut crosses in tops of chestnuts (important, to prevent explosion!) and roast in a metal pan for 15 to 20 minutes, or until hulls open up where cut and chestnuts give when squeezed. Remove chestnuts from oven and test one for doneness; if tender, immediately shell them all, peeling off hulls and inner skin (which has an acrid taste). Wrap them in a towel to hold their heat as you shell them (don't wait; chestnuts are much harder to shell once cooled). Discard any off-smelling or moldy sections. Break nutmeats into 2 to 4 pieces and set aside.

Turn oven heat up to 375°. Place rice in tight-lidded ovenproof casserole, rinse, and cover with boiling water. Bake rice for 45 minutes.

Meanwhile, prepare sausage (if desired): If sausage is in casing, remove meat from casing, then break off lumps of sausage meat and gently fry in a large skillet or Dutch oven with a minimal amount of oil. Set aside; drain fat.

Add 2 teaspoons olive oil to the pan and sauté onion until partly translucent. Add butter, celery, and garlic and sauté a minute more. Stir in seasonings, reserved chestnut meats, sausage, then finally the stock, scraping any browned bits from bottom of pan. Cover and turn off heat.

When rice is cooked, remove from oven and add to seasoned vegetable-sausage mixture, if in Dutch oven; otherwise, transfer rice to warmed serving bowl and toss with seasoned mixture.

Baked Brown Rice or Barley

Baking brown rice or barley is convenient and energy-efficient if you're baking something else at the same time, with no worry of the grains catching on. We bake more than enough for a meal, since these whole grains take longer to cook and leftovers reheat nicely (page 190) for a quick second appearance.

White rice and pearled barley can be baked the same way, with no rinsing needed; baking time is 30 minutes for rice, slightly longer for pearled barley.

Both brown basmati rice and whole barley are wonderful, fragrant, satisfying grains, whether served as a side dish or the base for a pilaf (as on pages 186 and 188). Brown rice goes well with anything, from egg, meat, and bean dishes to seafood and stir-fries. Barley is especially nice with roast lamb and onions, as an entrée or as leftovers made into Scotch broth.

 SERVES 4 TO 5

FOR RICE: 1 cup brown basmati rice
2 cups boiling water

FOR BARLEY: 1 cup whole barley, soaked
2 1/2 cups boiling water

Barley bakes best if the grains are soaked in water for a few hours or overnight. For rice, measure grains into lidded 1-quart baking dish; rinse with lukewarm water, and drain. Add boiling water, stir, and bake in preheated 375°F oven 45 minutes for rice, 50 to 60 minutes for barley (turn oven off for last 5 minutes). Remove baking dish from oven, keeping lid on until ready to serve; do not overbake.

Bulghur Pilaf

This pilaf, subtly seasoned with savory herbs and spices, goes well with Mediterranean and Middle Eastern dishes, especially lamb (leftover pilaf can be used in Baked Kibbeh, page 122). Although the pan-roasting and baking method is best for flavorful and fluffy grains, the pilaf is simple enough to make in a rustic stovetop kitchen, with the seasonings made up ahead in a foil spice packet.

 SERVES 4 TO 5

1 tablespoon olive oil
1/4 cup yellow onion, minced (*or* 1/4 teaspoon
   onion powder)
1 cup bulghur (cracked wheat)
1/2 teaspoon winter savory (*or* 1/4 teaspoon
   each Greek oregano and dried mint)

1 to 2 teaspoons dried lovage leaves
1/8 teaspoon allspice
1/2 teaspoon salt
Few grates black pepper
Tiny pinch cayenne pepper
2 cups boiling water

Preheat oven to 375°F. Heat oil in small (7 x 7-inch) tightly lidded Corningware or other ovenproof baking dish, and sauté onion in oil for a minute or so until translucent. Add bulghur and pan-roast over low-moderate heat for 1 to 2 minutes, stirring constantly. Add seasonings and boiling water, and cover with lid. Bake for 45 minutes (oven may be turned off after 40 minutes).

Mushroom-Barley Pilaf

I'll never forget my first whiff of home on arriving in Brooklin, late one November afternoon in 1981, where Zilla Daniel had offered to put me up during my first winter working for WoodenBoat. (Zilla and I had met at Findhorn in the community's publications department, and here again we were friends and colleagues working at WoodenBoat, she as proofreader and I as typesetter/copyeditor.) Bunny Gorski, a good friend of Zilla's (and soon mine), in the true neighborly spirit that is so alive and well in Brooklin and other coastal towns Downeast, had brought over a mushroom-barley pilaf she'd made and left to finish baking in Zilla's oven. Settling in while waiting for Zilla to come home from WoodenBoat, I breathed in that comforting aroma and felt grateful to be in a community of friends like these, so caring and such great cooks! After experimenting with the ingredients Bunny recalled using in that savory pilaf, I've enjoyed making it a couple times every winter since.

The technique of dry-roasting nuts in tamari is something I learned in the Findhorn kitchen, where we regularly tamari-roasted peanuts, hazels, almonds, and sunflower seeds to serve as a garnish.

SERVES 4

1 cup whole barley (or pearled)	1/4 teaspoon garlic powder
1 1/4 cups water	1/4 teaspoon salt
1 cup beef broth/bouillon (or vegetable stock)	Few grates black pepper
2/3 to 1 cup baby portabella mushrooms, cleaned and sliced	2 teaspoons dried lovage leaves
	1 teaspoon winter savory
1 tablespoon salted butter	4 teaspoons tamari
1 tablespoon olive oil	2/3 cup walnut halves, broken in half

Set water to boil in teakettle, and heat stock to a simmer. Preheat oven to 375°F. Rinse barley with cold water and place in small (7 x 7-inch) tightly lidded Corningware or other ovenproof baking dish. Add water and stock, cover and bake for about 45 minutes for whole barley (about 30 minutes for pearled).

Meanwhile, prepare the mushrooms and sauté in butter and oil until slightly browned and beginning to release their liquor. Stir in seasonings including 2 teaspoons of the tamari. When the barley has baked long enough to be al dente, remove from oven and stir in the seasoned mushroom mixture. Lower heat to 350° and return pilaf to oven, adding a little more liquid if necessary, and continue to bake covered for about another 20 to 30 minutes or until grains are tender and liquid is completely absorbed.

During the final half-hour of baking, oven-toast the walnut halves for a couple of minutes, till hot and lightly golden. Remove from oven, drizzle with remaining tamari, and shake pan to coat evenly. Return pan to oven for another 30 seconds to 1 minute until the tamari has dry-coated the nuts. When ready to serve, garnish the top of the pilaf with the nuts if you prefer them crunchy; otherwise, they can be stirred into the pilaf during last 15 minutes or so of baking.

Buckwheat (Kasha)

With the first cold raw autumn days, I start craving buckwheat for its bland light flavor and satisfying low-gluten texture, along with its warming (yang) effect. Usually we'll make a batch to have plain (with a little butter and tamari) alongside a savory dinner of pork or scallops and winter storage vegetables, but I'm always glad to have leftover buckwheat (kasha) as the basis for a lunch veggie stir-fry. Buckwheat tastes wonderful with stir-steamed brassicas and sweet root vegetables like onions or leeks, savoy cabbage, turnips, squash, or carrots, sprinkled with toasted nuts and tamari.

Buckwheat is also a fine breakfast cereal, a discovery I made living with Zilla Daniel, who loved starting the day with hot whole grains. Assemble a steaming bowlful of kasha deliciously dressed up with applesauce (or cranberry sauce, Zilla's favorite), yogurt, walnuts, cinnamon, and maple syrup; or (my favorite) dried currants, butter, cinnamon, maple syrup, toasted hazelnuts, and fresh orange juice.

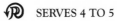 SERVES 4 TO 5

1 cup buckwheat groats
1 medium egg, beaten

2 1/4 cups boiling water

Rinse buckwheat in strainer with cold water, shaking out excess liquid. Turn into Corningware or other lidded stovetop/ovenproof baking dish. Stirring constantly, dry-roast grains over medium heat. Meanwhile, beat egg in small cup, and set water to boil in kettle. Preheat oven to 375°F.

When buckwheat is nearly dry and grains are hot and steaming, remove from heat and add egg, stirring to coat grains evenly. Stir 30 seconds more or until egg is set, then quickly stir boiling water into grains. Cover and bake 30 to 35 minutes, or until grains are puffed and all liquid is absorbed.

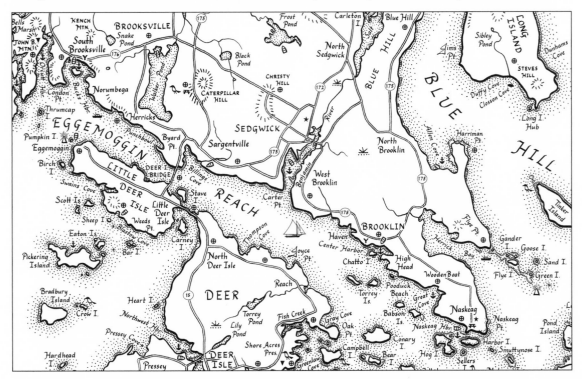

Pan-Roasted Couscous, Quinoa, or Millet

These light, mellow golden grains go especially well with grilled meats and dishes served with pan drippings or piquant, clear sauces, such as chicken and shrimp. Serve these fluffy cooked grains plain (a soothing choice for delicate digestions), or garnish with a few lightly toasted pumpkin seeds ("poor man's pistachios"), almonds, or hazelnuts as a simple pilaf. All are quick and easy carbos whether cooking at home or camp; directions for both methods (oven and stovetop) are given here.

Although these grains are best when freshly made, they reheat nicely as described below.

 SERVES 4 TO 6

1 tablespoon olive oil
1 cup dry couscous, quinoa, or millet

2 cups boiling water

Preheat oven to 375°F. Heat oil in small (7 x 7-inch) lidded Corningware or other ovenproof baking dish. Add grains and pan-roast over low-moderate heat for a couple of minutes, stirring constantly to prevent from scorching. When evenly dry-roasted to a very light gold, add boiling water, and cover with lid.

Bake couscous, a processed grain, for 20 to 25 minutes, turning the oven off after 10 to 15 minutes; this prevents overcooking and ensures fluffy couscous. Bake quinoa and millet, both nutty-tasting whole grains, for 25 to 30 minutes at 375°.

If camping or camp-cruising with just a stovetop, pan-roast grains in lidded heavy-bottomed pot over low heat. Add boiling water and place covered pot on flame-tamer or other heat diffuser to keep bottom from scorching. Gently cook couscous for 15 minutes, then turn off heat and leave on warm burner. Cook quinoa or millet over low heat for 30 minutes, checking with a chopstick for doneness.

REHEATING LEFTOVER GRAINS

In working around the limitations of cooking at camp, we discovered an easy—and superior—way to reheat leftover cooked grains such as kasha, bulghur and couscous, quinoa, millet, white or brown rice: Wipe a little olive oil around the bottom and sides of a metal pie plate, sprinkle the leftover grains evenly in the pan, cover with foil, and place over low heat—either toward the outer edge of a charcoal grill, or on a flame-tamer over a gas burner. Heat for about 10 minutes, stirring the grains around midway with a chopstick, and there you are—hot, fluffy, moist grains, with maybe some golden crispness around the edges of the pan.

The same idea works well at home, heating leftover cooked grains in the oven (or toaster oven, if the stove's oven is not already in use baking the rest of the meal): Simply crumble the leftover cooked grains into a lightly oiled metal pie pan, cover with foil, and heat for 10 to 12 minutes in a 375° oven, or until the grains are hot and steaming.

This method is also a good way to reheat leftover mashed potatoes, and much more reliable than trying to reheat leftover carbos in a saucepan, with damp, often gummy (or worse, stuck-on) results.

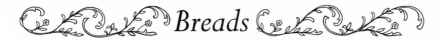

Breads

Whole-Wheat Biscuits

If you're hankering for the classic feather-light, buttery, yeast-bready variety, nothing is finer than a batch of Bakewell Cream biscuits, baked close together following the recipe on the can—delicious dipped in maple syrup or molasses for an old-time Downeast treat, as offered by Patty Hutchins at "Food Way Back When Along the Bagaduce," an afternoon of local food memories sponsored by the Bagaduce Watershed Association and the Wilson Museum in Castine.

The biscuits here, featuring whole-grain flours, are nutty-tasting, crusty, more like a scone. This recipe makes a smallish batch of biscuits, just the right size to fit on top of a Pot Pie (page 96) or round out the corners of a light meal—even breakfast, with honey or jam. Leftover biscuits freeze just fine.

MAKES 9 TO 12 BISCUITS

1 1/2 cups whole-wheat pastry flour (*or* 1 cup whole-wheat + 1/2 cup unbleached flour)
1/2 cup oat flour (or barley flour)
1/4 teaspoon salt
1 tablespoon baking powder

1/4 teaspoon baking soda
3 tablespoons chilled salted butter, diced
2 tablespoons olive (or vegetable) oil
2/3 cup cold milk mixed with a little yogurt (or buttermilk)

Measure dry ingredients in mixing bowl and toss together. Rub diced butter into flours with fingers until evenly distributed, then sprinkle oil over and stir to combine. Preheat oven to 425°F.

Add milk mixed with a little plain yogurt (or buttermilk) all at once and stir briefly to bring dough together. Turn dough out onto floured surface, and with floured hands, shape into a flattened ball. Turn to coat with flour, then pat out into a circle or square about 5/8 inch thick.

If making a Pot Pie, shape and bake biscuit squares as described on page 97. To make round biscuits, cut dough with a 2- or 2 1/4-inch biscuit or cookie cutter, or the top of a glass dipped in flour. Gather up dough remnants, reform, and recut till dough is used up. Transfer biscuits with floured spatula to oiled and floured baking sheet. Brush tops with milk for a golden crust.

Bake in top third of oven for 10 to 12 minutes, or until biscuits are golden. (It is a little harder to tell when whole-wheat breads and pastries are browned, so start checking after 8 minutes.)

Cranberry-Walnut Biscuits

I threw these fruit-and-nut biscuits together to go with a savory soup, only to find they are also nice for breakfast, reheated or fresh-baked, hot, split, and drizzled with honey. The colorful cranberries make them perfect for a holiday meal, especially with poultry as the centerpiece. Or try the dried-apple variation served with apple butter (page 273), a delicious idea I came across in Ruth Cousineau's friendly Vermont cookbook, Country Suppers. *This is a good recipe to pull out of the hat when you've run out of eggs.*

1 cup whole-wheat pastry flour	3 tablespoons chilled salted butter, diced
1/3 cup oat flour	2 tablespoons canola oil
1/3 cup unbleached flour	1/3 cup raw apple, finely chopped
3 tablespoons light brown sugar	1/2 to 1 teaspoon freshly grated orange zest
2 teaspoons baking powder	1/3 cup walnuts, coarsely chopped
1/4 teaspoon baking soda	1/3 cup cranberries, fresh or frozen
1/2 teaspoon salt (scant)	1/2 cup milk mixed with a little yogurt (or
Dash of cinnamon, allspice, and/or cloves	buttermilk) + milk to brush tops

Combine dry ingredients (flour through spices) in mixing bowl and rub butter into flours with fingers. Drizzle oil over dry mixture and toss until flours are evenly shortened and crumbly. Stir in chopped apples, walnuts, zest, and cranberries (cut cranberries in half if small; otherwise cut in thirds or quarters). Preheat oven to 425°F.

Add milk mixed with a little plain yogurt (or buttermilk) to dry mixture all at once, and stir briefly to bring dough together.

Oil a baking sheet and dust with flour. Turn dough out onto floured counter, and pat out with floured hands into a circle 5/8 to 3/4 inch thick. Using a 2- or 2 1/4-inch biscuit cutter or floured glass, cut dough into rounds, reforming scraps and recutting until dough is used up. Transfer to cookie sheet. Lightly brush tops with milk for a golden crust, if desired.

Bake biscuits in top third of oven for 16 to 18 minutes (longer with frozen berries), until golden.

Variation
DRIED-APPLE BISCUITS: Omit zest, and use 1/3 to 1/2 cup dried apples, snipped in small pieces and plumped in 1 tablespoon water or cider, in place of the fresh apple and cranberries.

Cape Breton Oatcakes

Some three decades ago, on a family trip to Cape Breton Island, Nova Scotia, I begged a recipe from the proprietress of a motel near Baddeck for her delicious oatcakes, served in a basket with every meal. Unlike the oatcakes I ate in Scotland, these are slightly sweet, somewhere between piecrust, crackers, and shortbread. I cut the butter with oil and enjoy them plain (using less sugar) as a snack—or as a sweeter tea biscuit, fancied up with cashews or a mix of coconuts, almonds, and apricots (variations).

MAKES 24 OATCAKES

3 tablespoons butter	1/4 teaspoon salt
1/3 to 1/2 cup light brown sugar, unpacked	1/3 cup canola oil (scant)
1 1/2 cups rolled oats	1/4 teaspoon baking soda
1 cup whole-wheat pastry flour	1/4 cup hot water

Cream butter with sugar, and rub together with oats, flour, and salt. Add oil and work evenly into flours. Add soda dissolved in hot water, and stir to form a crumbly dough.

With floured hands, form dough into a ball and roll out on floured surface into a rough square. Cut pastry into 2 x 2 1/2-inch squares and transfer to 2 unoiled baking sheets. Bake in preheated 350°F oven 12 to 20 minutes (depending on size and thickness of pans) until slightly browned around the edges.

Variations

APRICOT-ALMOND OATCAKES: Add 1/4 cup chopped soft apricots, 1/4 cup chopped whole almonds, and 1/3 cup unsweetened shredded dried coconut to dry ingredients. Roll out, cut, and bake as above.

CASHEW OATCAKES: Add 1/2 cup raw cashew pieces to dry ingredients. Roll out, cut, and bake as above.

Hearty Cornbread

Served with Richard's Chili (page 158) or any kind of Southwestern soup or stew, this flavorful cornbread (maybe with some stir-steamed kale alongside; see page 177) makes it a real meal. The kernel corn and pumpkin seeds add texture, but you can keep it simple and leave them out. Leftover cornbread, reheated or toasted, plain or spread with jam, is a golden addition to breakfast or brunch.

MAKES 9 SQUARES

2 tablespoons butter	1/2 cup kernel corn, fresh or frozen
2 tablespoons olive oil	and thawed (optional)
1 cup yellow cornmeal	1 large egg
1 cup whole-wheat pastry flour	2 tablespoons (1/8 cup) molasses
4 teaspoons baking powder	1 cup milk
1/2 teaspoon salt	1/4 cup raw pumpkin seeds (optional)

Preheat oven to 350°F. Melt butter and oil in 9 x 9-inch square baking pan or 8 x 8-inch baking dish. Meanwhile, assemble dry ingredients (cornmeal through corn) in separate bowl.

Beat egg in large mixing bowl, adding molasses, then half of milk. Remove melted shortening from oven and, if not too hot, stir in with rest of liquids; otherwise, combine with rest of milk before adding. Add dry mixture to wet and stir until flours are moistened.

Spread remaining butter-oil residue around baking pan and lightly dust with flour. Spread batter in pan and sprinkle with pumpkin seeds. Bake in top third of oven for 20 to 30 minutes or until done in the middle and pumpkin seeds are lightly toasted. Cut into tic-tac-toe squares, and serve hot.

Variation

CHILI CORNBREAD: Dust top of batter lightly with Chili Rub (page 68) before baking.

Savory Cheese-Poppyseed Scones

Scones don't have to be just for afternoon tea. A little richer than biscuits, scones lend themselves to all kinds of savory interpretations. This versatile golden multigrain scone recipe starts out with cheese and poppyseeds, then heads off in two different directions: to the Southwest (following in the footsteps of the Hearty Cornbread on page 194), and to Italy (inspired by a recipe in Simply Scones, *by Leslie Weiner and Barbara Albright). Make them in wedges or rounds.*

MAKES 10 TO 12 SCONES

1/2 cup corn flour (finely ground cornmeal)	2 tablespoons salted chilled butter, diced
1/2 cup unbleached flour	3 tablespoons olive oil
1/3 cup whole-wheat pastry flour	1/4 cup poppyseeds (scant)
1/3 cup oat flour	1/4 cup grated Parmesan, Romano, or
1 tablespoon semolina flour (or wheat germ)	Manchego cheese
2 teaspoons baking powder	1/4 cup grated cheddar, Asiago, or Gruyère
1/2 teaspoon organic sugar	1/2 cup milk (or buttermilk)
1/4 teaspoon salt (scant)	1 large egg

Combine dry ingredients (corn flour through salt) in large mixing bowl. Add butter and, using your fingers, rub into flour mixture. Drizzle oil over flour mixture and toss for a crumbly mixture. Add poppyseeds and cheeses (finely or coarsely grated, or a combination). Preheat oven to 400°F.

Using 2 baking sheets (1 large, 1 small), oil 3 circles 6 inches wide and dust with mixture of flour and coarse cornmeal. (If making cut-out biscuit rounds, oil and flour whole baking sheet.) Add egg to milk in measuring cup and beat together with knife or fork. Pour into dry mixture and stir briefly.

Spoon dough onto floured areas on baking sheets in 3 equal piles. With floured hands, pat each portion of dough into a circle about 4 1/2 inches diameter. Using a floured chef's knife, cut each circle into 4 wedges, making 2 perpendicular cuts, then space them a little apart. (Or for round scones, pat dough out on floured surface and cut with a 2- or 2 1/4-inch biscuit butter; then transfer to prepared baking sheet.) Brush tops with a little milk for a golden crust.

Bake in top third of oven 18 to 20 minutes for wedges, 16 to 18 minutes for biscuit rounds, or until lightly browned. Recut wedges along same lines. Place scones on rack to cool.

Variations

FOUR CORNERS SCONES: Add 1/2 teaspoon summer savory and a small pinch (1/8 teaspoon or less) of cayenne or Chili Rub (page 68) to dry ingredients. Replace poppyseeds with 1/3 cup fresh or frozen and thawed corn kernels. Place dough in 3 piles on floured baking sheets and pat into rounds, then cut each into 4 wedges. Brush with milk and sprinkle with raw pumpkin seeds, and bake as described above.

ITALIAN POLENTA SCONES: Add 3/4 teaspoon dried basil to dry ingredients. Replace poppyseeds with 2 or 3 dried tomato halves, snipped with scissors and "plumped" in a tablespoon of water. Brush top of patted-out dough with milk and press 1/4 cup raw pine nuts into surface of dough before cutting into wedges or rounds. Bake as described above.

Whole-Wheat Fennel Bread & Rolls

The fragrant fennel and fruity olive oil really shine through in this light-textured wheat bread. This recipe makes enough for 12 rolls, or 1 freeform loaf plus 6 rolls. Baked as cloverleaf rolls (using a muffin pan), they are wonderful with soup.

MAKES 1 LOAF PLUS 6 ROLLS

1 1/2 cups very warm water (or potato water, or whey)

1 packet dry active yeast (2 1/4 teaspoons)

2 teaspoons unsulphured Barbados molasses

1 1/2 cups whole-wheat bread flour

1/2 teaspoon salt

2 1/2 cups unbleached bread flour

1 1/2 to 2 teaspoons fennel seeds

1 1/2 tablespoons extra-virgin olive oil + 4 teaspoons to grease bowl and pans

Dissolve yeast in warm whey or water with molasses in large mixing bowl. Add whole-wheat flour, salt, and 1 1/2 cups of the unbleached flour, and mix together to form sponge. Let rest while you crush fennel seeds in mortar and pestle, then soak them in warm olive oil for about 5 minutes (a small stainless-steel bowl set in a warm oven works well).

Mix seeds and olive oil into sponge, then add remaining unbleached flour, or as much as dough will readily take up. Turn out onto floured surface and knead about 8 to 10 minutes, until dough springs back when dimpled with finger.

Clean mixing bowl and grease with additional olive oil. Roll ball of dough around bowl to coat with oil, cover with damp cloth, and let rise in warm place about 1 hour or until doubled in bulk.

Punch down dough and knead again briefly. To make 1 freeform loaf plus 6 rolls, shape 5/8 of dough into oval loaf and place on oiled baking sheet. Generously oil a 6-muffin stainless-steel pan with 3-inch cups and shape remaining dough into 18 pecan-sized balls, putting 3 in each muffin cup. (Or to make 12 rolls, divide dough in half, then form each portion into 6 round or oval rolls.)

Brush tops of loaf and rolls with lukewarm water, cover with clean plastic produce bag or damp cloth, and let rise in warm place about 20 minutes, or until almost doubled.

Preheat oven to 400°F. Bake 5 minutes in top third of oven, then lower heat to 375° and bake about another 20 minutes, or until bread/rolls are golden and sound hollow when tapped on bottom. Let cool 5 minutes, then remove from pans.

Oatmeal-Sunflower Bread

I've kneaded several recipes together for this oatmeal bread, including one my cousin Catie Bonello Filipelli brought home from her adventures out West working in a Montana bakery (having shrunk the recipe to one-eighth of its original Yellowstone proportions). It makes a loaf that's subtly sweet with honey or maple syrup and nicely textured with oats, sunflower seeds, and whole wheat, satisfying fresh or toasted.

MAKES 2 MEDIUM LOAVES

1 3/4 cups very warm water
1 packet dry active yeast (2 1/4 teaspoons)
3 tablespoons honey (or maple syrup)
    + 2 tablespoons warm water
2/3 cup quick oats
1 teaspoon salt

1/3 cup raw sunflower seeds
1 2/3 cups whole-wheat bread flour
2 cups unbleached bread flour
    + about 1/4 cup for kneading
1/2 tablespoon salted butter

In large, warm ceramic mixing bowl, dissolve yeast in warm water. Dissolve honey (or maple syrup) in 2 tablespoons water and add along with oats; let soak 5 minutes. Meanwhile combine salt, sunflower seeds, and whole-wheat flour in a separate bowl.

Add dry mixture to sweetened oat mixture and stir until whole-wheat flour is moistened, then mix in 1 cup unbleached bread flour. Mix in as much of the remaining 1 cup unbleached flour as dough will readily take up, then sprinkle the rest on counter. Let dough rest a few minutes, then turn out onto floured counter and knead 12 to 15 minutes or until firm and elastic, sprinkling additional flour as needed to keep dough from sticking. Shape dough into a ball.

Wash and dry mixing bowl, and grease with 1/2 tablespoon butter. Roll ball of dough around in bowl, coating all surfaces. Let rise under damp cloth in warm, draft-free place for about 1 hour or until doubled in bulk.

Punch dough down, knead briefly, and form into 2 freeform torpedo-shaped loaves (or 1 loaf plus 6 rolls). Place on 2 baking sheets oiled and sprinkled liberally with semolina flour. (Or, shape loaves to fit 2 rectangular 4 1/2 x 8 1/2-inch loaf pans or a double bâtard pan, pages 200–01, oiled and sprinkled with semolina flour.)

Brush or wipe loaves with a little warm water, cover loosely or drape with damp dishtowels or clean plastic bags, and let rise in warm draft-free place 40 to 45 minutes, or until nearly doubled.

Preheat oven to 400°F, setting racks in top third of oven for freeform loaves or rolls (use center position if baking in loaf pans or a bâtard pan). Bake at 400° for 5 to 8 minutes; remove loaves from oven and spritz surfaces with a plant mister filled with clean water, then reduce heat to 350° and bake for another 20 to 23 minutes (12 to 15 minutes for rolls), or until loaves are golden and sound hollow when tapped on bottom. (Loaves baked in loaf pans will take a little longer.)

When cool enough to handle, transfer to cooling racks.

Whole-Wheat Challah

This light, eggy Jewish holiday bread, braided and dusted with poppy or sesame seeds, looks so beautiful and festive—yet is no more trouble to make than any yeasted bread (as long as you don't mind staying close by your warm kitchen for an hour or two). Traditional recipes call for all white unbleached flour; this combination of white and whole-wheat flours gives you substance along with the light, moist texture you expect in a challah. Day-old challah makes wonderful French toast.

🅟 MAKES 2 MEDIUM LOAVES

2 packets dry active yeast (4 1/2 teaspoons)

Drop of honey

1 cup + 3 tablespoons very warm skim milk
    or water (or combination)

5 tablespoons salted butter

1 tablespoon vegetable oil

2 tablespoons honey

3 large (or 2 extra-large) eggs, beaten
    (reserve 1 1/2 tablespoons for egg wash)

3/4 teaspoon salt

2 cups whole-wheat bread flour

2 3/4 to 3 cups unbleached bread flour

3 to 4 tablespoons sesame seeds and/or
    poppyseeds (page 276)

Dissolve yeast in warm milk or water with drop of honey in large ceramic mixing bowl; let stand for about 5 minutes. Put butter, oil, and honey in small ovenproof bowl and set in warm oven (or in pot of hot water) to soften; then add eggs, mix well, and add to yeast mixture.

Stir in salt and whole-wheat flour and beat together for sponge. Gradually add 2 1/4 to 2 1/2 cups unbleached flour or enough to make an easily kneadable dough. Turn dough out onto clean countertop sprinkled with remaining 1/2 cup unbleached flour, and knead 12 to 15 minutes, or until ball of dough springs back when dimpled with finger.

Place dough in warm, clean, buttered bowl, rolling ball of dough around to coat top. Cover with damp cloth or clean plastic produce bag, and let rise in warm place 40 to 50 minutes or until doubled.

Punch dough down, knead briefly, and cut in 6 portions. Form dough into "snakes" about 13 inches long, 3 per loaf, rolling and stretching each piece of dough with your hands (no flour necessary). Place on oiled baking sheet, 3 per sheet. Add 1 tablespoon water to reserved beaten egg to make a wash.

Beginning in the middle of each loaf, braid to each end; then dampen "snake" ends with water, press together, and fold under end of loaf. Brush loaves with egg wash, and set to rise again under a warm, draft-free canopy (made by artfully draping 2 damp dishtowels above the trays) about 20 to 30 minutes or until almost doubled. (Don't let the loaves get overblown, or they will flatten.) Brush loaves once more with egg wash and sprinkle liberally with poppy or sesame seeds, or a combination.

Bake in top third of preheated 375°F oven for 20 minutes, then lower heat to 325° and bake another 5 to 10 minutes until loaves are lightly golden and sound hollow when tapped on the bottom. Be careful not to overbake.

When loaves are cool enough to handle, transfer to cooling racks.

Swedish Limpa Rye

This fragrant traditional Swedish rye bread is seldom found on bakery shelves, artisan or otherwise—I don't know why, as it's a lovely, tender bread, simple to bake and a nice foil for cold-cut sandwiches, toasted for breakfast or as a go-along with soup, or just fresh out of the oven with butter. The dough holds its shape well as a freeform loaf, or could be divided into rolls.

MAKES 1 LARGE LOAF, OR 12 ROLLS

1 package dry active yeast (2 1/4 teaspoons)

3/4 cup very warm water

2 teaspoons organic sugar

1 tablespoon salted butter

1 tablespoon canola oil

1 teaspoon whole anise seeds

1 1/2 tablespoons unsulphured molasses

2 to 3 teaspoons freshly grated orange zest

1 teaspoon salt

2 tablespoons fresh-squeezed orange juice

2 tablespoons milk (or buttermilk, or milk with a little yogurt)

1 cup stone-ground rye flour

1 cup stone-ground whole-wheat bread flour

1/2 cup unbleached bread flour + 1/4 cup for kneading

Sprinkle yeast and sugar into warm water in large, warm ceramic mixing bowl. Let proof 5 minutes. Meanwhile melt butter with oil in small metal bowl, then remove from heat and add anise seeds. Leave seeds to soak while you prepare the other wet ingredients.

Add the molasses, orange zest, and salt to lukewarm oils and seeds. Squeeze 2 tablespoons orange juice into measuring cup, then add 2 tablespoons milk (or buttermilk) or enough to measure 1/4 cup; add to other liquids in small bowl, then stir the resulting mixture into the dissolved yeast.

Measure rye and wheat flours into separate bowl, plus 1/2 cup unbleached flour. Reserve 1/4 cup unbleached flour for kneading.

Pour flours into liquid mixture and stir with large spoon to form a fairly firm dough. Turn dough out onto counter sprinkled with a little of the reserved flour, and knead 5 to 10 minutes, using additional flour as needed, until dough springs back when poked with a finger. Place in oiled or buttered bowl, cover with damp dishtowel, and let rise in warm place for 1 hour.

Lightly grease a heavy-bottomed baking sheet with a little butter or oil, and sprinkle with coarse cornmeal. When dough has about doubled, punch down and turn out onto counter. Knead briefly, then roll up into a narrow oval about 10 to 11 inches long. (Or divide dough into 12 portions and form into rolls.) Place on prepared baking sheet, cover with damp dishtowel, and let rise 50 minutes to 1 hour (less time for rolls), or until almost doubled.

Preheat oven to 375°F with rack in center of oven, and bake bread about 25 to 30 minutes, rotating pan halfway. (Rolls will take less time, 15 to 20 minutes.) At this point the bread should be almost done, sounding hollow when thumped on the bottom. Turn oven off and let loaf continue to bake another 3 to 5 minutes or until nicely browned.

When loaf or rolls are cool enough to handle, transfer to cooling rack.

Multigrain Baguettes

True French baguettes are a challenge to bake at home, what with their long rounded shape, two or three long risings, and hot/wet treatment to achieve a chewy, crackly crust. Might as well leave the real thing to the boulangerie. . . . *On the other hand, flavorful whole-grain baguettes are less easily come by and more expensive, so well worth a try. A great help is having one of those specialized pans for baking classic long, slender* baguettes—*or slightly shorter, plumper loaves, properly called* bâtards. *These double pans resemble two pieces of gutter pipe joined side by side, forming 3-inch-diameter loaves (baguette pan), or 4-inch bâtards (Italian bread pan). Even using regular baking sheets, though, you can still turn out respectable freeform crusty bâtards.*

This forgiving recipe makes two tasty loaves, with two average rising times. Including a larger measure of salt, along with some high-protein whole-wheat or spelt flour and semolina flour, gives structure to the loaf—along with color, texture, and the nice crust you expect from a baguette.

2 MEDIUM LOAVES

1 packet active dry yeast (2 1/4 teaspoons)	2 teaspoons salt
2 cups very warm water	1 cup whole-wheat bread flour (or spelt)
1 tablespoon organic sugar	1/4 cup wheat bran
1 teaspoon unsulphured Barbados molasses (or honey)	1/2 cup semolina flour
	2 3/4 cups unbleached bread flour
1/2 cup rolled oats	1/2 tablespoon unsalted butter

Pour water into warmed mixing bowl, sprinkle yeast, and stir to dissolve. Add sugar, molasses or honey, and oats, and set aside for a few minutes to proof yeast and moisten oats. (NOTE: If you haven't any organic sugar, use 2 teaspoons each white sugar and molasses or honey.) Meanwhile, combine dry ingredients except for unbleached flour (whole-wheat flour through salt) in small bowl. Measure unbleached bread flour into separate small bowl.

Stir mixed-grain dry mixture into yeast mixture. Then gradually mix in about 2 1/2 cups of the unbleached flour, or as much as the dough will take up. Let dough rest a few minutes.

Sprinkle 1 to 2 tablespoons of the remaining flour on countertop and turn dough out onto floured surface. Knead for 10 minutes, sprinkling more of the reserved flour a little at a time to prevent sticking, until dough is firm and elastic. (Depending on the humidity and moisture content of the flour, you may use a little less or a little more flour.) Roll dough into a ball.

Let butter soften in warm, clean mixing bowl. Roll dough around in buttered bowl, coating all sides. Cover with clean plastic produce bag or damp dishtowel, and let dough rise in warm, draft-free place for 1 to 1 1/4 hours, or until doubled in bulk.

If using a double baguette or bâtard pan, lightly oil and sprinkle with coarse cornmeal. For free-form loaves, lightly oil 2 baking sheets and sprinkle with cornmeal in the footprint of a long oval loaf.

Punch dough down and divide in two equal portions with sharp knife. Working one half at a time, transfer dough to lightly floured surface and knead a few times, then stretch dough out into a rectangle about 10 inches long. Rolling the dough away from you, shape it into a log: for bâtards, 10 to 12 inches is long enough; for baguettes, rock hands back and forth a few times, lengthening log to 13 or 14 inches (the loaves will lengthen several inches as they rise). Place bâtard-length loaves in prepared bâtard pan or on baking sheets; place baguette loaves in prepared baguette pan.

Brush loaves with warm water, then loosely cover (baking pans and all) with clean plastic produce bag(s) or under damp dishtowel(s). Let rise about 50 minutes, or until almost doubled.

Preheat oven to 425°F. Set roasting pan one-third full of hot water on lower shelf of oven. If using double bâtard/baguette pans, set rack in center of oven; for freeform loaves, set rack in top third. Spray loaves thoroughly with a plant mister filled with clean water.

When oven is preheated, slash top of each loaf with 3 or 4 diagonal (almost lengthwise) slits about 1/8 inch deep, using a very sharp knife or razor blade; then whisk loaves into the oven. After 5 minutes' baking time, spritz surface of loaves with water, and again after 5 minutes. Rotate pan(s).

Bake freeform loaves another 15 to 25 minutes (a total of 25 to 35 minutes), double baguettes or bâtards another 35 to 45 minutes (a total of 45 to 55 minutes), or until loaves are nicely browned and sound hollow when tapped on the bottom.

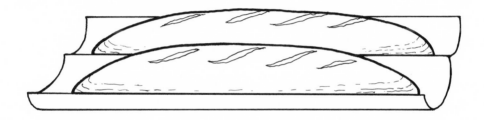

Freeform Loaves

Freeform loaves baked at home are seldom as lofty and plump as bakery loaves. I suspect the artisan bakers' secrets include gluten flour, baker's stones and peels, specialty bread pans, the ample size and temperature of a commercial oven—plus a pile of wisdom and experience.

For us home bakers, I can recommend several keys to success. First and foremost, always use fresh active yeast stamped with an expiration date well in the future (if in doubt, throw it out). Equally important, once you've formed the loaf or loaves, go for a minimal second rise—almost doubled, but don't let the loaf get overblown, or it may start deflating before you can get it into a fully preheated oven. If you slash the top (a good idea, to prevent ragged cracks from splitting the crust), wait until the absolute last minute before putting the bread in the oven, to minimizing deflating.

As further insurance against a flattened loaf, a neat trick is to bake baguette or bâtard loaves in one of those double pans, curved on the bottom (available at stores that cater to cooks, such as Rooster Brother in Ellsworth, www.roosterbrother.com). A baguette pan is designed to bake 2 long skinny loaves, 3 inches wide; an Italian bread pan can bake shorter bâtards, 4 inches wide by 14 inches long. Another way to bolster the sides of a freeform loaf is to use a ceramic casserole dish or stoneware bread baker, which conducts heat evenly like a baker's stone, producing a crusty bottom. An oval baking dish roughly 6 x 8 or 5 x 10 inches, 2 to 3 inches deep, forms a nice country loaf.

Olive Bread

This savory bread is inspired by the classic Greek olive bread, eliopitta. *The traditional leavening, baking powder, makes for a somewhat dense (though quick) bread; the same savory flavorings combine just as well in this yeasted version, which has a nice texture and chewy crust. As used in other Greek dishes, mint lightens the intensity of the olives (I use dried common mint leaves gathered from a local stream). Or give the bread an Italian accent by substituting rosemary (see first variation).*

Either version is delicious toasted and drizzled with olive oil as an accompaniment for soup, or in a toasted cheese sandwich. Or serve it fresh-baked as a meze *(appetizer); a simple spread of chevre (creamy goat cheese) or cream cheese lightened with lemon and other Greek flavors (page 16) nicely complements the olives. This recipe makes a medium loaf or two small bâtards, just enough to feed a dinner party of six or eight with appetites quickened by a winter outing, washed down with amber beer.*

MAKES 1 MEDIUM LOAF, 2 SMALL LOAVES

1/2 packet dry active yeast (1 1/8 teaspoons)	1/4 teaspoon salt
3/4 cup + 1 tablespoon very warm water	1 1/2 to 2 teaspoons dried mint
Drop of honey	1/2 cup finely minced onion
2 1/2 tablespoons extra-virgin olive oil	1/2 to 2/3 cup olives (marinated ripe olive
1/3 cup semolina flour	medley or brined Kalamata olives), pitted
2/3 cup whole-wheat bread flour	and sliced or coarsely chopped
1 1/4 cups unbleached bread flour + 1/4 cup	1 egg yolk
for kneading	1 tablespoon water

Dissolve yeast with warm water and honey in large mixing bowl. Add olive oil, then stir in semolina and whole-wheat flours to form sponge. Let sponge rest while you measure 1 1/4 cups unbleached bread flour with salt and mint in a separate small bowl. Chop onions and olives and add to unbleached flour mixture.

Add flour mixture to sponge in a couple of additions, stirring to form a fairly stiff but kneadable dough. If you are using 2/3 cup olives, you shouldn't need to add any water; kneading will express a little additional juice from the olives. If using 1/2 cup olives, add up to 1 tablespoon more water if the dough seems a bit dry.

Turn dough out onto clean counter sprinkled with 2 tablespoons of the reserved flour and knead about 10 minutes until smooth and elastic, sprinkling additional flour as needed to keep from sticking. Shape dough into a ball. Roll ball of dough in warm bowl greased with olive oil, cover with damp cloth or plastic bag, and let rise in warm draft-free place for about 50 to 60 minutes or until doubled.

Punch dough down and knead again briefly, then form into a loaf. For an elongated oval freeform loaf, rock dough back and forth, lengthening to about 10 inches, and center lengthwise on oiled baking sheet sprinkled with semolina flour or coarse cornmeal. Or, divide dough in half and form two bâtards about 8 inches long, setting them side by side in a double baguette pan oiled and sprinkled with coarse cornmeal. (See page 201 for more on baking freeform and baguette/bâtard loaves.)

Wipe loaf (loaves) with a little warm water and let rise, covered with damp towel or clean plastic bag, in warm draft-free place for about 30 to 40 minutes or until almost doubled. Preheat oven to 375°F, with rack set in top third of oven for a freeform loaf, or in center of oven for bâtards.

Bake in preheated oven for about 15 minutes. Meanwhile, mix egg yolk with water to make an egg wash. Remove loaf (loaves) from oven and brush surface with egg wash, then bake another 20 to 30 minutes (35 to 45 minutes in all) or until bread is nicely browned and hollow-sounding when tapped on the bottom. Remove to wire rack to cool.

Slice with a sharp serrated knife and serve with plain chevre, Lemon-Cream Cheese Spread (page 16), or toasted and drizzled with extra-virgin olive oil.

NOTE: What to do with the leftover egg wash and white? Either combine them and use in a muffin recipe, or incorporate them in a Coconut-Walnut Cake (page 248) or another recipe calling for extra egg white.

Variations

ROSEMARY-OLIVE BREAD: Use 1/2 teaspoon chopped fresh rosemary in place of the mint. Bake as described above. Serve with chevre or toasted with olive oil.

QUICK ELIOPITTA: Replace yeast with 2 teaspoons baking powder, assembling all of the dry ingredients, including onions and olives, together in large mixing bowl. Form a well in the flours, pour in the water mixed with olive oil, and stir until dough comes together to form a fairly stiff but kneadable dough. Knead as described in main recipe, then let dough rest 10 minutes (no rising time necessary). Form into an oval freeform loaf and bake as described above. Serve with Lemon-Cream Cheese Spread (page 16).

HAND VS. MACHINE

Food processors and bread mixers offer several advantages, including the obvious ones of saving the time and effort of kneading by hand, not to mention cleaning up a sticky counter. Another less obvious advantage is that with machine mixing, only a little extra flour is needed to prevent sticking while forming loaves. A moister dough tends to rise more easily, forming the bubbles so appealing in some of the rustic breads.

Yet for this neo-Luddite, in a two-person household, somehow the effort and noise of setting up, assembling, operating, dismantling, and washing all the parts and pieces of a mixer seems hassle enough that I'd just as soon roll up my sleeves and knead by hand—for the satisfaction of hand-crafting a loaf, combined with a peaceful 10-minute reverie. And so you'll find directions for hand-kneading throughout this chapter's recipes for yeasted breads. But if you're more comfortable using a mixer or food processor, by all means do.

Italian Seed Bread

Surrounded by talented local artisan bakers, it's easy to rely on their array of signature rustic breads, and forget any idea of baking at home. This recipe came about as an attempt to re-create one of my favorite bakery loaves, an Italian Five-Grain made by Kathy McCloskey, after the closing of her bakery Pain de Famille. Thankfully this and her other artisan breads are back at Blue Hill Hearth (and a similar loaf is made by Bagaduce Bread), but I'm glad to have figured out how to bake such a satisfyingly chewy Italian seed bread from scratch in my own kitchen—not just for the bread itself but the warm sense of self-reliance, especially when it saves a trip to town on an inclement day.

This loaf makes great toast, especially the variation with pecans, which toast along with the bread.

1 LARGE LOAF

1 1/4 cups very warm water	1/4 cup pumpkin seeds
1/2 packet dry active yeast (1 1/8 teaspoons)	2 to 3 tablespoons raw sunflower seeds
1/2 teaspoon honey (or organic sugar)	1 tablespoon flax seeds (optional)
1 1/2 tablespoons canola oil	1 1/8 teaspoons salt
2 cups unbleached bread flour + 1/3 to 1/2 cup for kneading	2 to 3 tablespoons whole sesame seeds (*or* 1 or 2 tablespoons pumpkin seeds)
1/2 cup whole-wheat bread flour	2 tablespoons coarse cornmeal

Sprinkle yeast over warm water in large, warm ceramic mixing bowl and stir to dissolve. Add honey and proof yeast for 5 minutes. Meanwhile, measure dry ingredients (flours, seeds, and salt) in separate bowl, reserving 1/3 to 1/2 cup unbleached flour for kneading.

Add oil to bowl with yeast, then add flour mixture in 3 stages, stirring with wooden spoon, until dough has taken up most of the flour. Let dough rest for a few minutes, then turn out onto clean counter along with any unabsorbed flour. Knead for about 10 minutes, working in flours plus reserved flour sprinkled a little at a time, until dough is smooth and elastic.

Grease warm, clean ceramic bowl with a little olive oil, then roll ball dough around in bowl to coat all sides. Cover with large, clean plastic produce bag (or damp dishtowel) and let rise at room temperature or in warm draft-free place until doubled, about 1 1/2 hours.

When risen, pull dough from bowl (without punching down) onto lightly floured surface. For a freeform loaf, gently stretch dough into a circle about 10 inches wide, then roll away from you to form a stout country loaf 10 to 11 inches long, seam-side down. Place loaf on a rectangular baking sheet lightly oiled and dusted with coarse cornmeal, or in an oiled and dusted oval baking dish (see page 201). Wipe surface of loaf with water and sprinkle with sesame (or pumpkin) seeds.

For a bâtard, rock log back and forth a couple times to lengthen to about 12 or 13 inches. Lay loaf in a 4-inch Italian bread pan, oiled and dusted with cornmeal. For a sesame crust, wipe surface of dough with wet hands and roll log in sesame seeds, as on page 206, coating all sides. (Or if you prefer pumpkin seeds, sprinkle them over the top after placing loaf in pan.)

Let rise 35 to 45 minutes at room temperature, until plump but not fully doubled. Preheat oven to 400°F, with rack set in top third of oven for a freeform loaf, or in the center if using a baking dish or bâtard pan. Spritz top of loaf with a plant mister filled with clean water. When oven is fully pre-heated, place loaf in oven.

For a crispy crust, spritz top twice more with plant mister during the first 15 minutes of baking. Bake loaf a total of about 35 minutes on a baking sheet, 40 to 45 minutes in a baking dish or bâtard pan, or until nicely browned and hollow-sounding when thumped on the bottom. When loaf is cool enough to handle, remove from pan or dish to cooling rack.

Variation

ITALIAN BREAD WITH PECANS: Replace the pumpkin, sunflower, and flax seeds in dry ingredients with 2/3 cup broken raw pecan halves. Form as a country loaf with a plain (not seeded) crust, and bake as described above.

Sesame Semolina Bread

Having sampled various bakery loaves, I wanted to try my hand at baking this traditional Italian bread with light, chewy texture and golden sesame crust. No leads turned up in any of the Italian cookbooks I could find (maybe because semolina bread is such a bakery staple), but Nick Malgieri's recipe in Baking with Julia *pointed in the right direction.*

King Arthur's unbleached bread flour (milled from high-protein hard spring wheat) is a good choice for this recipe; it includes malted barley flour as a built-in yeast nutrient, so only a pinch of sugar is needed in the sponge. Milled from durum flour (another hard wheat), semolina flour—also used in pasta, puddings, and pizza crust—gives the bread structure, a golden color, and a crispy crust, helped by a little steam while baking.

Semolina bread is best eaten fresh, but like all bread freezes well. It is delicious toasted for breakfast as a foil for fruit preserves.

1 MEDIUM LOAF

1 cup very warm water	3/4 cup semolina flour
1/4 teaspoon organic sugar (or barley malt)	1 teaspoon salt
1/2 packet dry active yeast (1 1/8 teaspoons)	1 tablespoon extra-virgin olive oil
1 1/2 cups unbleached bread flour + 1/4 cup	1/3 cup raw sesame seeds
for kneading	2 tablespoons coarse cornmeal

Combine hot water with sugar in large, warm ceramic bowl and sprinkle yeast over the surface. Let stand a few minutes to proof yeast, then mix in 1 cup unbleached bread flour to form sponge. Cover bowl and let rise at room temperature for 1 to 1 1/2 hours, or until sponge has doubled.

Combine semolina flour and salt, and stir into the sponge, along with olive oil. Stir in 1/2 cup of the remaining unbleached flour, or whatever the dough will take up while remaining moist and somewhat sticky, reserving the last 1/4 cup flour for kneading. Turn dough out onto clean countertop sprinkled with a little of the reserved flour and knead 10 minutes, using additional flour as needed to keep dough from sticking, until dough is firm and elastic.

Grease warm, clean mixing bowl with olive oil, and roll ball of dough around in bowl to coat with oil. Cover bowl with clean plastic bag and let rise at room temperature for 1 1/4 to 1 1/2 hours, or until doubled in bulk. Meanwhile lightly oil a rectangular baking sheet (or Italian bread/bâtard pan, pages 200–01) and sprinkle with coarse cornmeal in the footprint of an 11–12-inch loaf.

When dough has risen, punch down and turn out onto lightly floured surface, then fold dough in onto itself and form into an oblong loaf 10 to 11 inches long, seam-side down. Sprinkle sesame seeds evenly over the area of counter occupied by loaf. With wet hands, wipe surface of dough to moisten thoroughly; follow this with a light coating of olive oil. Roll loaf in sesame seeds, turning to coat all sides evenly, especially the top. Quickly transfer loaf to prepared baking sheet (or bâtard pan).

Cover loaf, baking sheet and all, with clean plastic produce bag, and let rise at room temperature for 45 minutes to 1 hour, or until almost doubled.

Preheat oven to 400°F. Using a plant mister filled with fresh water, spritz top of loaf thoroughly; sprinkle additional sesame seeds to fill any gaps in surface. Just before putting loaf in preheated oven, slash top with 3 or 4 diagonal cuts about 1/8 inch deep, using a razor blade or sharp paring knife.

Bake in top third of oven for about 10 minutes, then spritz surface of loaf once more with water. Rotate pan and bake another 25 to 28 minutes, or until loaf is golden and crusty and makes a hollow sound when tapped on the bottom.

Focaccia

This Italian staple is easy to buy, but just as easy to bake, and lends itself to various uses including appetizers (Crostini with Fresh Mozzarella, page 20), sandwiches (Toasted Vegetable-Cheese Pockets, page 25), or just fresh on its own. However, many focaccia recipes (and store-bought loaves, for that matter) seem oblivious to the fact that focaccia isn't focaccia without the characteristic bubbles and chewy crust. My first attempt at home-baked focaccia resulted in a disappointing cakey loaf with tiny uniform holes. Then, in Craig Kominiak's focaccia recipe in Baking with Julia *(a collection of recipes from America's best professional bakers, by Dorie Greenspan), I stumbled on the key: a final long, cool rise in the refrigerator, along with liberal spritzing with water while baking. Lo and behold, a perfect rustic loaf.*

1 LARGE ROUND LOAF

2/3 packet (1 1/2 teaspoons) highly active (rapid-rise) yeast	3/4 teaspoon salt
	2 cups unbleached bread flour
1 teaspoon organic sugar	1 teaspoon fresh rosemary, coarsely chopped
3/4 cup very warm water	1/2 to 1 teaspoon fresh thyme
2 tablespoons extra-virgin olive oil + 1 for oiling	Pinch (1/8 inch) coarse sea salt

Dissolve yeast in warm water with sugar, and proof for 5 minutes. Add 2 tablespoons olive oil. Measure unbleached flour into separate bowl and mix with salt, then gradually stir in as much flour mixture as the dough will readily take up. Pour remaining flour on counter to use for kneading. Turn dough out onto floured counter and knead 10 minutes. Gather dough into a ball.

Grease warm, clean mixing bowl with olive oil and return dough to bowl, rolling to coat with oil. Cover with damp dishtowel or clean plastic bag and let rise at room temperature for 30 minutes.

Fold dough into center of bowl to deflate it and let rise a second time, about 50 minutes or until doubled in bulk. Fold dough down again, then turn out onto floured surface and shape into a ball.

Wipe olive oil over surface area of dough and place in gallon-size ziplock bag. Seal and refrigerate for 24 to 36 hours for the third, cool rise, which creates the focaccia's characteristic bubbles.

When ready to bake the focaccia, remove dough from bag with oiled hands onto lightly floured surface. Lightly wipe top of dough with olive oil, cover with the same plastic bag (or wrap), and let rest 1 hour to come to room temperature.

Preheat oven to 450°F, with rack positioned in the middle of the oven. Lightly oil a round pizza pan and sprinkle with coarse cornmeal. Combine herbs and salt and set aside.

Press down on the middle of the ball of dough; then, with as little handling as possible (to keep the bubbles), gently pull and stretch dough into a circle about 10 inches in diameter. Let rest 10 minutes, then transfer to prepared sheet. Brush surface with a little more olive oil. With your fingertips or the end of a wooden spoon, dimple the top center 7 inches of the focaccia with indentations spaced about 1 inch apart. Sprinkle herbs and salt over the top.

Bake focaccia 15 to 20 minutes, using a plant mister to spritz top of loaf with water 3 times during first half of baking time. Focaccia is done when puffed up and golden on top and around the edges, and nicely browned and crusty on the bottom. Remove from oven, brush top edges with a little extra olive oil, and let cool.

Best eaten fresh, focaccia also freezes well.

BEYOND UNBLEACHED

Supermarkets may be bursting with choices, but in the realm of flour, natural food stores and co-ops rule. There you can find most any type or grind of flour imaginable, and usually (especially in a community of home bakers, with good turnover) fresher flours than in the baking aisle. A co-op store (as we have in Blue Hill), where a wide variety of flours and grains are sold in bulk, is a great opportunity to buy small amounts and experiment with unfamiliar flours.

Good old unbleached all-purpose flour is the stuff of many a baked good, but not everyone's digestive system gets along with wheat—which may be behind the availability of flours milled from other grains with little or no gluten, like corn, oats, and rice. And whether or not wheat agrees with you, it's still nice to have some variety combining different flours in multigrain breads, muffins, cookies, even pies and cakes. Each grain's flour has its own distinctive color, flavor, texture, and handling characteristics.

You'll find lots of examples of ways to use different grains and flours among the recipes, but here is a gathering of flours I've found most useful, with notes on what to bake of them:

CORN FLOUR (finely milled yellow cornmeal)—light-textured corn or anadama muffins, pancakes, polenta cake. Low in gluten, so best combined with some wheat flour.

CORNMEAL (medium to coarsely ground yellow cornmeal)—spoon bread, pancakes, cornbread, muffins (vary with blue cornmeal); sprinkle coarse cornmeal on baking pans to prevent scorching of bread, rolls, pizza. (Very coarse cornmeal can be used to make the side dish polenta, but it is better to use Italian-style polenta milled especially for cooking, not baking.)

OAT FLOUR (finely milled oats)—pancakes, waffles, muffins, cakes, cookies, scones, piecrusts; lends a nice, cakey texture to quick breads, and a nutty sweetness to piecrusts. Has little gluten, so best combined with some wheat flour.

OAT BRAN (outer husk, coarsely milled)—feature in piecrusts, muffins; add to scones, cookies, or anywhere extra texture and fiber are welcome. Absorbs moisture slowly, so let batter rest before baking.

OATS (rolled whole oats)—feature in cookies, granola, scones; add to muffins, breads for texture. (Whole oats are best in baked goods; "quick" cut oats, intended for porridge, can be used in small amounts in yeast breads, but tend to make scones and quick breads gummy.)

BARLEY FLOUR (finely milled barley)—use in biscuits, pancakes, in vegan and wheat-free baking; barley flour can help add moistness and loft in lieu of an egg.

BUCKWHEAT FLOUR (finely milled brown or white buckwheat)—pancakes, waffles, breads. Gluten-free. Brown buckwheat flour lends a satisfying earthy flavor and dense texture. Acadian light buckwheat flour, combined with wheat flour, makes golden, cakey muffins; also ployes (Acadian crêpes, page 95).

RYE FLOUR (finely milled or coarsely stone-ground rye)—yeast breads; slightly sour flavor, traditionally complemented by sweet flavorings like fennel, caraway, anise, molasses.

RICE FLOUR (finely milled brown or white rice)—cookies, muffins; can also be used as thickener or to dust baking pans. Gluten-free flour, best used in quick breads. Gives cookies a sandy texture, so best to combine a small amount with other flours. Absorbs moisture slowly, so let batter rest before baking.

SEMOLINA FLOUR (coarsely ground durum flour)—feature in homemade pasta, semolina bread; milled of hard wheat, so including some in pizza dough yields a crisper crust. Often used to dust baking pans to prevent scorching. Semolina can also be cooked as a porridge, then sweetened and cooled to form a pudding. Or a spoonful can be sprinkled on the bottom crust of a fruit pie or tart to absorb fruit juices.

SPELT (an ancient species of wheat, stone-ground)—breads, muffins; high in protein and low in gluten, though similar to whole-wheat bread flour in flavor, texture, and dough development. Digestible by some people who can't tolerate ordinary wheat.

WHOLE-WHEAT PASTRY FLOUR (finely milled or stone-ground wheat)—piecrusts, cookies, scones, quick breads; milled of softer wheat, which has less protein and gluten. Includes wheat germ and bran; with unbleached flour, these have been removed. A lighter "white whole-wheat flour" is also available.

WHOLE-WHEAT BREAD FLOUR (finely milled or stone-ground wheat)—yeast breads, pizza crust; milled of harder wheat, which has more protein and gluten. Includes wheat and bran; with unbleached bread flour, these have been removed. (Some unbleached flours, such as King Arthur's, include a small amount of barley malt to nourish the yeast.)

WHEAT GERM (oil- and protein-rich "seed" of wheat kernel)—add to muffins, cookies, cakes, breads, and cereals for sweet, nutty flavor and texture, vitamin E, and magnesium. Lightly toasted has best flavor, texture, and shelf life.

WHEAT BRAN (husk of wheat kernel)—add to muffins, breads, and cereals for fiber and texture.

Breakfast Specials

Date-Nut Granola

With so many tempting granolas available at natural food stores, why bother making your own? Well, first and foremost it's fun, also satisfying to reach for an airtight jar full of your own signature mix, lightly sweetened and just as crunchy, nutty, etc. as you like—super-fresh, probably cheaper too.

Let newly made granola "cure" for a day, then enjoy sprinkled over a breakfast bowl of fresh fruit (Valencias or clementines, apples, pears, bananas, blueberries, cherries, plums, nectarines) swimming in unfiltered natural fruit juice or nectar, topped with plain yogurt and maple syrup or honey.

MAKES 8 CUPS, ABOUT 12 SERVINGS

5 cups rolled oats

1/2 cup raw sunflower seeds

1/2 cup maple syrup (or maple syrup combined with honey or barley malt)

3 tablespoons warm water

1/3 teaspoon salt

1 teaspoon vanilla

1/3 cup canola oil

1/3 to 1/2 cup whole almonds, coarsely chopped

1/3 cup raw hazelnuts, coarsely chopped

1/3 cup raw pumpkin seeds

5 Medjool dates, thinly sliced (*or* 1/2 to 2/3 cup mixed dried fruit—dates, flame raisins, dried cranberries, apricots, apples, pears)

1/3 cup wheat germ

1/3 cup wheat bran (and/or dried coconut)

1/3 cup oat bran

Dash of cinnamon (optional)

Preheat oven to 350°F. Measure oats and sunflower seeds into mixing bowl. Assemble liquid ingredients in small pitcher or 1-cup measuring cup (altogether they equal about 1 cup). Stir combined liquids well with spoon or knife, then pour about 2/3 of liquid into oat-seed mixture and stir until grains are evenly coated. Pour remaining liquid into separate small bowl.

Spread mixture in 1 or 2 baking pans with sides, and bake 5 minutes. Meanwhile, chop nuts. Remove grain mixture from oven and turn thoroughly with spoon or spatula. Sprinkle nuts over top.

Reduce oven temperature to 325° and bake granola for about 5 minutes more, then turn again. Meanwhile, measure pumpkin seeds and dates (or dried fruits), and set aside. Add wheat germ and bran to remaining liquid and stir to combine.

When granola has toasted for 3 to 5 minutes more, turn thoroughly and sprinkle wheat germ–bran mixture over the top, then the pumpkin seeds and dates (or mixed dried fruits). Return granola to oven and bake for about 5 minutes, or until granola is evenly light gold and almost done. Turn one last time, turn off oven, and bake 3 to 5 minutes. (NOTE: Once the added sugar of the dried fruits—especially the dates—comes up to heat, the granola will tend to brown more quickly, so watch it like a hawk during this final phase to be sure it does not get away from you. Better to stay on the light side rather than risk scorching the granola, which makes it taste bitter.)

Remove from oven, dust with cinnamon if desired, and let cool completely; then store in jars.

Variation

CASHEW-COCONUT GRANOLA: Omit hazelnuts and pumpkin seeds, and add 1/2 cup raw cashews toward the end of baking, along with the dates. Sprinkle 1/3 to 1/2 cup unsweetened shredded dried coconut over the top for the last couple minutes of baking, stirring once, until coconut turns a light gold.

Homemade Yogurt

Even more satisfying than making your own granola is making your own yogurt. Once you have a system that works, and a good culture, you can stay on a roll producing yogurt with the milk and fat content you like best, at a fraction of the cost of store-bought—and (if you eat a lot of yogurt) without accumulating plastic containers! I use a trio of vintage square-shouldered 24-ounce Atlas mason jars that fit just right in both our stockpot incubator and our refrigerator door, using a half-gallon of milk per batch. (The same half-gallon would also make 2 quarts with a little milk left over.) Once a week, or as soon as we get into the third jar, I set aside the time—about an hour—to scald and cool the milk, sterilize jars and lids, and inoculate the milk with starter. Then I babysit the yogurt, checking on the water bath temperature once or twice during the day, until it has "yogged" or firmly set.

Not that there wasn't a learning curve, however . . . I've had my share of "disappointing yogurt" outcomes, with a consistency more like kefir. There are ways to deal with runny yogurt (see below), but the best prevention is to use a thermometer (one that registers up to 120°F) to get the right temperature, and give the yogurt all the incubation time it needs. Here's what works for me:

For a starter, simply use some of your current yogurt supply—either your last batch of homemade yogurt, or a quart of store-bought plain yogurt containing "live active cultures," including *Lactobacillus acidophilus*, *L. bulgaricus*, and *S. thermophilus*. (I find Butterworks Farm's plain yogurt works well as a starter, plus it's a good excuse to indulge in their delicious yogurt made from Jersey milk, topped with a rich layer of yogurt cream. Nancy's and Stonyfield plain yogurt are two other reliable choices for starter.) For each 1-quart jar you plan to make, spoon into a small, clean bowl 3 to 4 tablespoons of yogurt starter, or 2 1/2 to 3 tablespoons per 1 1/2-pint (24-ounce) jar. Stir out the lumps, then set the bowl out of harm's way to come to room temperature.

Using one of your clean yogurt jars, measure the milk (filling to jar shoulder level) into a saucepan comfortably sized for pouring. I like to use BGH-free homogenized local milk with 2 percent fat. Even if you are using pasteurized milk, it's a good idea to scald it to dispatch any organisms that could compete with your yogurt cultures. Heat the milk over moderate heat, stirring occasionally, until it's just beginning to steam and foam, then remove from heat and let it cool on a clean cake rack until the temperature drops to about 112°F.

Meanwhile, sterilize the jars and lids by boiling for 10 minutes in a lidded stockpot (the pot and jars should be a third full of water). It's okay to recycle used canning lids, since no seal is required.

When the milk temperature has dropped to 112°F, it's time to start the yogurt. (I can't tell you how often I have gone on to other projects, completely sidetracked, only to remember my now-chilly pot of milk. If this happens, simply warm it up over low heat to the magic temperature, and proceed.) Using clean tongs, remove the jars one by one from the pot, and briefly let them drain upside down on the rack, along with lids. Turn the jars right-side up and pour the milk, filling the jars evenly to just below shoulder level. Spoon the yogurt culture evenly among the jars, stirring it into the milk. Fit lids and tighten rings securely.

Meanwhile, begin preheating the oven (set on "warm" for a minute or two, just long enough to take the chill off), with the oven racks on the lowest rungs. Add enough cool or warm water to the stockpot hot-water bath to bring the water temperature to 110–112°F. Submerge the jars in the water bath, adjusting water level and temperature as needed (water should just cover jars), cover the pot, then gently place it in the turned-off warm oven. Look in on the yogurt after a few hours, adding hot water as needed to bring water bath up to temperature, being careful not to joggle the jars.

Alternatively, you could keep the yogurt warm by setting the pot on a sunny plant shelf or in the warm radius of a woodstove; just make sure the water temperature doesn't exceed 110–112°, which could "cook" the yogurt cultures.

You can expect yogurt to take anywhere from 6 to 10 hours to set firmly. Test firmness by gently tilting the jars. If at all in doubt, leave the jars in the lukewarm water bath for a few more hours, even overnight, before refrigerating.

NOTE: At the other end of the yogurt cycle, when all that's left in the jar is the dregs, I like to swish a little milk around with the yogurt—vigorously shake the jar—and pour the "milkshake" into a smaller jar for use in baking. You'll note that a lot of the baking recipes here call for milk mixed with a little plain yogurt in lieu of sour milk or buttermilk.

DISAPPOINTING YOGURT?

If for whatever reason (tired culture, temperature a little too hot or too cold) you end up with yogurt that hasn't set as firmly as you'd like, well, there's not much you can do except try again with a fresh batch of milk and fresh starter. Sometimes a culture just gets tired. My guess is that one or another of the "live active cultures"—perhaps *S. thermophilus*, whose Latin name means "likes heat"—doesn't get enough heat once the water bath cools, and gradually (over several batches of yogurt) dwindles in population, yielding a less custardy yogurt. If you find this happening a couple times in a row, you'll need to start fresh with a new container of store yogurt. Pay extra attention to holding the proper temperature, and you should be fine from here on.

But what to do with the disappointing kefir-like batch? Make yogurt sour cream! Yogurt cheese! Salad dressing! Use it like buttermilk (in baking, mashed potatoes, etc.). Make fruit gelatin puddings and pies, even popsicles (see Strawberry-Banana Popsicles, page 231). You can see I've had lots of experience. . . . If you're faced with two quarts of runny yogurt, though, you'll want to quickly shrink it down to size to reclaim your refrigerator, and the best way is to simply strain out the liquid or whey, leaving the yogurt solids in the form of a tangy, low-fat sour cream that you can season with herbs—say, tarragon, marjoram, perhaps a little garlic or lemon zest—like a boursin or dip.

To drain the yogurt, fit a clean, wet cloth (an old napkin or linen dishcloth) or a couple layers of cheesecloth over a strainer and secure around the edges with a wide rubber band. Set the strainer over a bowl and pour it full of runny yogurt. Go do something else, and let it drain. Stir periodically with a chopstick, adding more yogurt as space allows and decanting whey at it reaches the strainer (keep the calcium-rich whey to use as liquid in baking). When all the yogurt has been drained, use a rubber spatula to scrape the "sour cream" into a smaller bowl or container. Season to taste, and enjoy.

Muesli

This simple Swiss-style breakfast cereal is a healthy, quick alternative to baked granola. The key is to use fresh ingredients and make only a small batch at a time. Serve as you would granola, sprinkled over a bowl of fresh fruit and juice topped with yogurt and maple syrup. Or serve Muesli the traditional way, mixed with grated raw apples, yogurt, and honey.

 MAKES 2 2/3 CUPS, 4 TO 5 SERVINGS

1 1/2 cups rolled oats

1/4 cup raw sunflower seeds

1/3 to 1/2 cup raw almonds (or combination almonds and hazelnuts), coarsely chopped

1/4 cup raw pumpkin seeds

3 Medjool dates, thinly sliced

3 to 4 dried apricots, chopped

2 dried pear halves, sliced

Combine ingredients. Muesli will keep fresh for a few weeks stored in an airtight jar.

Dressed-up Oatmeal

Good old porridge hardly needs a recipe, but I offer this as a basic formula with suggestions for a few nice variations. Plain oatmeal is honest fare, but dress it up a little and you have a heart-warming, delicious if not glamorous breakfast—one well suited for a winter camp foray, traveling easily in the food box. Hold back on the water for a thicker porridge, or use the full 3:1 for a creamy consistency.

For another hot cereal with possibilities, consider buckwheat (kasha) gussied up for breakfast with fruit, nuts, and maple syrup (page 189).

 SERVES 2

1 cup rolled oats (1/2 cup per serving)

Salt, a wee pinch

2 2/3 to 3 cups water (1 1/3 to 1 1/2 cups per serving)

Combine oats, water, and salt in small pot and slowly bring to a boil, stirring frequently. Simmer for a few minutes, stirring constantly. When thick and creamy, and oats are tender, add dried fruit (see variations below). Cover pot and simmer over very low heat for 1 or 2 minutes more.

Divide steaming-hot oatmeal among bowls. Serve with a small pat of butter (if desired), milk or half-and-half, maple syrup, a dash of cinnamon, and dried fruit and nuts of your choice.

Variations

DATE-HAZELNUT OATMEAL: When oatmeal is almost done, add 2 Medjool dates, chopped, per serving. Garnish each serving with about 8 to 10 halved raw hazelnuts.

RAISIN-WALNUT OATMEAL: When oatmeal is almost done, add 1 to 2 tablespoons flame or muscat raisins per serving. Garnish each serving with chopped walnuts, and sweeten with molasses or brown sugar.

Prune-Almond Oatmeal: When oatmeal is almost done, add 2 prunes, cut in bite-sized pieces, per serving. (Or substitute 1 tablespoon dried currants.) If desired, add a single small drop of orange oil to the pot along with the dried fruit. Garnish each serving with 8 to 10 halved or chopped raw almonds.

Whole-Grain Waffles

This recipe started out as a way to keep up with an abundant supply of duck eggs, back when we were raising ducks. Made with duck or chicken eggs, these flavorful, toothsome waffles are worth the effort as a weekend breakfast treat. The mix of whole grains makes for a surprisingly light-textured waffle.

For a quick fix for two, the recipe is easily halved. Or make a full or double recipe for enough extra waffles to freeze and enjoy on busy weekday mornings, quickly reheated in a toaster oven. We use a non-stick Belgian waffle maker with deep holes yielding crisp waffles 4 inches square.

Serve waffles with fresh (or thawed frozen) fruit or berries, plain yogurt, maple syrup, and a sprinkling of nuts. Or enjoy them with grated apples, chunky applesauce, or other fruit sauce.

10 WAFFLES, SERVES 5

1 cup whole-wheat pastry flour, fine-ground	1/4 teaspoon salt
1/4 cup quick oats (or oat flour)	1 cup + 1 tablespoon milk
1/4 cup wheat germ (or unbleached flour)	1 teaspoon vanilla
1/4 cup oat bran (*or* 3 tablespoons oat flour)	2 extra-large eggs
2 1/4 teaspoons baking powder	2 tablespoons canola oil
1 tablespoon white or organic sugar	

Combine dry ingredients (flour through salt) in batter bowl or mixing bowl. Measure wet ingredients into separate small bowl or large measuring cup and use paring knife to whisk together, beating egg. Pour into dry mixture and let rest 5 minutes while the waffle maker preheats.

Spoon 1 large serving spoon full of batter (more or less, depending on the size of your waffle maker) into each waffle compartment, close lid, and bake until waffles are done. Serve as baked; or remove waffles to cooling rack until batter is used up, then bring the whole batch up to heat in oven or crisp in toaster oven and serve at once with your favorite embellishments.

Freeze any leftover waffles in a single layer in a ziplock bag; they'll reheat quickly in an oven or toaster oven set at 375° to 400°F.

Variation
Wildberry Waffles: Toss 1/2 cup fresh or frozen raspberries and/or blueberries with the dry mixture.

Pecan Waffles

These are a nice, nutty variation on the previous recipe, made exactly the same way. The pecans become lightly toasted as they bake.

8 WAFFLES, SERVES 4

3/4 cup whole-wheat pastry flour, fine-ground
1/4 cup oat flour
1/4 cup quick oats (or unbleached flour)
2 tablespoons toasted wheat germ
1 tablespoon white or organic sugar
2 1/4 teaspoons baking powder

1/4 teaspoon salt
1/3 cup pecans, chopped
2 large eggs
2 tablespoons canola oil
3/4 cup milk
1 teaspoon vanilla

Variation

ORANGE-PECAN WAFFLES: Use fresh-squeezed orange juice in place of 1/4 cup of the milk, and add 1/2 teaspoon freshly grated orange zest to the batter.

DUCKS

For about six years Richard and I raised ducks. Ostensibly we were doing this for a supply of their creamy free-range eggs and rich, gamy-tasting meat . . . but really, as it turned out, the main benefit of keeping ducks was a constant source of entertainment, an ongoing backyard duck carnival and rodeo. Who knew ducks were such fun, irrepressibly cheerful, social, sexy animals! The main challenge was keeping them supplied with clean swimming water in kiddie pools (lacking a farm pond), and protected from predators—and each other's domination antics.

We started with four Indian runners, the ones that look like Dr. Seuss characters outfitted in sleeveless brown sweaters, known for their characteristic upright-bottle posture. Any strange noise, and up periscope, heads a-swivel scanning the field. Over that first summer we sadly lost three of the original four to raccoons, leaving poor lonely Mr. Duck. We knew he was longing for female companionship, and we were hankering for some eggs, but the only locally available ducks at the time were two Australian spotted mallards, a pair of siblings. Despite the difference in size and breed, we took them on, calling them Mrs. Duck and the Little Drake.

From there, things got a lot more interesting, ranging from wild courtship displays (catch-me, catch-me round the pool) to a series of springtime broods. Mrs. Duck proved a good and determined mother, hatching several clutches of beautiful light brown Mallard x Indian Runner ducks, some laying light blue-green eggs like hers, some white. For several years our flock of ducks—as many as 34 birds at one point—kept us well supplied with eggs, which we ate, sold, and froze (beaten with a drop of honey, then poured into ice cube trays). One fall we culled some of the drakes (with ducks it's important to keep a good balance of males to females, to avoid tensions in the flock) and put them in the freezer, for a winter of delicious dinners of free-range roast duck followed by soup (page 44).

After the initial three, which had such engaging personalities they quickly became pets, we stopped naming them—a good thing, since we ultimately had to decommission the duckyard: too many birds, too much work, too much cholesterol. (We sold or gave away as many as we could, and made duck dinners of the rest.)

But it sure was fun while it lasted: dear, broody Mrs. Duck; the adorable fluffy peeps trailing her around yard and field; the total delight in a fresh supply of clean water; the head-bobbing foreplay and victory lap around the pool; the joyous chorus greeting anyone coming up the driveway; the playful dives across the snow . . . The time the ducks joined in with my cat in batting about a stunned vole . . . The gummy snacking on garden slugs . . . Ah, good company, and good eating.

Fruit-Filled Ployes

Ployes, a traditional Acadian pancake (or eggless crêpe) made of light buckwheat flour (page 95), make a quick and light alternative to pancakes. The trick is to use a very hot pan or griddle. Although it is not necessary to grease the pan if hot enough, we find a light wipe of oil good insurance, especially with the first ploye.

Ployes can be served like pancakes, in a stack, or served rolled like crêpes around a fresh-fruit or other filling. Maple syrup and yogurt are the obvious choice, or you could serve them with sweetened whipped cream for a la-di-da breakfast or dessert.

2 to 2 1/2 cups fresh fruit salad (2 to 3 ripe
    fruits: cherries, peaches, strawberries,
    blueberries, raspberries, grated apples)

1 cup ployes mix + 1 1/3 cups water
Whole almonds, halved (page 60) or sliced
Plain yogurt and maple syrup

Combine ployes mix with water and let stand 5 minutes. Heat skillet or griddle and wipe lightly with oiled piece of paper towel. Following directions on ployes mix package, fry them in 1 or 2 batches, depending on the size of your pan or griddle and the size ployes desired, spreading batter with spoon to make 6 medium (7-inch) ployes or 4 larger ones. Stack on a plate and keep warm in oven.

To serve, spoon fruit along center of each ploye and fold/roll up, placing seam-side down on plate. Serve sprinkled with almonds and a dusting of cinnamon, along with yogurt and maple syrup.

Richard's Anadama Pancakes

Pots rattling downstairs on a weekend morning means pancakes are on the way! The corn flour and molasses give such a warm, round flavor, these pancakes hardly need butter—just maple syrup.

SERVES 3 TO 4

1/2 cup whole-wheat pastry flour
1/2 cup unbleached flour
3 tablespoons cup corn flour (finely ground
    cornmeal), scant 1/4 cup
1 3/4 teaspoon baking powder
1/2 teaspoon salt

1 tablespoon canola oil
1 tablespoon butter
1 to 2 tablespoons unsulphured molasses
1 large egg
1 cup + 1 to 1 1/2 tablespoons milk (as
    needed for spreadable consistency)

Combine dry ingredients in batter bowl. Heat oil and butter in large flat-bottomed stainless-steel skillet until just melted. Break egg into small bowl and add molasses, then melted shortening; whisk together and add 1 cup milk. Add wet ingredients to dry mixture and whisk until well blended. If batter seems a little thick, add 1 tablespoon or so more milk; batter should be thin enough to spread out some, but thick enough for a somewhat fluffy pancake. Let batter rest for a few minutes.

Sop up remaining oil and butter residue in frying pan with small folded pad of paper towel, and fry first batch of pancakes (3 per pan) over medium-high heat; use medium-low heat thereafter. Wipe pan between batches with oiled paper towel.

Freeze any leftover pancakes, to reheat in the oven (page 214). Serve with your favorite accompaniments—fresh fruit or fruit sauce (page 232), maple syrup, nuts or sunflower seeds, yogurt.

Variation
BLUEBERRY PANCAKES: Toss 1/2 to 2/3 cup fresh or frozen wild blueberries into combined flours before adding liquid ingredients.

Apple-Oat Streusel Muffins

Who can resist a sugar-and-spice streusel-topped muffin? Especially studded with nuts. They are best served hot, with a little butter and perhaps honey.

MAKES 6 MUFFINS

3/4 cup whole-wheat pastry flour

1/2 cup oat flour

1/4 cup oat bran

1/4 cup rolled oats

1 large egg

1 1/4 teaspoons baking powder

1/2 teaspoon baking soda

1/4 teaspoon salt

1/2 teaspoon cinnamon

2/3 cup chopped raw apple (or pear, or fresh or frozen blueberries)

2 tablespoons light brown sugar, packed

2 tablespoons canola oil

1/2 teaspoon vanilla

Enough milk (or milk with a little yogurt) to measure 1 cup + 2 tablespoons liquid

STREUSEL TOPPING

1 tablespoon brown sugar, packed

1 tablespoon salted butter

1/4 teaspoon cinnamon (or combination nutmeg and allspice)

1 tablespoon toasted wheat germ

1 tablespoon each oat flour and oat bran

1/2 teaspoon vanilla

1/3 cup chopped hazelnuts or walnuts

Combine dry ingredients (flour through fruit) in large mixing bowl. Make streusel topping, first rubbing butter into dry ingredients with fingers, then adding vanilla and nuts; set aside.

Preheat oven to 400°F. Combine wet ingredients in a measuring cup: Using a paring knife (or fork), beat egg right in the measuring cup, then whisk in remaining ingredients in order listed (all except last 2 tablespoons milk), for a total liquid measure of 1 cup. Pour into dry mixture, add remaining 2 tablespoons milk, and mix briefly with spoon until flours are evenly moistened.

Spoon batter evenly into oiled or paper-lined 6-muffin stainless-steel pan. Sprinkle streusel topping evenly over the tops. (Clean up any stray sugar from surface of muffin pan, to prevent it from scorching.) Bake for about 15 to 18 minutes, or until muffins are done and the nuts nicely toasted.

TWICE AS NICE

Muffins are so much nicer straight out of the oven—if not fresh-baked, then reheated. To warm day-old muffins, peel off any papers, wrap muffins together in foil (or a metal pie plate covered with foil), and heat in a 350°F oven or toaster oven (or on a trivet on top of a woodstove) for 10 to 15 minutes. Or simply slice muffins in half, set cut-side down on oven rack, unwrapped, and reheat the same way.

Blueberry-Almond Bran Muffins

Maine blueberries, whole grains, and nuts—plus two magic ingredients—take the humble bran muffin beyond healthy to delicious. A touch of almond extract along with some toasted wheat germ help lighten the muscular flavor of the bran, lending a sweet nuttiness. And why use the traditional raisins when you have wild fresh (or frozen) fruit?

Any kind of berries work well, but I especially love using frozen wild blueberries or raspberries foraged on expeditions to camp—many of them making a return trip back to camp tucked inside muffins. These freeze well, so I'll often cache part of a batch in the freezer, ready to grab and go. They make a healthy, sustaining breakfast just as they are, or slathered with almond butter and honey.

MAKES 6 MUFFINS

1 cup fresh wheat bran	3 to 4 tablespoons almonds, coarsely chopped
1/3 cup toasted wheat germ	2/3 cup fresh or frozen blueberries
2/3 cup whole-wheat pastry flour	1 large egg
1 teaspoon baking powder	2 1/2 tablespoons canola oil
1/2 teaspoon baking soda	1/2 teaspoon pure almond extract
1/4 cup light brown sugar, packed	Enough milk (or milk with a little yogurt)
1/4 teaspoon cinnamon	to measure 1 cup + 3 tablespoons
1/4 teaspoon salt	liquid ingredients

Assemble dry ingredients in order listed in mixing bowl, berries last, and mix till evenly blended.

Preheat oven to 400°F. Combine wet ingredients in a measuring cup: Using a paring knife (or fork), beat egg right in the measuring cup, then whisk in remaining ingredients in order listed (all except last 3 tablespoons milk), for a total liquid measure of 1 cup. Pour into dry mixture, add remaining milk, and mix briefly with spoon until flours are evenly moistened.

Spoon batter evenly into oiled or paper-lined 6-muffin stainless-steel pan. Bake for 18 to 22 minutes (or longer if using frozen berries), or until muffins are done and nicely golden on top.

Variations

APRICOT-ALMOND BRAN MUFFINS: Use 6 soft dried apricot halves, snipped, in place of the blueberries.

BLUEBERRY-BANANA BRAN MUFFINS: Replace half of the blueberries with 1/3 cup chopped banana, and use equal parts cinnamon and nutmeg.

APPLE-BLACKBERRY BRAN MUFFINS: Use 1/3 cup fresh blackberries and 1/4 cup coarsely chopped walnuts in place of the blueberries and almonds.

RASPBERRY-PECAN BRAN MUFFINS: Use 2/3 cup fresh or frozen raspberries (wild ones best) and 1/4 cup pecan pieces in place of the blueberries and almonds.

CRANBERRY-WALNUT BRAN MUFFINS: Use 2/3 cup fresh or frozen cranberries and 1/4 cup broken walnuts in place of the blueberries and almonds; omit cinnamon, and add the grated zest of 1/2 orange and 2 tablespoons freshly squeezed orange juice to the liquid ingredients before topping up with milk.

BERRY-PICKING

Summer just isn't summer without abundant ripe berries, fresh-picked from a local patch. Of course, it's easier to pick up a quart at a local farm stand, but somehow those that taste the best are the ones you foraged for free in a secret thicket, bursting with vitamin W—for the wild adventure of picking them, complete with deerfly bites, scratched shins, and maybe a glimpse of "Blackie" (the Maine black bear) who loves them too.

Raspberries come first, then lowbush and highbush blueberries, although in most parts of Maine there are a couple of weeks from late July into early August when the wild crops overlap. When the time is ripe, you can head out with two "buckets" (recycled yogurt containers) and pick some of each, for a week's worth of patriotic breakfasts and desserts.

Raspberries thrive in cut-over woodlands, and in Maine (unfortunately) we have no shortage of those. After many seasons of picking wild berries, I've determined that although the canes spring up prolifically in cut areas, sunny fields, and log landings, the biggest, most luscious raspberries are found in moister areas, in part shade, sheltered by bushes, trees, and large boulders, and on coastal islands. They especially like piles of slash and downed woody debris, which calls for artful footwork picking them—raspberry tai chi—but the prize berries are worth it, and the taller canes easier to reach. Razzle-dazzled, I can keep picking them till sunset—and dream about them all night.

Lowbush blueberries can crop up most anywhere around old fields or ledgy summits. You'll find good picking in grown-over old blueberry ground. Be conscious and considerate of land ownership. Conservation land is usually open to folks picking a few quarts for personal use. Some landowners with small, unsprayed berry fields may let you pick some for free or for a reasonable price. As with raspberries, the best picking is usually around bushes, rocks, and other places that hold moisture and shade.

For me, blueberry heaven is picking from highbush blueberries on the shore of a not-too-developed lake, as can still be found in parts of Hancock and Washington Counties and farther north. Highbush blueberries are happy with their feet wet, as am I getting to them by canoe. Toting a few lidded quart containers in a daypack or little cooler, I'll pick away, for the double pleasure of having lakeside blueberries both fresh and frozen to bake with through the winter.

Blueberries are easy to freeze: Simply pick out leaves, stems, unripe berries, and errant bugs, put in pint plastic containers, and freeze. I never wash wild berries unless I have a reason to suspect dust or spray, easily avoided by picking away from roadsides, clearcuts, and commercial fields.

Raspberries are best spread in a single layer on waxed paper, frozen, then put in plastic freezer containers. This way they'll stay whole and you can shake out however many you need for muffins, scones, and whatnot. To thaw enough to sprinkle over waffles or pancakes, spread them out on a warm plate, wait a few minutes, and they'll be almost like fresh-picked.

Wild blackberries tend to be too seedy to freeze well, and though delicious as an occasional treat, I find them not worth tangling with their vicious thorns. But sometimes you'll get lucky and find a few canes with dead-ripe fruit arching conveniently within reach. Eaten fresh with yogurt or cream, or baked in a cobbler or pie, they are berry fine!

(Opposite) Blueberry heaven, at Nicatous Lake

Berry-Almond Corn Muffins

Corn flour (finely ground cornmeal) combined with oat flour and a touch of almond makes for a lighter-tasting, less gritty corn muffin—or combine with Acadian light buckwheat flour, for a similar light gold muffin with cakey texture. Gild the lily by sprinkling the tops with organic sugar.

MAKES 6 MUFFINS

2/3 cup corn flour (*or* 1/4 cup corn flour +
    1/3 cup Acadian light buckwheat flour)
1/3 cup oat flour
1/2 cup whole-wheat pastry flour
1/4 cup unbleached flour (scant)
1/4 cup organic sugar + for sprinkling tops
1 3/4 teaspoons baking powder
1/2 teaspoon salt

1 large egg
2 1/2 tablespoons canola oil
1/4 teaspoon almond extract (or vanilla)
Enough milk (or milk with a little yogurt) to
    measure 1 cup + 2 tablespoons liquid
1/3 cup almonds, chopped (or sunflower seeds)
2/3 cup fresh or frozen raspberries, blueberries,
    or cranberries (halved if large)

Assemble dry ingredients (flour through salt) in mixing bowl, and mix till evenly blended.

Preheat oven to 400°F. Combine wet ingredients in a measuring cup: Using a paring knife (or fork), beat egg, then whisk in oil, almond extract, and enough milk for a total liquid measure of 1 cup + 2 tablespoons. Add almonds (or sunflower seeds) and fruit and toss to coat berries with flour. Pour liquids into dry mixture, and mix briefly until flours are evenly moistened.

Spoon batter into oiled or paper-lined 6-muffin stainless-steel pan. Sprinkle tops with sugar. Bake 16 to 20 minutes (or longer if using frozen berries), or until muffins are done and nicely golden.

Variations

RHUBARB-WALNUT CORN MUFFINS: Replace berries with 2/3 cup fresh or frozen "strawberry" rhubarb (page 232), thin red stalks chopped in 3/8-inch pieces. Use vanilla, and replace almonds with walnuts.

BLUEBERRY-LEMON MUFFINS: Using blueberries, add 1 teaspoon finely minced fresh lemon peel to dry mixture; replace almonds with walnuts. Use vanilla along with 1 teaspoon lemon juice in wet ingredients.

Blue Corn-Pecan Muffins

What to do with blue cornmeal? Try these Southwest-inspired muffins, studded with toasted pecans.

MAKES 6 MUFFINS

3/4 cup blue cornmeal

1/4 cup unbleached flour

1/3 cup whole-wheat pastry flour

1/3 cup oat flour

2 tablespoons light brown sugar

1 1/2 teaspoons baking powder

1/4 teaspoon baking soda

1/4 teaspoon salt

2 tablespoons liquid (warm) honey

1 extra-large egg

2 tablespoons fresh-squeezed orange juice

2 1/2 to 3 tablespoons canola oil

Enough milk (or milk with a little yogurt) to
measure 1 cup + 2 tablespoons liquid

2/3 cup raw pecans, coarsely chopped

Assemble dry ingredients (cornmeal through salt) in large mixing bowl. Drizzle with honey.

Preheat oven to 400°F. Combine wet ingredients in a measuring cup: Using a paring knife (or fork), beat egg in the measuring cup, then add oil, juice, and enough milk for a total liquid measure of 1 cup + 2 tablespoons. Pour into dry mixture, and stir briefly until flours are evenly moistened.

Spoon batter evenly into oiled or paper-lined 6-muffin stainless-steel pan. Press pecan pieces into top of batter. Bake for about 16 to 20 minutes, or until muffins are done and nicely golden on top.

Raspberry-Hazelnut Muffins

Crusted with toasted hazelnuts and tucked with bright raspberries, these muffins give a promising start to the day. Or if you haven't a cache of frozen raspberries or blueberries (page 220), make them plain (or with a simple streusel topping in lieu of the hazelnuts, page 224) as a foil for jam. This versatile multigrain muffin also combines well with the warm flavors of orange, maple, and pecans.

MAKES 6 MUFFINS

1/2 cup oat flour

1 cup whole-wheat pastry flour

1/4 cup wheat germ or unbleached flour
(or combination)

1/4 cup light brown and/or organic sugar

1 1/2 teaspoons baking powder

1/4 teaspoon baking soda

1/4 teaspoon salt

1 extra-large egg

2 1/2 to 3 tablespoons canola oil

1 to 2 tablespoons fresh-squeezed orange
or clementine juice

Enough milk (or milk with a little yogurt)
to measure 1 cup + 2 tablespoons liquid

1/3 cup hazelnuts, coarsely chopped

2/3 cup frozen raspberries (or blueberries)

Assemble dry ingredients (flour through salt) in large mixing bowl, and mix till evenly blended.

Preheat oven to 400°F. Combine wet ingredients in a measuring cup: Using a paring knife (or fork), beat egg right in the measuring cup, then stir in canola oil, juice, and enough milk for a total liquid measure of 1 cup + 2 tablespoons. Toss berries with dry mixture, then pour in combined liquids and mix briefly until flours are evenly moistened.

Spoon batter evenly into oiled or paper-lined 6-muffin stainless-steel pan. Sprinkle tops evenly with hazelnuts (plus a little organic sugar if you like a crunchy crust). Bake 20 to 25 minutes (the longer time if using frozen berries), or until muffins are done and nicely browned on top.

Variation

ORANGE-PECAN MUFFINS: Replace 1 tablespoon of the sugar with dark maple syrup, added to the liquid ingredients along with 1 to 2 drops pure orange oil. Sprinkle 1/2 cup broken raw pecans over the tops.

Carrot Spice Muffins

For those who'd feel just a little guilty eating Carrot Cake (page 246) for breakfast, these muffins are for you. The wheat germ, sunflower seeds, and coconut give them a sweet, nutty flavor and tender texture. Good just by themselves, they'd also make fine cupcakes with a gilding of Vanilla Buttercream or Cream Cheese Frosting (page 245).

MAKES 6 MUFFINS

3/4 cup whole-wheat pastry flour	1/4 teaspoon coriander
1/3 cup toasted wheat germ	1/4 teaspoon allspice
1/3 cup oat flour	1/3 cup raw sunflower seeds (or walnuts)
1 rounded tablespoon wheat bran	1/4 cup sultanas or Thompson raisins
1/4 cup unsweetened dried shredded coconut	1 cup shredded carrots
1/3 cup light brown sugar, lightly packed	1/4 cup + 1 tablespoon canola oil
1 1/2 teaspoons baking powder	1 large egg
1/4 teaspoon baking soda	1 teaspoon vanilla
1/2 teaspoon salt	Enough milk (or milk with a little yogurt) to
1/4 teaspoon cinnamon	measure 1 cup + 2 tablespoons liquid

Assemble dry ingredients (flour through spices) in large mixing bowl, and mix till evenly blended. Add seeds (or nuts), raisins, and carrots, and toss until well combined.

Preheat oven to 400°F. Combine wet ingredients in a measuring cup in order listed, beginning with oil, then add egg, stir with a paring knife, and add vanilla and milk, for a total liquid measure of 1 cup + 2 tablespoons. Pour into dry mixture, and stir briefly until flours are evenly moistened.

Spoon batter evenly into oiled or paper-lined 6-muffin stainless-steel pan. Bake 22 to 26 minutes, or until muffins are done through and golden on top.

Blueberry Cake

This cake is fashioned after my Mom's Downeast blueberry cake, which she'd serve fresh out of the oven as part of a special brunch, lunch, or light supper. Though my adaptation favors the more natural ingredients we have available now to bake with (over the traditional white flour, white sugar, and Crisco), I think of this more as a breakfast or dessert cake—especially when decorated with a creamy frosting and walnuts. Fresh blueberries are best, being less likely to stain the batter than frozen ones.

9 TO 12 SERVINGS

1/4 cup light brown sugar, packed
1/4 cup organic or white sugar
1/2 cup oat flour
1/2 cup whole-wheat pastry flour
3/4 cup unbleached flour
1 3/4 teaspoons baking powder
1/2 teaspoon salt
1/4 to 1/2 teaspoon nutmeg
3/4 to 1 cup fresh or frozen blueberries

2 tablespoons salted butter
3 1/2 tablespoons canola oil
1 extra-large egg
1/2 teaspoon vanilla
2/3 cup + 1 to 2 tablespoons milk (or milk with a little yogurt)
Vanilla Buttercream or Cream Cheese Frosting (page 245) (optional)
Walnut quarters (optional)

Assemble dry ingredients (sugar through nutmeg) in large mixing bowl. In preheating oven set to 375°F, melt butter with oil in small stainless-steel bowl or pan. Meanwhile beat egg in small bowl and stir in vanilla, then the warm (not hot) butter/oil and the milk.

Grease 8 x 8-inch square (or 9-inch round) ovenproof baking dish with oil/butter residue, and dust with flour. Add blueberries to dry mixture.

Pour wet ingredients into dry mixture and stir briefly until flours are moistened. Spoon and scrape into prepared pan. Bake in preheated oven for 35 to 45 minutes (the longer time if using frozen berries) or until lightly browned around the edge and a toothpick inserted in the middle comes out clean. Let cool 5 minutes, then turn out on rack.

Serve plain as a breakfast coffeecake. Or, for more of a dessert cake (or cupcakes), spread Vanilla Buttercream or Cream Cheese Frosting over top of cooled cake, and decorate with walnut quarters.

NOTE: This batter makes just enough for a batch of 6 large blueberry muffins or cupcakes.

Variations

BLUEBERRY-GINGER CAKE: Use just a pinch of nutmeg, and add 2 to 3 teaspoons finely minced candied ginger to cake batter (or frost cake with Ginger-Cream Cheese Frosting, page 245).

BLUEBERRY-APPLE CAKE: Use equal parts blueberries and chopped raw apple.

APPLE-WALNUT CAKE: Use 1 cup chopped apple, and add 1/2 cup coarsely chopped walnuts to dry ingredients rather than using as decoration.

STREUSEL-TOPPED BLUEBERRY CAKE: Sprinkle the top with a simple dusting of 2 tablespoons each organic sugar and toasted wheat germ, 1/4 cup chopped walnuts, and a dash of allspice and cinnamon.

Rhubarb Coffeecake

This is one breakfast special that, lightly frosted, can pass as dessert—although it's just the thing to wake up sleepy taste buds. The cake itself is sweetened just enough to take the pucker out of the rhubarb, leaving room for the sweetness of the topping, whether you go for the streusel or the amazingly simple sour cream frosting.

If you have some of the early thin stalks of "strawberry" rhubarb (page 232), those are most berrylike. A little later in the season, peaches, plums, or pears could make a nice variation, a good way to use up disappointing fruit (not juicy enough for out-of-hand eating).

9 SERVINGS

1 1/2 cups chopped "strawberry" rhubarb,
    fresh or frozen and partially thawed

1 1/4 cups fine-ground whole-wheat pastry flour

1/4 cup unbleached flour (or whole-wheat)

1/3 cup oat flour

2 tablespoons oat bran

1/3 cup walnuts (optional, if using Sour
    Cream Frosting)

1/3 cup light brown sugar, lightly packed

1/3 cup organic or white sugar

2 teaspoons baking powder

1/4 teaspoon cinnamon

1/2 teaspoon salt

Streusel Topping (or Sour Cream Frosting)

1 tablespoon salted butter

1/4 cup canola oil

1 extra-large egg

1 teaspoon vanilla

Enough milk (or milk with a little yogurt) to
    measure 1 cup + 1 tablespoon liquid

STREUSEL TOPPING

2 tablespoons salted butter

3 tablespoons light brown sugar, packed

1 tablespoon each oat flour, wheat flour,
    oat bran, and toasted wheat germ

1/2 cup rolled oats

1/4 teaspoon each cinnamon and allspice

1/3 cup walnuts, coarsely chopped

3/4 teaspoon vanilla

SOUR CREAM FROSTING

1 cup full-fat sour cream

1/3 cup confectioners' sugar

If using fresh rhubarb, trim ends of stalks and chop in 3/8- to 1/2-inch pieces. Combine dry ingredients (flour through salt) in mixing bowl. Toss rhubarb, fresh or frozen, with dry ingredients.

For a crumb-topped coffeecake, make Streusel Topping: Cream butter with sugar, then add grains and flours and rub crumbs together with fingers; add cinnamon, nuts, and vanilla, and a small pinch of salt to taste. Or for a frosted coffeecake, combine sour cream with confectioners' sugar; set aside.

Preheat oven to 350°F, with rack set in center of oven. Melt butter in oven in a small metal bowl. Add oil and cool to lukewarm. Meanwhile, butter an 8 x 8-inch square or 9 x 9-inch round ovenproof baking dish and dust with flour.

Beat egg with knife or fork in measuring cup, then stir in vanilla and enough milk for a total liquid measure of 1 cup + 1 tablespoon. Stir into lukewarm shortening.

Pour wet ingredients into flour mixture and mix with a few strokes, until flours are moistened. Spoon batter into prepared baking dish. Leave plain to frost later, or sprinkle evenly with Streusel

Topping. Bake 40 to 50 minutes (less time for a plain cake, more with the Streusel Topping or if using partially thawed frozen fruit), or until coffeecake is nicely golden on top and a toothpick inserted in center of cake comes out clean. Let cool to lukewarm before serving.

For a frosted cake, spread Sour Cream Frosting over top of cooled cake. Store in covered container to keep frosting from drying out.

Variations

BLUEBERRY COFFEECAKE: Reduce amount of brown sugar in batter to 1/4 cup, and use 1/4 to 1/2 teaspoon nutmeg in dry ingredients instead of cinnamon. Use 1 cup fresh or frozen blueberries in place of rhubarb.

PEACH, PLUM, OR PEAR COFFEECAKE: Reduce amount of brown sugar in cake batter to 1/4 cup, and add 1/4 to 1/2 teaspoon nutmeg and/or allspice to dry ingredients in place of cinnamon. Use 1 1/3 cups chopped fresh peaches, plums, or pears in place of the rhubarb.

Banana-Hazelnut Bread

Looking for a whole-grain, subtly sweet banana breakfast loaf, it took me many tries to get it right, finding a happy balance between flours, liquids, and sugars. Bananza! The moist, tender banana bread encrusted with toasty hazelnuts (or macadamia nuts) makes for a nice contrast of textures. Or bake it the traditional way, with walnuts mixed into the batter (see variation).

MAKES 1 MEDIUM LOAF

3/4 cup whole-wheat pastry flour	1 tablespoon salted butter
1/4 cup oat flour	1/4 cup canola oil
1/3 cup unbleached flour	1 1/2 large (or 2 small) ripe bananas,
2 tablespoons wheat germ	about 3/4 cup mashed
2 tablespoons oat bran	1 extra-large egg
1 1/4 teaspoons baking powder	2 rounded tablespoons organic sugar
1/2 teaspoon baking soda	2 tablespoons maple syrup
1/4 rounded teaspoon salt	1 teaspoon vanilla
1/4 teaspoon nutmeg	2 tablespoons milk (or buttermilk, or whey)
1/8 teaspoon allspice	1/2 cup hazelnuts (or macadamias), chopped

Combine dry ingredients (flour through spices) in small bowl. Set aside.

Preheat oven to 350°F. Melt butter with oil in 3 1/2 x 7 1/2-inch or 4 1/2- x 8 1/2-inch loaf pan, then cool to lukewarm. Mash bananas in mixing bowl; then cream in egg, sugar, maple syrup, vanilla, milk, and lukewarm shortening. Spread shortening residue around cooled loaf pan and dust with flour.

Pour dry mixture into creamed mixture, stirring until flours are moistened. Let batter rest a few minutes to let flours take up liquids, then scrape into prepared loaf pan. Coarsely chop hazelnuts (or macadamias) in halves or thirds and gently press into top. Bake 45 to 50 minutes, or until lightly browned on top and a toothpick stuck in center comes out clean. Let cool on baking rack.

Serve plain, or spread each slice with a little sour cream drizzled with honey.

Variation

BANANA-WALNUT BREAD: Replace hazelnuts with 2/3 cup chopped walnuts, added to dry ingredients.

Apple-Walnut Bread

This bread came along with me and my friend Jan Carpenter on an expedition Downeast one raw November day, doing a soil test for a pit privy on my island in First Chain Lake. The soil scientist, Dean Bradshaw, ferried us over in a canoe to the island, where we savored the bread and hot tea as a comforting snack when the work was done.

As it turned out, Dean (with his wife Nan) was also an organic cranberry grower, en route back from the processor, and he sent us each home with a bag of ripe cranberries—inspiring me to throw some in with the apples next time I baked a loaf. You could also use up firm or mealy pears (see variation). The whole wheat and spices make for a richly flavored loaf generous with fruit and nuts.

MAKES 1 LARGE LOAF

2 1/4 cups whole-wheat pastry flour (scant)	1 1/2 cups whole raw apples (or equal parts apples and cranberries), chopped
1/4 cup toasted wheat germ	2 tablespoons butter
1 1/2 teaspoons baking powder	1/2 cup brown sugar, packed (+ 1 rounded tablespoon if using cranberries or tart apples)
3/4 teaspoon baking soda	
1 1/4 teaspoons cinnamon	
1/2 teaspoon ginger	1 extra-large egg
1/2 teaspoon ground cloves	3 tablespoons canola oil
1/2 teaspoon salt	1 cup milk with a little yogurt (or buttermilk)
2/3 cup walnuts, coarsely chopped	

Combine dry ingredients (flour through fruit); set aside. In a large mixing bowl, cream butter and sugar, then beat in egg. Mix in oil, then milk (or buttermilk). Pour dry ingredients into wet mixture and stir until all flours are moistened. (Add 1 more tablespoon milk if batter seems too stiff.)

Preheat oven to 360°F. Butter and flour a 4 1/2- by 8 1/2-inch Pyrex loaf pan; scrape batter into pan. Bake 1 hour, or until top of loaf is nicely browned and toothpick inserted in center comes out clean. Cool 5 minutes, then turn out of pan onto rack to finish cooling.

Variation

PEAR-WALNUT BREAD: Use firm ripe pears in place of apples. For spices, use 1/4 to 1/2 teaspoon nutmeg or allspice, 1/4 cinnamon, and 1/4 teaspoon cloves.

Christmas Stöllen

I learned to make this lovely Old World Christmas bread from my mother-in-law, Dolly Washburn, using her German mother's recipe. I've lightened up just a little on the original recipe's shortening, and substituted oil for some of the butter; also a little whole-grain flour seems to enhance the texture without making it heavy. I've made Stöllen with the traditional mixed candied fruit, but have come to prefer it with the simpler golden raisins and dried cherries.

This recipe makes two good-sized loaves, or three smaller ones, which works best for our small household—one to enjoy at home, one to give, and one to freeze (unfrosted) for later. Dolly, who has a full house for Christmas, makes it as one large loaf, which takes a little longer to bake and has a slightly denser texture.

MAKES 3 SMALL LOAVES OR 1 LARGE LOAF

1 1/4 cups milk

1/2 cup (1 stick) salted butter

1/4 cup canola oil

2 tablespoons very warm water

2 packets dry active yeast (1 1/2 tablespoons)

1 cup white sugar (including 1 teaspoon
    for yeast mixture)

3 large eggs, room temperature

5 cups unbleached flour

1 to 1 1/2 cups whole-wheat pastry flour

1/2 teaspoon salt

Seeds of 10 to 12 cardamom pods, ground in
    mortar and pestle

1/2 cup golden raisins (or equal parts golden
    raisins and dried cherries)

1/2 to 1 cup candied fruit (either mixed fruit,
    or candied lemon and orange peel)

2/3 cup walnuts, coarsely chopped

~ DECORATION ~

About 3/4 cup confectioners' sugar + enough
    tangerine/ clementine juice to make a glaze

Walnut quarters and dried cherries

In small saucepan, scald milk, then melt butter in the hot milk over low (or no) heat. Add oil and sugar, and let cool to lukewarm. Meanwhile, in large, warmed mixing bowl, dissolve yeast in warm water with 1 teaspoon of the sugar. Add lukewarm milk-shortening-sugar mixture. Beat in eggs. Combine flour, salt, and cardamom and gradually add to wet mixture, stirring after each addition.

Turn dough out onto floured countertop or other surface, and knead for about 6 minutes until firm and elastic. Let rise in warm, buttered mixing bowl, covered with damp cloth, in oven or other warm place until doubled.

Punch dough down, then turn out on lightly floured surface. Working with floured hands, spread dough out into a large, flat oval and sprinkle evenly with fruit and nuts. Fold into thirds, and knead briefly until fruit and nuts are evenly worked into dough, then divide and form into two or three oval loaves. Place freeform loaves on greased cookie sheets. (Or, keep as one large single loaf, and place in buttered rectangular baking pan.) Let rise again until nearly doubled (better to err on the firm and lofty side than risk flattening).

Bake in preheated 325°F oven for about 40 to 50 minutes, depending on loaf size, until done but not too brown. Let cool on cake rack; meanwhile mix confectioners' sugar with enough juice to form glaze. Drizzle glaze over cooled loaf (loaves) in zigzag pattern, and decorate with walnuts and a few dried cherries if desired.

Pies & Cakes, Etc.

Strawberries

I've been picking strawberries since I was a little wild one myself, tagging along behind my mother who loved picking the tiny wild fruits each summer. We'd go berry-picking in fields she knew of growing up in Hancock, and in the fields out back of our house in Cumberland Center where I grew up. Then she'd serve them, simply hulled and sprinkled with a little sugar, with shortcakes and whipped cream as a special treat.

I still love foraging for wild strawberries, but for more than a handful, a nice summer ritual is a trip to the nearest pick-your-own strawberry place, ours being Silveridge Farm in North Bucksport. Picking there in the old farm fields sloping down to Silver Lake with a view to Great Pond Mountain, in company with people of all ages all focused on the same pleasant task, is just as much a treat as the berries themselves. And what berries! Oh, just one more quart . . . Unless it's a year to make jam, though, 6 quarts—4 to freeze, 2 to eat fresh—are usually enough for just us plus occasional company.

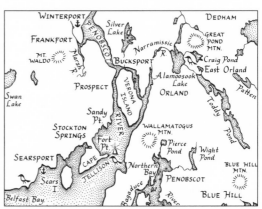

We cut most of the berries in half, big ones in thick slices, then spread them in a thin layer on waxed paper on trays to freeze. Once frozen, they're zipped into 1-quart freezer bags. Freezing them as halves or slices (maybe also a few whole smaller berries, to use as glamorous ice cubes) keeps them from glomming together, so you can shake out as many as you need. Let the berries thaw slowly in the refrigerator, then sweeten as desired and serve on waffles and shortcakes, on vanilla ice cream, or use in popsicles, sauces, pies. . . .

Strawberry Preserves (MAKES ABOUT 6 HALF-PINTS)

Bright strawberry preserves are like "summer in a jar" (quoting Greg Brown), a fragrant winter treat.

2 quarts firm, ripe small to medium strawberries, washed, hulled, and halved	4 1/2 cups white or organic sugar 2 to 2 1/2 tablespoons lemon juice

Combine berries with sugar and lemon juice in a large nonreactive pot or saucepan. Heat slowly, stirring constantly, until berries release some juice and sugar is dissolved, then cook uncovered at a slow boil for 15 to 18 minutes or until mixture is almost at the jellying point (almost sheets from a spoon). Skim foam, then ladle into 6 hot clean half-pint jars, leaving 1/4 inch headroom. Cover jars with new lids soaked in hot water, secure with rings, and process in boiling-water bath for 10 minutes. Let cool, check seals, and store in pantry or other cool dark place.

Strawberry-Banana Popsicles

These humble little popsicles grew out of a need to use up the occasional "disappointing" (not-as-thick-as-hoped) batch of homemade yogurt (page 212) along with a backlog of frozen strawberries. The banana gives a smooth texture, taking the place of the cream, egg, or carrageenan used in regular ice creams. These aren't cloyingly sweet or artificial-tasting like some commercially made fruit popsicles— all you need is a little honey, lemon, and sugar to bring out the natural tart sweetness of the fruit.

You can use a blender for a uniform pourable puree, but I find the fork method less hassle, plus a little fruit texture is nice. Lacking popsicle forms, I just spoon the smoothie-like mixture into 3-ounce bathroom-sized paper cups and insert a small recycled (or improvised) hardwood popsicle stick or sundae spoon upright in the middle of each one to freeze in place.

Keep the frozen popsicles on hand in the freezer, wrapped in a plastic bag, for a quick summertime pick-me-up. Grab one as you're heading out, let it thaw for a few minutes in its little cup, and enjoy a healthy frozen treat.

 MAKES 15 POPSICLES

3 medium ripe bananas, thoroughly mashed

1 quart fresh or thawed frozen strawberries, thoroughly mashed

1/2 teaspoon lemon juice

1/2 cup honey (scant)

2 to 4 tablespoons organic or white sugar

2 cups plain yogurt

Use a fork to mash the fruit in large ceramic bowl, or puree in blender. Add lemon juice, honey, sugar to taste, and yogurt, and mix well.

Set about 15 bathroom-sized (3-ounce) paper cups on a small tray. Spoon about 1/3 cup fruit mixture into each cup. Freeze about 1 1/4 hours or until a skin has formed on top, then insert a small wooden stick in center of each popsicle. (Or if you'd rather set them to freeze all at once, you can poke the sticks through a piece of foil to hold them upright.) Freeze until solid, then enclose the whole batch in a plastic bag. Popsicles should keep up to 2 months in the freezer.

Strawberry Rhubarb?

Perhaps, like me, you've always thought of strawberries and rhubarb as a time-honored pairing. Or so I did, until coming across a recipe in an old-time Downeast cookbook by Elsie Boynton referring to "strawberry rhubarb" as the variety with red stalks. Hmm, could our strawberry-rhubarb combination have evolved from a miscommunication? If so, a happy mistake!

But the old-timers were right in identifying the lower, red part of the stalk as the sweetest part of the "pie plant," as rhubarb was once called. The strawberry-colored lower stalk is sweeter and less stringy than the upper green part (closer to the leaves, which are poisonous), especially early in the season. Sweetest of all is the whitish-pink base of the stalk, which you'll get if you pull the rhubarb stalk up from the base of the plant, rather than cutting: gently rock the stalk back and forth until the plant releases it, then trim off the leaf and the "beard" at the base of the stalk.

Here in Maine, our strawberry and rhubarb seasons don't always coincide as well as their flavors. Of course you can find them together in the supermarket, along with other trucked-in produce, but we hunter-gatherer types would rather wait to pick them both in season. Rhubarb is usually prime from late May to early June. By cutting back the plant and flower head, you can probably keep your rhubarb going until late June and early July, when pick-your-own strawberries are in season, but the stalks won't be as sweet as earlier on. Here's where a freezer pulls its weight: you can combine fresh rhubarb with the last of last year's pick-your-own strawberries; then continue the cycle by picking, chopping, and freezing a fresh supply of "strawberry" rhubarb while it's at its sweetest, to thaw and add to fresh-picked strawberries to make pies, sauces, conserves, or whatever you fancy.

Strawberry-Rhubarb Sauce

This simple sauce is delicious over vanilla ice cream for dessert, or as a sauce for waffles or pancakes, along with plain yogurt. Or use it in a Strawberry-Rhubarb Gelatin Pie (page 234). The amount of sweetener assumes using the naturally sweet lower rhubarb stalk and ripe strawberries; otherwise you may want to add a little more honey or sugar, or reverse the proportions of strawberries to rhubarb.

℞   MAKES 3 PINTS

1 1/2 quarts fresh (or frozen, thawed) "strawberry" rhubarb, 1/2-inch chunks
1/4 cup water (including juice from thawed fruit)

1 quart fresh (or frozen, thawed) strawberries
3/4 to 7/8 cup honey (*or* 1 1/4 cups sugar)
1/4 teaspoon cinnamon (optional)

Put rhubarb and water in large saucepan; cover, and cook over medium-low heat for 6 to 8 minutes. Meanwhile, wash and stem strawberries (cut in half or thirds if large). When rhubarb is tender, stir in honey (or sugar), then add strawberries and finally cinnamon if desired. Cook fruit an additional 5 to 8 minutes, just long enough to bring sauce to a boil. Turn off heat.

Meanwhile sterilize 3 pint jars by boiling 10 minutes in a hot-water bath. Drain jars, then fill with hot sauce, leaving 1/2 inch headroom. Wipe jar mouths, place new lids soaked in hot water over tops, secure with rings, and process 15 minutes in boiling-water bath. Let cool; check seals, and store.

Rhubarb Pie with Lattice Crust

Here is the ultimate spring dessert, made with the first product of your garden: fresh "strawberry" red rhubarb. The lower stalks should give the filling a nice blush, but with a little crop management (see page 232) you can combine garden rhubarb with native strawberries for a deeper red (variation). The whole-grain crust and vanilla ice cream make it a special dessert—although people have been known to eat rhubarb pie for breakfast, along with plain yogurt and maple syrup.

Most rhubarb pie recipes call for a lot of sugar. If you use fresh early-season rhubarb, favoring the naturally sweet bottom half of the stalk, the amount of sugar suggested here should be plenty sweet.

SERVES 8

4 to 4 1/2 cups "strawberry" rhubarb, sliced
1 cup organic sugar (*or* 1/4 cup light brown
    sugar + 3/4 cup white sugar)
1/3 cup unbleached flour

Dash cinnamon (1/8 teaspoon)
1/2 tablespoon salted butter, diced small
Whole-Wheat Pastry, Double-Crust Recipe
    (page 238)

Rinse rhubarb, trim "beards" from base of stalks, and slice with serrated knife in 3/8- to 1/2-inch pieces. Set aside in covered bowl. Measure sugar, flour, and cinnamon into separate bowl.

Make the Whole-Wheat Pastry, Double-Crust Recipe (page 238), and divide in two unevenly sized balls (proportioned 5/8 to 3/8). Roll the larger ball of dough out on a lightly floured surface to about 13 inches in diameter. Transfer to 9-inch deep-dish Pyrex pie plate, and align evenly across bottom and up sides of pie plate, with about 1/2 inch extra pastry folded over top lip of plate.

Pour flour-sugar-spice mixture over rhubarb, toss to coat, then pour into center of pastry and level out evenly. Dot with butter.

Preheat oven to 425°F. Roll out smaller ball of pastry on lightly floured counter into a long oval about 7 inches wide by 10 to 11 inches long. Using a non-serrated dinner knife, cut pastry into strips about 1/2 inch wide; transfer lattice strips one at a time to top of pie, weaving a lattice crust, working from the center outward. You will need 12 to 14 strips to weave the crust.

Fold under extra pastry at ends of lattice strips together with excess bottom crust, to form outside edge. Crimp edge, alternating thumbs and index fingers of both hands.

Bake pie at 425° for 10 minutes, then lower heat to 350° and bake for 40 minutes more, or until crust is golden brown and rhubarb filling is tender and bubbling.

Serve either warm or cold with vanilla ice cream.

Variation

STRAWBERRY-RHUBARB PIE: Replace 1 1/2 to 2 cups of the rhubarb with fresh (or frozen and thawed) sliced strawberries. Decrease sugar to 2/3 to 3/4 cup.

Fresh-Fruit Gelatin Pie

I've been selling my map wares at the Machias Blueberry Festival for over two decades, but not as long as Helen's Restaurant has been serving up pies and other Downeast delicacies. One of the first times there, my booth-mate (Richard) and I shared a piece of Helen's fresh blueberry pie slathered with whipped cream as a post-festival treat, and found their fresh-fruit approach a revelation.

Many experiments later, I've found my own natural-foods touch with this idea of combining fresh (uncooked) fruit with a gelatin filling, crisp pastry, and cream topping. It's a little more effort than a baked pie, but what a way to celebrate the ripe fruits of summertime! Or deep in winter, maybe your pantry holds the makings for a gelatin pie using last summer's strawberries and rhubarb (see variation).

SERVES 8

3 cups fresh strawberries, blueberries, or raspberries (or stoned, sliced peaches or cherries sprinkled with 1 teaspoon lemon juice)

2 cups unfiltered fruit juice or nectar of the same featured fruit

1 1/2 packets plain unflavored gelatin

1/3 cup honey

1/2 cup plain yogurt (optional)

Oatcake Piecrust (page 235) or Oaty Piecrust (page 242)

Pick through fruit, removing stems, leaves, etc. If using strawberries, halve or slice if large.

Dissolve gelatin in 1/2 cup of the fruit juice and set aside. Heat remaining 1 1/2 cups juice in double boiler to very hot and add gelatin mixture, stirring until well dissolved and hot. Remove from heat and add honey. Let cool in boiler top to room temperature. For a smoother, creamier consistency, mix a little of the cooled juice in with the yogurt (if desired), then stir yogurt into juice mixture.

Crush 1 cup of the berries (or mash 1 cup of the fruit slices) and add to juice mixture. Add 1 cup whole berries or fruit slices, reserving the last cup to spread on top of the pie. Chill filling in refrigerator or freezer, stirring frequently, until it begins to gel. Meanwhile make the Oatcake (or Oaty) Piecrust, and pre-bake shell in a 9-inch deep-dish Pyrex pie plate, as described on page 235.

When gelatin mixture is beginning to set, spoon into baked and cooled pie shell. Press remaining berries or fruit halves/slices into top of pie. Refrigerate for another hour or two, until pie is set. Top each serving with sweetened whipped cream.

NOTE: Gelatin pies are best eaten the same day they are made. Any left over will keep for another day at cool room temperature; this is better than refrigerating, which may produce a soggy crust.

Variation

STRAWBERRY-RHUBARB GELATIN PIE: Thaw 1 to 1 1/2 cups thawed frozen strawberries. Dissolve 1 1/2 packets gelatin in 1 cup strawberry juice (unfiltered juice plus juice drained from strawberries) and heat in double boiler. Remove from heat and stir in 1 pint Strawberry-Rhubarb Sauce (page 232), 1/4 cup honey, and thawed strawberries. Chill filling and when it begins to gel, spoon into pre-baked Oatcake or Oaty Piecrust. Refrigerate until set and serve with whipped cream.

OATCAKE PIECRUST

This dessert piecrust reminds me of the thin, nutty-tasting oatcakes I ate while living in northern Scotland and visiting the Western Isles. Although they used steel-cut oats, oat bran in a pastry context gives a similar texture—rich and crumbly, a little like a cracker or crumb crust, but that's just fine with a chilled gelatin-based fruit filling.

1/2 cup whole-wheat pastry flour	1/4 teaspoon salt
1/4 cup unbleached flour	2 tablespoons chilled salted butter, diced
1/2 cup oat bran	2 1/2 tablespoons canola oil
1/2 cup oat flour	3 to 4 tablespoons ice water, as needed

Preheat oven to 425°F. Combine dry ingredients in mixing bowl, and rub butter evenly into flours with your fingers. Drizzle with oil and stir with spoon until mixture resembles coarse oatmeal.

Add water, adding 2 tablespoons water, then 1 to 2 tablespoons more as needed to bring dough together. Pastry will crumbly, but malleable enough to pat into bottom and up sides of 9-inch pie plate to form a slightly crimped edge. Prick bottom and sides of crust with fork.

Bake for 6 minutes, then lower heat to 375° and bake another 5 minutes or until light gold. Let cool on wire rack.

Coconut Cream Pie

A similar approach to the Fresh-Fruit Gelatin Pie, using the same Oatcake Piecrust, makes a melt-in-your mouth coconut cream pie, simple and considerably lighter than your usual coconut custard. Although opening and grating a whole coconut (page 249) is a project you'll probably only want to tackle once in a while, the fresh taste and smooth texture are a treat.

Like all gelatin pies, this is best eaten the day it is made, while the crust is still crisp.

SERVES 8

1 1/2 tablespoons gelatin (1 1/2 envelopes)	1 1/4 cups unsweetened shredded dried coconut
2 cups milk (*or* 1 1/2 cups milk + 1/2 cup light-	(*or* 1 1/2 cups shredded fresh coconut)
ened coconut milk or fresh coconut liquid)	1/3 cup honey
1 1/4 cups light cream	3/4 teaspoon vanilla (*or* 2 teaspoons dark rum)
Pinch of salt	Oatcake Piecrust or Oaty Piecrust (page 242)

Dissolve gelatin in 1/4 cup of the milk. Pour remaining milk and cream into double boiler, along with coconut and salt, and heat to scalding (until milk steams and frothy bubbles begin to form). Remove from heat and add dissolved gelatin, honey, and vanilla. Let cool for about an hour; then chill in refrigerator for 1 to 2 hours, stirring occasionally, until filling is beginning to set.

Meanwhile, make the piecrust, and pre-bake shell in a 9-inch deep-dish Pyrex pie plate, as described above.

Spoon chilled coconut filling into cooled pie shell, and smooth surface. Refrigerate for another hour or two, until pie is set. Serve plain or with a dollop of sweetened, stiffly whipped cream.

Because of the cream, any leftover pie should be refrigerated.

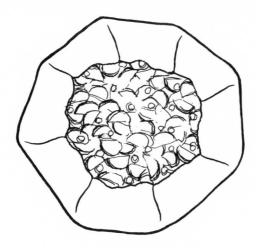

Rustic Fruit Tart

There are as many ways to make one of these charming freeform tarts—called galettes *in France—as there are combinations of summer fruits, berries, and preserves. How you choose to sweeten the tart will depend on the type of fruits you are using and how ripe and juicy they are. If using berries or juicy stone fruits (plums, peaches, apricots, nectarines, cherries), dusting with sugar and cornstarch is a better bet; with denser fruits and pomes (apples and pears), a fruit glaze is* merveilleux. *Like all pies, fresh-fruit tarts are best kept at room temperature and eaten within a day or so.*

SERVES 8

Tart Crust (page 237)
3 1/2 to 3 3/4 cups fresh red plums, apricots,
    nectarines, peaches, cherries, pears, or apples
    (or combination), sliced
1 tablespoon beaten egg + 1/2 teaspoon water

1/4 cup plum, apricot, peach, or red currant
    preserves + 2 tablespoons hot water
    (*or* 1/4 cup sugar + 1 to 1 1/2 tablespoons
    cornstarch)
1 tablespoon organic sugar for sprinkling

Make Tart Crust and chill in the refrigerator. Meanwhile prepare fruit, leaving skin on but removing any blemishes and bruises, cores, and pits. Cut stone fruits in 1/2-inch crescents; apples and pears in slices 1/8 to 1/4 inch thick.

Combine beaten egg with water in small bowl for egg wash (refrigerate rest of beaten egg for another use such as muffins or scones).

If using firmer fruits, make a fruit glaze by spooning preserves into saucepan, cutting up any large pieces of fruit. Add water and stir over low heat until preserves melt into a thin glaze. If using mostly ripe, juicy fruit, combine sugar with cornstarch, smoothing out lumps, and toss with fruit, rather than sweetening tart with glaze. Preheat oven to 400°F, setting racks in lower third or center of oven.

Roll dough out onto lightly floured surface into a large circle, 13 to 13 1/2 inches in diameter and a little over 1/8 inch thick. (Don't worry about raggedy edges; that's part of the tart's rustic appeal.) Roll pastry up onto rolling pin, and unfurl over center of baking sheet. (NOTE: If using a lightweight pan, such as a 12-inch round pizza pan, dust center with a little semolina or pastry flour to prevent scorching bottom of crust; or roll the pastry out on a lightly floured piece of baker's parchment and place in center of baking sheet.)

Lightly brush center 8 inches of pastry with egg wash, then arrange fruit slices, leaving a margin of 2 to 2 1/2 inches of pastry around the outside. If sweetening with glaze, drizzle glaze evenly over the fruit. Fold pastry border over perimeter of fruit, spacing pastry folds about 3 inches apart while gently patting in place (about 8 folds around a 9-inch tart). Brush egg wash over top of crust and sprinkle with organic sugar.

Bake tart about 35 minutes or until fruit is tender and tart crust is nicely golden. Cool for about 5 minutes, then use spatula(s) to transfer tart to cooling rack. Cool thoroughly, then slide tart onto a plate or platter and slice into wedges. Serve plain, or with whipped cream or vanilla ice cream.

Variation

BERRY-FRUIT TART: Toss 2 1/2 to 2 2/3 cups sliced nectarines, peaches, apricots, apples, or plums with 1/4 cup sugar and 1 1/2 tablespoons cornstarch, and arrange in center of tart. Sprinkle evenly with 1 cup fresh blueberries or raspberries (or frozen berries, partially thawed). Finish assembling tart and bake as described above.

TART CRUST

3/4 cup unbleached flour	5 tablespoons chilled salted butter, diced
1/2 cup whole-wheat pastry flour	1 tablespoon chilled Neufchatel or cream
1/3 cup oat flour	cheese, diced
1 to 2 teaspoons white sugar	2 tablespoons canola oil
1/4 teaspoon salt	4 to 5 tablespoons ice water

Combine dry ingredients (flour through salt). Rub butter into flours, then cream cheese. Drizzle oil over crumbly mixture and toss with fork. Add ice water 1 tablespoon at a time until dough clumps together when pinched with fingers.

Turn dough out onto lightly floured surface roll out into a small rectangle. Fold in thirds, and repeat. Gather dough into a ball and refrigerate, covered with plastic, for 20 to 30 minutes while you prepare the fruit and other ingredients. Finish tart as described above.

ORGANIC SUGAR

Why use organic sugar rather than the standard, cheaper white? Because organic sugar is a very nice product: light gold, clear, somewhat larger crystals that actually taste like something (sugar cane!), bringing more flavor to baked goods, plus sparkle if sprinkled on top. Organic sugar is grown without the use of pesticides. I can't certify it's good for you, but it's better!

Piecrusts

I have to admit, my favorite part of any pie is the crust—providing it's freshly made from scratch, and not overbaked. Using mostly whole-grain flours, honest butter and oil, and a light hand with salt makes for a sweet, nutty-tasting, soul-satisfying crust. I know those pre-made piecrusts may seem convenient, but they can't come close to a real piecrust using fresh whole ingredients—you really can taste the difference. In this and other chapters, you'll find crusts for many occasions: a corn-wheat crust for savory pies, a subtly sweet crust for tarts, oaty and nutty crusts for dessert pies, and an easy-rolling whole-wheat pastry for double-crust pies, turnovers, and tarts.

Whole-Wheat Pastry, Double-Crust Recipe

This two-crust pastry recipe, using a good balance of whole-wheat, unbleached, and oat flours, works equally well with dessert and savory pies. It's easy to handle, and makes just the right amount for a batch of tarts or turnovers. When making something savory, such as pasties (page 28), use extra-virgin olive oil instead of canola to give the pastry extra flavor. For a slightly richer, more delicate dessert crust, use 4 tablespoons ice-cold butter, grated or minced.

1 cup whole-wheat pastry flour, brown or white	3 tablespoons chilled salted butter, diced
1 cup unbleached pastry flour	4 brim-ful tablespoons (or scant 1/4 cup)
1/2 cup oat flour	canola oil
1/3 to 1/2 teaspoon salt	7 to 8 tablespoons ice water

Combine dry ingredients in mixing bowl. Rub butter into flours with fingers until evenly distributed. Drizzle with oil and toss until mixture resembles coarse oatmeal. Sprinkle with ice water, adding the last few tablespoons one at a time as needed to bring dough together into a ball. Pastry should not be dry or crumbly, but moist enough to roll out easily on floured surface.

Green Tomato Mincemeat Tarts

The old-timers relied on suet and deer meat, but I'll take green tomatoes as a base for mincemeat any day. Fruity and full of vitamin C, this richly flavored vegetarian mincemeat only gets better with time; you can eat it within a year, but wait another few years and you'll have a blue-ribbon dessert worthy of the Exhibition Hall. Bake the mincemeat in tarts (or turnovers, or a pie), serve with vanilla ice cream, and oh my! Thanksgiving should come more often.

The same crust and handling work well with two other Thanksgiving flavors, cranberry and pecan (see variations). Cranberry tarts have been around since Colonial times; this date-sweetened cranberry filling is from our earlier cookbook. The pecan filling is a scaled-down (three-fourths) version of Don Drew's recipe, which my Dad bakes as a beautiful pie with the pecans arranged in concentric rings like a golden sunflower.

Whole-Wheat Pastry, Double-Crust Recipe   1 to 1 1/2 pints Green Tomato Mincemeat

Make pastry dough and divide into 10 equal portions for tarts (or turnovers, as made on page 240). Lightly flour clean countertop. Preheat oven to 400°F.

Roll out each ball of pastry into a round about 1/8 inch thick and large enough to fit in a 4-inch non-stick tart pan, allowing a little extra pastry to crimp edges. Fill each tart shell with 1/4 cup (or slightly less) mincemeat. Place tarts on 2 baking sheets, to make moving them in and out of the oven easier. (If you're a little shy on filling, and have some mini cookie cutters, a nice touch is to cut the 10th round of dough into holiday shapes—holly leaves, stars, bells—small enough to fit on the top of each tart, as decoration. Or cut the pastry into simple shapes freehand using a paring knife.)

Bake at 400° and bake for 14 to 18 minutes or until pastry is golden. Remove to cooling rack. Serve tarts with a dollop of vanilla ice cream or sweetened whipped cream if desired.

Variations

CRANBERRY TARTS: Put 2 cups chopped apples in a saucepan with 1/2 cup cider and heat to a simmer. Add 1 3/4 cups raw whole cranberries; when they begin to pop, stir in 1/2 cup chopped dates, 1/3 cup packed brown sugar, 1 tablespoon honey, a dash of cinnamon, and 3/4 teaspoon orange zest. Cook covered until fruit softens and sauce thickens. Divide filling among 10 tart shells pre-baked at 400°F for 8 to 10 minutes, or fill pastry with sauce and bake as above. Serve with whipped cream or or vanilla ice cream.

PECAN TARTS: Cream 1/2 cup packed brown sugar with 2 tablespoons melted butter, 2 teaspoons flour, and 3/4 cup dark corn syrup. Beat in 3 large eggs, 1 1/2 teaspoons vanilla, and 1/8 teaspoon salt. Divide filling among 10 tart crusts. Place 12 pecan halves on top of each tart. Bake at 375°F for 28 to 30 minutes.

GREEN TOMATO MINCEMEAT (MAKES 8 PINTS)

2 quarts green tomatoes, seeded and chopped	3 cups brown sugar, lightly packed
1 tablespoon salt	1/2 cup honey
Freshly grated zest of 1 orange	1/2 cup + 1 tablespoon cider vinegar
Fruit of 1 orange, peeled, seeded, and chopped	2 teaspoons cinnamon
1 1/2 quarts apples, peeled, cored, and chopped	1 teaspoon nutmeg
3/4 cup golden raisins	1 teaspoon ground cloves
1 3/4 cups Thompson raisins	2 tablespoons fresh ginger root, skinned,
1/2 cup canola oil	thinly sliced, and minced

Prepare tomatoes and sprinkle with salt. After 1 hour, cover tomatoes with boiling water and let soak 5 minutes; then drain thoroughly. Put in large pot with remaining ingredients, and cook over medium-high heat for 15 minutes, stirring frequently, until sauce thickens to filling consistency.

Fill 8 clean pint jars with hot mincemeat, leaving 1/2 to 3/4 inch headroom. Remove air bubbles. Wipe jar mouths, fit with new lids soaked in hot water, and secure with rings. Process in boiling-water bath for 25 minutes. Let cool, check seals, and store in pantry or other cool dark place.

Apple Turnovers

Subtly sweet with old-fashioned spices, this mixed fresh-and-dried fruit filling is reminiscent of mincemeat—especially with the rich "aged" flavor of dried pears, if you have some (see variation).

This amount of filling should work out just about right with the amount of pastry—but if you run short, wondering how to fill one last lone round of pastry, here's a chance to improvise with whatever you have on hand. One of my favorite quick fillings is to cut up a few soft dried apricots, add a tablespoonful of apricot preserves and some coarsely chopped walnuts, and call it good!

MAKES 10 TURNOVERS

3 1/4 cups chopped apples, about 4 medium
  (such as Cortlands or Empires), skins on
1/2 to 2/3 cup cider (or equal parts water and
  apple butter)
1/3 cup Thompson or flame raisins
1/4 cup light brown sugar, packed
Small pinch of salt

1/2 to 3/4 teaspoon cinnamon
1/4 teaspoon nutmeg
1/8 teaspoon cloves
1 teaspoon salted butter
1/4 cup walnuts, lightly toasted and chopped
Whole-Wheat Pastry, Double-Crust Recipe
  (page 238)

Cut apples in quarters, core, trim any bruised spots or blemished skin, and slice or chop into bite-sized pieces. Place in saucepan with cider and cook over medium to low heat, partly covered, for 6 to 8 minutes, until fruit is tender but not mushy. Stir or shake pot frequently to keep fruit from catching on. Remove from heat. Stir in raisins, sugar, salt, spices, butter, and walnuts (baked at 325°F for 3 to 4 minutes until very lightly toasted, then chopped). Let filling sit while you make the pastry.

Divide dough into 10 portions the size of a walnut. One at a time, roll out balls of dough on lightly floured surface into pastry ovals about 4 1/2 x 6 1/2 inches. It helps to first flatten the ball of dough with the palm of your hand, flipping the pastry several times as you coax the perimeter into an oval shape with both hands, before rolling it out further to the desired dimensions.

Working one freshly rolled-out pastry oval at a time, spoon a portion of filling (about 1/4 cup) onto the front third (facing toward you) of pastry, leaving 1/2 inch margin around front edge. Use your finger dipped in a little water to moisten around filled edge. Fold rest of pastry back over filling, align edges, and pat edges of turnover together; gently crimp with fork. Preheat oven to 425°F.

Arrange turnovers on 2 lightly oiled baking sheets, 5 per sheet, keeping corners of pastries away from outside edges of pan so they won't scorch. (The first tray-ful can be baking while you assemble the second batch.) Using a round toothpick (or the tines of a fork), poke a few holes (or sets of holes) in top of each turnover to let steam escape. Lightly brush tops with a little milk, if desired, for a browner crust. Reduce temperature setting to 400° and bake turnovers for 18 to 20 minutes or until nicely golden. Remove to cooling rack.

Variation

APPLE-PEAR TURNOVERS: Soak 8 dried pear halves in 3/4 cup water or apple cider for 30 minutes to 1 hour, then pour into saucepan with soaking liquid and 2 1/4 cups chopped apples. Add remaining ingredients and cook filling, then assemble and bake turnovers as described above.

Pumpkin Cheesecake Pie

This and the following recipe are a couple of gild-the-lily versions of pumpkin pie, an American favorite harvest dessert from New England on south, made variously (and interchangeably) with pumpkin, squash, and sweet potatoes, maple syrup, brown sugar, and molasses.

I had no idea how regional a favorite until living in England and Scotland, where pumpkins and "yams" are not as widely celebrated as here and seldom found at the greengrocer's. In the Findhorn Community kitchen, some of us homesick Americans went to great lengths one autumn getting a batch of pumpkins from a local farmer (an American expatriate!) so we could bake some pumpkin pies and share a cherished tradition.

This pie is sweetened lightly with maple syrup, which allows the flavors of the pumpkin-ricotta "cheesecake" filling to come through. Use the Nutty Dessert Crust, or if you'd prefer a pastry crust, the Oaty Piecrust (page 242) is a good choice—for pie, or pumpkin tarts!

SERVES 8

Nutty Dessert Crust (recipe follows)	1/8 teaspoon salt
2 extra-large (or 3 large) eggs	3/4 teaspoon cinnamon
2/3 cup ricotta	1/2 teaspoon ground ginger
1 to 1 1/3 cups mashed cooked pumpkin or	1/4 teaspoon nutmeg or mace
winter squash (such as Sweet Dumpling)	1/4 cup half-and-half
2 tablespoons light brown sugar	1/4 cup milk
1/3 cup maple syrup	1/4 teaspoon vanilla

Make piecrust and press into a 9-inch pie plate (see recipe below). Cook the pumpkin (or a golden winter squash such as Sweet Dumpling) by boiling, steaming, or baking until tender, then skin and mash in mixing bowl. (NOTE: To bake squash, cut in half, scoop out seeds, fill halves with water, and bake in pan covered with foil at 375°F for about 45 minutes.) Beat in eggs, then ricotta. Stir in brown sugar and maple syrup. Add spices, then half-and-half, milk, and vanilla.

Preheat oven to 425°F. Pour in filling, and bake for 5 minutes; then lower heat to 350° and continue baking another 45 to 50 minutes, or until set in the middle and light golden on top. Serve with a dollop of sweetened whipped cream and a dash of cinnamon.

NUTTY DESSERT CRUST

1/3 cup quick or rolled oats	2 tablespoons light brown sugar
3/4 cup whole-wheat pastry flour	2 tablespoons chilled salted butter, diced
1/4 cup oat flour or oat bran	2 tablespoons canola oil
1 to 2 tablespoons wheat germ (optional)	1/4 cup finely chopped walnuts (or pecans)
1/4 teaspoon salt	2 1/2 to 3 tablespoons ice water, as needed

Combine dry ingredients in mixing bowl, and work butter evenly into flours with fingers. Drizzle with oil and stir until mixture resembles coarse oatmeal. Add nuts. Sprinkle with 2 1/2 to 3 tablespoons ice water, as needed to bring dough together. Pastry will be rich and crumbly, but malleable enough to pat into the bottom and about 1 1/4 inches up sides of pie plate.

Sweet Potato Pie

The filling is lightly spiced and sweetened with maple syrup, letting the sweet potato be at the forefront. Go with more or less maple syrup and half-and-half, depending on the consistency and sweetness of your sweet potatoes. A crusty pecan topping, inspired by a wonderful pie made by Norma Rössel for the potluck dessert table at a WoodenBoat Christmas party, gives a toasty golden touch.

SERVES 8

1 1/2 cups mashed baked sweet potato
   (1 large or 2 small sweet potatoes)
2 extra-large (or 3 large) eggs
1/2 cup milk
1/4 to 1/3 cup half-and-half
2 tablespoons light brown sugar
2 to 3 tablespoons maple syrup
1/4 teaspoon salt
1/2 teaspoon cinnamon

1/4 teaspoon nutmeg
1/4 teaspoon allspice
1/2 teaspoon vanilla
Oaty Piecrust (recipe follows)
~ TOPPING ~
3/4 to 1 cup raw whole pecans, chopped
2 tablespoons maple sugar, if you have some
   (otherwise, light brown sugar)
1/4 teaspoon cinnamon

Hopefully you've thought ahead and baked 1 or 2 extra sweet potatoes (at 400°F for 1 hour). Remove skin from baked potatoes, along with any dark areas under skin. Put sweet potato pulp in large mixing bowl and mash with fork. Beat in eggs, milk, half-and-half, sugar and maple syrup, spices, and vanilla.

Make Oaty Piecrust and line 9-inch deep-dish pie plate. Preheat oven to 425°F. Chop pecans into separate small bowl, and combine with sugar and cinnamon.

Scrape filling into prepared crust and smooth surface. Bake at 425° for 10 minutes, then reduce temperature to 350° and bake another 10 minutes. Remove pie from oven and sprinkle top evenly with nut mixture. Return to oven and bake 35 to 40 minutes more, until knife inserted in center of pie comes out clean and nut topping is lightly browned. Serve plain or with a little whipped cream sweetened with organic sugar or maple syrup.

OATY PIECRUST

Oat flour (finely ground oats) brings a nice nutty flavor and texture to piecrust. With a larger ratio of oat flour to wheat flour (and less gluten development), this pastry tends to be a bit fragile, so is best suited to single-crust pies. For two-crust pies, turnovers, or other pastries that need more handling, use the Whole-Wheat Pastry recipe (page 239), which includes more wheat flour. With savory pastries, olive oil (in place of canola) adds flavor to the crust.

2/3 cups whole-wheat pastry flour
1/3 cup unbleached flour
2/3 cup oat flour
1/4 teaspoon salt

3 tablespoons chilled salted butter, diced
2 tablespoons canola oil (or olive oil)
4 1/2 tablespoons ice water

Combine dry ingredients in mixing bowl, and work butter evenly into flours with fingers. Drizzle with oil and stir with spoon until mixture resembles coarse oatmeal. Add water, sprinkling a few drops more ice water as needed to bring dough together.

Roll out dough on floured surface into circle about 12 inches in diameter, lightly brushing top with unbleached flour to keep from sticking. Roll up on rolling pin and transfer to 9-inch deep-dish pie plate, adjusting crust to fit sides. Crimp edges.

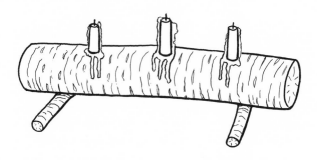

GRANDMA'S CAMP KITCHEN

Back in the early 1930s, my grandparents (Glenn and Gwendolyn Crosen) had a cabin built of native hemlock, pine, and cedar on a northern cove of Beech Hill Pond, north of Ellsworth. Grandma and Grandpa (a chemistry professor), both from the Midwest, were thrilled to be able to spend summers on a pristine Maine lake, and made the cabin their home away from home.

Over the next three generations the Old Cabin would host many a family house party, with "backrubs, warm laughter, and game competition, and fabulous meals from our intimate kitchen . . . Fifty-odd years of Hearts, Bridge, and Spoons, under kerosene lamplight, serenaded by loons" (from a poem I scribbled in the camp logbook). The place fairly gleams with all the good times and conversations had there. I savored many summer vacations there with my family while Grandma and Grandpa were alive—and though the lake has gotten more built up, the camps more modern, and Richard and I have our own more rustic camp way Downeast, I still check in each summer to reconnect with my brother and his family, my parents, aunts, and cousins.

The pale-green lake and sandy beach are as beautiful as ever, but my favorite spot is the cozy little kitchen in the Old Cabin, with its peeled-log half-timbering, vintage dishes and pine cupboards, Grandma's homemade dishtowel curtains and canisters she painted with lake scenes, and many of the same pots and utensils she used in baking, all from scratch, countless lemon meringue and blueberry pies, birthday cakes, sticky buns, and of course chocolate chip cookies. By her definition, any special occasion was an occasion for special baking—and vice versa. One cake in particular stands out in my memory, a square one she made for my mother's birthday: a cocoa cake frosted with orange buttercream, decorated with candles set in little pinecone holders Grandpa fashioned out of red spruce cones (see next page, also the picture facing page 280).

Though tiny (no more than 6 by 8 feet), the Old Cabin kitchen, open to the porch through a hinged serving window, still turns out memorable meals, continuing Grandma's tradition of gracious sit-down dinners, folks lingering around the big pine table with its birch log candelabra over dessert and tea, talking and laughing with the loons. . . .

Cranberry-Apple Cake

I bake this cake in a darkened 9 x 9-inch square baking pan that belonged to my Grandma, Gwendolyn Crosen, who delighted in baking special desserts both at home and at camp. An 8 x 8-inch baking dish or a round cake pan would do as well. Whatever the shape, this lip-smacking but healthy cake is wholesome enough even for breakfast! I usually make it with half and half cranberries and apples, but it's equally good using either all cranberries or all apples—or applesauce (variation).

SERVES 8 TO 12

1 cup whole-wheat pastry flour

1/3 cup toasted wheat germ

1/3 cup oat flour

1/3 cup unbleached flour

1/3 cup light brown sugar, packed

1/3 teaspoon salt

3/4 teaspoon baking powder

3/4 teaspoon baking soda

1/2 teaspoon cinnamon

1/4 teaspoon cloves

1/4 teaspoon allspice

1/2 cup walnuts, broken or coarsely chopped

1/2 to 2/3 cup cranberries, fresh or frozen

1/2 to 2/3 cup raw apple, chopped (1/2 apple)

1 large or extra-large egg

1/3 cup canola oil

3/4 teaspoon vanilla

1 1/2 tablespoons honey

1/2 cup milk

1 tablespoon yogurt or cider

Vanilla or Orange Buttercream (page 245)

12 to 16 walnut quarters (split halves)

In large mixing bowl, combine dry ingredients (flour through spices); add walnuts, cranberries (halved if large), and apple. In smaller bowl beat together wet ingredients (egg through yogurt/cider).

Preheat oven to 350°F. Butter a 9 x 9-, 8 x 8-, or 7 x 11-inch baking pan/dish and dust with flour.

Pour wet mixture into dry and mix briefly till flours are moistened, adding another 1 to 2 teaspoons milk or cider as needed for a spreadably moist batter. Scrape batter into prepared pan or dish, and spread evenly. Bake 30 to 40 minutes (the longer time if using frozen cranberries) or until cake is lightly browned on top and a toothpick inserted in center comes out clean. Let cool on wire rack.

When cake has cooled completely, carefully transfer to cake box lined with waxed paper. Frost top of cake with Vanilla or Orange Buttercream Frosting and decorate with walnut pieces.

Variation

APPLESAUCE CAKE: Omit cranberries and apple. In wet ingredients, replace honey and milk with 1 cup lightly sweetened applesauce, 2 tablespoons sultanas plumped in 2 tablespoons cider, and 1 tablespoon melted butter. Spread batter in pan/dish and bake as above. Frost with Cream Cheese Frosting, page 245.

BUTTERCREAM FROSTING

A simple, honest buttercream really makes a cake—especially one with tart fruits, nuts, and whole-grain textures. On the other hand, too much sugary frosting can be cloying—especially if the cake makes an appearance at breakfast or tea break. The amounts here are modest, enough to frost the top of a single-layer cake, and perhaps the sides. To frost two layers, make half again as much.

VANILLA BUTTERCREAM FROSTING (MAKES 1/2 TO 2/3 CUP)

2 tablespoons salted butter

1 1/2 to 2 tablespoons yogurt, sour cream, or milk

Few grains salt

1/2 teaspoon vanilla

Enough confectioners' sugar for good spreading consistency (about 1 cup)

ORANGE BUTTERCREAM FROSTING (MAKES 2/3 CUP)

1 1/2 tablespoons salted butter

2 tablespoons cream cheese or sour cream

1 tablespoon fresh-squeezed clementine, tangerine, or orange juice

Few grains salt

1/4 teaspoon vanilla

1 drop pure orange oil (*or* 1/4 teaspoon orange zest)

Enough confectioners' sugar for good spreading consistency (about 1 1/4 cups)

LEMON BUTTERCREAM FROSTING (MAKES 1/2 TO 2/3 CUP)

2 tablespoons salted butter

2 tablespoons sour cream, yogurt, or cream cheese

Few grains salt

1/2 teaspoon freshly grated lemon zest

1/2 teaspoon fresh-squeezed lemon juice

1/4 teaspoon vanilla

Enough confectioners' sugar for good spreading consistency (about 1 cup)

Using a fork, cream butter with cream cheese, yogurt, sour cream, or milk in small mixing bowl. Add flavorings. (NOTE: If using orange oil, be careful to measure just 1 small drop, as the flavor is very concentrated.) Gradually cream in enough confectioners' sugar for a fairly stiff but smooth spreading consistency. Makes enough frosting to cover top of an 8 x 8- or 9 x 9-inch square cake. If you prefer a cake with less frosting (say, to serve as a breakfast or coffeecake rather than as a dessert), pipe a smaller amount in a leafy mandala, woodland scene, or whatever strikes your fancy.

CREAM CHEESE FROSTING (MAKES 2/3 CUP)

1 tablespoon salted butter

3 tablespoons Neufchatel or cream cheese

1/2 to 1 teaspoon milk

1/4 teaspoon vanilla

1/2 teaspoon lemon juice

1 to 1 1/4 cups confectioners' sugar

Cream butter and cream cheese with fork in small mixing bowl. Add milk, vanilla, and juice, then gradually cream in sugar until smooth (more sugar will only liquefy the cream cheese).

Variation

GINGER-CREAM CHEESE FROSTING: Cream 3 ounces Neufchatel cream cheese with 2 tablespoons honey. Add 2 teaspoons minced candied ginger; beat until fluffy. Or add ginger to Cream Cheese Frosting, above.

Carrot Cake

Carrot cake is one of many good reasons to grow (or buy from a local farmer) a supply of storage carrots, so much sweeter than their pale trucked-in cousins. Early Nantes "candy carrots" are lovely, crunchy and sweet for eating fresh in salads, and will keep fresh refrigerated for four months or so. Stouter varieties like Bolero are the best keepers, for savory stews and carrot cake through the winter.

There are more sumptuous versions of carrot cake, with canned pineapple, coconut, more eggs, sugar, and shortening. . . . This whole-grain interpretation is moist and rich in flavor and texture without being too heavy or sweet. For another healthy variation, try the Carrot Spice Muffins (page 223), baked as a cake or cupcakes.

SERVES 9 TO 12

3/4 cup whole-wheat pastry flour
1/3 cup oat flour
1/3 cup wheat germ
1/2 cup unbleached pastry flour
2 teaspoons baking powder
1/4 teaspoon baking soda
1/2 teaspoon salt (scant)
1 teaspoon cinnamon
1/4 teaspoon nutmeg
1/4 teaspoon ground cloves
1 3/4 cups shredded raw carrots

2/3 cup chopped walnuts
1/4 cup golden raisins or sultanas
2 tablespoons salted butter, softened
1/2 cup light brown sugar, packed
2 large eggs
1/3 cup canola oil
1 teaspoon vanilla
1/4 cup milk
1/3 cup pear (or pineapple) juice
Cream Cheese Frosting (page 245)
Walnut quarters

Assemble dry ingredients (flour through spices) in medium-sized bowl; fluff with fork to "sift." Stir in carrots, nuts, and raisins (or if raisins are dry, soak them in juice to add with wet ingredients).

In large mixing bowl, cream together butter and sugar, then beat in eggs, oil, vanilla, milk, and juice. Preheat oven to 350°F. Butter a 9 x 9-inch square or 7 x 11-inch rectangular baking dish (or 2 round 8-inch cake pans) and dust with flour.

Stir dry mixture into liquid mixture in thirds, stirring after each addition. Batter will be moist.

Using a spoon or cake spatula, pour and spread batter in prepared baking dish or pans. Bake in center or top third of oven for 30 to 45 minutes (less time for 2 layers, longer for a single layer) until browned on top and a toothpick inserted in center comes out clean. Let cool on wire rack.

When cake has cooled completely, carefully transfer whole cake (or bottom layer) to a plate or cake box lined with waxed paper. Frost single-layer cake with 1 recipe Cream Cheese Frosting (or Vanilla or Lemon Buttercream Frosting, page 245). For a 2-layer cake (using round 8-inch layers, or a rectangular cake cut in half), make a recipe and a half of frosting and frost top and between layers. Decorate top of cake with walnut quarters.

Variation

CARROT-COCONUT CAKE: Use 1 tablespoon butter in wet ingredients, and replace juice and milk with 2/3 cup lightened coconut milk (page 71). Frost with Vanilla Buttercream or Cream Cheese Frosting.

Zucchini Bread

*T*hough usually made as a tea bread, this zucchini bread qualifies as an elegant dessert topped with vanilla ice cream, as served by my friend Jan Carpenter of Penobscot. (On the rare occasion that the loaf "bathtubs" or balks about coming out of the pan, it goes by the less elegant but exotic name of Zucchini Bungle.) Likely it's the natural ingredients—whole wheat, organic sugar or evaporated cane juice, fresh walnuts and garden zucchini—that bring such rich flavor and cakelike texture to the loaf.

Here are two versions of the recipe—as Jan makes it in a large loaf pan, or scaled down as a tea bread—along with a variation using winter squash or pumpkin.

If you have a lot of zucchini (or a lunker that didn't get picked quite soon enough), Jan suggests freezing recipe-sized portions of grated zucchini for winter baking; thaw and add, along with any juice, to the wet ingredients.

MAKES 1 LARGE LOAF

3/4 cup whole-wheat pastry flour, stone-ground	1/2 to 2/3 cup walnuts, coarsely chopped
3/4 cup unbleached flour	1 cup shredded fresh zucchini
2 teaspoons baking powder	1 extra-large egg (or 2 medium eggs)
1/2 teaspoon baking soda	2/3 to 3/4 cup organic sugar (or cane juice)
1/2 teaspoon salt	1/2 cup olive or canola oil (or combination)
1 1/2 teaspoons cinnamon	1 1/2 teaspoons vanilla

MAKES 1 MEDIUM LOAF

2/3 cup whole-wheat pastry flour, stone-ground	1/3 to 1/2 cup walnuts, coarsely chopped
1/3 cup unbleached flour	1 cup shredded fresh zucchini
1/4 cup toasted wheat germ	1 extra-large egg
1 teaspoon baking powder	1/2 to 2/3 cup organic sugar (or cane juice)
1/2 teaspoon baking soda	1/3 cup olive or canola oil (or combination)
1/3 teaspoon salt	1 tablespoon milk
1 teaspoon cinnamon	1 teaspoon vanilla

Combine dry ingredients (flour through walnuts); set aside. Preheat oven to 325°F. Generously butter a large (4 1/2 x 8 1/2-inch) or medium (3 1/2 x 7 1/2-inch) loaf pan and dust with flour.

Beat egg(s) in large bowl. Beat in sugar and oil, then add milk (if making smaller recipe) and vanilla. Stir in zucchini. Mix dry ingredients with wet and stir until flours are moistened.

Spoon batter into pan and bake 55 minutes to 1 hour for large loaf, 50 to 55 minutes for smaller loaf, or until bread tests done and top is nicely browned. Set on cake rack until cool enough to turn out of pan without bungling. Serve in slices with vanilla ice cream.

Variation

PUMPKIN (OR SQUASH) BREAD: Use the same dry ingredients as in the larger recipe, with 1 teaspoon cinnamon and 1/2 teaspoon allspice. Vary the wet ingredients by using a scant 1/2 cup organic sugar, 1/3 cup oil, 2/3 to 3/4 cup mashed cooked pumpkin (or winter squash), and 1/4 cup milk, plus the same amounts of egg and vanilla.

Coconut-Walnut Cake

Based on a classic Italian cream cake, this recipe has a lighter touch on the usual proportions of sugar, butter, and eggs, with a lighter frosting—yet is every bit as moist and delicious, and shouldn't weigh on your conscience (or ribs). The nicely textured sponge-type cake is a perfect backdrop for the coconut and lightly toasted walnuts, or the variation with orange, pecans, and sour cream.

SERVES 10 TO 12

2/3 cup unsweetened shredded dried coconut
2/3 cup lightened coconut milk (page 71)
3 tablespoons salted butter, softened
1 1/3 cups white sugar (scant)
3 tablespoons canola oil
2 large eggs, separated
1 to 2 additional egg whites
1 teaspoon vanilla
3/4 to 1 cup walnuts

1 cup unbleached all-purpose or cake flour
2/3 cup whole-wheat pastry flour, fine-ground
1/3 cup oat flour
1 teaspoon baking powder
1/2 teaspoon baking soda
1/4 teaspoon salt
1/2 cup milk with a little yogurt (or buttermilk)
Sour Cream Frosting (page 249), Vanilla
    Buttercream (page 245), or whipped cream

Place coconut in small bowl and add coconut milk, so coconut can take up some of the liquid. (If using fresh grated coconut, page 249, you can increase the amount of coconut by 2 tablespoons.)

Cream butter with sugar in large mixing bowl, then add oil and egg yolks and beat until fluffy. Stir in vanilla. Stir soaked coconut into creamed mixture.

Preheat oven to 350°F. Spread walnuts on baking sheet and lightly toast in preheating oven for 3 to 4 minutes, just enough to bring out their flavor. Let cool, then rub off any loose skins and coarsely chop. Meanwhile assemble remaining dry ingredients (flour through salt) in small bowl, and "sift" flours by fluffing with spoon or fork. Add chopped walnuts to flour mixture.

Whip egg whites in separate bowl until fairly stiff. Lightly butter two or three 9 x 9-inch cake pans (or two 8 x 8-inch ovenproof baking dishes) and dust with flour.

Add flour mixture to creamed mixture by thirds, alternating with the milk-yogurt mixture (or buttermilk). Fold whipped egg whites into batter.

Divide batter between prepared pans, and bake at 350° for 25 to 28 minutes, or until light gold and a toothpick inserted in the center comes out clean.

When completely cooled, assemble the cake, frosting the top and between layers.

Variations

COCONUT-WALNUT BUNDT CAKE: Pour batter into a buttered and floured 10-inch bundt pan. Bake 45 to 50 minutes or until done. Serve each slice with a dollop of sweetened whipped cream.

ORANGE-PECAN SOUR CREAM CAKE: Omit coconut and coconut milk, substituting 1/2 cup sour cream thinned with 2 tablespoons milk (2/3 cup total). Add a few drops (1/8 teaspoon) orange oil to the creamed mixture. Use 1 cup chopped pecans in place of walnuts, and add to dry mixture 1/2 teaspoon ground coriander. For liquid, use 1/4 cup milk (or buttermilk) plus 1/4 cup fresh-squeezed orange/clementine juice.

Sour Cream Frosting

Here is an elegantly simple recipe for a creamy, subtly tart frosting—just the right finish for a sweet, rich cake like this one. Sweet-tooths, don't be tempted to add more sugar, as it will only make the frosting syrupy; in fact, you could use even less than the amount suggested here, just enough to offset the tang of the sour cream. Unlike more sugary frostings, which harden, or whipped cream, which separates, this sour cream frosting keeps its smooth texture, at room temperature or in the refrigerator.

1 1/2 cups full-fat cultured sour cream   1/2 to 2/3 cup confectioners' sugar

Measure sour cream into small mixing bowl. Add sugar and gently stir until evenly blended. Spread over cooled cake, or refrigerate until ready to use. (NOTE: It's best to keep the frosted cake covered in a cake box, to keep the frosting from drying out.)

What About the Yolks?

How to use up a couple lonely egg yolks whose whites have helped leaven and moisten a cake? Well, there's hollandaise sauce, or Béchamel Sauce (page 164) . . . or you could cook the broken yolks in a non-stick pan until set, then chop or crumble them over a spinach salad (page 58). Or, thin the yolk with water and brush on a tart (page 202) or loaf of bread (page 236) for a golden glaze.

Fresh Coconut

Opening and grating a fresh coconut is worth the occasional bother: softer, fresher-tasting, and more flavorful than dried coconut, also cheaper. A good-sized coconut will yield about 5 cups grated coconut, enough to use fresh in a pie and freeze the rest, in ziplock bags or packed in containers in recipe-sized portions to use in Coconut Cream Pie, Coconut-Walnut Cake, Carrot Spice Muffins. . . . (When baking with fresh coconut, use a little more than the amount of dried coconut called for in a recipe, as noted.)

Here's how to deal with a fresh coconut: You'll know you've picked a good one if the "milk" swishes inside when you shake it (otherwise, the liquid has probably leaked out through a soft spot). (NOTE: Fresh coconut liquid, erroneously called "milk," is different from coconut milk, which is the creamy liquid expressed from grated fresh coconut steeped in hot water.) Using a hammer and icepick, puncture two of the three "eyes" and drain out all the liquid. Then bake the empty coconut in a preheated 400°F oven for 15 minutes, to release the shell. Strike the hot coconut with a hammer to break it open and into pieces.

Baking the coconut should have helped separate the hull from the meat, but you may have to use a paring knife on stubborn pieces or tough sections of inner husk. If you prefer your coconut snowy-white, pare off all of the thin brown inner husk before grating; otherwise leave some on (it's fine to eat and contrasts nicely with the white coconut). Grate the coconut with a hand grater or in a food processor. Use fresh or freeze.

Polenta Cake with Fresh-Fruit Ambrosia

This simple fresh-fruit dessert is like johnnycake crossed with strawberry shortcake—add sweet, juicy oranges, coconut, and maple syrup, and it becomes ambrosia, food of the gods! Or for variety, serve the cake twice, two different ways, one half with Ambrosia and the other with summer fruits (variation).

SERVES 8 TO 12

3/4 cup unbleached flour

1/2 cup corn flour

1/2 cup oat flour

1 teaspoon baking powder

1/2 teaspoon baking soda

1/4 teaspoon salt

3 tablespoons salted butter

2/3 cup white or organic sugar

2 medium to large eggs

2 tablespoons canola oil

1 teaspoon vanilla

1/2 cup milk with a little yogurt (or buttermilk)

Fresh-Fruit Ambrosia

1 to 1 1/4 cups flaked dried coconut (preferably large flakes), lightly toasted

1 1/2 to 2 cups cream, whipped (*or* 3 to 4 cups whole plain yogurt, or a combination)

Maple syrup or organic sugar to taste

Assemble dry ingredients (flour through salt) in small bowl, stir to combine, and set aside. Lightly butter a 9-inch Pyrex deep-dish pie plate. Preheat oven to 350°F.

Cream butter with sugar in mixing bowl. Beat in eggs, oil, and vanilla. Add dry mixture to creamed mixture alternately with milk and yogurt (or buttermilk), stirring after each addition. Scrape batter into prepared pie plate. Bake 30 to 32 minutes or until cake is golden on top and tests done in the center. Turn off heat.

While cake cools, prepare fruit. Meanwhile, spread coconut in a pan and toast briefly in still-warm oven (careful, it only takes a minute; shake pan a couple times to toast evenly). Whip cream (or combine equal parts whipped cream and yogurt) and sweeten with sugar or maple syrup.

Cut cake in 8 to 12 wedges, then slice each piece horizontally. To assemble each serving, place bottom layer of cake on dessert plate, and spoon portion of Ambrosia over bottom slice. Drizzle with a little of the fruit juice, and sprinkle with toasted coconut. Top with upper slice. Serve with sweetened whipped cream or yogurt-cream, or yogurt drizzled with a little maple syrup.

FRESH-FRUIT AMBROSIA

1 1/2 pints to 1 quart fresh strawberries (or frozen and thawed), halved or sliced if large

2 Valencia or Minneola oranges (*or* 4 clementines), sections seeded and halved

3 to 4 tablespoons maple syrup (or honey)

Combine fruit with syrup (or honey), and serve over Polenta Cake. Best eaten within a day or so.

Variation

POLENTA CAKE WITH SUMMER FRUITS: For Ambrosia fruits, use chopped ripe, juicy nectarines or plums, and/or red raspberries. Replace coconut with 2/3 cup lightly toasted almonds (page 74), thinly sliced.

Fresh-Fruit Shortcakes

The quintessential summertime dessert. Freshness—ripe juicy fruit, lush whipped cream, just-baked cake—is what it's all about, so the recipes are scaled small to be enjoyed at one sitting. Layer one featured fruit or two, at the height of their season, with whipped cream on golden shortcakes or individual sponge cakes sweetened with honey. Or, any time of year, layer the sponge cake with dried fruit and sweetened ricotta in a small, simple cassata, a traditional Sicilian dessert (variation).

SERVES 3

Shortcakes or Sponge Cakes (below)

1 2/3 cups fresh fruit (strawberries, cherries, peaches, nectarines, plums, raspberries)

1 tablespoon honey + 1 teaspoon lemon juice

1/3 to 1/2 cup whipping cream

1 to 2 tablespoons plain yogurt (optional)

Drop of vanilla (optional)

1 rounded tablespoon organic sugar

Make Shortcakes or Sponge Cakes. Prepare fruit and drizzle with honey; if it will be a little while before serving, sprinkle with lemon juice and refrigerate. (Ripe fruit is best prepared just ahead, while the cakes are cooling.) Whip cream, stir in yogurt and vanilla if desired, and sweeten with sugar.

Split cakes in half horizontally. Spoon a portion of fruit over each bottom layer. Add a generous dollop of whipped cream, then set remaining cake half on top.

SHORTCAKES

1/3 cup whole-wheat pastry flour, fine-ground

1/3 cup unbleached flour (scant)

2 level tablespoons oat flour

1 1/4 teaspoons baking powder

1/8 teaspoon salt

1 tablespoon chilled salted butter, diced

2 teaspoons canola oil

1 level tablespoon honey (*or* 2 full teaspoons)

1/4 cup half-and-half (or combination of cream + milk)

Measure flours in cup, then combine with remaining dry ingredients in small bowl. Rub in butter with fingers, then drizzle oil over flours and stir in. If honey is cold, warm by setting jar in hot water, then drizzle honey thinly over flour mixture and work in with fingers, for a crumbly mixture. Add half-and-half and stir dough together with just a few strokes.

With floured fingers, divide dough into 3 small mounds on baking pan oiled and dusted with flour. Pat dough down slightly, pattycake style, to shape biscuit rounds 3/4 to 1 inch thick.

Bake in preheated 400°F oven for 8 to 10 minutes, until puffed and golden. Cool on rack.

SPONGE CAKES

1 tablespoon salted butter

1/4 cup white sugar

1 large egg, separated

1 tablespoon canola oil

1 tablespoon honey

1/4 teaspoon vanilla + 2 drops almond extract

1/4 cup whole-wheat pastry flour, fine-ground

2 level tablespoons oat flour

1/3 cup unbleached flour

3/4 teaspoon baking powder

1/8 teaspoon salt

1/4 cup milk (or milk with a little yogurt)

Cream butter with sugar in mixing bowl. Mix in egg yolk, oil, honey, and extracts. In separate small bowl sift together flours (2/3 cup total) with baking powder and salt.

Preheat oven to 350°F. Lightly butter 3 small (about 4 inches diameter) non-stick cake pans.

Add dry mixture to creamed mixture a third at a time, alternating with milk. Whip egg white in small bowl until fairly stiff, and fold into batter using a flexible scraper. Divide batter among prepared pans. Bake cakes about 20 minutes or until tops are lightly browned. Let cool on rack.

Variation

CASSATA WITH CHERRIES: Soak 1/4 cup halved dried cherries in 2 tablespoons orange-flavored liqueur (or brandy or golden rum + 2 drops orange oil). Bake 1 recipe Sponge Cakes in buttered 3 1/2 x 7-inch non-stick loaf pan 25 minutes at 350°F. Cool, then slice cake lengthwise in thirds. For filling, press 3/4 cup ricotta through a sieve with back of spoon, then stir in 1 rounded tablespoon sugar, 1 tablespoon cream, and the cherries and liqueur. Spread filling between layers. Sprinkle shaved bittersweet chocolate over top of cake, and chill until firm. Serve in wide slices. Best fresh; leftover cassata keeps 1 to 2 days refrigerated.

Plum-Apple Crumble

Cobbler, crisp, crunch, crumble—all similar baked fruit desserts distinguished by their toppings. I think of a cobbler as having a biscuit crust, and a crisp as being sprinkled with a streusel of sweet rich crumbs. In England and Scotland they're fruit crumbles, made with oaty toppings and served with custard sauce like most every other "pudding" (dessert). Crumbly with oats and toasted hazelnuts, I guess crumble is what we'll call this fragrant fruit dessert—or breakfast, served with plain yogurt.

SERVES 6

3 to 4 ripe red plums, sliced	3/4 cup rolled oats
2 apples, partially peeled, cored and sliced	1/2 cup whole-wheat pastry flour
1/3 cup honey	1/3 cup oat flour
3/4 to 7/8 cup unfiltered plum nectar	1/4 teaspoon salt
1/8 teaspoon cinnamon	1/4 teaspoon baking soda
1/8 teaspoon allspice	3/4 teaspoon baking powder
~ TOPPING ~	2 tablespoons canola oil
2 tablespoons chilled salted butter, diced	1 teaspoon vanilla
1/4 cup light brown sugar, unpacked	1 to 2 teaspoons water (or cider), as needed
1/4 cup organic sugar	1/2 cup raw hazelnuts, coarsely chopped

Butter an 8 x 8-inch ovenproof baking dish and fill with sliced fruit. Combine honey with plum juice and spices and pour over fruit. (Or use canned plums packed in light syrup, sweetened to taste.)

Preheat oven to 365°F. Rub butter into sugars in mixing bowl. Add dry ingredients (oats through baking powder) and toss with butter-sugar for a crumbly mixture. Drizzle with oil, vanilla, and water (or cider) and stir until topping clumps together. Add hazelnuts, and spoon topping evenly over fruit.

Bake 45 minutes or until juice is bubbling and topping is lightly golden. Let cool. Serve with vanilla ice cream, yogurt, or whipped cream.

Variation

APPLE CRUMBLE: For fruit, use 5 sliced cooking apples. Replace juice and honey with 7/8 cup apple cider sweetened with 1/2 cup unpacked light brown sugar. Sprinkle with topping and bake as above.

Fruit Cobbler

This comforting dessert is a nice finish for a fall or winter dinner party, and easy to assemble if you have some canned fruit on the pantry shelf. I like using Oregon-brand canned fruit (especially their red tart cherries) packed in water, adding enough extra juice to submerge the fruit in a generous sauce sweetened with honey. Or, if you have a summer bounty, use your own canned fruit—or fresh fruit, as in the variation. Fruit cobbler also makes a nice not-too-decadent breakfast, served with plain yogurt.

SERVES 6

1 pint (14.5-ounce can) canned fruit packed
    in water (cherries, peaches, apricots,
    raspberries)
1/3 to 1/2 cup unfiltered fruit juice or nectar,
    same as the featured fruit
1 1/2 tablespoons unbleached flour (or cornstarch)
1 raw apple, chopped (optional)
1/3 cup honey
1 teaspoon butter
1/8 teaspoon almond extract (if using cherries)

1/2 cup whole-wheat pastry flour, fine-ground
1/4 cup oat flour (or unbleached flour)
1/4 cup quick oats (or unbleached flour)
1/4 cup white sugar
1 teaspoon baking powder
Pinch of salt
1 1/2 tablespoons chilled salted butter, diced
1 1/2 tablespoons canola oil
1/3 cup milk
Organic sugar

Drain off canning liquid packed with fruit, and combine with additional fruit juice in small saucepan (about 1 cup total). Dilute flour (or cornstarch) in a little of the juice and stir back in. Cook over low heat until juice thickens slightly. Add chopped apple (if using to stretch fruit) and honey and simmer sauce a couple of minutes more. Add butter (and almond extract if using cherries).

Place drained canned fruit in buttered 8 x 8-inch ovenproof baking dish. Pour sauce over fruit. Preheat oven to 400°F.

To make cobbler crust, assemble dry ingredients (flour through salt) in mixing bowl. Rub butter evenly into flours with fingers. Drizzle oil over and work into flours for a crumbly mixture. Add milk and stir as needed to pull dough together. Spoon dough onto floured sheet of waxed paper, knead a few times, then pat into a square slightly smaller than top of baking dish. Transfer pastry on waxed paper to top of fruit. Sprinkle with a little sugar, and bake at 400° for the first 5 minutes; then reduce heat to 375° and bake another 20 minutes until bubbling around edges and crust is lightly browned.

Serve cooled or slightly warm, with vanilla ice cream, whipped cream, or plain yogurt.

Variation

FRESH-FRUIT COBBLER: Use fresh fruit in season, heating the fruit in the thickened sauce as with the optional apple in the main recipe. Raspberries and peaches are a good fresh-fruit combination (and a way to use up "disappointing" peaches). Other good pairings include apples and blueberries or blackberries, apples and plums, nectarines and blueberries. Depending on the ripeness and juiciness of your fruits, you'll need 3/4 to 1 1/4 cups unfiltered juice for the sauce, sweetened and thickened as above.

Huguenot Torte

The Huguenots came from France in search of religious freedom, settling in various parts of America. I came across this elegant dessert in several cookbooks, one of them featuring recipes from the South Carolina Low Country. I was intrigued, having a French Huguenot family ancestor (an Aunt Jane, no less) who lived in Missouri . . . which correlates with the "Ozark Pie" variation in yet another cookbook. Some Huguenots may have settled in the Southwest as well, guessing by a similar "Harvest Torte" recipe in a New Mexican cookbook.

This is a lovely dessert, kind of a cross between apple crisp and pecan pie—really quite light and simple, yet deliciously crusty and flavorful.

SERVES 8 TO 9

1 cup pecans, lightly toasted, coarsely chopped
1 1/4 cups raw apple, coarsely chopped
1 teaspoon lemon juice
1/4 cup unbleached flour
2 teaspoons baking powder
1/4 teaspoon salt

2 large eggs
2/3 cup white or organic sugar
1 tablespoon maple syrup
1 1/2 teaspoons vanilla
Whipped cream sweetened with a little
    maple syrup

Preheat oven to 325°F. Spread pecans in baking pan and bake about 4 to 6 minutes, shaking pan a couple of times, until lightly toasted. Let cool, then chop or break into large pieces. While pecans are toasting, core and chop apple (skin on), and sprinkle with lemon juice. Combine dry ingredients (flour through baking powder); set aside.

Beat eggs in a large mixing bowl until frothy, then add sugar and maple syrup and continue beating until mixture is light and thick. Add vanilla, then stir in dry mixture. Fold in apples and nuts.

Scrape batter into liberally buttered 9 x 9-inch square or round baking pan. Bake at 325° for 35 to 45 minutes, or until top is golden and crusty. Cut in squares or wedges.

Serve cooled or slightly warm, with a dollop of whipped cream sweetened with maple syrup.

Cookies & Scones

Good Cookies

This cookbook could have been nothing but cookie recipes—that's how much I love to invent and bake cookies. For me, it's the perfect way to unwind, focus scattered energies, or call up the creative Muse. Thank heavens I have a husband with a sweet tooth, and a freezer to stash away half of each batch, or my cookie-baking hobby would show more than it does.

After sorting through scores of cookie and scone experiments—most of them more or less successful—scribbled on scraps of paper over two decades, I've somehow managed to narrow them down to these repeat customers, the best of the repertoire.

As you read through these recipes, I think you'll find they tend to call for less sugar and fat, and more whole grains and flours, than your average cookie. Most of them use a relatively light hand with saturated fats, stretching the butter and oil with the addition of some liquid—often orange juice (though occasionally cider, water, maple syrup, apple butter, even sweet potatoes). I think the subtle orange flavor combines nicely with many cookie ingredients—pecans, peanuts, and especially chocolate; also the acidity activates and balances the baking soda.

Do keep in mind that here, as in any baking, the flour and liquid measurements are approximate. As noted under "Baking" in the introduction, the exact amounts needed will depend on the humidity of your home, the protein and moisture content of your flours and grains, the size of your eggs, your precision in measuring. . . . Don't hesitate to follow your intuition and add a little more (or less) flour or liquid to get the "right" consistency.

Also you may need to adjust baking temperatures and times to suit your own oven, baking pans, and taste. Suggested oven temperatures range from 350° to 375°F, depending on the type of cookie, pans, and desired consistency. Heavier, shiny stainless-steel cookie sheets are a good investment—they'll take a little longer but bake more evenly than thinner, darkened pans. If using lightweight pans, a lower setting (say, 365° rather than 375°) may be a safer bet, to prevent scorched bottoms. Also—especially with moist-dough and sugar-rolled cookies—dusting the greased pans with semolina or brown rice flour is good insurance against scorching; baker's parchment is another option.

If you (like me) prefer your cookies baked to a crumbly-crisp, nutty, golden turn, go for slightly lower temperature settings and longer baking times, use well-greased pans, and flatten the dough with a fork to encourage spreading. For soft, chewy cookies, use slightly hotter temperatures and less time; substitute honey, molasses, or maple syrup for some of the sugar; and drop the dough in larger spoonfuls, unflattened. (These and other whys and hows of the alchemy of cookie baking are revealed in a fascinating little kitchen guide, *The Inquisitive Cook*, by Anne Gardiner and Sue Wilson.)

Bake cookies and scones in the top third of the oven. If you can't fit two pans side by side on the same rack, set two racks close together and juggle the pans, swapping their positions in the oven. Most ovens boast of baking evenly, but just to make sure I rotate pans at least once midway through baking, while taking a peek to gauge how close the cookies or scones are to being done. Of course this lets some heat escape, but better safe than sorry. My best advice is to keep a close watch on the cookies and the time, especially near the end of baking, to capture that "nicely browned" moment.

All cookies are by definition "good" (who ever heard of a bad cookie?)—but sometimes it all comes together just right for *Good cookies!* So I offer these household favorites as a kind of "cookie walk," in celebration of our collective cookie creativity—because really, most of these are healthy spin-offs of traditional recipes. Feel free to experiment and spin off delicious variations of your own!

Chocolate-Hazelnut Oatmeal Cookies

I've made these cookies (or variations thereof) so many times I can do it in my sleep. A home and camp staple, they are nutty, oaty, golden, and not too sweet—more toothsome and less decadent than Nestle's and Ghirardelli's back-of-the-bag tollhouse classic. Here butter, sugar, and chocolate play more of a supporting role to the whole grains, nuts, and other good things. Freeze half the batch so you can vary the cookie menu and enjoy them fresh and crisp, at their best.

22 TO 24 COOKIES

4 tablespoons salted butter, softened

1/2 cup light brown sugar, lightly packed,
 + enough white sugar to make 2/3 cup

1 large egg

3 tablespoons canola oil

1 teaspoon vanilla

1 1/2 tablespoons fresh-squeezed orange juice

1 1/2 cups rolled oats

1/3 to 1/2 cup oat bran (*or* 1/4 cup quick oats
 + 1 tablespoon brown rice flour)

1 cup whole-wheat pastry flour

1/3 cup oat flour (or unbleached pastry flour)

Dash of allspice or cinnamon (optional)

1/3 cup Thompson raisins (optional)

1/2 cup hazelnuts or almonds (*or* 2/3 cup
 walnuts), coarsely chopped

1/3 to 1/2 cup chocolate chips (or chunks)

1 teaspoon baking powder

1/2 teaspoon baking soda

1/4 teaspoon salt

In large bowl, cream together sugar and butter; cream in egg, oil, vanilla, and juice. In separate bowl, combine dry ingredients. Pour dry ingredients into wet and mix until flours are moistened.

Preheat oven to 365°F. Lightly oil 3 cookie sheets; if using lightweight pans rather than steel, dust them with a little brown rice flour or semolina flour to keep bottoms of cookies from scorching.

Form spoonfuls of dough and space comfortably on cookie sheets, holding them together with your fingers as needed (the oaty dough, studded with treats, may need a little coaxing into shape). Flatten slightly with a fork. Bake 12 to 18 minutes until golden, then transfer to cooling racks.

Variation

ASSORTED FLAVORS: Hold the raisins and divide dough into thirds. Add to each third one of the following: 1/3 cup shredded dried coconut, 1/2 teaspoon fresh orange zest or 2 drops orange oil, or 2 tablespoons raisins (or leave plain). Form and bake as above.

Chocolate-Walnut Wheat Cookies

These are just right to munch sitting on the beach after a swim in the pond—drying out in the summer sun, which has warmed the chocolate chips. At least that's the fantasy that inspired the first batch of these cookies, which my Craig Pond swim buddy Susan White pronounced "good-tasting and healthy."

20 TO 24 COOKIES

3 tablespoons salted butter	1/4 cup toasted wheat germ
1/2 cup brown sugar, packed	3/4 teaspoon baking powder
1 large egg	3/4 teaspoon baking soda
2 tablespoons canola oil	1/3 teaspoon salt
2 tablespoons freshly squeezed orange juice	1/4 teaspoon cinnamon
1 teaspoon vanilla	1/4 teaspoon ground ginger (or allspice)
1 1/2 cups rolled oats	1/2 cup semisweet chocolate chips
3/4 cup whole-wheat pastry flour, stone-ground	2/3 cup walnuts, coarsely chopped

In large bowl, cream together sugar and butter; cream in egg, oil, juice, and vanilla. In separate bowl, combine dry ingredients. Pour dry ingredients into wet and mix until flours are moistened.

Preheat oven to 365°F. Place spoonfuls of dough on 2 to 3 lightly oiled cookie sheets. Flatten slightly. Bake about 8 to 12 minutes until nicely browned, then transfer to cooling racks.

Variation

CAROB-WALNUT TOFFEE COOKIES: Reduce amount of oats to 1 cup and wheat germ to 1 tablespoon (for a chewy-crisp lace-type cookie). Instead of chocolate chips, use 1/2 cup malt-sweetened carob chips (or a combination of carob and chocolate) and 1/4 cup flame raisins.

Mounds Bar Cookies

Inspired by Mounds bars, these cookies have that same chewy combination of coconut, almonds, and dark bittersweet chocolate. Like the candy, they are just a little too good.

16 TO 20 COOKIES

2/3 cup unsweetened shredded dried coconut	1/4 to 1/3 teaspoon salt
1/4 cup raw whole almonds, coarsely chopped	2 tablespoons salted butter
1/3 to 3/8 cup chunked dark chocolate (a chopped chocolate bar, or halved chocolate chips)	1/3 cup light brown sugar, packed, + enough organic sugar to equal 1/2 cup
3/4 cup rolled or quick oats	1 large egg
1 cup whole-wheat pastry flour, finely ground	3 tablespoons canola oil
1 teaspoon baking powder	1 tablespoon water, fresh orange juice, or cider
1/2 teaspoon baking soda	1/4 teaspoon almond extract

In small bowl, combine dry ingredients (coconut through salt) and mix evenly. In large mixing bowl, cream together butter and sugar; cream in egg, oil, water or juice, and almond extract. Pour dry ingredients in with the creamed mixture and stir until flours are moistened.

Preheat oven to 365°F. Lightly oil 2 cookie sheets and dust with rice or semolina flour to prevent scorching. Form walnut-sized spoonfuls of dough and space evenly on pans. Flatten slightly with fork.

Bake cookies about 12 to 16 minutes until golden, then transfer to cooling racks.

Variation

MACADAMIA-CHIP COOKIES: Replace up to half (1/3 cup) of the coconut with oat bran, and use roasted macadamia nuts in place of the almonds. Replace almond extract with 1/2 teaspoon vanilla.

Orange-Pecan Brownies

Brownies are the epitome of baker's alchemy: toasted nuts, adequate sugar, the minimum of flour and leavening, quality chocolate gently heated. . . . And then there's just something about orange and chocolate together, warm sweet synergy. These brownies are modestly sweet and full-flavored, with a soft texture that contrasts nicely with the toasted pecans.

16 BROWNIES

1/3 cup unbleached flour	1/2 cup white or organic sugar
2 tablespoons whole-wheat pastry flour	1/4 cup unsweetened Dutch process
2 tablespoons oat flour	cocoa
1/4 teaspoon salt	1 tablespoon honey
1/3 teaspoon baking powder	1 teaspoon vanilla
1/2 cup semisweet chocolate chips	1/4 teaspoon pure orange oil
4 tablespoons salted butter, diced	2 large eggs
2 tablespoons canola oil	1 tablespoon milk
1/4 cup light brown sugar, packed	3/4 to 1 cup raw pecan halves, broken

Assemble dry ingredients (flour through baking powder) in small bowl. Preheat oven to 350°F.

Place next 3 ingredients (chocolate chips through canola oil) in small metal bowl or pan, and set in preheating oven to melt; this will only take a few minutes. Let cool. Meanwhile, measure sugar and cocoa into a mixing bowl. Stir in cooled chocolate-shortening mixture, add honey, then beat in eggs, vanilla, and orange oil (or extract). Finally stir in milk.

Butter and lightly flour a 9 x 9-inch square baking pan. Add dry mixture to wet mixture. Stir until flours are moistened, then scrape into prepared pan. Sprinkle nuts evenly over top of batter. Bake 15 minutes at 350°, then reduce heat to 325° and bake another 10 to 12 minutes, or until brownies are set and toothpick tests clean, and the nuts lightly toasted. Let cool, then cut in squares.

Pecan Sandies

Carrying on a Christmas tradition started by my grandparents, my Dad generously treats us with a precious hoard of raw pecan halves, which we keep fresh in the freezer to use the coming year in baking. This is just one of several recipes that have become favorite ways to showcase pecans.

16 TO 22 COOKIES

3 1/2 tablespoons salted butter

1/3 cup light brown sugar, packed

1/3 cup white sugar (or maple sugar)

1 large egg

2 1/2 tablespoons canola oil

1 teaspoon vanilla

1 1/2 tablespoons fresh orange juice (or water)

1 1/3 cups rolled oats

1 cup fine-ground whole-wheat pastry flour

2 tablespoons unbleached flour

1 tablespoon brown rice flour

1 teaspoon baking powder

1/2 teaspoon baking soda

1/3 teaspoon salt

1/4 teaspoon ground coriander (optional)

3/4 cup raw pecans, coarsely chopped

2 tablespoons white or organic sugar +

    1 tablespoon brown rice flour (for rolling)

Cream together wet ingredients (butter through juice) in large mixing bowl. Combine dry ingredients (oats through pecans) in separate bowl; toss remaining sugar with rice flour in small bowl for rolling. Pour dry mixture into wet mixture and stir until flours are moistened.

Preheat oven to 365°F. Drop walnut-sized spoonfuls of dough into bowl with rolling mixture and coat evenly. Place on oiled and dusted cookie sheets, and flatten once or twice with fork. Bake for 10 to 16 minutes, or until set and lightly golden. Cool slightly and remove to rack.

Variation

COCOA-SPICE PECAN COOKIES: Replace oats and flours in dry ingredients with the following: 2/3 cup oats, 1/3 cup oat flour, 1 cup + 2 tablespoons whole-wheat pastry flour, 2 tablespoons unsweetened Dutch process cocoa, and 1 tablespoon Toffee-Spice Tea mix (page 267) or toasted wheat germ. Spice with a dash of allspice and cinnamon. Shape, roll, and bake cookies as above.

Pecan Sugar & Spice Cookies

Somehow I had never thought of featuring nutmeg in cookies . . . until one spring day when Linda Best and I went on a midmorning hike up Great Pond Mountain in Orland, sharing a picnic lunch on our favorite flat rock overlooking Craig Pond. Linda offered some wonderful sugar-and-spice oatmeal cookies she had made (one of those signature recipes, different every time) studded with pecans and golden raisins, with the old-fashioned aroma of nutmeg and "grandma's kitchen." Craving more, I fooled around in my own kitchen until I got it right. If you want to add a touch of chocolate, carob or malt-sweetened chocolate chips are mellow enough to go with the nutmeg and raisins.

23 TO 25 COOKIES

3 1/2 tablespoons salted butter

1/2 cup light brown sugar, packed, + enough
    white or organic sugar to equal 2/3 cup

1 large egg

1 teaspoon vanilla

2 1/2 tablespoons canola oil

1 2/3 to 2 tablespoons fresh orange juice

1 3/4 cups rolled oats

1 cup whole-wheat pastry flour

1/3 cup oat flour

3/4 teaspoon baking powder

3/4 teaspoon baking soda

1/2 teaspoon salt

1/2 to 3/4 teaspoon nutmeg

1/8 teaspoon allspice

1/2 cup sultanas (or half-and-half golden
    and Thompson raisins)

1/3 cup carob, malt-sweetened, or milk
    chocolate chips (optional)

2/3 cup pecans, coarsely chopped (or
    walnuts, or combination)

White or organic sugar for rolling

In a large bowl, cream together sugar and butter, then cream in egg, oil, and flavorings. In a separate bowl, combine dry ingredients. Pour dry mixture into wet and stir until flours are moistened.

Preheat oven to 365°F and prepare cookie sheets with oil. Dust the oiled pans lightly with a little brown rice or semolina flour, to prevent the bottoms of the sugar-coated cookies from scorching.

Roll walnut-sized balls of dough in sugar and place on cookie sheets, about 8 to 11 per sheet. Flatten slightly with fork. Bake the cookies about 10 to 15 minutes until nicely golden, then transfer to cooling racks.

FROM A DISTANCE

Another time Linda and I made plans to meet for a midmorning hike up the mountain happened to be September 11, 2001. We heard the news on the way but decided to hike anyway. Somehow I don't remember what we ate for our picnic that day, but I'll never forget the two of us singing Nanci Griffith's "From a Distance" from the top of Great Pond Mountain, as we looked out over the beautiful, precious area we call home—Blue Hill, Mount Desert Island, Craig Pond and Alamoosook Lake, Penobscot Bay . . . even Isle au Haut far to the south, visible on a clear day (as this one so memorably was). Our friendship, and the landscape, sustained us that day as it has many days since.

(Left) View of Craig Pond from Great Pond Mountain

Peanut-Orange Cookies

Though peanut-butter cookies are an all-American favorite, I've never been all that "nuts" about them. Maybe it's the dark-roasted sludginess of most peanut butter, even the chunky variety. Peanut cookies made with whole, lightly roasted peanuts, however, are a different matter. Unsalted canned Old Virginia peanuts give these cookies an irresistible sweet, nutty crunch—naughty, but nice! To remove temptation, put some in the freezer for another time.

24 TO 26 COOKIES

1 cup lightly roasted or Old Virginia unsalted peanuts, coarsely chopped (see Note)

4 tablespoons salted butter

2/3 cup brown sugar, lightly packed

1/3 cup white sugar

2 tablespoons canola oil

1 large egg

1 teaspoon vanilla extract

3 tablespoons fresh-squeezed orange juice, about 1/2 orange (or water with 1 drop orange oil)

1 cup + 2 tablespoons whole-wheat pastry flour

1/3 cup oat flour

1/2 cup unbleached flour

2/3 cup rolled oats

1/4 cup brown rice flour (or semolina flour)

1/4 to 1/3 teaspoon salt

Dash of cinnamon (about 1/8 to 1/4 teaspoon)

1 teaspoon baking soda

1 teaspoon baking powder

Roast and shell peanuts (see Note); rub off skins, and chop. (Or chop Old Virginia peanuts.)

Cream together wet ingredients in large bowl. Combine dry ingredients in separate bowl, and add to wet mixture. Mix with spoon until flours are moistened.

Lightly oil 2 to 3 cookie sheets. (If using thin pans, it helps to sprinkle the oiled pans with a little semolina or brown rice flour to prevent scorching the bottoms of these sugar-crisp cookies.) Drop spoonfuls of dough onto prepared cookie sheets; flatten slightly with fork. Bake at 365°F for 8 to 12 minutes or until cookies are set and light gold; less is more.

NOTE: For a light touch on the roasted peanuts, and an honest peanut taste, we'll sometimes get unhulled raw peanuts in the shell from our local Feed & Seed store and roast them at home. Spread a layer of raw peanuts on a cookie sheet and roast them for about 20 to 30 minutes in a 250°F oven (they'll fill the house with a heavenly aroma). Shake them from time to time when roasting, and sample often enough to be sure they don't get overdone. Once they've cooled for 5 minutes, you can shell them and rub off the skins, then coarsely chop what you need for the cookies. Equally delicious, though more expensive, are Old Virginia peanuts, fresh from the can; these are blanched, lightly toasted, and wonderfully crunchy. They're available unsalted; if using salted peanuts, rub or rinse off some of the salt before chopping them, or reduce the salt in the recipe to a small pinch.

FRESH FROM THE OVEN

To restore just-baked crispness to day(s)-old cookies, give them a quick warm-up in a toaster oven right before eating. A couple of minutes at 350°F does the trick. This treatment is especially nice for cookies made with chocolate chips, which become warm and molten all over again.

Halloween Cookies

Even though we seldom get trick-or-treaters anymore, I still like making these cookies at Halloween—treats for grown-ups! Studded with colorful Peanut M&Ms, they are festive, nutty, and wheaty, using Wheatena cereal as one of the flours.

18 TO 20 COOKIES

5 tablespoons salted butter

5/8 cup light brown sugar, lightly packed

1 large egg

2 tablespoons canola oil

Juice of 1/3 orange, about 2 1/2 tablespoons (or water)

1 teaspoon vanilla

Peanut M&Ms, 3 per cookie

3/4 cup dry Wheatena (cracked wheat and bran) cereal

1/2 cup toasted wheat germ

1/4 cup oat flour

1 1/2 cups whole-wheat pastry flour

1 teaspoon baking powder

1 teaspoon baking soda

1/4 teaspoon salt

Cream together wet ingredients in large mixing bowl.

Sort M&Ms into about 20 groups of 3 complementary colors. Combine remaining dry ingredients (Wheatena through salt) in separate bowl and add to wet mixture. Mix until flours are moistened.

Preheat oven to 365°F, and oil 2 cookie sheets. Spoon evenly sized lumps of dough onto cookie sheets, about 8 per sheet, and press 3 different-colored Peanut M&Ms into the top of each one, to both decorate and flatten the cookie. Bake for about 12 to 15 minutes, or until a light nutty brown; be careful not to overbake. Cool slightly and remove to rack.

HOME-BREWED VANILLA

Pure vanilla extract becomes ever more expensive, but I would never think of buying the artificial stuff—so have turned to the pleasant home economy of making my own. Granted, whole vanilla beans are not cheap either, but two of them immersed in a tall slender bottle or jar with pure vodka yield a generous cup-and-a-half of vanilla extract, perhaps even a refill with the addition of a fresh bean. A recycled 10- to 14-ounce glass bottle with a clean, tight cap, about 2 inches diameter and 7 inches tall, is a good size—clear, so you'll know when the vanilla bean has steeped long enough. Use only 100-proof vodka (not 80-proof), and either score the vanilla bean or use kitchen scissors to cut tiny slits up and down the sides to encourage release of the vanilla essence. The vanilla extract will be ready to use in about 2 weeks.

Apricot-Almond Bars

When you feel like a change from chocolate, try these bars featuring the warm, fragrant flavors of apricots and honey layered between rich crumbs and toasted almonds. The main recipe has the streusel topping traditionally found on date bars, as in the first variation. The second variation rearranges the ingredients a bit, adding an egg to the filling for an apricot tart. Either way, hold off (if you can) before sampling the bars; their flavor and texture will be even richer the next day.

For an apricot-almond tea biscuit, see the Cape Breton Oatcakes variation on page 193.

12 TO 16 BARS

2/3 cup dried sulphured apricots, soaked	1/3 cup oat flour
1 cup soaking liquid + 1/4 cup water	2/3 cup rolled oats (divided)
3 tablespoons white sugar	1/4 teaspoon salt
2 tablespoons honey	1/2 teaspoon cream of tartar (Bakewell Cream)
~ CRUST ~	3 1/2 + 1/2 tablespoons canola oil
3 tablespoons salted butter, softened	1 to 2 teaspoons water
1/3 cup light brown sugar, packed	1/2 teaspoon vanilla
1 cup whole-wheat pastry flour	1/4 teaspoon ground nutmeg
2 tablespoons unbleached flour	1/4 cup whole almonds, halved or chopped

Cover dried apricots with water and let soak a couple hours or overnight. Drain soaking liquid, reserving 1 cup. Cut apricots in small pieces with paring knife, and cover with reserved liquid plus 1/4 cup water in saucepan. Bring to boil, then simmer covered over low heat, stirring frequently, for 30 to 35 minutes or until apricots are tender and have begun breaking down into a sauce. (Depending on how long you soaked the apricots, and how much steam escapes while cooking, you may need to add or boil off a little liquid.) Add sugar and honey and simmer a few minutes more until you have a nice, thick conserve (about 1 1/3 cups), the consistency of cherry pie filling.

Meanwhile, make crust: Cream butter with brown sugar in large mixing bowl. Combine flours, 1/3 cup rolled oats, salt, and cream of tartar, and work into creamed mixture with fork and/or fingers. Drizzle with 3 1/2 tablespoons oil and work in. Sprinkle and stir 1 to 2 teaspoons water into the shortened crumbs to make a somewhat packable mixture. Preheat oven to 365°F.

Pack about two-thirds of the crumbs into bottom and 1 inch up sides of an 8 x 8- or 9 x 9-inch baking dish, and bake 8 to 10 minutes or until crust is puffed up slightly and beginning to brown. Meanwhile add 1/3 cup rolled oats, 1/2 tablespoon oil, the nutmeg, vanilla, and almonds to remaining crumb mixture for streusel topping. (NOTE: See page 60 for tips on halving whole almonds.)

Remove baking dish or pan from oven and spread apricot filling evenly over bottom of partially baked crust. Then sprinkle streusel topping evenly over all.

Bake for another 22 to 26 minutes, until almonds and topping are lightly toasted. Let cool, then cut into bars. Cover dish with plastic or store bars in covered container to keep from drying out.

Variations

DATE BARS: Substitute 1 cup dates for apricots; soak for 1 to 2 hours before stewing. Omit sugar from filling and add 1 to 2 tablespoons honey to taste, along with 1/4 teaspoon coriander and a little lemon zest. Use cinnamon and walnuts in the topping in place of nutmeg and almonds. Bake as in main recipe.

APRICOT-ALMOND TART SQUARES: Make filling as in main recipe. Rather than reserving a portion of crumbs for streusel topping, combine all crust ingredients (butter through vanilla), reserving almonds and nutmeg. Pat shortened crumbs into bottom and 1 inch up sides of 8 x 8-inch baking dish. Bake 8 to 10 minutes in 365°F oven. Add 1 beaten egg to cooled filling, along with nutmeg, 1 tablespoon flour, and 1/3 teaspoon baking powder; spread over baked crust. Sprinkle with almond halves. Bake as in main recipe.

Raspberry-Hazelnut Thumbprints

Ah, raspberries and hazelnuts, two woodland ingredients that go together like a hot drink and a good story—and a cookie, of course! A little toasted wheat germ enhances the nutty fragrance. These cookies are best fresh, hence the small batch. They can be made as thumbprint drop cookies, or even better, with a little more effort, rolled out and sandwiched with jam as Linzer cookies (variation).

14 TO 16 COOKIES

1/3 to 1/2 cup hazelnuts (or pecans or Brazil nuts), finely chopped	3 tablespoons salted butter
3/4 cup whole-wheat pastry flour	1/4 cup light brown sugar, lightly packed
1/3 cup toasted wheat germ	3 tablespoons white sugar
1/3 cup oat flour	1 large egg
1/2 teaspoon baking powder	1/2 teaspoon vanilla
1/4 teaspoon baking soda	2 tablespoons canola oil
1/4 teaspoon salt	2 teaspoons fresh orange juice (or water)
	Raspberry jam to fill thumbprints (1/3 cup)

Assemble dry ingredients (nuts through salt) in small bowl. In large mixing bowl, cream butter with sugar, and beat in egg, vanilla, oil, and juice or water. Preheat oven to 365°F.

Add dry ingredients to creamed mixture and stir until flours are moistened. Place walnut-sized lumps of dough on 2 lightly oiled cookie sheets, evenly spaced. With your thumb, gently press into the center of each cookie to form a teaspoon-sized hollow. Reshape cookie edges as needed.

Bake for about 8 minutes, then remove cookies from oven and press again for a slightly deeper hollow. Fill center of each cookie with a rounded 1/2 teaspoon-ful of raspberry preserves. Return cookies to oven and bake another 8 to 12 minutes or until nicely browned. Transfer to cooling rack.

Variation

LINZER COOKIES: Roll dough out on floured surface to 1/8 inch thick. Cut into 2 3/4-inch rounds, then cut a "doughnut hole" in each top half. Lay base rounds on lightly oiled cookie sheets; spread a spoonful of raspberry jam in center of each base round, and cover with top. Bake as described above.

Tangerine-Walnut Biscotti

Why buy biscotti, when you can make your own? These gift-worthy traditional Italian treats are not too sweet, satisfyingly crusty, and amenable to various flavor combinations, from citrus to chocolate to the classic anise (thank you, Betsy Bott, for a delicious reminder!). They're fine just plain or with the extra elegance of a vanilla or chocolate glaze. The whole-grain flour gives a more tender crumb to these twice-baked rusks, but they'll still take to dunking in hot tea, coffee, or toffee dessert tea between bites.

30 BISCOTTI

5 tablespoons salted butter, melted	1 teaspoon vanilla
1 cup white sugar	1 1/2 cups whole-wheat pastry or spelt flour
3 to 4 teaspoons freshly grated tangerine, clementine, or orange zest	1 1/2 cups unbleached flour
Several drops orange oil (less than 1/8 teaspoon)	1 teaspoon baking powder
3 tablespoons fresh tangerine or orange juice	1/2 teaspoon baking soda
3 medium to large eggs	1/4 teaspoon salt
	2/3 to 3/4 cup coarsely chopped walnuts

Melt butter over low heat on stove or in preheating 350°F oven; let cool. Combine sugar, zest, oil, and juice in large mixing bowl. Beat in eggs, vanilla, and lukewarm butter.

Mix together dry ingredients (flour through nuts) and add to wet mixture, stirring until flours are moistened. If dough seems very sticky, add another 1 to 2 tablespoons flour. Butter 2 cookie sheets.

Divide dough into 2 equal portions. One at a time, turn out each portion of dough onto a clean surface sprinkled with 2 tablespoons whole-wheat pastry flour and with floured hands, knead about 10 strokes, then form into a log. Transfer to cookie sheets and, using floured hands, coax each log into a loaf 10 to 11 inches long, flattened to 1 inch thick. Bake 25 to 28 minutes.

Remove from oven, transfer to wire rack, and cool 2 to 3 minutes; meanwhile, scrape cookie sheets with spatula to remove crumbs. Lower oven heat to 325°.

Place loaves, one at a time, on a dry, clean cutting board and slice diagonally with a sharp serrated knife into 5/8 to 3/4-inch slices. Spread slices on same 2 cookie sheets (ungreased) and bake 8 to 10 minutes until just beginning to turn golden; flip biscotti and bake about 8 minutes on the other side. Let cool on wire racks. Store in airtight container; biscotti also freeze well.

Variations

LEMON-WALNUT BISCOTTI: Use lemon zest, oil, and juice in place of tangerine/orange.

HAZELNUT BISCOTTI: Omit zest, oil, and juice, and replace with 3 tablespoons Frangelico hazelnut liqueur or vanilla-hazelnut dessert tea. Use an equivalent amount of hazelnuts—lightly toasted at around 350°, skins rubbed off, and coarsely chopped—in place of the walnuts.

ANISE-ALMOND BISCOTTI: Omit zest and oil, and soak 1 teaspoon crushed anise seeds in the melted butter. Replace juice with amaretto liqueur or an almond-flavored dessert tea such as Almond Sunset, or water. Replace walnuts with 1/2 cup coarsely chopped lightly toasted almonds.

Toffee-Spice Tea

This recipe came about after the demise of one of my favorite dessert teas—a delicately spiced malted barley tea marketed as French Vanilla. Not to be deprived, I rounded up all the ingredients except carob, which seemed like it might muddy the clear amber liquor and malt and spice flavors. The resulting mix brews a comforting, mellow, thirst-quenching hot drink that goes just right with most any kind of cookie. The malted barley has a subtle natural sweetness of its own, but the tea could be sweetened with a touch of honey. If you can find some carob pods or coarsely ground carob meal, try the variation for a more robust brew.

You'll find Munton's roasted crystal barley malt where home-brewing supplies are sold (including John Edwards Market in Ellsworth). Whole vanilla beans can be bought singly at most natural food stores, along with other herbs and spices. (When making this tea, I just pull a steeping vanilla bean out of a jar of home-brewed vanilla extract, page 263.) Cinnamon bark, coarsely ground into chips, is sometimes sold as a bulk herb; otherwise you can make enough for the tea using a mortar and pestle or spice grinder. The cinnamon bark should be fairly fine before it goes into the blender.

For bags, I recycle silk tea bags, saved from another favorite tea made by Mighty Leaf. (Though expensive, the silk bags seem too elegant to use just once. I cut off a side corner of the bag, squeeze out the spent contents, rinse out the bag and air-dry, then use a narrow half-inch funnel to spoon in the barley-spice mix and sew the bag shut with a single thread. If this seems like a lot of work, consider the economical cost of this special home brew, a third of the price of boxed dessert teas.) Or you could steep the tea in a fine-mesh basket or make it up in tea filter bags (both available at most natural food stores). Store the tea mix and/or teabags in an airtight jar.

MAKES 42 TO 48 CUPS/TEABAGS

2 cups roasted crystal malt barley	1/4 to 1/2 teaspoon ground or freshly
5 to 6 cardamom pods, seeds	grated nutmeg
2 tablespoons coarsely ground cinnamon bark	1 whole vanilla bean, snipped fine

Put half the malted barley in blender jar and pulse 2 to 4 times, stir with spoon or chopstick; repeat 5 or 6 times, or until barley resembles medium-grind meal. Pour into a cup or small bowl.

Put spices, vanilla, and remaining barley in blender and pulse as for the first batch, stirring larger pieces up from the bottom and sides of the blender jar. Add reserved barley meal and pulse and stir a few more times, until most of the mixture is ground into a coarse meal.

Pour mixture into a clean, dry, airtight pint jar. Fill teabags, using 2 level teaspoons barley-spice mix per bag, or brew with mesh basket, using 2 level teaspoons per cup.

Variation

CAROB TOFFEE TEA: Replacing 1/2 cup of the roasted barley with carob meal (carob pods coarsely ground in a spice grinder) gives the tea a deeper color and richer toffee flavor. Enjoy as tea, or as a heart-warming toddy with a jigger of golden rum (2 tablespoons) per brewed cup.

Cardamom-Walnut Shortbreads

Here's a lightened version of a type of shortbread cookie made in various Eastern European countries, especially Greece where kourambiedes *are a tradition during the winter holidays and at Easter. These melt-in-your-mouth nuggets are richly nutty, not overly sweet, fragrant with cardamom and lemon, and irresistible (hence the small batch). With no egg as a binder and a light touch on butter, it's a nice recipe to fall back on when you're running low on ingredients (or high on cholesterol)—plus there's no need to chill the dough before handling. Thanks to Anne Martina for the inspiration!*

Measure carefully, as there's a delicate balance between liquid and dry ingredients in this recipe. Though it's tempting to try one of the shortbreads right away, they'll taste even better the next day.

The cookies are just as good (and less messy) without the traditional powdered-sugar coating.

16 COOKIES

2/3 to 3/4 cup walnuts, lightly toasted, then chopped

3 tablespoons salted butter, softened

1/3 cup white sugar + enough packed light brown sugar to equal 1/2 cup)

3 tablespoons canola oil

1 teaspoon vanilla

1/2 teaspoon freshly grated lemon zest (or finely minced Meyer lemon peel)

2 teaspoons freshly squeezed lemon juice

2/3 cup confectioners' sugar

1/3 to 1/2 teaspoon freshly ground cardamom

1/4 cup oat flour

1/4 cup whole-wheat pastry flour

1 cup unbleached flour

1/3 teaspoon salt

1/4 teaspoon cream of tartar (Bakewell Cream)

1 teaspoon water (if needed)

To toast walnuts, place on baking sheet in 325°F oven and bake for 3 to 5 minutes, shaking once. Watch carefully to make sure they are only very lightly toasted. Let cool, then chop.

Cream butter with sugar in mixing bowl. Cream in oil, vanilla, lemon zest, and juice. Put confectioners' sugar in a waxed-paper-lined cookie tin. Grind cardamom (seeds of about 6 pods) in mortar and pestle, and add about one-fourth of the ground spice to the confectioners' sugar.

Preheat oven to 350°. Carefully measure flours into mixing bowl, then toss with other dry ingredients (salt, cream of tartar, chopped walnuts, and remaining ground cardamom). Stir into creamed mixture to form a crumbly, rich dough. Add 1 teaspoon water if needed to bring dough together. Dough should be just moist enough to hold together when squeezed in the palm of your hand to form 1- to 1 1/4-inch balls.

Place balls of dough on oiled and floured cookie sheet, and flatten slightly with fingers. (Or shape into the traditional crescents or triangles; you may need to add a touch more oil and water to moisten the dough for handling.) Bake for 25 minutes or until lightly golden around edges.

Remove from pan and let cool to slightly warm, then roll cookies in spiced confectioners' sugar, coating both sides. Leave uncovered until cooled completely, then store in tin with remaining sugar.

Variation

HAZELNUT SHORTBREADS: Replace walnuts with hazelnuts; rub off hulls before chopping toasted nuts. Omit lemon zest, and replace juice with water. Use less cardamom, or combine with nutmeg and allspice.

Whole-Wheat Rolled Spice Cookies

This is the only Christmas cookie I need to bake—there is just something so simple and honest about the wheat flours and spicing, and the ritual of rolling, cutting into shapes, and decorating is festive and satisfying. The shortbready cookies, at least undecorated, really are quite wholesome (what the Brits might call wholemeal biscuits), so you don't have to eat just one. I make them around the time of the Winter Solstice, and use my coziest cutters to shape them as cats, teapots, houses, wreaths, birds, and fir trees, each artfully decorated with Vanilla Buttercream Frosting and chopped walnuts.

30 TO 32 COOKIES

2 1/2 tablespoons salted butter

1/2 cup light brown sugar, lightly packed

2 rounded tablespoons white or organic sugar

1 large egg

4 tablespoons (1/4 cup) canola oil

1 tablespoon water (or cider)

1 teaspoon vanilla

1/3 cup toasted wheat germ

1/3 cup oat flour

1/3 cup unbleached pastry flour

1 1/4 cups whole-wheat pastry flour

2 teaspoons baking powder

1/4 teaspoon salt (scant)

1/2 teaspoon cinnamon

1/4 teaspoon ground ginger

1/4 teaspoon nutmeg

1/4 teaspoon allspice

1/8 teaspoon ground cloves

Seeds of 2 cardamom pods, ground in mortar and pestle (1/8 to 1/4 teaspoon)

1/2 recipe Vanilla Buttercream (page 245)

1/2 cup chopped walnuts

Cream butter and sugar together in a large mixing bowl, and beat in rest of wet ingredients. Combine dry ingredients in separate bowl, mix well, and add to wet mixture. Mix until flours are moistened, and bring together into a somewhat firm ball. There is no need to chill the dough (although this kind of dough can be made ahead, wrapped in plastic, and stored in the refrigerator to bake at a later time).

Preheat oven to 350°F (or 340° if using lightweight pans). Divide the ball of dough in half, keeping one portion covered in mixing bowl. Dust counter with flour and knead dough a few times, then roll out on floured surface to about 3/16 inch thickness (this makes a nice shortbread-like cookie; any thinner, and they'll tend to brown too quickly). Cut in shapes and transfer to lightly oiled cookie sheets. Gather up dough remnants, reform, and recut till dough is used up.

Bake for about 6 to 8 minutes or until just set and lightly golden. Transfer to wire rack and cool. Make one-half recipe Vanilla Buttercream Frosting to a spreadable consistency (using a combination of milk and yogurt or clementine juice as liquid). Decorate, using a toothpick or the pointy end of a chopstick, and sprinkle frosted areas with chopped walnuts.

Like any cookie, these are nicest when fresh. I'll often bake the whole batch, then put half of them, left plain, in the freezer, to bring out and decorate later.

Fig Newtons

Homemade Fig Newtons are a whole different breed from store-bought ones. A little orange zest brightens the fig filling, sandwiched between two pastry circles like a flying saucer. They are fun to make, flavorful, and satisfying—just the thing on a chilly afternoon after hiking or working outside.

14 COOKIES

~ FILLING ~
2/3 cup chopped dried figs
1/3 cup water
1/4 cup white sugar (scant)
2 tablespoons freshly squeezed clementine
    or orange juice
1 teaspoon clementine or orange zest
~ PASTRY ~
4 tablespoons salted butter
1/3 cup light brown sugar, firmly packed
    + enough white sugar to equal 1/2 cup

1 large egg
2 tablespoons canola oil
1/2 teaspoon vanilla
2 tablespoons clementine or orange juice
1 3/4 cups whole-wheat pastry flour (*or*
    1 1/2 cups whole-wheat flour + 1/4 cup
    wheat germ)
1/4 cup oat flour
1/4 cup unbleached flour
1 1/2 teaspoons baking powder
1/4 teaspoon salt

To make the filling, put chopped figs in small saucepan with water and simmer, covered, over low heat, stirring occasionally, until figs have softened and are beginning to form a sauce. (If using very dry figs, presoak them a little while before stewing.) Stir in sugar, clementine or orange juice, and zest and simmer uncovered for a few more minutes until the consistency of preserves. Let cool. (NOTE: If available, store-bought fig preserves could be used instead of stewed dried figs, combining 2/3 cup preserves with 2 tablespoons orange juice and 1 teaspoon zest to make filling.)

For cookie pastry, cream together wet ingredients (butter through clementine/orange juice) in large bowl in order listed. Assemble dry ingredients (flour through salt) and stir into wet mixture. Form dough into a ball and divide in two. Working with one half of pastry at a time, knead dough on floured surface 10 or 12 strokes, then roll out to about 1/8 inch thick. Cut in 2 1/2- or 2 3/4-inch rounds using a smooth- or "pinked"-edge biscuit cutter. You will need 2 rounds per cookie.

To assemble cookies, lay base round on lightly oiled cookie sheet and spoon about 1/2 tablespoon filling into the center. Moisten perimeter of dough with water, then lay top round over filling and pat around edge to seal; gently crimp edge with fork, if desired. Preheat oven to 350°F, and repeat with remaining dough, gathering up dough remnants to roll out and recut until dough is used up.

Using a toothpick, poke 4 small vent holes in top of each cookie (to let steam escape). Bake 12 to 15 minutes or until lightly browned (check bottoms to make sure they don't get too brown).

Variation

DATE-FILLED COOKIES: Stew 2/3 cup pitted dates in 1/3 cup water instead of the dried figs to make filling. Replace orange zest with 1/4 teaspoon ground coriander. Shape and bake as described above.

Date Hermits

Here's my whole-grain interpretation of hermits, an old-fashioned favorite, toothsome with oats, walnuts, and mellow dates (preferably Medjool) rather than the traditional plummy raisins. These are spicy and rich-tasting, yet lighter in saturated fat.

20 TO 24 HERMITS

1 1/4 cups whole-wheat pastry flour	1/2 to 2/3 cup dates (or sultanas, flame raisins)
2 tablespoons toasted wheat germ	2/3 cup walnuts, coarsely chopped
1/4 cup oat flour	3 1/2 tablespoons salted butter, softened
2/3 cup rolled oats	1/2 cup light brown sugar, unpacked
1 teaspoon cinnamon	1/3 cup unsulphured molasses (or combina-
1/2 teaspoon ground ginger	tion of molasses and honey)
1/2 teaspoon nutmeg	1 large egg
1/4 teaspoon cloves	3 tablespoons canola oil
1/2 teaspoon salt	1 teaspoon vanilla
1/2 teaspoon baking powder	3 tablespoons apple cider (or fresh orange
1/4 teaspoon baking soda	juice, or water)

Combine dry ingredients (flours through soda). Slice dates and add, along with walnuts; set aside. In large mixing bowl, cream butter, sugar, and molasses. Beat in egg, oil, vanilla, and cider or juice.

Add dry ingredients to wet mixture and stir until flours are thoroughly moistened. Let stand 5 minutes; meanwhile oil 2 rectangular cookie sheets and dust with rice flour. Preheat oven to 350°F.

Spoon dough onto cookie sheets in 4 narrow rows, 2 per sheet, then use spoon and fingers to shape each portion into a long flattened oval 2 1/2 inches wide by 10 inches long.

Bake in preheated oven for about 10 minutes, then rotate pans and bake another 6 to 9 minutes or until ovals are nicely browned along edges and set. Remove from oven and, while still warm, slice diagonally with serrated knife into 1 1/2- to 2-inch hermits, 5 to 6 per oval. Transfer to cooling rack.

Date-Caramel Fruit & Nut Cookies

For my belated 50th birthday party, my friend Lane Fisher brought a batch of her sunflower-raisin-oatmeal cookies. Though made without butter (Lane is lactose-intolerant), they're richly flavored with the caramel-like combination of wheat germ, oil, vanilla, and date sugar; crisp around the edges yet slightly chewy in the center. Smitten, I begged the recipe.

Date sugar, available at natural food stores, can be kind of expensive, so I make my adaptation of Lane's recipe with equal parts date/brown sugar, using a variety of dried fruits and nuts spiked with a little orange zest. I crave these especially in the fall and winter, combined with outdoor adventures.

1 cup canola oil (scant)

2 medium to large eggs

3/4 cup light brown sugar, unpacked

3/4 cup date sugar

1 tablespoon vanilla (that's right, 1 tablespoon)

1 cup rolled oats

1 cup whole-wheat pastry flour

1/2 cup toasted wheat germ

3/4 to 1 teaspoon salt

1 teaspoon baking powder

1 teaspoon baking soda

1/3 cup raisins

1/2 cup dried apples, snipped in small pieces

1/2 cup raw sunflower seeds

1/3 cup chopped roasted peanuts (optional)

1 teaspoon fresh orange zest

Stir together wet ingredients in large mixing bowl. Combine flours (oats through soda) and add to wet ingredients, mixing thoroughly. Stir fruits and nuts into the dough, which will be very thick.

Preheat oven to 325°F. Drop spoonfuls of dough onto oiled cookie sheets; no need to flatten since they'll spread some in baking. Bake 10 to 16 minutes, until golden brown around the edges, and remove to rack.

Sweet Potato Cookies

Ever wonder how to recycle one cold, lonely, leftover sweet potato? Here's an elegant solution! Few people can resist these unusual, walnut-studded, pumpkin-pie-spiced cookies. The sweet potato gives them a nice consistency, moist but not too rich. They go perfectly with autumn and tea or hot cider.

 12 TO 14 COOKIES

2 tablespoons salted butter, softened

2 tablespoons light brown sugar

1 medium leftover baked sweet potato, skinned

1 large egg

2 tablespoons maple syrup

2 tablespoons canola oil

1 teaspoon vanilla

1 cup whole-wheat pastry flour

2 tablespoons unbleached flour

1/4 teaspoon salt

1 teaspoon baking powder

1/2 teaspoon baking soda

1/2 teaspoon cinnamon

1 tablespoon minced candied ginger

1/4 teaspoon ground cloves

1/4 teaspoon nutmeg

1/4 teaspoon allspice

1/3 (or 1/2) cup Thompson raisins

2/3 (or 1/2) cup walnuts, coarsely chopped

1/4 cup white, organic, or maple sugar

Cream butter with brown sugar in large mixing bowl; mash sweet potato and cream into butter and sugar. Beat in egg, maple syrup, oil, and vanilla. Assemble dry ingredients (flour through walnuts) in separate bowl, then add to creamed mixture. Measure white sugar into small bowl for rolling.

Preheat oven to 365°F. Oil 2 stainless-steel cookie sheets and dust with brown rice flour. Drop spoonfuls of dough into sugar, roll to coat, and place on cookie sheets. Flatten with fork, dipping fork in sugar to prevent sticking. Bake 8 to 12 minutes until lightly browned; be careful not to overbake.

Apple Butter Cookies

*B*eing *the recreational cookie baker that I am, I rarely buy cookies, but an apple cookie from Little Notch Bakery in Southwest Harbor was memorable enough to inspire a baker's dozen experimental batches till I came up with something close. These are appley and good, tender yet chewy-crisp.*

14 TO 16 COOKIES

1/2 cup apple butter (recipe below)

2/3 to 3/4 cup dried apples, finely chopped

4 tablespoons salted butter, softened

2/3 cup light brown sugar, firmly packed

1 tablespoon unsulphured Barbados molasses

1 large egg

1 teaspoon vanilla

3 tablespoons canola oil

1 cup rolled oats

1 cup finely ground whole-wheat pastry flour

1 teaspoon baking soda

1/2 teaspoon salt

1 teaspoon cinnamon

1/4 teaspoon ground cloves

1/8 teaspoon allspice

2/3 cup walnuts (or pecans), coarsely chopped

1/4 cup Thompson or flame raisins (optional)

1/2 cup white or organic sugar

Add chopped dried apples to apple butter, giving them a little time to "plump" while you prepare the other ingredients. Cream butter with brown sugar and molasses in large mixing bowl, then beat in egg, vanilla, and oil. Stir apples into creamed mixture. Assemble dry ingredients (oats through nuts and optional raisins) in separate small bowl and set aside.

Stir dry combination into creamed mixture. Dough will be moist, to encourage spreading; if it seems a bit wet, add 1/2 to 1 tablespoon more flour. Let dough stand 5 minutes. Meanwhile, preheat oven to 365°F; oil 2 cookie sheets (preferably heavy-gauge stainless steel) and dust with semolina or pastry flour. Measure white sugar into a small bowl.

Drop generous spoonfuls of dough (about 1/4 cup each) onto floured cookie sheets, allowing ample room for spreading. Using a wide (2 1/2- to 3-inch) flat-bottomed jar or glass dipped in sugar, flatten and sugar-coat tops of cookies, pressing them out to 3 inches diameter. (It helps to first wipe bottom of jar with a little water or oil so sugar will stick; dip again in sugar before each pressing.)

Bake 16 to 18 minutes, or until set and lightly browned. Cool 1 minute, then transfer to rack.

APPLE BUTTER (MAKES 4 TO 5 HALF-PINTS)

4 pounds cooking apples (such as Wolf Rivers)

2 cups apple cider

3/4 to 1 cup light brown sugar, lightly packed

1/3 to 1/2 cup honey

3/4 teaspoon cinnamon

1/4 teaspoon each allspice and cloves

Wash apples, cut in sixths, and trim bad spots. Add cider and cook covered over medium heat until soft. Put applesauce through a China cap or food mill and spread purée in a 10 x 12-inch baking dish; stir in sugars and spices. Bake at 300°F for 1 hour, stirring every 10 to 15 minutes; reduce heat to 275° and bake, stirring more often, until apple butter is thick and caramel-colored. Put in 4 to 5 hot clean half-pint jars, leaving 1/4 inch headroom, and process 10 minutes in a boiling-water bath.

Lemon Squares

Lemon squares combine a shortbready crust with a zingy lemon-and-honey filling, with all the lip-smacking flavor of lemon pie but a little less fuss. Like the pie, they are best kept at room temperature and eaten within a day or two. Choose a juicy, deep yellow, preferably organic lemon for the zest.

12 TO 16 SQUARES

4 tablespoons salted butter	1/4 cup honey
1/4 cup white sugar	3 large or 2 extra-large eggs
2 teaspoons canola oil	2 tablespoons unbleached flour
1/2 cup whole-wheat pastry flour, fine-ground	1/2 teaspoon baking powder
1/2 cup unbleached flour	Pinch of salt
1/8 teaspoon salt	2 teaspoons freshly grated lemon zest (1 lemon)
~ FILLING ~	1/3 cup fresh lemon juice (1 1/2 to 2 lemons)
1/3 cup white sugar	1 tablespoon confectioners' sugar (optional)

For crust, cream butter with sugar; add oil, then rub in flours with fingers for crumbly mixture. Press crust into bottom and 3/4 inch up sides of 8 x 8- or 7 x 11-inch baking dish. Bake in preheated 350°F oven for 12 to 15 minutes, until crust begins to turn gold around the edges; remove from oven.

Meanwhile, make the filling: Using a fork, cream sugar with honey in nonreactive mixing bowl. Beat in eggs until frothy. Combine flour with baking powder and salt, smoothing any lumps, then add to creamed mixture. Stir in lemon zest and juice. Pour/scrape filling into warm crust, then return dish to oven and bake 14 to 16 minutes at 350°, or until lemon filling is puffed and set and crust is golden.

Remove to cooling rack. When lemon custard has cooled, sift confectioners' sugar over the top if desired. Cut into squares.

POPPYSEEDS

One summer we grew one of the edible varieties of poppies ("Breadbox" or "Breadseed") in our vegetable garden, and for quite a few years thereafter have managed to keep ourselves in poppyseeds simply by encouraging the volunteer seedlings that spring up in the same corner of the garden. Wait until the gaily colored flowers have gone by and the calyxes have turned brown, then make the rounds with a brown paper bag, snipping the tops and putting them heads-down in the bag. Give them a couple of days to finish drying, then shake out the last seeds, winnow out any husk fragments, and store in clean, airtight jars. Much thriftier and more satisfying than store-bought poppyseeds.

Lemon-Poppyseed Cookies

These cookies are full of flavor and not too rich—unless you opt for the gild-the-lily variation of frosting them together in pairs. Either way, they're a nice change from chocolate chip! Nicer yet if you have a Meyer lemon (if so, finely mince the tender peel rather than trying to grate it).

The rolled-and-cut cookies are more of a wafer, the icebox cookies more like a zesty shortbread. For ease of shaping and cleanup, I'd recommend the icebox approach.

32 TO 36 ICEBOX COOKIES, 24 TO 26 ROLLED

Freshly grated zest of 1 lemon (about 1 1/2 to 2 teaspoons)

3 to 3 1/2 tablespoons freshly squeezed lemon juice (2/3 to 1 lemon)

4 tablespoons salted butter, softened

1/4 cup light brown sugar, packed, + enough white sugar to equal 2/3 cup

1 large egg

1 tablespoon canola oil

1 cup whole-wheat pastry flour

1/4 cup unbleached flour

1/2 cup oat flour

1/4 cup brown rice flour (or equal parts rice flour and oat bran)

1/4 teaspoon salt

3/4 teaspoon baking powder

1/2 teaspoon baking soda

1/3 cup poppyseeds

Wash and dry lemon, then grate rind and squeeze juice. Cream butter with sugar, and add egg, oil, zest, and juice.

Assemble dry ingredients (flour through poppyseeds) in separate bowl and add gradually to creamed mixture, for a fairly firm but not stiff dough.

Spread a 16-inch sheet of waxed paper on counter, and sprinkle lengthwise with a mixture of 1 tablespoon each: brown rice flour, unbleached flour, and white sugar. Turn out dough onto dry mixture, shaping into a fat log of even diameter, about 12 to 14 inches long. Roll dough back and forth in dry mixture to evenly coat, then roll up in waxed paper. Transfer to tray or chopping board and chill in freezer compartment for about 3/4 hour. (Or, skip this step and make shaped wafers as described below.)

Preheat oven to 325°F. Remove dough from freezer and cut into 3/8-inch slices, wiping knife with a damp paper towel every 4 or 5 cuts to remove stickiness; or wrap dental floss around the log, cross ends, and work as scissors to shear off slices. (Alternatively, roll dough out 1/4 inch thick on floured surface and cut in 2 1/4-inch rounds. Or, for a sugared surface, place balls of dough on cookie sheets and flatten with bottom of glass dipped in white sugar.) Place on lightly oiled cookie sheets.

Turn oven temperature up to 350°, and bake about 12 to 14 minutes for icebox cookies, or 8 to 10 minutes for rolled cookies, until set and light gold but not overbrowned. Transfer to rack to cool.

Variation

LEMON-POPPYSEED "OREOS": For sandwich cookies, roll out dough and cut in 2 1/4-inch rounds, and bake as described above. When cooled, put them together in pairs, back to back, spreading about 1 tablespoon Cream Cheese Frosting (page 245) per pair, stiffened with a little extra confectioners' sugar. Makes about 1 dozen.

Sand Dollars

These crisp sugar cookies, decorated with almonds, resemble the delicate flat sea urchins found washed up on the beach. Their light spicing can be varied with toffee, anise, or candied orange peel.

18 TO 22 COOKIES

3 tablespoons salted butter, softened

1/2 cup light brown sugar, unpacked

1/3 cup organic or white sugar + for rolling

2 tablespoons canola oil

1 large egg

1 teaspoon vanilla

1 cup whole-wheat pastry flour

1/3 cup brown rice flour (scant)

1/4 cup toasted wheat germ

1/4 teaspoon salt

1 teaspoon baking powder + 1/4 teaspoon soda

1 teaspoon allspice

1/2 teaspoon cinnamon and/or ground ginger

1/4 cup chopped chocolate chips + 1 tablespoon Toffee-Spice Tea mix, page 267 (*or* 2 tablespoons minced candied orange peel; *or* 1/2 teaspoon crushed anise seeds)

Almond halves (page 60), 5 per cookie

Cream butter with sugar in mixing bowl. Cream in oil, egg, and vanilla. Combine dry ingredients, add to wet mixture, and stir until flours are moistened. Preheat oven to 365°F. Halve almonds.

Form dough into 1 1/4-inch balls, roll in sugar, and place on oiled steel cookie sheets, well spaced (they will spread). Flatten slightly with fork, then press 5 almond halves (skin-side up) like a star in the top of each one. Bake 8 to 12 minutes, until light gold. Let cool briefly, then transfer to wire rack.

SCONES

Scones—a cross between biscuits and cookies, breakfast and dessert—are a fun and no-fuss baked good, involving few dishes and many possible combinations. In the British Isles they are pronounced "scuns" and, in the classic cream tea, served with clotted or whipped cream, raspberry jam, and lots of hot tea. While living in London and Scotland I encountered everything from "rock cakes," drop scones lumpy with chocolate chips and nuts, to the classic currant-studded biscuits or wedges.

Back home in Maine, a sweet little book called *Simply Scones*, by Leslie Weiner and Barbara Albright, set me to exploring the wider world of scone-making (including savory scones, page 195). Although scones are traditionally quite short, I like to lighten up on the butter and use a combination of whole-grain flours. The following recipes and their variations will give you some ideas.

Scones will stay fresh for several days, stored in an airtight container. As with cookies, day-old scones can be restored to just-baked freshness by warming them in a toaster oven before serving.

Date-Walnut Scones

Even though this recipe centers on dates and walnuts, the basic scone batter lends itself to improvisation. Feel free to juggle the proportions of oats and flours—just keep the total to 2 cups to stay in proportion with the other ingredients. Try dried pears, apricots, currants, or prunes (chopped and soaked in a little water or juice if dry) in place of the dates, substituting a dash of nutmeg, cinnamon, or allspice for the zest and coriander. Or, try the Lemon-Poppyseed variation.

You'll notice this is one of several recipes calling for Medjool dates. Though "dearer" than regular pitted dates, these are well worth the price for their warm, full flavor and creamy consistency (due to their higher sugar content), which makes them easier to slice.

8 TO 12 SCONES

2/3 cup rolled oats

1/3 cup oat flour

3/4 cup whole-wheat pastry flour

1/4 cup unbleached flour

1 3/4 teaspoons baking powder

1/4 teaspoon baking soda

1/3 cup light brown sugar, packed

1 1/2 to 2 teaspoons freshly grated orange
(or lemon) zest

1/4 teaspoon salt

1/2 teaspoon ground coriander

3 tablespoons chilled salted butter, diced

2 1/2 tablespoons canola oil

1 large egg, beaten in measuring cup

2 tablespoons freshly squeezed orange juice
(*or* 1 tablespoon lemon juice)

1/2 teaspoon vanilla

Enough milk (or milk + yogurt, or buttermilk)
to bring liquid measure to 2/3 cup

2/3 cup walnuts, coarsely chopped

1/2 cup Medjool dates, pitted and chopped

White or organic sugar for sprinkling

Combine dry ingredients (oats through coriander) in large mixing bowl. Add butter and, using fingers, rub into flour mixture. Drizzle oil over flour mixture and work in. Add fruit and nuts. Preheat oven to 375°F.

Combine wet ingredients (egg through milk) in measuring cup, adding enough milk so that the liquid ingredients measure exactly 2/3 cup. Pour into dry mixture and combine with a few strokes. Add 1 or 2 teaspoons more milk as needed for a spoonable batter. Let batter rest 5 minutes.

To make 12 wedge-shaped scones, use 1 rectangular or 2 round baking sheets (such as pizza pans) and oil and generously flour 2 circles about 8 inches in diameter. Spoon half of dough in center of each floured circle and, with lightly floured hands, pat each into a disc about 6 inches in diameter. Brush surface with milk to moisten (if needed) and sprinkle sugar evenly over the top. Using a chef's knife dipped in flour, cut each disc into 6 wedges, 3 cuts meeting in the center. (Or for larger, narrower scones, make a single circle 8 inches in diameter, and slice dough into 8 wedges.)

Bake at 375° in top third of oven for 22 to 26 minutes, or until lightly browned and toothpick in center comes out clean. Recut scones along same lines, then transfer wedges to rack to cool.

Variation

LEMON (OR ORANGE)-POPPYSEED SCONES: Use 2 to 3 teaspoons fresh lemon or orange zest, and 1/3 cup poppyseeds in place of the dates and walnuts.

Prune-Walnut Scones

This recipe, though similar to the previous one, makes a smaller batch of dessert scones with an intriguing combination of prunes, walnuts, lemon, and dark chocolate. The proportions of oats and shortening, with a light touch on the sugar, make for a rich crumbly scone, just right with a cup of tea.

8 SCONES

1/3 cup rolled oats	1/3 cup walnuts, coarsely chopped
1/3 cup oat flour	1/4 to 1/3 cup pitted prunes, chopped
1 cup whole-wheat pastry flour, fine-ground	3/4 teaspoon fresh lemon peel, finely minced
1 1/2 teaspoons baking powder	2 tablespoons dark chocolate, slivers or chunks
1/2 teaspoon baking soda	1 large egg, beaten in measuring cup
1/4 teaspoon salt	Enough milk (or milk with a little yogurt)
1/3 cup organic or white sugar (scant)	to equal 1/2 cup liquid
3 tablespoons chilled salted butter, diced	Organic sugar for sprinkling (2 tablespoons)
3 tablespoons canola or light olive oil	1 teaspoon vanilla

Combine dry ingredients (oats through sugar) in large mixing bowl. Add butter and rub into flour mixture with fingers. Drizzle oil over flour mixture and toss to combine. Add nuts, prunes, lemon, and chocolate. Preheat oven to 400°F. Oil a cookie sheet or round pizza pan and dust with semolina, brown rice, or pastry flour.

Beat egg in measuring cup, and add enough milk (or milk plus yogurt) to bring liquid measure to 1/2 cup. Add vanilla, then pour liquids into dry mixture and stir just enough to bring dough together.

Pile dough in center of prepared baking sheet and, with floured hands, pat out into an 8-inch circle. Sprinkle top generously with organic sugar. Using a floured chef's knife, slice into 8 wedges.

Bake in top third of preheated oven for 5 minutes, then lower heat to 375° and bake 12 to 15 minutes more, or until scone surface is lightly browned and a toothpick inserted in the center comes out clean. Recut along same lines, let cool 5 minutes, then transfer wedges to cooling rack.

Variation

PRUNE-ALMOND SCONES: Use 1/4 cup chopped almonds instead of walnuts. Replace lemon peel with 3/4 to 1 teaspoon finely minced fresh orange peel, and use 1/2 teaspoon vanilla plus 1/8 teaspoon almond extract. Bake as above.

Cranberry-Almond Scones

These scones came into being as refreshments for a Penobscot Comprehensive Planning workshop. Thinking what kind of cookies to bring, I remembered some frozen cranberries Richard and I had picked in one of Penobscot's little bogs, which seemed just right for the occasion.

As scones go, these are more like cookies—especially the chocolate-cherries variation, ditto dried cranberries. Fresh-cranberry scones are more of a fruity, tart-sweet biscuit.

You haven't lived until you've experienced schlepping (and schlurping) around in wading sandals or knee-high rubber boots from hummock to wiggly hummock in a wild cranberry bog, going after the big dark red berries. Get them in the fall, before the hard frosts.

15 TO 18 SCONES

1 cup + 2 tablespoons whole-wheat pastry flour
2 tablespoons toasted wheat germ
1/3 cup oat flour
1/3 cup unbleached flour
1/4 cup oat bran
1/3 cup white sugar
2 1/4 teaspoons baking powder
1/4 teaspoon salt
4 tablespoons chilled butter, diced
2 tablespoons canola oil

1 tablespoon honey
2/3 to 3/4 cup fresh or frozen cranberries, halved if large (or 1/2 cup dried cranberries)
1/4 cup golden raisins or sultanas
1/4 cup whole almonds, coarsely chopped
1/3 cup milk + 1 tablespoon plain yogurt
1 large egg
1/4 teaspoon almond extract
1/3 cup white or organic sugar for rolling

Combine dry ingredients (flour through salt) in large mixing bowl, add butter, and rub into flour mixture with fingers. Drizzle with oil and honey and toss until mixture resembles rich crumbs. Add fresh or dried cranberries, raisins, and nuts. (NOTE: If using frozen cranberries, do not thaw but toss them with the dry mixture just before mixing in the liquid ingredients, to avoid staining the dough.)

Combine milk with yogurt in measuring cup. Add egg and whisk together with milk using a knife or fork. Add almond extract. Put white or organic sugar in a separate small bowl for rolling.

Pour liquids into dry mixture and stir until flours are moistened, for a rather sticky dough (add a tablespoon more whole-wheat pastry flour if dough seems too wet). Preheat oven to 375°F. Lightly oil 2 cookie sheets and dust liberally with semolina or pastry flour.

One at a time, drop walnut-sized spoonfuls of dough in the sugar, and roll to coat all sides (rinsing fingers as needed). Place on cookie sheet, and gently flatten with fingers to about 3/4 inch thick. Bake 12 to 15 minutes (the longer time if using frozen cranberries), or until lightly golden.

Variations

CHERRY-CHOCOLATE SCONES: Use 1/2 cup dried cherries (halved if large) in place of the cranberries and golden raisins. Add about 1/4 cup small (or chopped) bittersweet chocolate chips or dark chocolate shavings. Lightly toast almonds if desired. Bake as described above.

FLORENTINE SCONES: Replace fruit and nuts in batter with 1/2 cup Thompson raisins. Press about 1/2 tablespoon raw pine nuts into the top as you flatten each ball of dough. Bake as described above.

Apple & Spice Scones

Good for breakfast, dessert, or a tea break, especially fresh out of the oven—and a nice multipurpose baked good to bring along to camp. This basic recipe lends itself to other fresh-fruit variations, handy if you happen to have a "disappointing" (not juicy) peach, pear, or plum that needs using up.

MAKES ABOUT 12 SCONES

2/3 cup whole-wheat pastry flour, fine-ground	1/4 teaspoon ground cloves
2/3 cup unbleached flour	1/8 teaspoon ground ginger
1/3 cup oat flour	3 tablespoons chilled salted butter, diced
1/4 cup toasted wheat germ (or rolled oats)	3 tablespoons canola oil
1/3 cup light brown sugar, packed	3/4 cup chopped raw apple, peel left on
1 1/4 teaspoons baking powder	1/2 to 2/3 cup walnuts, coarsely chopped
1/2 teaspoon baking soda	1/3 cup milk + 1 tablespoon yogurt
1/2 teaspoon salt	1 teaspoon vanilla
1 teaspoon cinnamon	1 large egg
1/4 teaspoon nutmeg	1/3 cup white or organic sugar (optional)

Combine dry ingredients (flour through spices) in large mixing bowl. Rub butter into flours using your fingers. Add canola oil and work in evenly, then add apples and walnuts to shortened mixture.

Preheat oven to 375°F. Oil 2 cookie sheets and dust with pastry flour. Measure milk + yogurt (or buttermilk) into measuring cup, then add vanilla and egg and "whisk" with paring knife. Pour into dry mixture and stir briefly, until flours are moistened.

Form balls of dough one at a time, about 1 3/4 inches diameter, and roll just the top half of each ball in sugar (not the bottom, as the sugar would scorch). Place on cookie sheets, 6 scones to a sheet. Bake 18 to 20 minutes, or until nicely golden. Remove to rack and cool. (NOTE: In humid weather, the sugar coating may wick moisture; if scones become sticky, reheat in toaster oven before serving.)

Variations

PEACH (OR PEAR) SCONES: Use firm peaches or pears instead of apples; spice with 1/8 teaspoon nutmeg.

PLUM-ALMOND SCONES: Use fresh firm (not overripe or juicy) plums instead of apples, and replace walnuts with 1/4 cup coarsely chopped almonds. Replace "apple pie" spices with just 1/4 teaspoon allspice.

Beech Hill Pond circa 1911, before the Old Cabin was built in the early 1930s; Dad, Mom, Richard, and me struck silly by our cockeyed canoe; Grandma's tiny camp kitchen; serving up dessert and good conversation in the Old Cabin; the kitchen pass-thru window to the porch; the very cake I remember watching Grandma make for my Mom's birthday (page 243).

Overleaf, more rustic kitchens: Richard stirring up supper at Billfish Pond in Baxter State Park; loaded canoe, with gear in waterproof "package"; our camp kitchen at Webster Lake; happy camper prepping dinner at our island campsite on First Chain Lake; our mainland camp kitchen and porch (we're still "camping in" as we fix up the inside of the old camp).

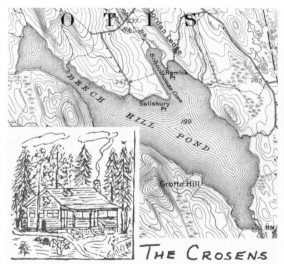

The Crosens

Camp Kitchen ~ *Ashore & Afloat*

Just because you're roughing it—be it car-camping, cabin-camping, canoe-camping, camp-cruising—doesn't mean the food has to be anything less than you'd eat at home. "Eating out" in a beautiful setting close to nature, each day full of adventure, exertion, earth, air, water, and wildlife, brings on an appreciative appetite for fresh, nicely prepared food—nothing artificial—and plenty of it. Unless you're on an extended backpacking trek or a long voyage (beyond the scope of this book), there's no reason that with good planning and thoughtful food storage, your meals in the wild can't be varied, well-balanced, fresh, and delicious.

That said, there are certain limitations cooking in an off-grid kitchen, including weight; storage; lack of refrigeration and hot running water; smaller and fewer burners, pots, and pans; little light; and vagaries of weather—all of which the camp cookee or galley cook needs to factor into meal planning.

You'll find examples of camp-friendly soups, salads, and entrees highlighted as such throughout the book (and it goes without saying that most breads, cookies, breakfasts and desserts are camp-friendly in the eating, if not in the baking). The sample menus that follow offer further suggestions on ways to combine foods in a series of meals. Ideally most rustic-kitchen dishes will include relatively few ingredients (or have sauces or other components that can be put together ahead of time) and need only a stovetop or grill to prepare. Better yet if some dishes—such as leftover grilled chicken or pork, potatoes, beans, sautéed veggies—can reinvent themselves as part of a sandwich, salad, soup, or stew (as highlighted with a "pot luck" or "recyclable" symbol, page 7). Also with just a cooler for refrigeration, the raw materials need to travel well or be used up quickly if very perishable.

The recipes and recommendations here come from some 20 years of canoe-camping adventures Richard and I have had on and around remote and semi-remote Maine lakes, from Baxter State Park (Webster Lake) to northern Hancock County (Nicatous, Duck, and Gassabias Lakes) and Washington County (Rocky Pond, and my island in First Chain Lake). Nothing like making do with a table, tarp, windscreen, and one- or two-burner stove to inspire practicality! After our early adventures backpacking to remote ponds in Baxter, canoe-camping with a boatload of food and two coolers seemed downright luxurious. Now, with our little off-grid lakeside kitchen in our mainland camp at First Chain Lake, we are getting soft, sheltered from the elements as we cook and eat. But it's still a fun, satisfying challenge, eating well at camp.

Food Planning & Packing

A camp getaway seriously begins when I reach for a little square of notepaper from my "camp menu" block and rough out a menu. First the headings: Breakfasts, Lunches, Dinners, and how many of each meal, plus Hors d'Oeuvres, Drinks, and Desserts. Then a long poke-around in the refrigerator and freezer, scouting for meal-makings already on hand. Usually a few ingredients inspire an idea for one meal, leading to more, and before we know it, there's a plan—sometimes a weekend's worth of good eats without a trip to the store, although three to five days' worth takes more concerted provisioning.

The goal is a variety of nice yet fairly simple meals similar to what we'd make at home, but with some prepping done ahead to save lugging too many ingredients. For example, marinades are a fine thing to make ahead, then pour into a ziplock bag along with chicken or other meat already trimmed and the packaging disposed of at home. Grilled meats also cut down on greasy pans, which are more of a challenge to wash in a primitive scullery where hot water doesn't come out of the tap. Marinades contain citric or other acids and sugars, wines, garlic/onion, salt, and oil, all of which act as preservatives, prolonging color and freshness while flavoring the meat. Marinating meats can "chill" in the cooler for up to three days, lending flexibility to the menu in case you need to wait for decent grilling weather.

Along with marinades, sometimes we'll make meals ahead—chili or beef stew, spaghetti sauce and meatballs, pea soup—and freeze them, banked away for the next time we need an easy meal. All of these are good camp food for inclement weather, quick to heat up on early nights, and they'll keep things cold in the cooler as they slowly thaw. But mostly I like cooking from scratch at camp in our little kitchen away from home. Its rustic amenities—candles and kerosene lamps for light, lugged or hand-pumped lake water for washing, SunShower for warm-water rinse—only add to the adventure.

There's no oven as yet, which means we have no way to bake breads and other goodies at camp, so often the first scribbles on the menu have to do with baking: muffins and granola for breakfast, cookies and cakes for desserts. I'll pick away at the camp baking beforehand, and pop things in the freezer to stay fresh until we're ready to go.

PACKING

Once we have a menu and most items premade, preassembled, or procured, I'll begin departure day by making a pile of dry goods (pasta, grains, teas, nuts, breads, crackers) to go in our traveling pantry: a waxed heavy-duty fruit box, begged from the produce department at the grocery store, rigged by Richard with rope handles for carrying. Anything that doesn't need to go in the cooler gets packed in the food box (and then, at the appointed time, into the car). Our current "Jersey Fruit" nectarine box has lived to survive many canoe-camping trips and three- to five-day stays at camp.

Working with my scrap of a menu, I'll methodically round up all needed food items, dry and perishable, until everything is accounted for. Then I stash the menu in the food box for a brief memory jog if we're away for more than three days. After that, it gets zipped away with all its brethren for posterity. With all the times Richard and I have been camping together, each trip launched with one of these scribbled menus, you can imagine the collection that has accumulated!

An assortment of them are combined on the pages that follow as sample camp menus.

Since we bring drinking water from home and use untreated lake water for all other washing, I pre-wash most green leafies and other produce that we'll be eating raw, store them in plastic bags, and organize them in the fridge along with all the other cold stuff—yogurt, juice, cheese, and condiments in downsized bottles and jars—so everything that's coming with us is segregated from what's staying at home. This way when it's time to go, it's all right there and nothing (we hope!) gets forgotten. The idea is to avoid extra stops along the way, or having to leave camp for a food foray—at least if our time away is short. (After four or five days in the "wild," it can be a nice adventure to head into town to stock up on ice, fresh bread, and local news and culture.)

For drinking water, we'll usually fill up gallon-sized plastic jugs from our home tap, a general rule of thumb being a half gallon to three quarts per person per day (counting on lake water for cooking and washing, and bottled water at a local store should we run out).

To save trips to the "ice box," we make our own block ice by filling clean half-gallon cider or milk jugs three-quarters full (to allow for ice expansion) and freezing them in our home chest freezer. Three of these (four in high summer) fit in the cooler and keep things plenty cold for three days. Beyond that, a block from the nearby store every other day does the job. Avoid ice cubes, which melt more quickly. As long as your plastic ice jugs are intact, they won't leak the way bagged ice will, creating arctic puddles in the bottom of the cooler that can zap tender fruits and vegetables.

Our green Coleman 54-quart cooler, which has been camping with us all this time, is still going strong and holds enough ice, beverages, meat, fruits, vegetables, cheese, and condiments—loaded from left to right, bottom to top, in order of coldness—for three to five days. For a longer stay, a small Playmate cooler chilled by bottles of meltwater drained from the ice jugs stretches the refrigerator capacity, also serving as a paddling lunchbox.

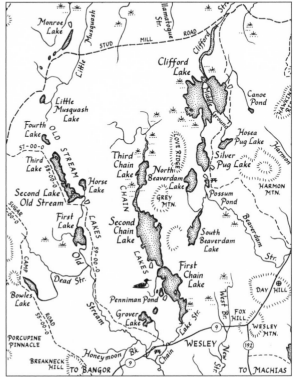

There is an art to packing a cooler, one key caveat being: Don't put tender perishables (greens and fruits) too close to ice or frozen foods, or they will get frostbitten. Use cold bottled water, drinks, and meat as a buffer between ice and fresh produce. Resting a blanket of foam, bubble wrap, or an upside-down plastic tray over the cooler contents can help keep your cool. And to minimize rummaging (which bruises vegetables and lets cold escape), sequester small items in a tray that rides on the top rails inside the cooler. Tender greens could go here, but herbs like basil will do even better unrefrigerated, sprinkled with water and kept in ziplock bags. Most fruits, including tomatoes and avocadoes, are best left to ripen at room temperature.

Closing in our departure, everything works its way toward the front door where, after making one last check, it gets loaded into the car.

Whatever the menu, always bring a little more than you expect to eat, just in case the weather interferes with your grilling plans or keeps you hunkered down for another day—or maybe you might decide to stay a little longer, or invite friends to join you for a meal. On the other hand, with perishability and weight being concerns in a primitive kitchen, you don't want to bring too much food either. Besides, running a little short on some item can be a good excuse to get a line wet or go foraging, whether in a wild berry thicket, streamside, or in a local market.

Serendipity goes for cooking and serving, too: With all the variables in adventuring outdoors, it's enough simply to plan the number of meals and dishes, but leave the timing up to choice and factors like how long a frozen food takes to thaw, the weather and temperature (making a hot meal or cold meal a better choice), perishability (what needs to be used up first), availability of leftovers, and last but not least, what people feel like eating.

Then there's that dash of ingenuity in planning meals around some of the same ingredients, with, say, breakfasts that can double as dessert, hors d'oeuvres as snacks. This "multipurpose foods" concept fits right in with the practical spirit of camping, where it's always a plus if you can use gear for more than one purpose to save lugging specialty items, thereby trimming bulk and streamlining planning.

Sample Camp Menus

Our camp menus tend to follow the seasons, using whatever's available, appealing, and travels well. These are typical examples, with some foods used in more than one meal. Drinks might include coffee, cocoa, assorted teas, water, juices, limeade, beer, wine, toddies (tea with rum, sipping whisky).

3 days, May/June

Breakfasts (3)
Raspberry Hazelnut Muffins; orange sections with yogurt and honey
Fruit bowl with sliced apple, banana, grapes, plum nectar, yogurt, maple syrup, Date-Nut Granola
Rhubarb Cake with Sour Cream Frosting; orange juice

Lunches (3)
Focaccia Grilled-Cheese Sandwiches; Tomato-Basil Soup (homemade or Knorr)
Focaccia pockets with olive oil, turkey breast, lettuce, olives, scallions, plum tomatoes, yellow pepper
(Leftover grilled) Chicken sandwiches on Italian Seed Bread with Tomato-Eggplant Tapenade, arugula

Dinners (3)
Grilled Lemon-Herb Chicken; pasta bowties; sautéed onion, zucchini, and plum tomatoes
Grilled Orange-Teriyaki Steak; leftover white/brown rice, reheated on grill; stir-steamed onions,
    scallions, broccoli, baby bok choy, carrot, fresh cilantro
Richard's Chili with grated Manchego, pumpkin seeds, cilantro; quinoa; sautéed onions and zucchini

HORS D'OEUVRES/SNACKS
Almonds, olives, Jarlsberg/gouda/cheddar, grapes, Tomato-Eggplant Tapenade on choice of bread

DESSERTS
Chocolate-Hazelnut Oatmeal Cookies
Rhubarb Cake with Sour Cream Frosting

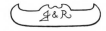

4 DAYS, MID-JULY

BREAKFASTS (4)
(2) Fruit bowl with yogurt, peaches, foraged raspberries, plum nectar, maple syrup, Date-Nut Granola
Sesame Semolina toast with almond butter and cherry jam; orange sections with yogurt and honey
Blue Corn-Pecan Muffins; butter and honey; plums and orange sections with yogurt and honey

LUNCHES (3)
Quick Minestrone (with leftover Cajun Chicken, sautéed veggies, shaved Manchego); bread & butter
Chicken & Peach Tabbouleh (with leftover grilled chicken and quinoa, cukes, cilantro)
Niçoise Salad with hardboiled egg and cukes; Sesame Semolina Bread and butter

DINNERS (4)
Cajun Chicken with sautéed onions, summer squash, green beans, tomatoes; Rice-Noodle Pilaf
Pasta e Fagiole with Pork & Plum Tomatoes; whole-wheat spirals; stir-steamed zucchini
Grilled Lemon-Herb Chicken; quinoa; stir-steamed spinach and green pepper
Grilled Halibut in Lime-Garlic Marinade; leftover pilaf; stir-steamed beans, peppers, tomatoes

HORS D'OEUVRES/SNACKS
Raclette/morbier cheese, plums, almonds, marinated olives, sesame breadsticks ("cigars")

DESSERTS
Chocolate-Walnut Wheat Cookies
Peaches and chocolate

4 DAYS, LABOR DAY

BREAKFASTS (4)
Scrambled eggs; toasted bagels with almond butter and raspberry jam; orange juice
(2) Fruit bowl with nectarines, blueberries, blueberry juice, yogurt, maple syrup, Date-Nut Granola
Blueberry-Apple Cake with Cream Cheese Frosting; cantaloupe

LUNCHES (4)
(Leftover hot-smoked) Pork sandwiches on walnut-dill bread; mustard, lettuce, peperoncini, red onion
(Leftover grilled) Steak Sandwiches with Dill-Horseradish Sauce; cherry tomatoes, lettuce, and cukes
Marinated Green Bean Salad with feta/goat gouda and grapes or cherry tomatoes; bread
(Leftover grilled at home) Apple-Smoked Steelhead Trout, German Potato Salad, lettuce and cukes

DINNERS (4)

Grilled chuck steak with salsa; corn-off-the-cob; Everyday Tossed Salad with olives, fresh cilantro, and cherry tomatoes, Orange-Coriander Vinaigrette

Mediterranean Lamb Kebabs; Pan-Roasted Rice; stir-steamed onions, summer squash, green beans, rainbow chard, plum tomatoes

(Leftover grilled or hot-smoked at home) Pork summer veggie stew with onions, summer squash, green beans, plum tomatoes, basil; boiled new potatoes with fresh summer savory

Shell beans with (leftover grilled) lamb, onions, plum tomatoes, rosemary, stir-steamed rainbow chard; leftover Pan-Roasted Rice

HORS D'OEUVRES/SNACKS

Almonds, pistachios, olives, feta/goat gouda, red grapes, wheat crackers

DESSERTS

Pecan Sugar & Spice Cookies
Blueberry-Apple Cake with Cream Cheese Frosting

3 DAYS, OCTOBER

BREAKFASTS (3)

Cranberry-Apple Cake with Buttercream Frosting; orange sections
Multigrain toast with almond butter and strawberry jam; orange sections with yogurt and honey
Blueberry-Almond Bran muffins; almond butter and honey; pears with plum juice and yogurt

LUNCHES (3)

Curried Squash Soup with Chicken; sesame breadsticks ("cigars")
Richard's Chili; Savory Cheese-Corn Scones; fresh parsley
Cheddar/goat gouda sandwiches on multigrain bread; Tomato-Basil Soup (homemade or Knorr); cabbage slaw with vinaigrette
Lamb & Lentil Soup sprinkled with fresh parsley; multigrain toast drizzled with olive oil

DINNERS (3)

Grilled Orange-Ginger Pork Spareribs; leftover brown rice (baked at home), reheated on grill; stir-steamed onions and broccoli
Chicken Sausage with Green Beans, Feta & Dried Tomatoes; whole-wheat spirals
Leftover roast lamb (cooked at home) with sautéed onions, garlic, and rosemary; steamed beet greens; whole barley (presoaked and stovetop-simmered)

HORS D'OEUVRES/SNACKS

Almonds and dried pears, olives, cheddar/gouda/feta cheese, sesame breadsticks ("cigars")

DESSERTS

Fig Newtons
Cranberry-Apple Cake with Buttercream Frosting

STOVES

At this point we've been content to outfit our camp with just a Coleman two-burner propane camp stove. Although there are some limitations to being without an oven, between the cooktop and the charcoal grill (a Weber Smoky Joe) and an airtight woodstove for cooler seasons, we can cook most anything. We've even mastered the art of using an old metal pie plate, oiled and covered with foil, as a rustic toaster oven, to heat up leftover grains or make grilled cheese sandwiches (page 23)—either on the cooktop with a flame-tamer (simply a piece of 1/4-inch aluminum plate), on top of woodstove on an old cast-iron burner plate, or on the side of the grill over moderate coals.

Once replaced by a four-burner camp stove with oven (ah, the possibilities!), the Coleman can resume its former life as a canoe-camping stove. For short canoe-camping and backpacking trips, we've found the small disposable canisters the most convenient way to carry propane, although staying at our mainland camp (essentially car-camping) allows the more earth-friendly choice of using a refillable 10-pound gas bottle. We also have a 20-pounder which goes us most of a year.

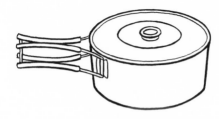

SAVE A DISH

We've learned a thing or two in our off-grid cooking about dirty-dish frugality. Less is definitely more in situations where hot water is only available at the expense of time, effort, and fuel (even with the help of a SunShower). Here are dish-saving measures worth applying at camp or anywhere:

- When measuring liquid ingredients totaling 1 cup or less, add them to a measuring cup in such an order that you can measure and mix them in the cup without using a bowl.

- Grill meats or fish, when possible, for one less greasy pan—you'll clean the grill (after dinner or next time you grill) by brushing/scraping off the charred remains heated over the hot coals.

- If the timing works right, serve grilled meat or fish on a plate or pot lid already used in preparing the rest of the meal. (Exception: Don't use a plate that has held raw meat.)

- If making a meal such as Pasta e Fagioli (pages 147–48), where two or three ingredients (sausages, shell beans, pasta) need to be boiled, cook them one after the other using the same pot (refreshing the water in between). They'll all end up in the same dish anyway.

- When draining pasta, carefully hold the lid (using a potholder) closely against the top of the pot and pour off the water, rather than draining through a colander; or use a slotted spoon as a drain or scoop. Use bowls or plates as a catch basin for hot drainwater, to warm them before serving.

- Serve food from the pots used for cooking, kept warm buffet style on the counter or stove.

- Use paper plates when appropriate—perhaps a second time if nearly pristine.

- If your stove lacks a pilot, light a candle to relight from as you cook—you'll save matches, too.

Index to People & Places

Index to Recipes & Ingredients

About the Author

A self-taught mapmaker and freelance editor, Jane Crosen has always been at home with words and art, but discovered publishing as a way to put them together while living in the Findhorn Community in Scotland in her twenties. On returning to Maine, a couple of typesetting jobs led to a two-year post at DeLorme Publishing as editor and girl Friday, immersed in maps, recreational guides, and gazetteer listings—and a new desire to explore the backcountry treasures of her home state.

A move to the Blue Hill Peninsula brought further opportunities over the next 25 years to explore and grow as a copyeditor and proofreader for WoodenBoat in Brooklin and various other publishers, editing hiking and outdoor recreation guides, travel journals, boat-building books, cookbooks, New England history and ecology, and conservation/resource management plans. Meanwhile her affinity with maps, Maine, and design blossomed into a series of hand-drawn maps of Maine coast and lake regions. The maps, available as posters, postcards, notecards, coasters, and T-shirts, can be seen at www.mainemapmaker.com, or ask for a brochure (Jane Crosen, Mapmaker, 207–326–4850, janecrosenmaps@gwi.net). They are also sold in a number of stores along the Maine coast and inland.

Jane and her husband, Richard Washburn, live in rural Penobscot, Maine, in a house they designed and built themselves. They enjoy cooking and writing, music and fiber arts, tending home and garden, exploring old woods roads and trails, and being near or on water in any form—lake, stream, or ocean.

Getting ready for an open house